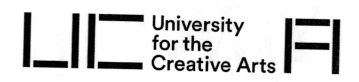

Fort Pitt
Rochester
Kent
ME1 1DZ

Tel: 01634 888734
E-mail:
gatewayrochester@uca.ac.uk

THE ARCHITECTURE OF
THE LOUVRE

THE ARCHITECTURE OF
THE LOUVRE

❧

GENEVIEVE BRESC-BAUTIER

❧

PHOTOGRAPHS BY

KEIICHI TAHARA

❧

PREFACE BY

PIERRE ROSENBERG

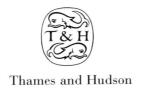

Thames and Hudson

On the endpapers
Projects by various architects, from Bernini in the mid-17th century
onwards, to link the Louvre (top) and the Tuileries (bottom). In some,
an attempt is made to disguise the change of axis between the two
palaces. (Engraving by Drouet, 1811. Musée Carnavalet, Paris)

Illustration credits
© Ruben Alterio: drawings on pp. 8, 190
© Collection de la Banque du Louvre, Paris: pp. 40–41
© Bibliothèque Nationale, Paris: p. 21
Photothèque des Musées de la Ville de Paris, © by SPADEM 1995
(Musée Carnavalet): endpapers, pp. 13, 43, 88, 118, 128, 129, 146
© Pei Cobb Freed & Partners: pp. 192–93, 195, 206 (© photo
National Geographic), 207 (© photo Stéphane Couturier,
Archipress, Paris)
© Photo RMN: pp. 38, 71, 74, 80, 96

Translated from the French by Emily Lane

First published in Great Britain in 1995 by
Thames and Hudson Ltd, London

©1995 by Editions Assouline, Paris

British Library Cataloguing-in-Publication Data
A catalogue record for this book is available from the British Library

ISBN 0-500-34142-7

Printed and bound in Italy

Contents

Preface

'Louvre'... No one has so far convincingly explained the original meaning of what has become one of the most famous French words in the world. To everyone it simply means 'museum', and by a sort of conditioned reflex it at once conjures up images of the *Mona Lisa*, the *Winged Victory*, the *Venus de Milo* and Michelangelo's *Slaves*.

But in thinking of the museum, people forget the palace, which is in its own right a museum of painting and sculpture, as well as an epitome of six centuries of architecture. It is this other museum, so often unnoticed, that Geneviève Bresc reveals here, as she skilfully relates its long and complex history. And it is this other museum that visitors to the Louvre will soon discover. When the Richelieu wing opened, after the departure of the Finance Ministry, it was easy to imagine that the reorganization of the collections was finished, but that is far from being the case: at the present moment, work is in progress over an area totalling 25,000 square metres (some 6 acres).

The work involves six of the seven departments of the Louvre – all except for that of sculpture (which accordingly occupies a privileged position in this book). It affects the historic fabric, presenting architects, planners and curators with the thorny problem of showing to best advantage both the setting and the collections, both the container and the things contained; of making the architecture, the decorative stucco and the paintings harmonize equally happily with Egyptian sculpture, Greek vases, antique terracottas and Middle-Eastern bronzes... To restore this setting, to give it the care and respect it deserves – more, perhaps than has been given it in the past – is one of our constant concerns and one of our most urgent tasks.

A single example may make the point: the Galerie d'Apollon. It is unquestionably the finest gallery in France after the Galerie des Glaces at Versailles, but how many people are aware of that today? Over a period of two hundred years, from Le Vau to Delacroix, from Le Brun to Pierre, from the Marsy brothers to Callet, architects and Surintendants des Bâtiments, stuccoists and painters have competed with one another to produce the sumptuous setting that would one day serve to display the crown jewels. Yet who now, on entering the Galerie d'Apollon, can suppress a sigh, or not feel a pang of sorrow on seeing the neglected state of these majestic spaces – spaces which, we are convinced, will when they are restored be among the most popular and the most admired in all the Louvre?

That 'new' Louvre which visitors will discover is in fact the older part. Set beside the modern Louvre created by I. M. Pei and his various teams, it is surely what will come as the greatest surprise to the readers of Geneviève Bresc's work.

They will discover the Louvre as it was, they will see it as it is today, and they will be able to imagine it as it will be tomorrow, restored and revealed. The three lists that accompany the text – the list of architects, the list of painters and the (particularly impressive) list of sculptors, from Jean Goujon to Jean-Baptiste Carpeaux, – will make plain that there is quite another way to visit the Louvre. That alternative exploration will soon be possible, when the planned signage explaining the historic fabric is installed. In the meantime, we beg the readers of this book to bear with us over the numerous building works that are in progress.

And as you wander round the stupendous collections of works of art that are displayed here, never forget all those – from Raymond du Temple, master of the works to Charles V in the second half of the fourteenth century, to Braque who in 1953 added his painted blue and white birds to the carved woodwork of Scibecq de Carpi, from Bernini to Ingres, from Percier and Fontaine to Ferran, from Sarazin to Barye, from Chaudel to Rude, from Poussin to Gros – who have made for them a setting worthy of their greatness.

PIERRE ROSENBERG
Président Directeur
Musée du Louvre

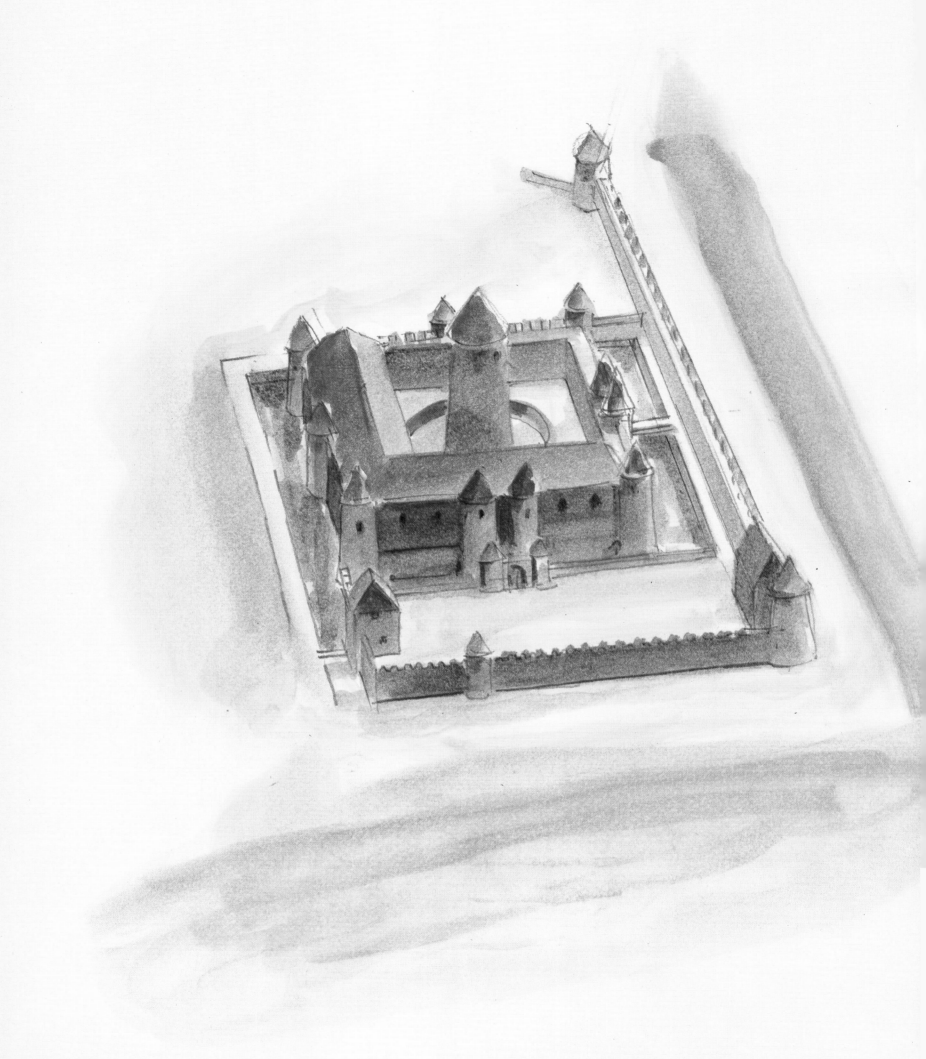

Reconstruction of the *donjon* of Philippe Auguste's Louvre, at the western edge of the walls of Paris.

The Medieval Fortress

Late twelfth–thirteenth centuries: the Great Tower of the Louvre

The story of the Louvre begins in the time of Philippe Auguste, one of the great statesmen of the Middle Ages. When he came to the throne Paris was a burgh of no great significance, and the King of France was a feudal lord based in his realm of the Ile-de-France. By the time of his death, in 1223, Paris was beginning to be recognized as the capital of the kingdom of France, its university was the centre of intellectual life, and the King, since his victory at Bouvines in 1214, was one of the political leaders of Christendom. It was he who decided on the building of a new castle in Paris.

Medieval Paris was a small fortified town with narrow streets, built on the two banks of the Seine enclosing the Ile de la Cité, on which stood the palace which had been a royal residence since the time of the Merovingians. Around the town were largely rural suburbs, punctuated by a few great houses on the roads leading away from the town gates, and large religious establishments. The area outside the walls to the west was known as 'Louvre'. The name is first recorded in 1186, in connection with the foundation of the Hospital of St Thomas 'of the Louvre'. Its meaning is still uncertain, despite the best efforts of philological ingenuity: the Latin word, *Lupara*, and its French form have been scrutinized etymologically to produce a range of possible meanings, some more fanciful than others: Saxon fortress? leper hospital? signal tower? kennel for wolf-hunting? stand of oak-trees? red place?

Traces of human activity in Neolithic times have been found in the area; under the Romans, when Paris was Lutetia, there were fields under cultivation and claypits a little further out, where the Cour du Carrousel is now. In the Middle Ages it was a suburb of gardens, protected from the high waters of the Seine by a clay dyke, and inhabited by rather dubious people.

In 1190, on the eve of setting out on Crusade, Philippe Auguste determined to protect his town, and the royal palace on the Ile de la Cité, against invaders from the west – by which was meant the English. His biographer Rigord tells us that he compelled the burghers to enclose the town within a new wall (subsequently known as the Wall of Philippe Auguste) which ran between the built-up centre and the suburbs. At the point where the wall met the river, a tower known as the 'Tour du Coin' (corner tower) formed a defensive pincer with the Tour de Nesle on the left bank. Beside it rose not a simple bastion but a strong fortress, the 'Tower of the Louvre'. That name first appears in a document of 1202, where it is given as the example to be followed for the construction of another castle, Dun-le-Roi. Thus from the outset it was perceived as a model.

The fortification of Paris is part of the story of the endless war between the Capetian kings of France and the Plantagenet kings of England. The young Philippe Auguste had already defeated the aged Henry II, who had died in 1189. Anxious to build on his success, he set off on crusade to Jerusalem with the new king of England, his brother-in-law, Richard the Lionheart. Officially it was a joint expedition, but in practice they were not allies. The Plantagenets were dukes of Normandy and counts of Anjou, and from his mother Eleanor Richard had inherited control over Poitou and Guyenne. English territory in Normandy was not far away, threatening the fragile royal state of the Ile de France, so Paris had to be protected. The need would become less pressing after 1204, when the successful French siege of Château-Gaillard and capture of Rouen drove the Lionheart's brother, King John, back towards Aquitaine. The building of the Louvre, however, also reflected Philippe Auguste's determination to show himself as the protector of his people, and as a great builder, a good administrator, and an organizer capable of drawing creatively on the human and financial resources of an increasingly self-conscious nation.

Overleaf Philippe Auguste's *donjon* or 'Great Tower' (right), in its dry moat.

9

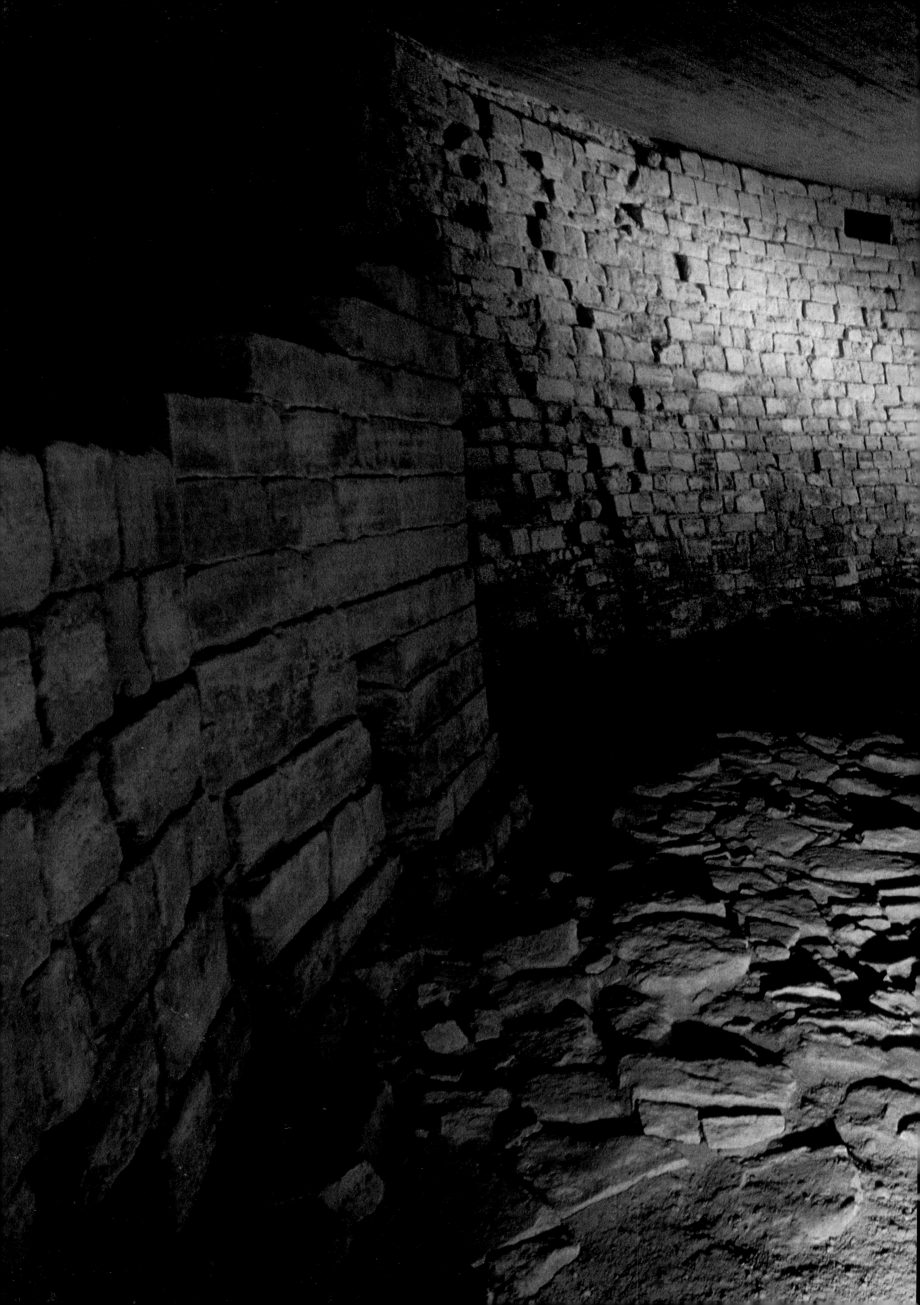

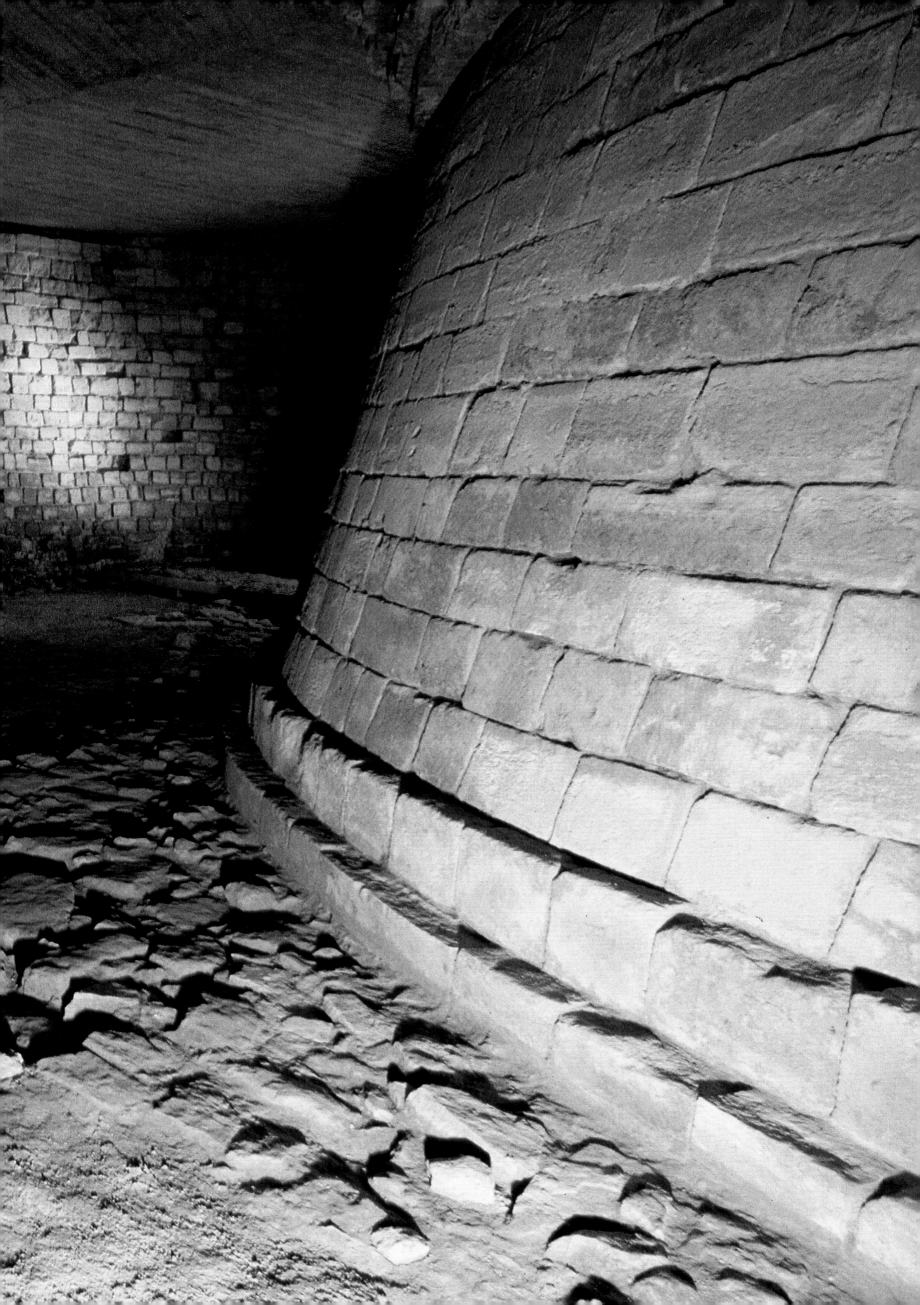

The castle of the Louvre was erected by the finest of Philippe Auguste's military master masons. Were they influenced by castles in the Holy Land that they had seen on Crusade with the King? or did they know those already, since a majority of previous crusaders had been French? The fortress does have some features in common with castles built on level sites in the East: it was a thick-walled rectangle, measuring some 72 metres (235 feet) east–west by 78 metres (255 feet) north–south, surrounded by moats fed from the river, and strengthened at the corners by circular towers. The two gates, one at the south towards the river and one at the east towards the town, were flanked by massive semi-circular towers. What was novel in the design was its extreme compactness: there was no outer bailey, no chapel, no other buildings – nothing but the rectangular castle, with, at its heart, slightly off-centre, the 'grosse tour' or Great Tower, a perfectly circular structure 15 metres (50 feet) in diameter and probably originally some 30 metres (100 feet) high, surrounded by a dry moat 6 metres (20 feet) deep and 10 metres (33 feet) wide. Remains of this castle had been discovered during excavations in 1866 by Adolphe Berty in the south-west corner of the Cour Carrée, but it was the archaeological work of Michel Fleury and Venceslas Kruta in 1984–85 that led to the exposure of the lower walls of the great fortress, and the rediscovery of its smooth walls of fawn ashlar on which the masons had carefully inscribed their marks. Thereafter, a tour of the moats of the medieval Louvre was to become part of a visit to the museum.

What was known as the 'Tower of the Louvre' was, like the Tower of London, a defensive castle on the river, outside the city walls. It was a fortress of last resort, with its own wells to supply it in case of siege. It could also serve as a prison and as a treasury: after his defeat at Bouvines in 1214, Ferdinand of Portugal, Count of Flanders, was held there for thirteen years, and in 1295 the royal treasury, hitherto entrusted to the Templars, was moved there by Philip the Fair when he began his relentless campaign against the order.

The 'Tower' also had a symbolic function in the body politic: vassals of the realm held their fiefs from it, and it continued to be referred to as a legal entity even after the slighting of the donjon. The king often came to the Louvre, and the assemblies held here included the one that determined Anagni's attempt on the life of Pope Boniface VIII, promoted by Philip the Fair.

Only the west and south ranges contained residential accommodation. There was a great hall, presumably on the first floor, which under Charles V was known as the Salle Saint-Louis. That name is now given to a room at a lower level, with walls dating back to the time of Philippe Auguste and remains of a later thirteenth-century rib vault, which was rediscovered by chance during works in 1882. Its columns with carved capitals evoke the austere grandeur of the medieval palace, tempered only by the humorous grotesque masks that support the ribs at their springing from the walls. In this vaulted space, given dramatic lighting by Richard Peduzzi in 1989, display cases show a number of objects found during the excavations of 1984–85. Notable among them is a gilt parade helmet decorated with coloured enamels, which was discovered in pieces at the bottom of a well. It had presumably been stolen from a palace storeroom for its precious metals, and then thrown there by the thief. The royal inventories for 1411 mention a 'gilt chapel' which, like this helmet, was decorated with winged stags, the device 'En bien', the lilies of France in enamel, and a coronet of fleurs-de-lis. This refined symbolism was used by Charles VI and by the Dauphin, the future Charles VII, and the helmet must have belonged to one of them.

1364–80: residence of Charles V

A hundred years after its construction, the Louvre changed its character. Paris was enjoying the effects of the intellectual and economic flowering that characterized the 'century of St Louis', and the suburb of the Louvre had come of age: St Louis founded a hospital for the blind there, the Quinze-Vingts; manors were established, such as that of the rich Lombard banker Ernoul le Fin, taken over by Pierre des Essards, father-in-law of Etienne Marcel, the famous Provost of the Merchants; streets of houses had been built to the west of the castle.

A romantic – and somewhat fanciful – vision of the medieval castle.

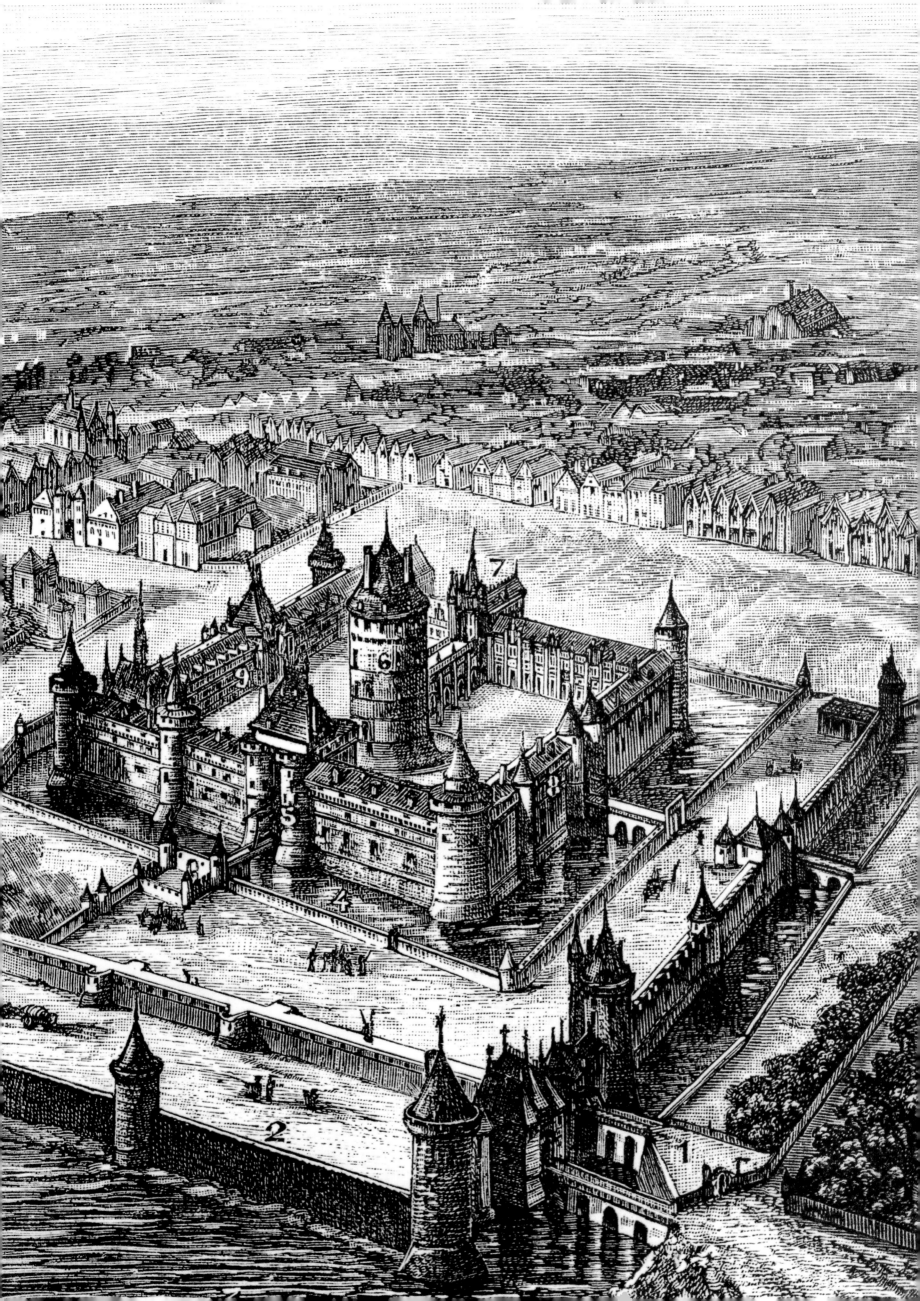

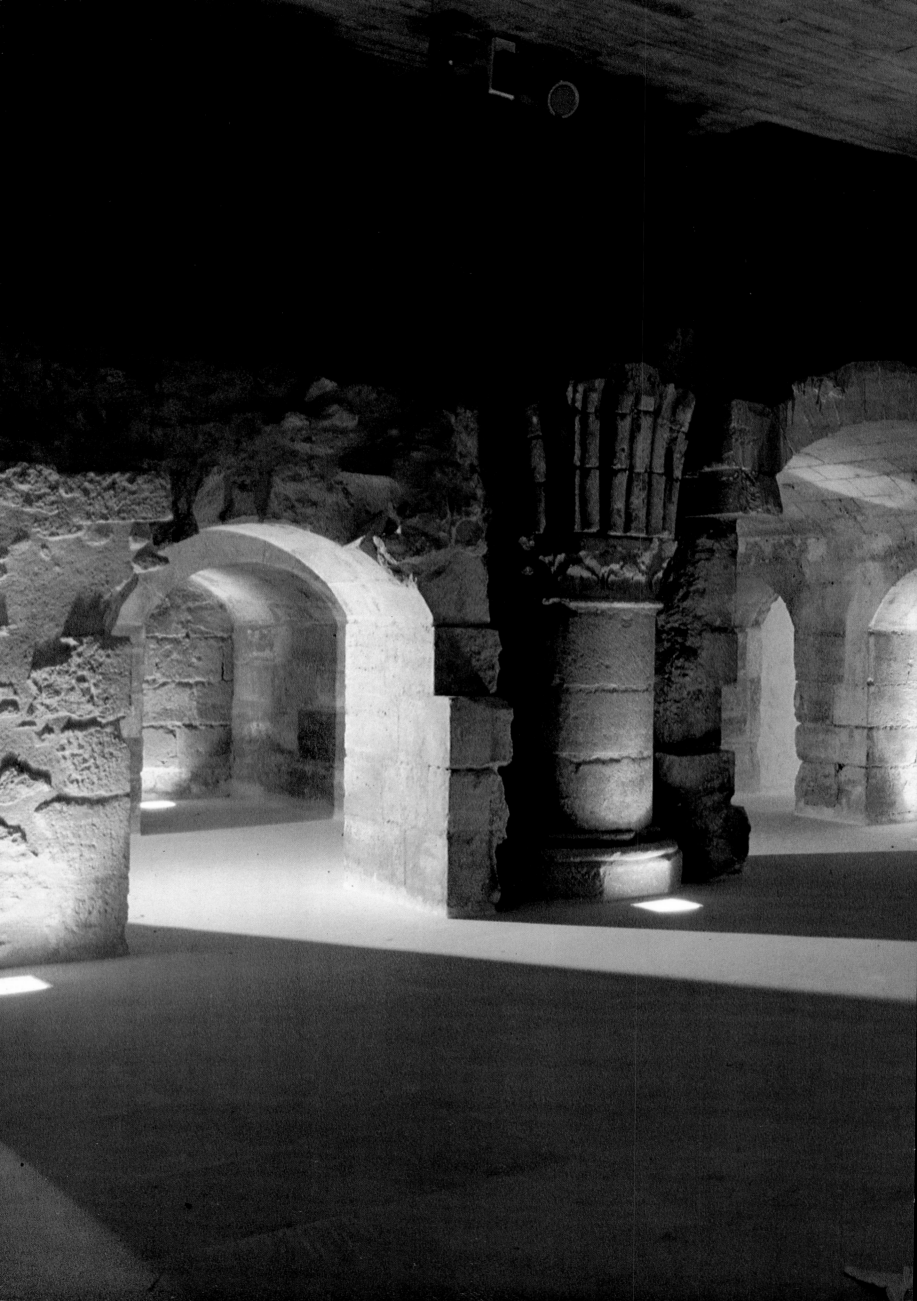

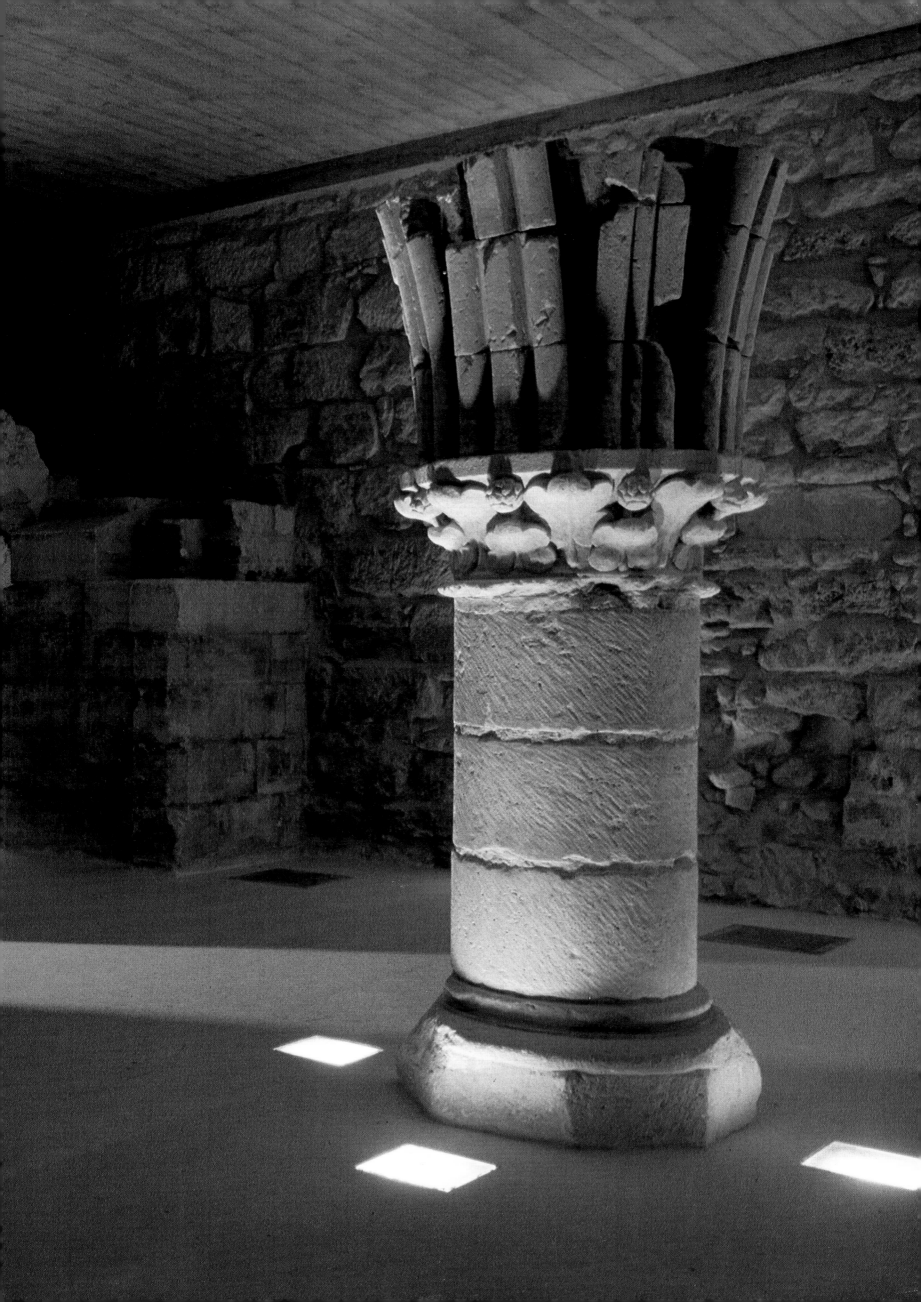

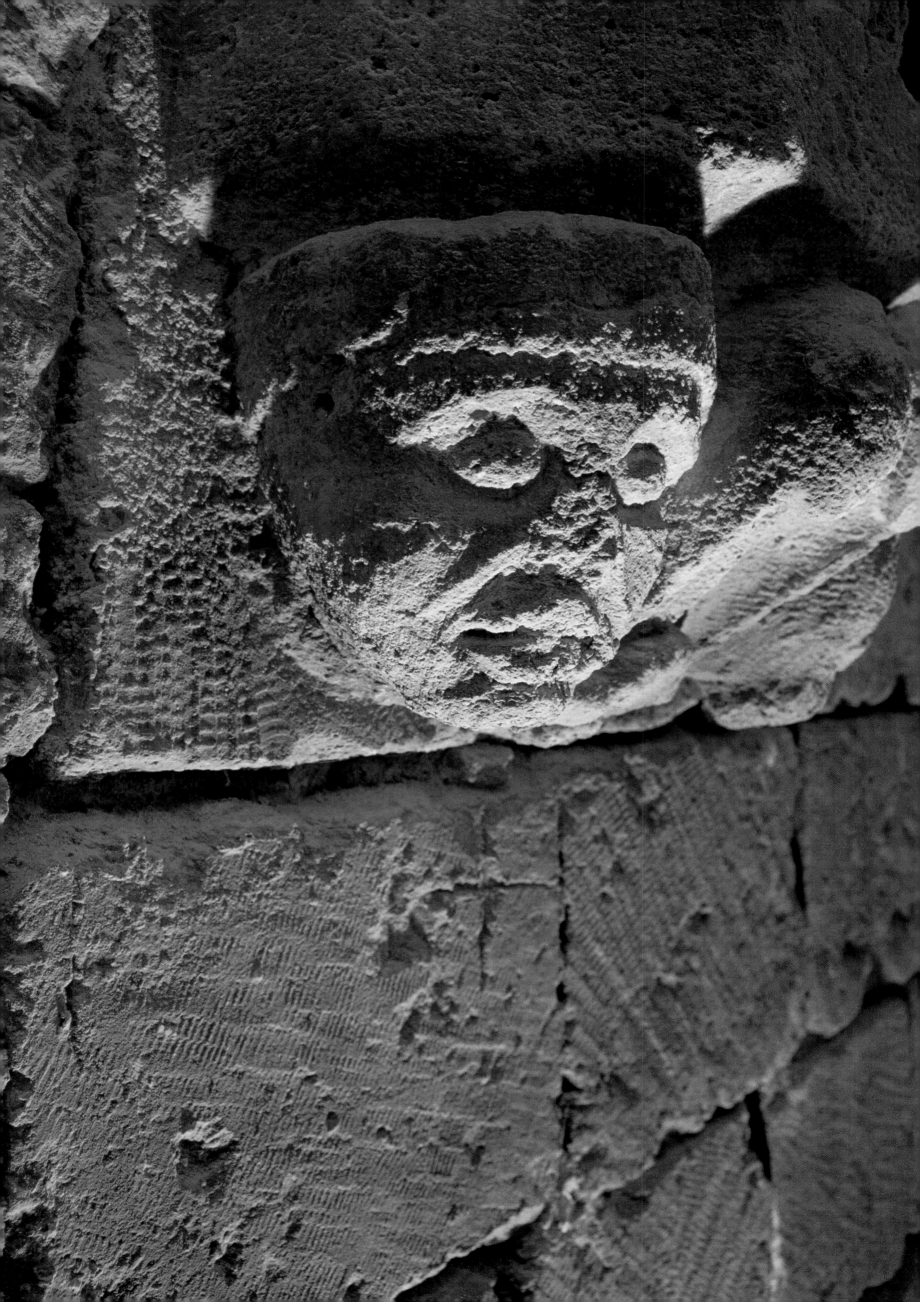

The dramatic clashes of the Hundred Years War were taking place far away, and the Louvre seemed to have lost its defensive function, when in 1357 the citizens' revolt led by Etienne Marcel broke out. Paris was by then a much larger town, and to protect it Etienne Marcel in 1358 had an earthen rampart constructed to the west of the expanding quarter of the Louvre. The Dauphin Charles, regent of France during his father Jean le Bon's captivity in England, defeated the rebels and completed the rampart in the following year. The result, known as the Wall of Charles V, consisted of a very broad band of earthen defences with a deep moat fed by the Seine. The excavations of Paul Van Ossel in 1990 exposed these massive works. They were altered in the early sixteenth century with the construction of a low wall and a tower for artillery: this last stage of the fortifications can be seen today in the underground complex of the Carrousel.

If the Louvre had lost its key role in the defence of Paris, it now acquired a new purpose: to protect the king himself. Charles V had bad memories of the old palace on the Ile de la Cité, where Etienne Marcel had forced him to look on as his marshals were executed, and had made him wear a hat in the colours of the city. He now sought both a secure home for himself and a place from which the rebellious citizenry could be held under military control. Between 1360 and 1384 he transformed the Louvre into a residence, well protected from the city and from the river by a system of walls and dry moats. It was not his main residence: the palace of the Cité occupied a unique position as the chief royal seat, for it was consecrated by the presence of the Sainte-Chapelle containing the relics that had been acquired by St Louis. Both in Paris and in the surrounding country Charles also had a number of other residences, including the Hôtel Saint-Pol and the castles of Vincennes and Beauté. And like all medieval kings, he did not stay long in one place but was often on the move – hunting, visiting his domains, and keeping the peace within his realm.

Shortly after his accession, Charles V commissioned his master mason, Raymond du Temple, to carry out building work at the Louvre to make the fortress habitable. New lodgings were created, with separate chambers and halls for the King and Queen, new large windows, and a chapel. Outside, both to the north and towards the river to the south pleasure gardens were laid out, with porticoes and pavilions made of wood, and even a menagerie (as at the Hôtel Saint-Pol), affording rural pleasures. Charles V was also a man of letters and ideas, and a patron of the arts – hence the name by which he is sometimes known, Charles the Wise. The north-west tower, formerly the mews or falconry, became the Library Tower, housing part of the large royal collection of manuscripts (973 works are listed in the inventory drawn up in 1373 by the librarian, Gilles Malet); the floor was paved with glazed tiles decorated with coats of arms. A spiral stair of eighty-three steps, corbelled out over the moat surrounding the *donjon*, led up to the state rooms. This 'Grande Vis', built in 1364–69, was the masterpiece of Raymond du Temple: its rise was punctuated by statues of the King and Queen, of the King's brothers, and of two sergeants-at-arms. (One of the latter was perhaps a portrait of the architect, who enjoyed that title.) A similar emphasis on the image of the ruler – common in antiquity, and seen also on the Emperor Frederick II's monumental gate at Capua – recurred in other works of Charles V, such as the fortresses of the Bastille and Vincennes, and the portal of the church of the Célestins. Significantly, this work at the Louvre was put in hand immediately after the death of Jean le Bon and the succession of Charles.

A proud, isolated structure confronting the city, white, bristling with towers and turrets, weathercocks and banners: thus the Louvre of Charles V appears in the rare images we have of it, all slightly later in date – in a miniature in the *Très Riches Heures* of the Duc de Berry (Musée Condé, Chantilly) and, later still, in the background of two famous altarpieces, the *Pietà of Saint-Germain-des-Prés* and the *Retable of the Parliament of Paris* (both in the Louvre).

Pages 14–15 The Salle Saint-Louis, below the western range of the medieval castle (now the Lescot wing).
The outer walls of the room are part of Philippe Auguste's castle. The columns, and the springers of the now destroyed stone vault,
belong to a thirteenth-century remodelling. The arches, vaults and solid walls in the background
are connected with the planned central staircase of the Lescot wing, begun in 1546.
Opposite A corbel in the form of a grotesque face.

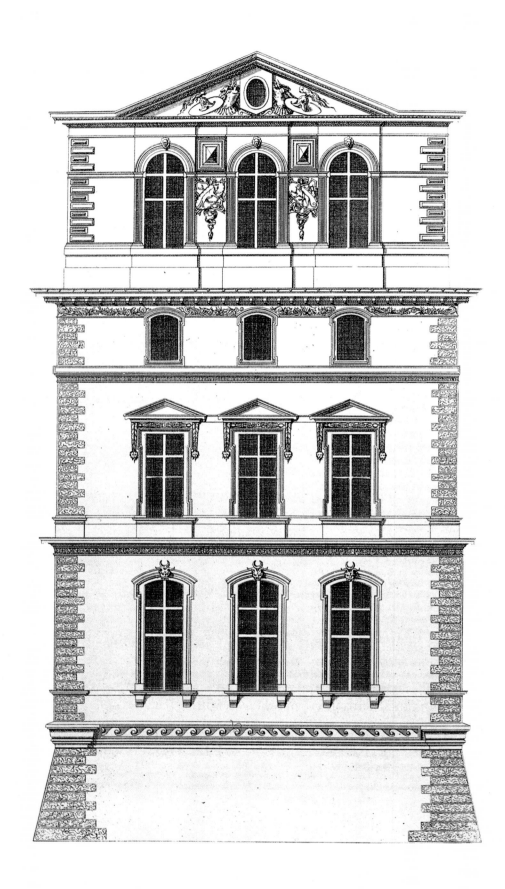

The river façade of the Pavillon du Roy, built under Henri II to contain the King's State Bedchamber and Council Chamber.

The Renaissance Palace

François I decides to remodel the Louvre

The late Middle Ages were not a good time for the Louvre. Paris was at risk during the struggles at the end of the Hundred Years War, and was in the hands of successive factions until 1420 when it was occupied by the English and the young Henry V took up residence in the castle.

After peace had finally been restored, the French kings from Charles VII to Louis XII abandoned the capital in favour of the Loire Valley. New Renaissance châteaux were built there, while the Louvre remained in its medieval state. Eventually, however, at the end of a reign that had seen such splendid architectural achievements as the castles of Chambord, Blois, Villers-Cotteret, the Château de Madrid, and especially Fontainebleau, François I turned his attention to his old Parisian stronghold. François' taste was for things Italian, and he had invited a number of Italian artists to France, including Leonardo da Vinci, Andrea del Sarto, Francesco Primaticcio, Rosso Fiorentino and Benvenuto Cellini; he was a lover of splendid pageantry (such as that of his meeting with Henry VIII of England at the Field of Cloth of Gold); he encouraged writers, and fostered a renaissance of the arts. A passionate huntsman in his early years, he had found little to attract him to Paris.

Yet on 15 March 1528, returning from his captivity in Madrid, the King announced to the magistrates of Paris that he intended to take up residence in the capital, and chiefly at the Louvre, 'knowing that our castle of the Louvre is the most commodious and fitting place for us to lodge in'. He had decided to 'cause the said castle to be repaired and put in order'. What had been the main entrance, to the south, was blocked, in favour of the eastern gate facing the city. Thus an east-west orientation was established that conditioned the future development of the great axis of Paris, which was eventually to extend from the Porte d'Honneur of the Louvre as far as the heights of the Défense. François I must have found the old fortress a gloomy place, for in February 1528 he had already had the great round tower demolished, its moat filled in, and the resulting courtyard paved, letting in light and air. New apartments were created, some with frescoes of nymphs and satyrs in the modern taste. The services were reorganized around the perimeter, with kitchens to the west and a tennis court to the east. The bank between the river and the moat was improved to create a passage 40 metres (130 feet) wide leading to the Tuileries, where he had bought a small estate in 1518 for his mother, Louise de Savoie. This eventually became the Quai du Louvre.

The castle retained its former function – if not as a prison, certainly as a treasury, for the Trésor de l'Epargne was installed there in 1523, together with the War Treasury and the Finance administration. At the same time, it was also a residence: the King lived there for a time in 1534, and festivities were staged, such as those for the marriage of the Duc de Guise and Mademoiselle de Longueville, and for the reception of the King of Scotland. Most splendid of all were the celebrations held during the visit to Paris of François I's great rival, the Emperor Charles V, on 1 January 1540: the courtyard of the old castle, still medieval but dressed up by recent works, was the scene of one of the magnificent feasts for which the King was famous; the centrepiece was a giant statue of Vulcan holding a torch.

Was the King embarrassed by his old castle? By the end of 1540 two major Italian architects had made their appearance at the French court: Giacomo Vignola, who accompanied Primaticcio bringing with him casts of antique statues, and Sebastiano Serlio, whose *Sixth Book of Architecture* includes a design for a '*casa del Re in città'*. Was this invitation connected with a project for the Louvre, as André Chastel suggested? Whatever was in his mind, nothing happened until the very end of his reign.

It was not until 2 August 1546 that François I commissioned Pierre Lescot to begin a radical remodelling of the castle, with 'a great range of lodgings where the great hall now is'. The western range, which was the largest and would have contained the great hall, was taken down to basement level and a new building was erected above. In a way that was satisfying both symbolically and economically, it occupied the exact site of its predecessor, and required no expropriations or purchases of additional land.

The architect chosen, Pierre Lescot, lord of Clagny, was a Frenchman, a Parisian, and a cleric. (He was almoner in ordinary to the King and commendatory abbot of Clermont, near Laval.) A new generation of French architects was in the ascendant, and the work at the Louvre appears as a turning-point in the appropriation of the Renaissance language of architecture not only by master masons but by men of culture such as Lescot and Philibert Delorme. Serlio quietly left the scene.

1546–59: the great work of Henri II

The first king to live at the Louvre for a significant length of time was Henri II. His court – and indeed that of his sons and their successors – remained itinerant, moving from château to château and even in Paris residing for part of the time at the elegant Hôtel des Tournelles. But the Louvre became a chief place of residence, where the King held council and from which he directed his kingdom. Fitting apartments were therefore necessary for a brilliant, professedly modern court, governed by a new etiquette.

One of Henri's motives in completing his father's project was manifestly the glorification of the monarchy. Royal power was to be expressed by a new building which departed completely from traditional architectural forms: in its structure, the iconography of its sculpture, the arrangement of its apartments, and the theatricality of the new great hall, the Louvre was to be a royal palace unlike any that had gone before.

The King reaffirmed Lescot's commission, while appointing Philibert Delorme superintendent of all other royal building projects. Work on the principal range extended from 1546 to 1566. The ground floor was built, and the central oculus was decorated by 1548 (we know the date from the notarized contract for the gilding of the inscription over the door) – undoubtedly by Jean Goujon, though no contract for this carving survives. This opening marks a projection where a stair was to rise in straight flights. The foundations of the stair can still be seen, in the form of supporting walls that cut across the medieval lower hall, known today as the Salle Saint-Louis.

On 10 July 1549 a change of plan was announced by the King: from centre of the range, the staircase was to be shifted to the north to allow the creation of one large hall instead of two smaller ones. The change meant a radical alteration to the design of the façade, to accommodate the staircase to the north, and the 'Tribunal' of the great hall to the south. Lescot accordingly created a strongly marked rhythm, with projecting bays emphasized by columns alternating with slightly recessed ranges whose ground floor is articulated by arcades creating the effect of a loggia. From the press of sculptors eager for the commission to decorate the new projecting bays at the ends, Jean Goujon was chosen in December 1549: it is to him that we owe the allegorical sculptures surrounding the oculi.

A second change of plan while work was in progress in 1553 substituted for the traditional high French roof an Italian-style attic storey and a double-pitch roof, of which the lower part is concealed behind a carved stone cresting. Two architectural innovations appeared at the Louvre: the double-pitch roof, which was to enjoy a long vogue in France, and polychromy – for into the creamy limestone of the façade are set a hard, fine-grained, white stone for the oculi and their surrounds, and various coloured marbles in the form of oval plaques, cartouches and lintels.

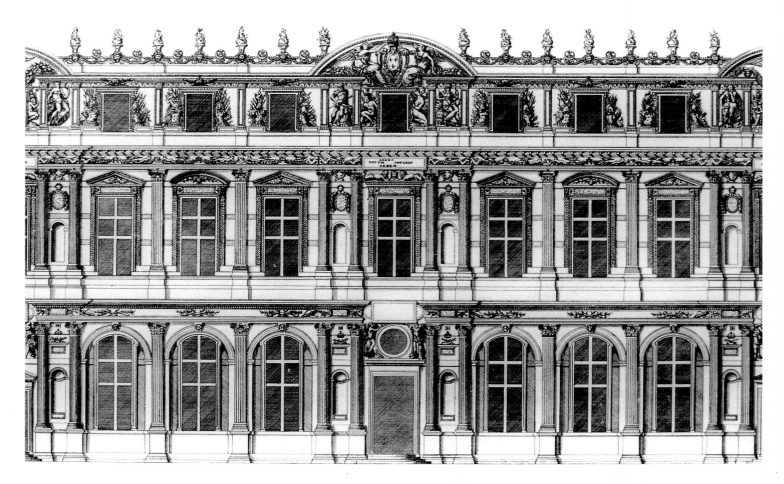

Thus the Henri II wing or Lescot wing was completed. Inside, it had a staircase with straight flights, the 'Grand Degré' (great stair), which ascends below a vault splendidly decorated in 1553–55 with sculptures on the theme of the hunt, featuring dogs, satyrs, and the figure of the goddess Diana (an allusion to the King's mistress, Diane de Poitiers). On the upper floor, the doorway was given a large relief of playful cherubs, those chubby putti derived from Italian art, which three hundred years later, in 1855, were to serve as models for the decoration of the Passage Richelieu in the new Louvre of Napoleon III. The entire ground floor was given over to a single great hall, which came to be known as the Salle des Cariatides. At its southern end, on a slightly higher level and separated from the rest of the room by four columns, was the Tribunal, where the King sat. At the opposite end, forming a portico around the entrance door, was a musicians' gallery supported on four tall stone caryatids – described in the contract of 1550 as 'term-like figures serving as columns'. They were the work of Jean Goujon, who besides being a sculptor was also an architect, had illustrated an edition of Vitruvius, and had written on the architecture of the ancients. Here he managed to be classical and decorative at the same time.

On the exterior, the Lescot wing is clearly articulated both horizontally and vertically: horizontally, in three storeys, each of which is emphatically characterized – a ground floor with an applied arcade of round-headed arches, a first floor with large windows, and a richly decorated attic storey, with pediments filled with figures and trophies carved by Jean Goujon; vertically, by the alternation between the three projecting bays, with doors surmounted by large oculi flanked by lithe allegorical figures, sculpted in shallow relief by Goujon (1548–50), and the two recessed sections. In May 1552 Goujon contracted to carve the first-floor window-heads: in the projecting bays we find a symmetrical motif consisting of the head of Diana framed between two hounds, while in the recessed sections there are male and female satyr heads. He then carved the frieze, with its playful putti holding swags, the royal cipher H, and the crescent moon, symbol of the goddess Diana. All these decorative elements have a strong sculptural presence.

The most remarkable part of the decoration is the attic storey, which Goujon contracted in May 1554 to 'enrich with figures in three great pediments on the top storey of the building'. The monumental figures are almost brutally powerful. Their emphasis is very probably due to Goujon's wish faithfully to follow

Lescot's façade as it was illustrated in *Les Plus Excellents Bastiments de France* by Jacques I Androuet du Cerceau.

Vitruvius' advice that sculptures placed far from the viewer should be clearly visible; but such an appetite for sculptural density and for the expression of force must also owe much to Michelangelo. Goujon must have known the Sistine Chapel: the allegorical figure of a virtue that crowns the tomb of a member of the Dreux-Brézé family in Rouen Cathedral, of which he is said to have been the architect, clearly looks back to one of Michelangelo's Sybils. Now, at the Louvre, he could bring into play two opposing strains of Mannerism, in the swirling, supple elegance of the female figures that flank the oculi, and the dynamism of the giants at attic level. The sculptural richness of the courtyard façade was in marked contrast to the austerity of the (now lost) elevation to the outside world, but what that faced was merely the service court or kitchen court.

Goujon, who was active at the Louvre from 1548 to 1562, was unquestionably Lescot's most prestigious collaborator, and one might almost say that he was the co-author of this highly three-dimensional façade, where sculpture plays a role unequalled in French architecture. Lescot and Goujon had already worked together brilliantly as a team on the *jubé* or rood screen of Saint-Germain-l'Auxerrois, where the parapet displayed a large relief of the Lamentation over the Dead Christ and four small reliefs of the Evangelists (now in the Department of Sculpture at the Louvre). It is suggested that the two men also collaborated on the Fontaine des Innocents in 1549. But we must not forget that Goujon claimed to be an architect as well as a sculptor, and it was in that role that he had worked at the château of Ecouen for the Connétable Anne de Montmorency, a great patron and friend of Henri II.

At the Louvre, the sculptural programme reflects the aspiration of Henri II – the 'most Christian King' – to a power that was not merely secular but quasi-mystical. The imagery expounds a highly philosophical view of royal power. Theoretically, the monarchy represented divine order; it mediated between the King's subjects and the world of ideas, nature, and knowledge. On the central projecting bay we see the embodiment of power: in the pediment are the royal arms, held by figures of Fame, while below two deities of war, Mars and Bellona, flank chained prisoners. On the right-hand projection, a figure of Science or Learning, holding a caduceus, in the pediment surmounts two ancient philosophers (Euclid and Archimedes?) with attendant genii depicted reading and writing. On the left-hand projection, we see Nature holding a cornucopia, surrounded by the gods of plenty: Ceres and the harvest, Bacchus and the vine, Pan and the forests, and Neptune and the oceans. Thus Nature and Science are complementaries, held in a cosmic equilibrium, whose point of balance is divine/royal Concord. The philosophical notion of Concord was one that preoccupied contemporary political philosophers, notably Guillaume Postel.

In 1556 Lescot erected the Pavillon du Roi, or *'gros pavillon'*, at the southern end of the new range. This tower-like structure faced the river with an austere elevation whose only decoration was a pediment filled with trophies. Here Lescot introduced another new feature to France: alternately long and short quoins with vermiculated rustication. The motif came from the Palazzo Farnese in Rome; Lescot clearly liked it, and used it again at the château of Vallery (Yonne). It was to feature in all the subsequent building campaigns at the Louvre, reaching a flamboyant climax in the work commissioned by Napoleon III. Two other distinctive features of the external façade of the Pavillon du Roi were also to have a long life: three tall round-headed windows on the top storey forming a belvedere – a motif that reappears in the pavilions built in the seventeenth and nineteenth centuries – and masks or grotesque heads on the keystones of the ground-floor windows.

Internally, the Pavillon du Roi had four storeys, of which the lowest level housed the Council Chamber while above, on the *piano nobile*, enjoying a magnificent view, were two royal bedchambers. The finer of the two was the State Bedchamber, which was square, with an ornate timber ceiling designed by Lescot and executed in 1556 under the direction of Francisque Scibecq de Carpi, a cabinet-maker from Lombardy who had already distinguished himself in the Galerie François I at Fontainebleau and at Anêt. The room itself disappeared during later alterations, but the ceiling survives, re-erected under the Restoration on the first floor of the Colonnade wing.

The upper part of the central bay of the Lescot wing, with winged figures of Fame, Mars and Bellona, and captives in chains.

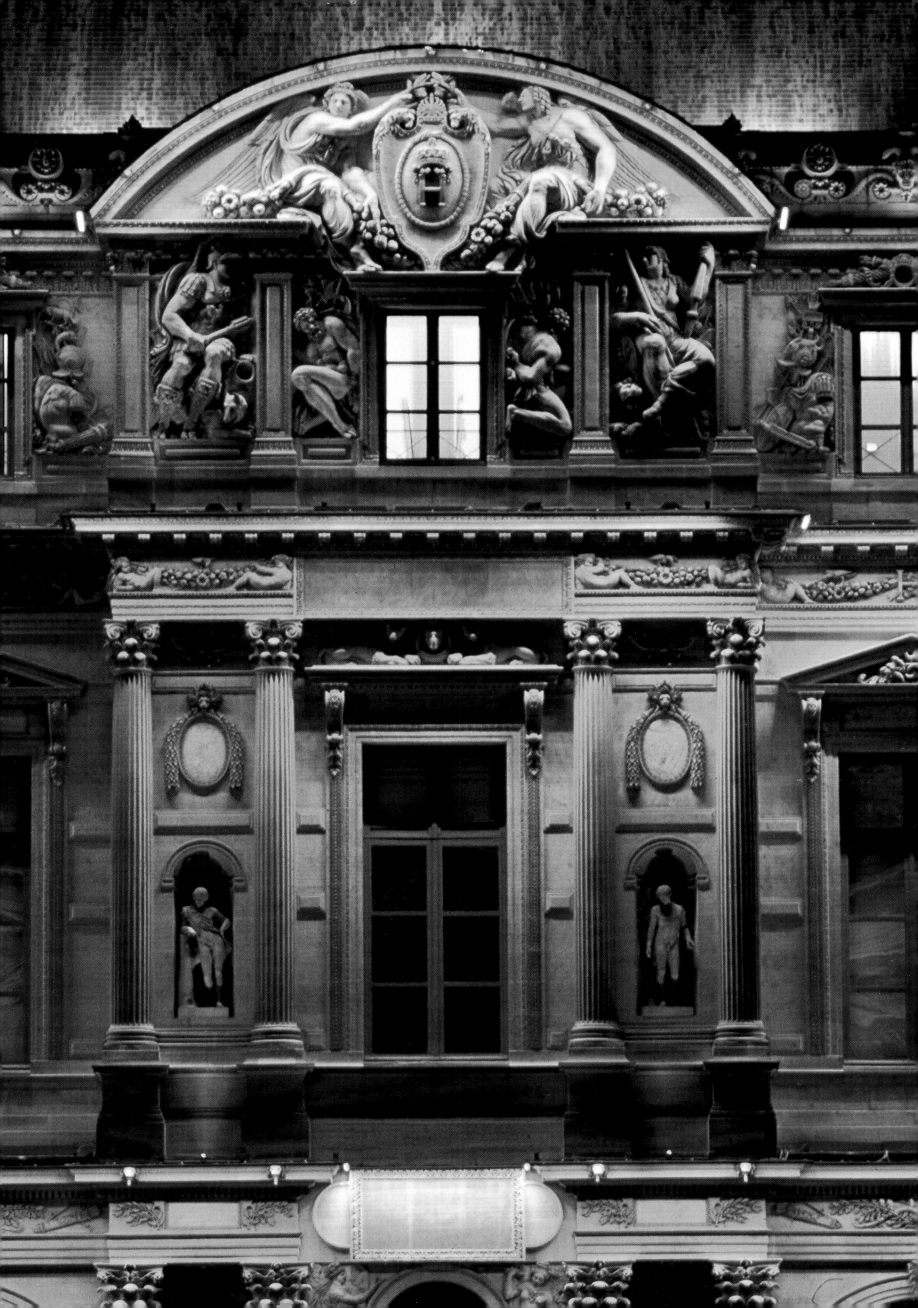

From the first floor of the Lescot wing you entered a great antechamber – now known as the Henri II Vestibule – of which the ceiling was also carved by Scibecq de Carpi, with the assistance of François Carmoy, in 1557–58 (in 1953 its central field was filled with Georges Braque's *Birds*), and that room led to a vast guardroom, much altered over the centuries, where antique bronzes are now displayed.

1560–88: the palace of the last Valois

Jacques I Androuet du Cerceau tells us that Henri II, 'finding himself so greatly satisfied at the sight of so perfect a work, considered extending it around the other three sides, to make this court a nonpareil'. And indeed, Lescot began to demolish the southern range of the medieval fortress, to replace it by a new wing, the elevation of which would continue the design that he had just built. This wing would house the queens – the Queen Mother on the ground floor, and Henri II's Queen above. One unit, a recessed section flanked by two projecting bays, was built. Through the ciphers of Henri II and his successor Charles IX carved on it we can follow the progress of the works. In 1562–63 the Lheureux brothers and Martin Lefort carved the frieze of swags, putti and birds; in 1564–65, Etienne Carmoy and Martin Lefort produced the trophies on the attic storey, together with lion heads and swags of oak leaves. This is probably also the date of the attic stages of the projecting bays, which used episodes from ancient history to illustrate Charles IX's device, 'Justice and Charity'. The reliefs were taken down in 1806 under Napoleon, when the attic storey was rebuilt, but they are displayed today in a rotunda on the way from the Pyramid to the medieval Louvre: the subjects are the justice of Cambyses, the justice of Zaleucus, Roman Charity, and what is probably a Roman priest-king. The pediments, containing allegorical figures of Charity and Justice, were carefully salvaged by Napoleon's architects, the Neoclassicists Percier and Fontaine, who were great admirers of the French Renaissance, and re-erected in 1806 in the Passage Saint-Germain-l'Auxerrois.

The splendid new palace that now existed was the setting for the excesses and intrigues of the last of the Valois. By now its military function was minimal; the Arsenal had moved in 1572 to the Quai des Célestins (where the Bibliothèque de l'Arsenal still is today). The Louvre was the scene of royal festivities and marriages, such as those of Claude de France and the Duke of Lorraine, of the future François II and Mary Stuart in 1558, and of Henry of Navarre and Marguerite of France – the future Henri IV and Reine Margot – in 1572. But it also witnessed the St Bartholomew's Day Massacre, in the night of 23 August 1572, when the bell of Saint-Germain-l'Auxerrois gave the signal for a general slaughter of Protestants. With the exception of Henry of Navarre and his cousin the Prince de Condé, who were protected as descendants of St Louis, all the Protestants in the palace were cast out to the murderous frenzy of the mob. Within the palace itself, bloodshed extended even into the room of Henri III's sister Marguerite, Queen of Navarre. Charles IX was accused of having taken part in the murders himself. The image of the killer-king haunted the Louvre for Republicans, to the extent that in the nineteenth century the window of the Petite Galerie looking towards the Seine was mistakenly identified as the 'Balcony of Charles IX' from which he was said to have shot down escaping Protestants with a crossbow.

Henri III was a man of paradoxical contrasts – religious yet depraved, capable of refined literary judgment yet cruel, intelligent yet disliked. When he left the Louvre, it was often to take part in mystically inspired processions. Inside the palace, he presided over his learned academy, which was the first in France to bring together men of letters and artists. Again, blood was spilled: the blood of pages, punished for laughing at religion; of Saint-Mégrin, the King's favourite, stabbed as he left the Louvre by followers of the Duc de Guise; even that of the lions in the royal menagerie, deliberately shot to death with crossbows after the King had a terrifying dream. Finally, at the end of the Journée des Barricades in May 1588, cornered by a crowd of the people of Paris, Henri III escaped from the Louvre by the passage to the Seine as the rebels took over the palace.

The stone vault of the 'Grand Degré', carved with allusions to the hunt.

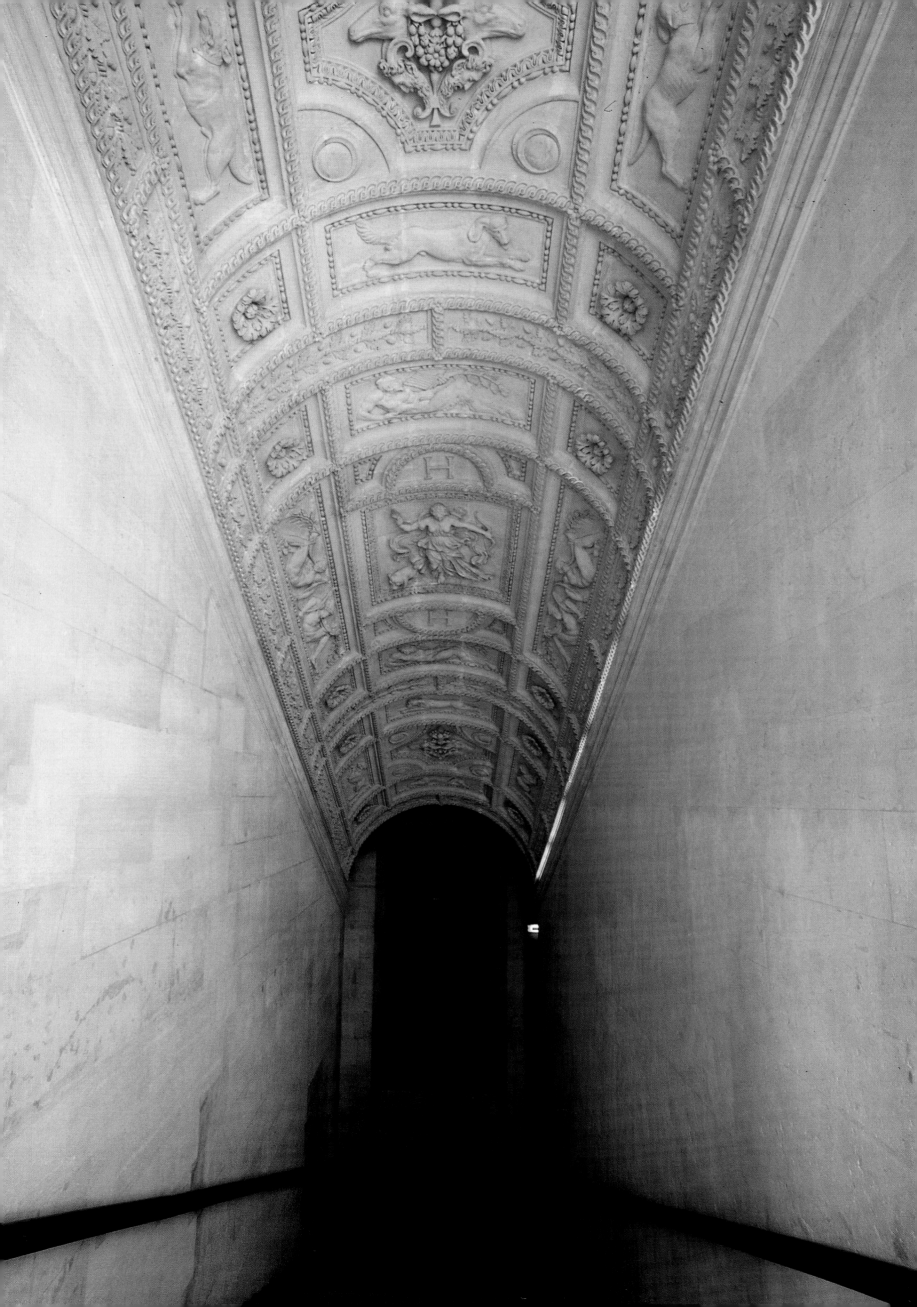

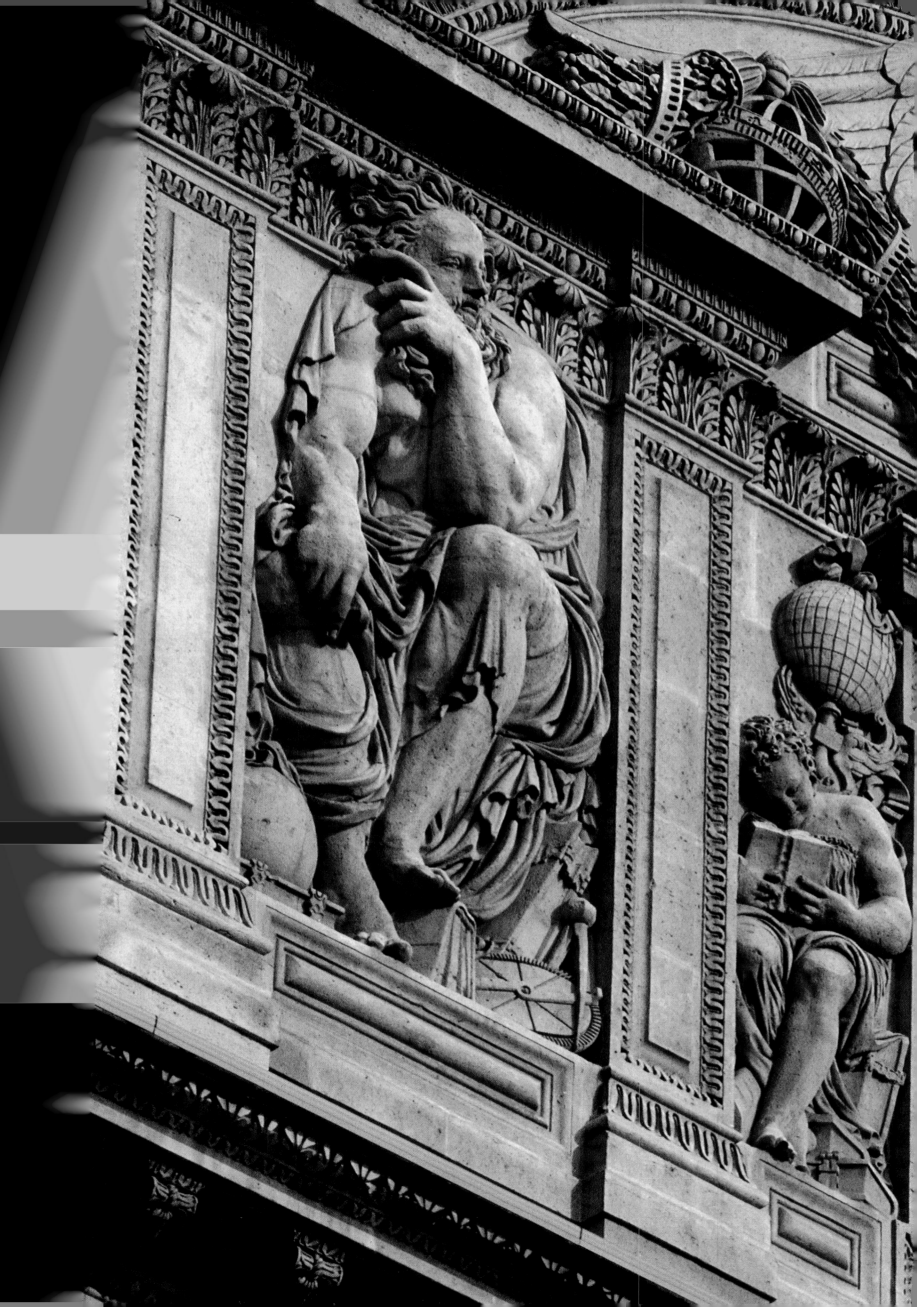

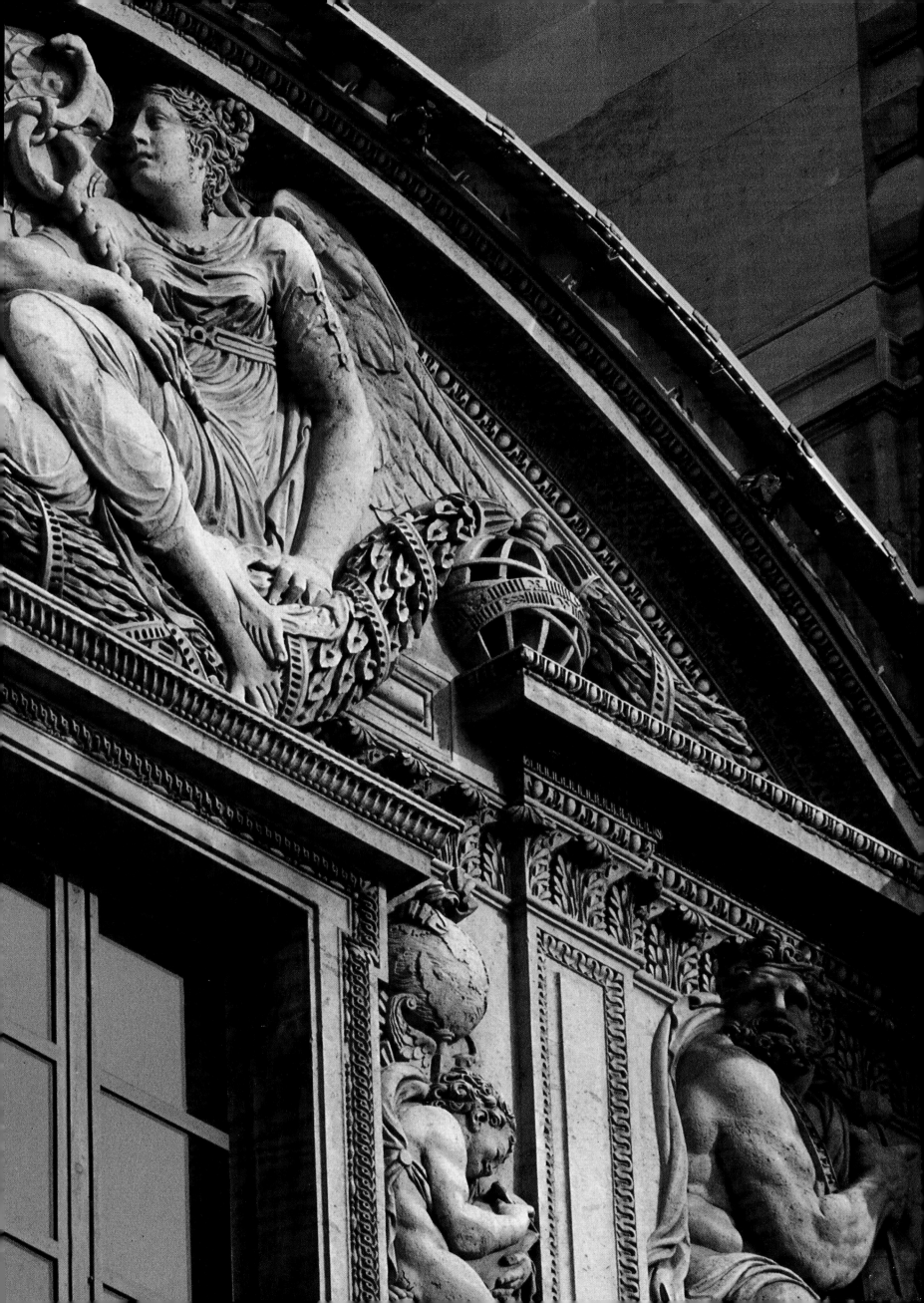

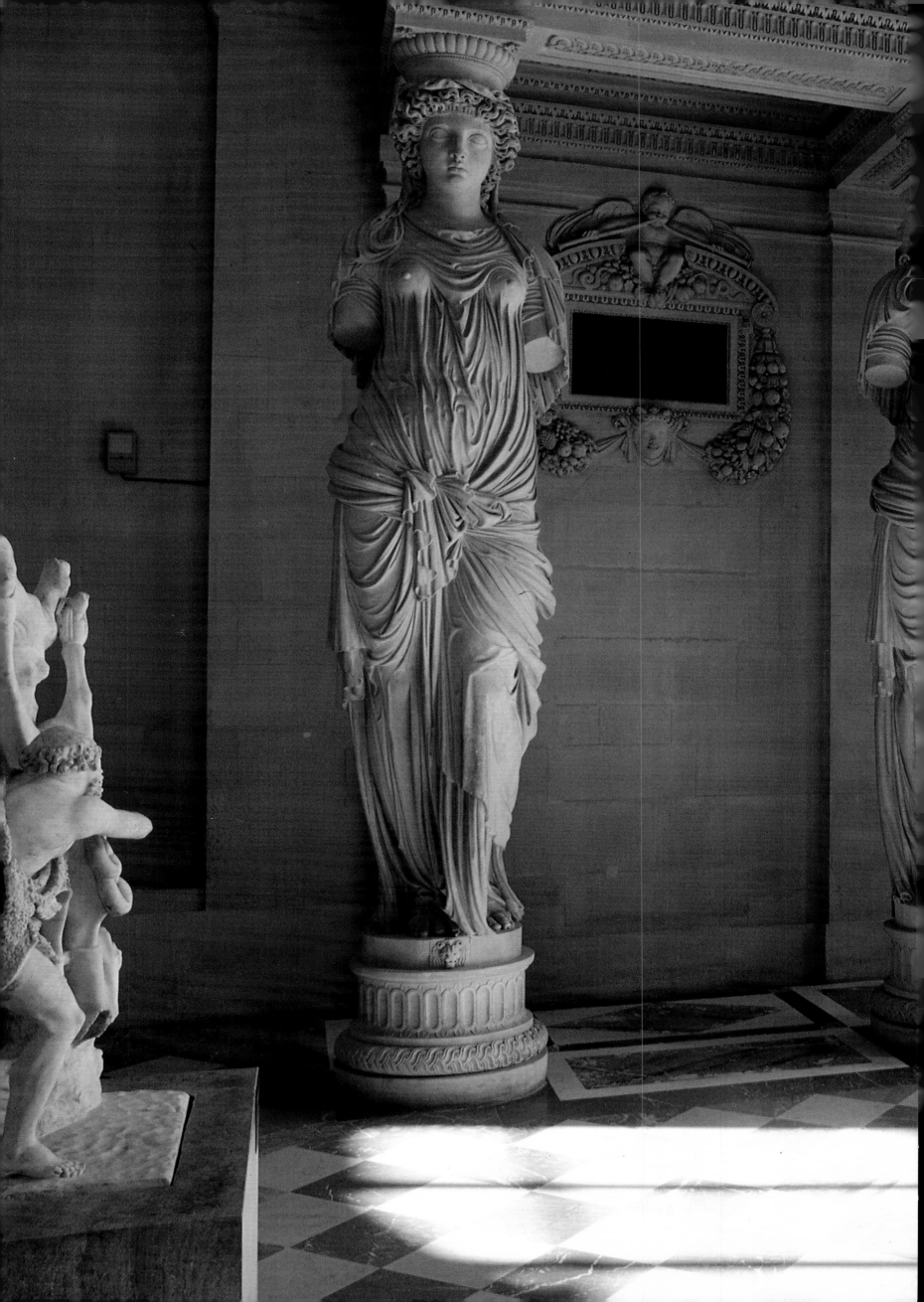

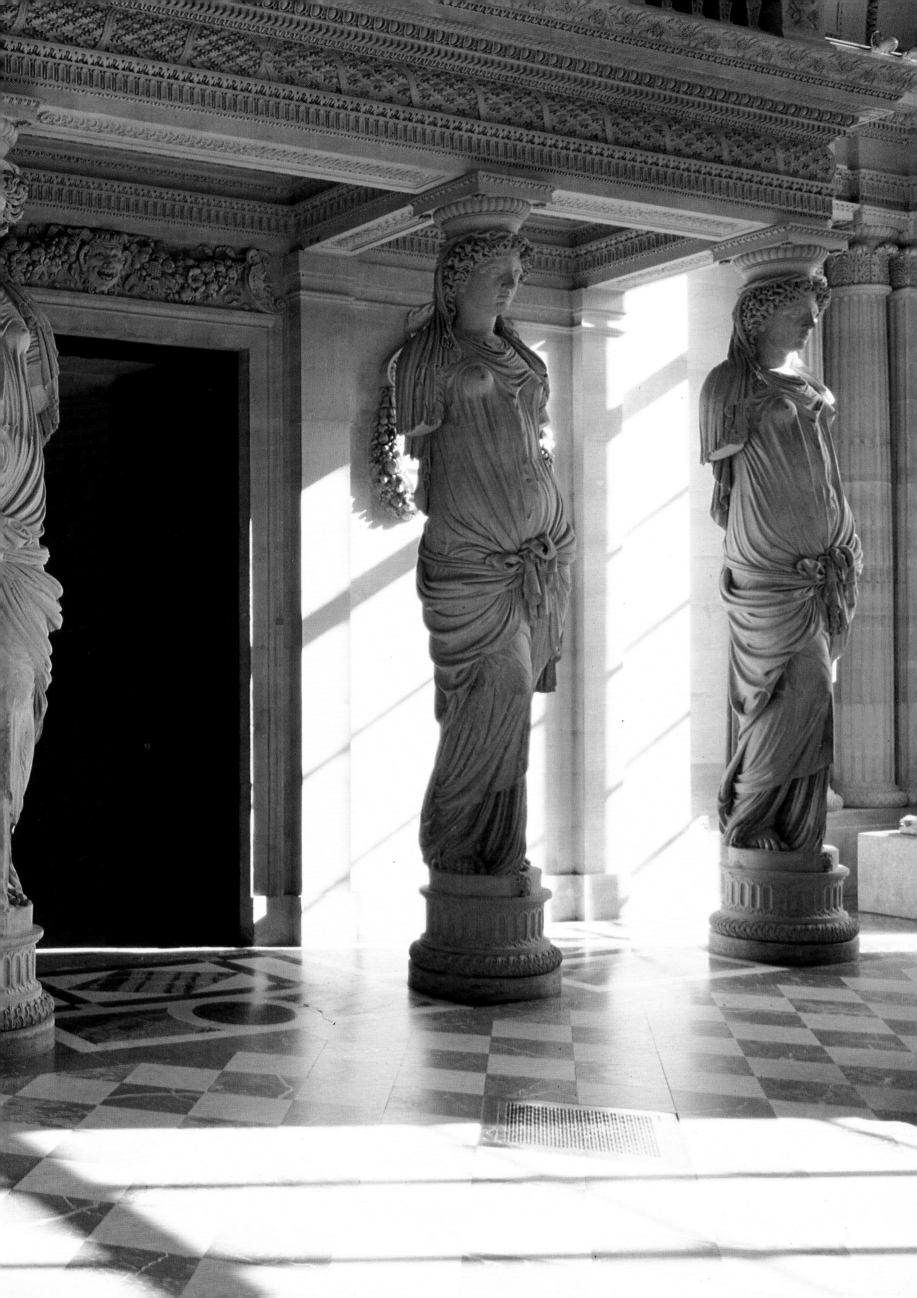

Pages 26–27 The attic stage of the northern pavilion of the Lescot wing. The robust figures, sculpted by Goujon, depict Science or Learning holding a caduceus, at the top; two ancient philosophers, perhaps Euclid and Archimedes, accompanied by instruments of measurement; and two genii reading and writing. The numerous globes and armillary spheres are allusions to science and also to Henri II's dream of French imperial power.

Pages 28–29 The musicians' gallery in the Salle des Cariatides. Goujon contracted to sculpt the caryatids, from which the room takes its name, in 1550.

Opposite A view from the Tribunal end of the Salle des Cariatides, looking towards the musicians' gallery. Under the direction of Percier and Fontaine, in 1806, the room was given fluted columns supporting a stone vault, and transformed into part of the Musée des Antiques. It now houses Roman copies of Greek sculptures, including the famous *Diane à la Biche* (*Diana with a Doe*), seen in the centre.

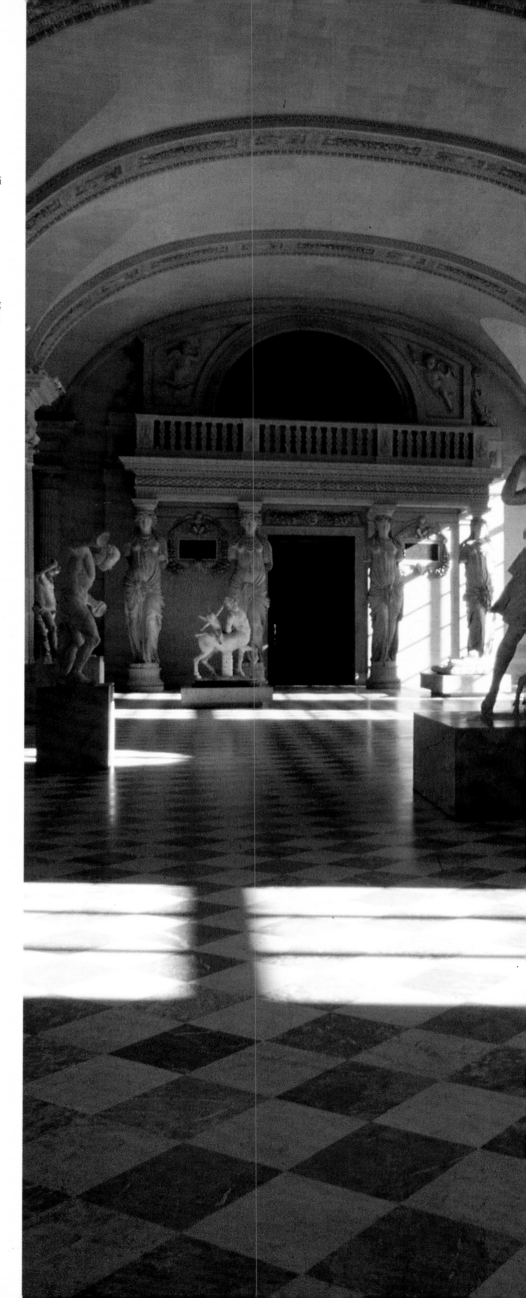

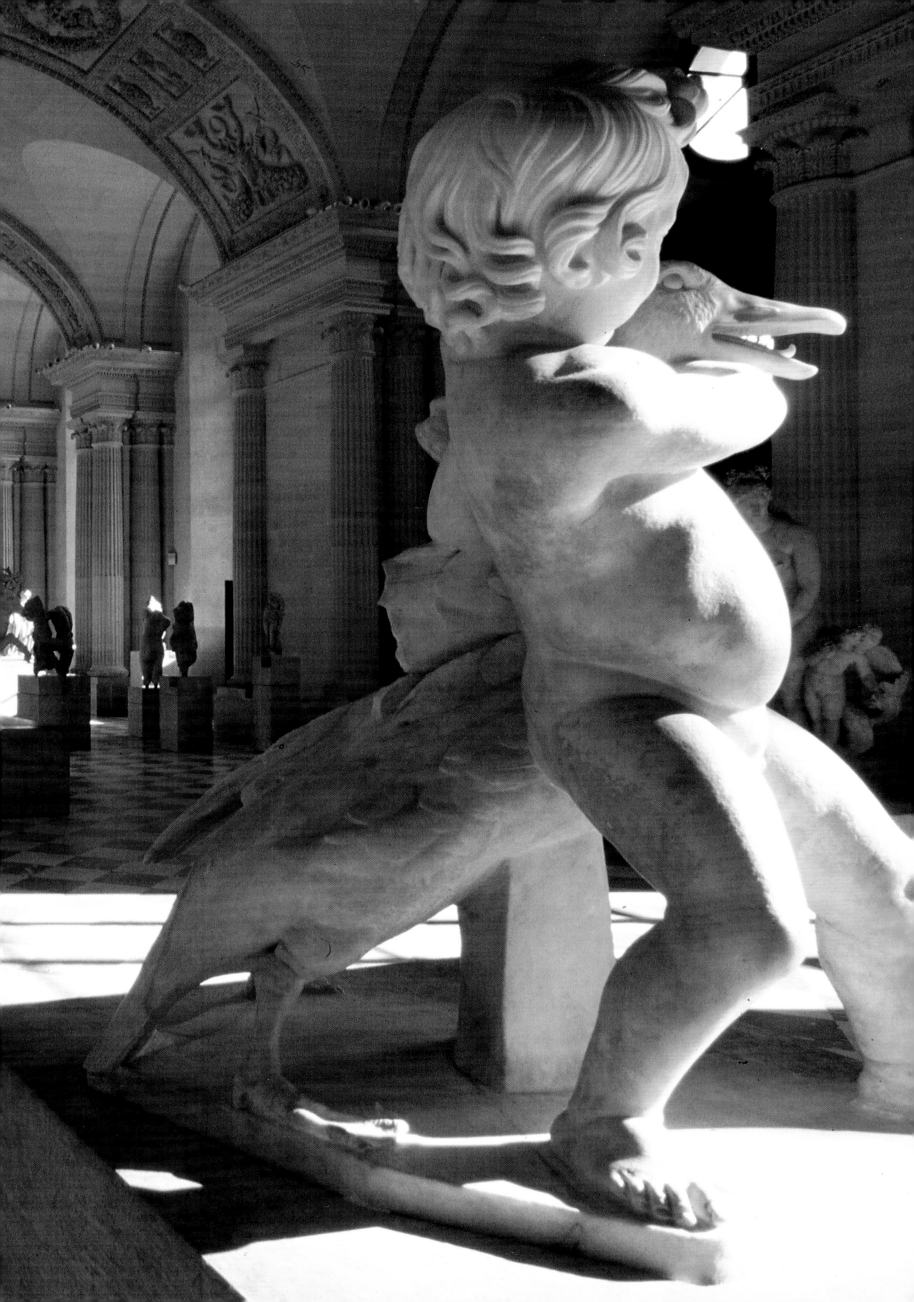

His excesses were followed by those of the Catholics of the League. In December 1591 Mayenne chose the beams of the Salle des Cariatides as the gibbet from which to hang the Sixteen, the Parisian leaders who had executed President Brisson. Shortly afterwards, in January 1593, the States of the League met in the upper hall, and in April of the same year it was at the Louvre that Mayenne received Philip II of Spain's claims to the throne of France.

And so the palace remained unfinished. Or, one should say, the palaces – for a few hundred yards to the west, the Queen Mother, Catherine de Médicis, had begun a new château, called the Tuileries from the tile-makers' workshops that had formerly occupied the site. Her architects were Philibert Delorme, from 1563 until his death in 1570, and then Jean Bullant. Delorme was an architect and theorist from Lyons; he had been in charge of royal works under Henri II, and had built the château of Anêt for Diane de Poitiers and the château of Saint-Maur for the Queen. His project for the Tuileries was vast and magnificent. The scheme illustrated by Du Cerceau in his *Les Plus Excellents Bastiments de France* (which owes something to the illustrator's imagination) shows a vast rectangle measuring 188 by 118 metres (617 by 387 feet) around a central courtyard; ancillary courtyards may also have been envisaged. Delorme had begun by erecting the *corps de logis* to the west, and had laid the foundations of two wings at right angles to it (discovered in recent excavations). He then gave up work on the wings, and concentrated on the central pavilion, which was later given a dome, and on its two lower wings, provided with terraces. The façades displayed rich and profuse decoration, including Ionic columns encircled with bands of ornament that were to have a long posterity in French architecture. Some survive, rescued when the palace was demolished in 1882; their design had already been taken up in the Louvre of Napoleon III, or more precisely in those parts of the new building closest to the Tuileries. Many of the sculptures, marble inlay and gilt-bronze decoration on the Tuileries façades reflected the taste of the Queen Mother, who was born a Medici. The commission to the sculptor Ponce Jacquiot lays particular stress on the many carved figures reclining on the pediments, in the manner of Michelangelo's Medici tombs at San Lorenzo in Florence. Delorme was also keenly interested in the interior of the palace: the centre was occupied by a famous staircase, elliptical in plan, where the steps rose around a hollow centre ringed with columns – a technical tour de force of luminous elegance.

Delorme's successor on his death in 1570 was Jean Bullant, who had built the châteaux of Ecouen and Chantilly for the Connétable Anne de Montmorency. Work began to the south on the 'Pavillon Bullant', a two-storeyed structure with Ionic and Corinthian orders superimposed in canonical fashion. This remained incomplete, and a pavilion to the north never rose above foundation level.

At the same time, the Tuileries Gardens were created, in an area away from the buildings to the west, between the Seine and the property boundaries along the Rue Saint-Honoré. In this vast space, 300 metres wide by 500 metres long (985 by 1640 feet), a Florentine gentleman, Bernard de Carnessequi, created a world of fantasy and animation of the sort for which Tuscan villas are still celebrated today. *Berceaux* (tunnel arbours) and trellises, woods planted as wildernesses, and a vegetable garden laid out in neat rows combined to form a microcosm of nature. There were special features, too, for this was already a park designed to be visited for entertainment: an echo, a 'Daedalus' or labyrinth, fountains, and a most remarkable grotto, decorated with glazed ceramics commissioned by the Queen in February 1570 from the brilliant Protestant craftsman and scholar Bernard Palissy.

Some of Palissy's material was subsequently discovered in kilns on the site of the Cour du Carrousel – first in 1865, and then as recently as 1990. Plaster moulds, earthen impressions, unglazed casts and others bright with enamel colours, and experiments with transparent glazes show us all the stages in a patient process of making casts from natural objects and then recreating them by means of highly complex techniques.

Opposite One of the caryatids sculpted by Jean Goujon in the Salle des Cariatides.

Pages 34–35 The ceiling of the Henri II Vestibule, carved by Scibecq de Carpi with the assistance of François Carmoy. Braque's *Birds* replaced earlier paintings in 1953.

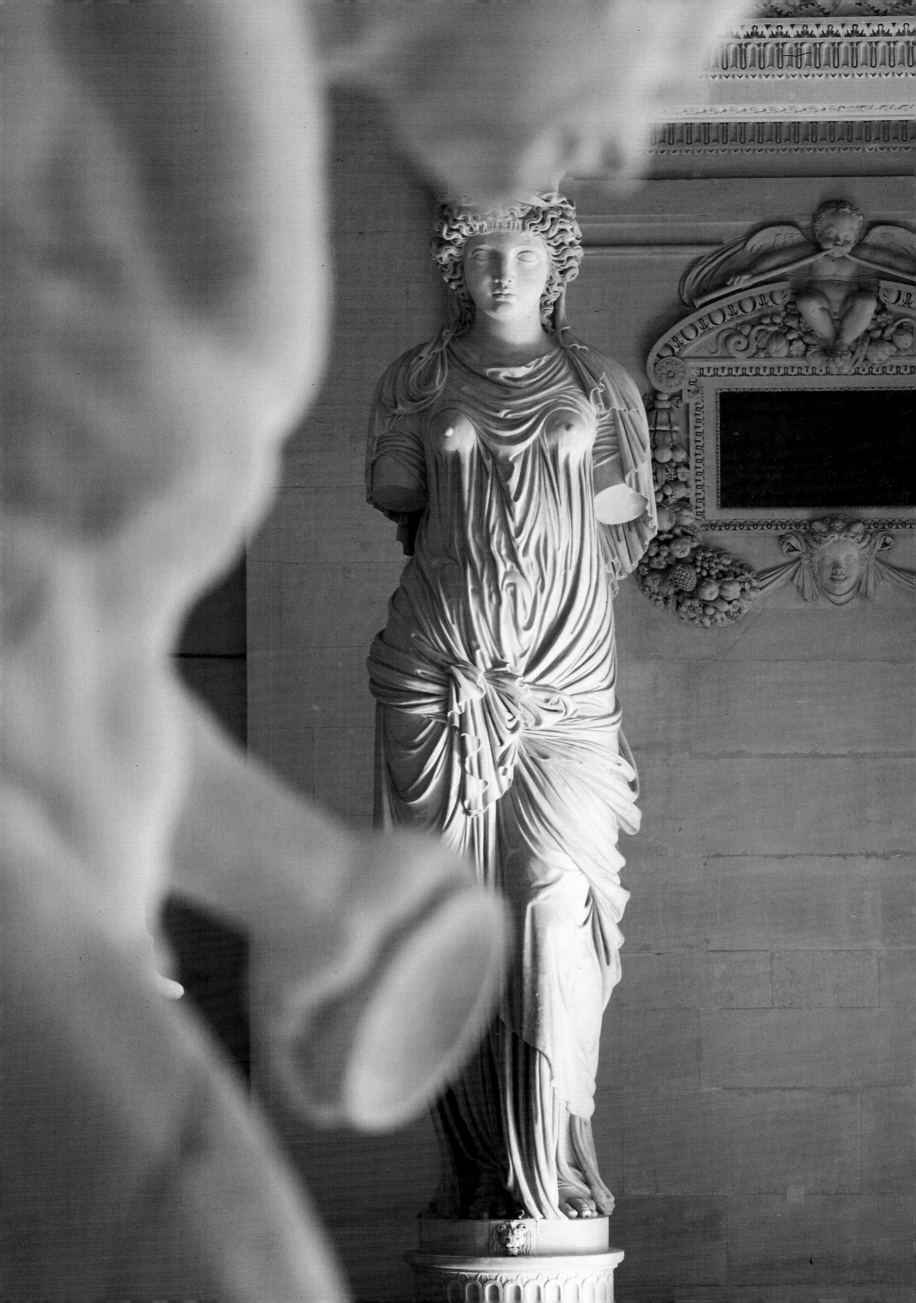

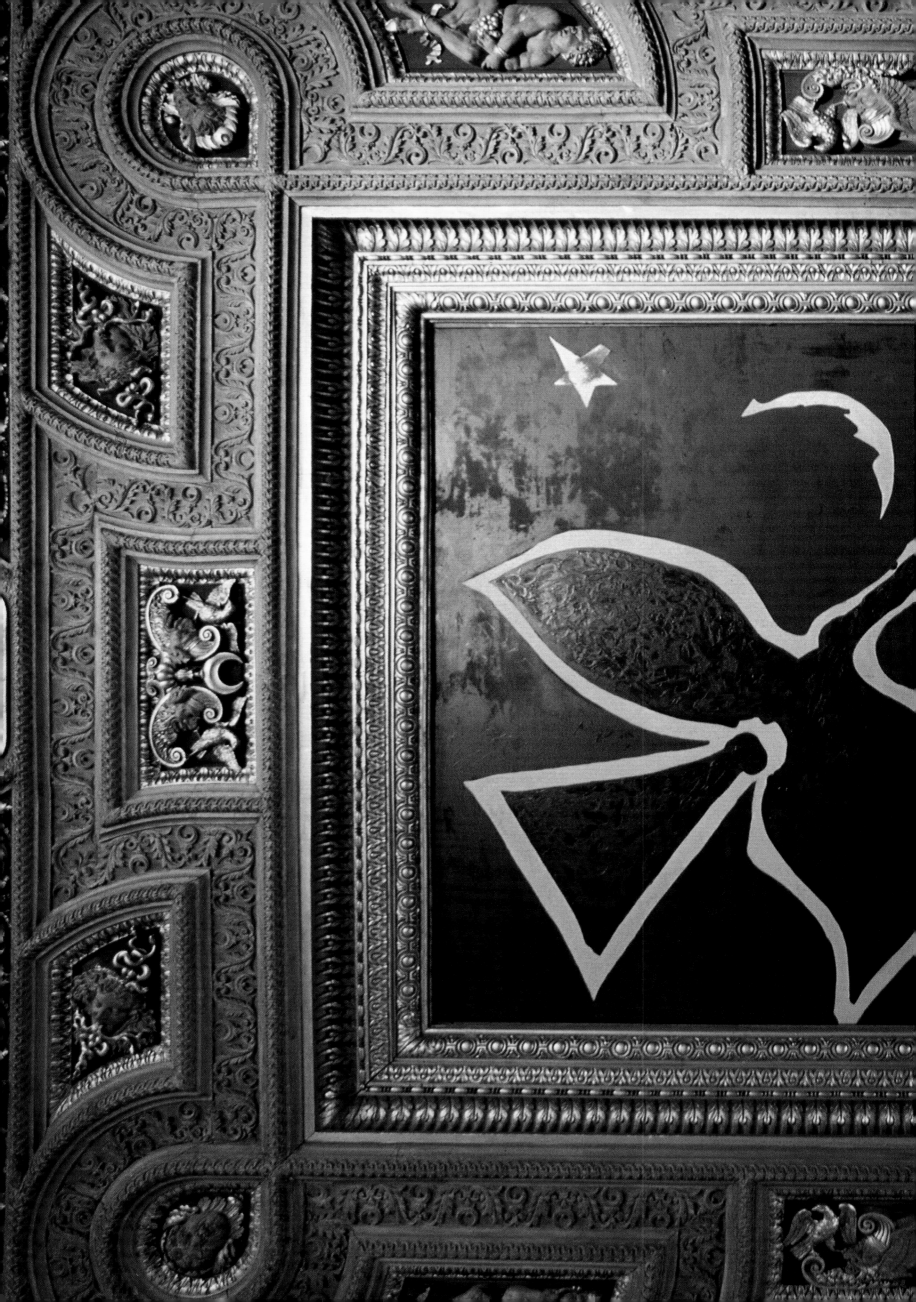

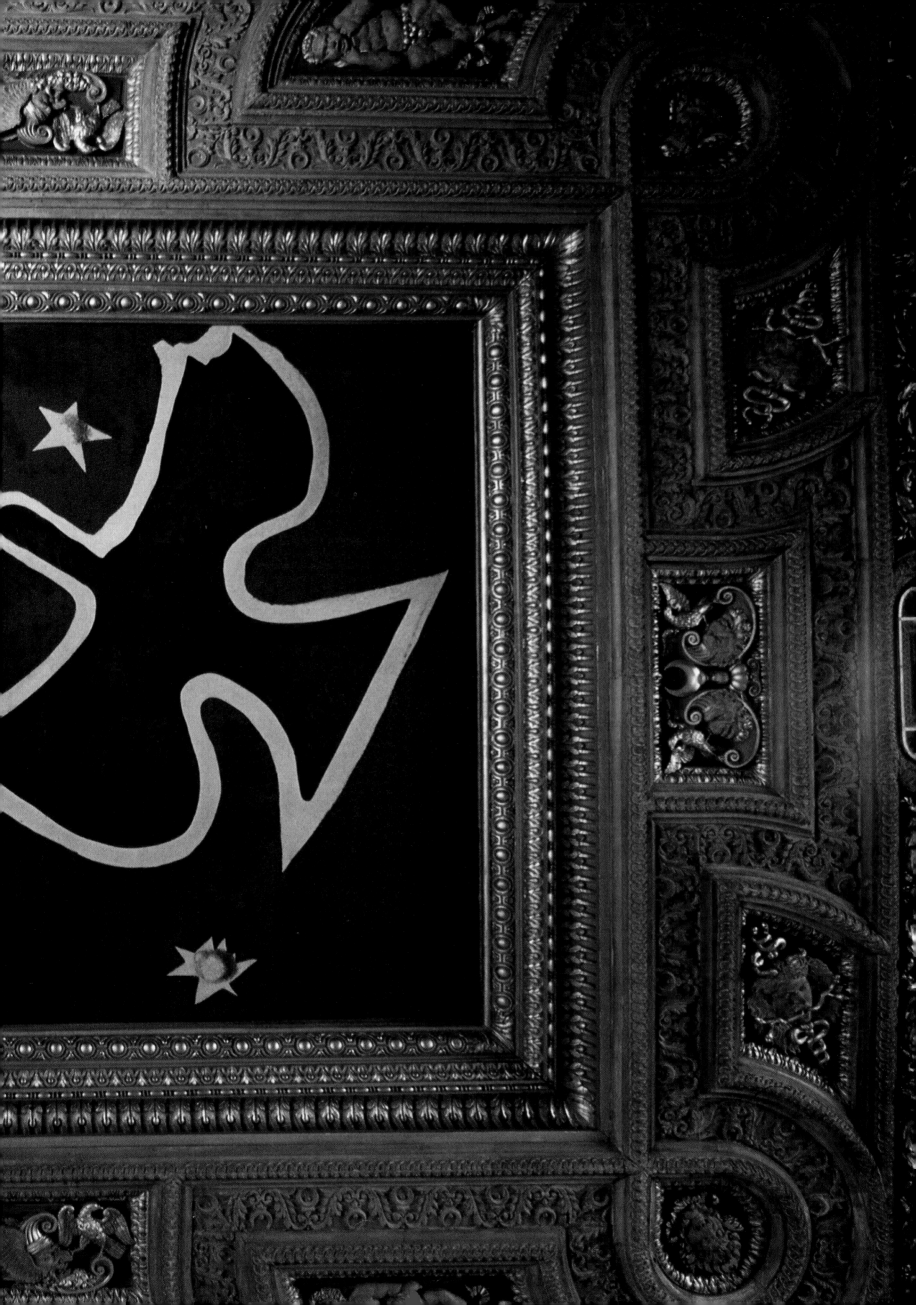

In these techniques, Palissy played with the textures and colour of clay and enamels. Some complete decorative elements were also found, intended for a grotto (probably that of the Tuileries, but possibly Ecouen), as well as medallions, spoons made of glazed earthenware, modelled animals – chiefly snakes, lizards and frogs – swags of fruit, moulds of figures and animals, reliefs (the arms of Catherine de Médicis, the sword of the Connétable de Montmorency, the head of a man), and the ingredients for great ceramic dishes which were decorated with plants and animals and sometimes also medallions. Here, piled into a kiln, was material that gave a unique insight into the work of one of the most famous French humanists, whose reward for all his work at the Tuileries was not glory but prison and a painful death.

Work went on at an amazing pace between 1564 and 1572, but the Queen then wearied of her unfinished palace. Was she daunted by the immense, endless cost of the vast project? Or was she afraid that the site was too exposed – although Charles IX had had a further bastioned wall thrown round the Tuileries Gardens in 1556, with a gate where the Orangerie now stands? Legend has it that the superstitious Catherine de Médicis was reacting to a prophecy: she was told that she would meet her end under the patronage of St Germain, and therefore fled the palace set in the parish of Saint-Germain-l'Auxerrois, and removed to the Hôtel de Soissons, near the Halles, of which the extraordinary astronomical column still survives today next to the Bourse de Commerce.

Charles IX's projects also remained incomplete. In 1566 he had initiated the building of the Petite Galerie, between the Pavillon du Roi (at the end of the Lescot wing) and the Seine, which was to be followed by another gallery beside the river linking the Louvre and the Tuileries, on the model of the corridor that linked the Uffizi to the Pitti Palace in Florence. Lescot began work, perhaps with the assistance of Pierre II Chambiges (according to the account given by Henri Sauval a century later). He probably built a single-storey structure, linked to the Pavillon du Roi by a narrow corridor across the western moat, and crowned by a terrace. The central part of this still survives, a seven-arched loggia in which the middle arch forms a monumental entrance. It is remarkable for the polychromy of the Doric pilasters, where cream-coloured stone alternates with black marble plaques, and for the rich sculptural decoration, comprising allegorical figures in the spandrels of the arches and a fully classical triglyph frieze.

Pierre Lescot died in 1578. He was succeeded by Baptiste Androuet du Cerceau, who built one more bay of the southern range of the old Louvre courtyard. It was a very small contribution by the last of the Valois to his family's grand schemes. And the decoration bears not his cipher but that of the next dynasty, from which all the French kings until the end of the monarchy were to come: 'HDB' for Henri de Bourbon, who ascended the throne in 1589 as Henri IV.

The carved wooden ceiling of the State Bedchamber of Henri II.

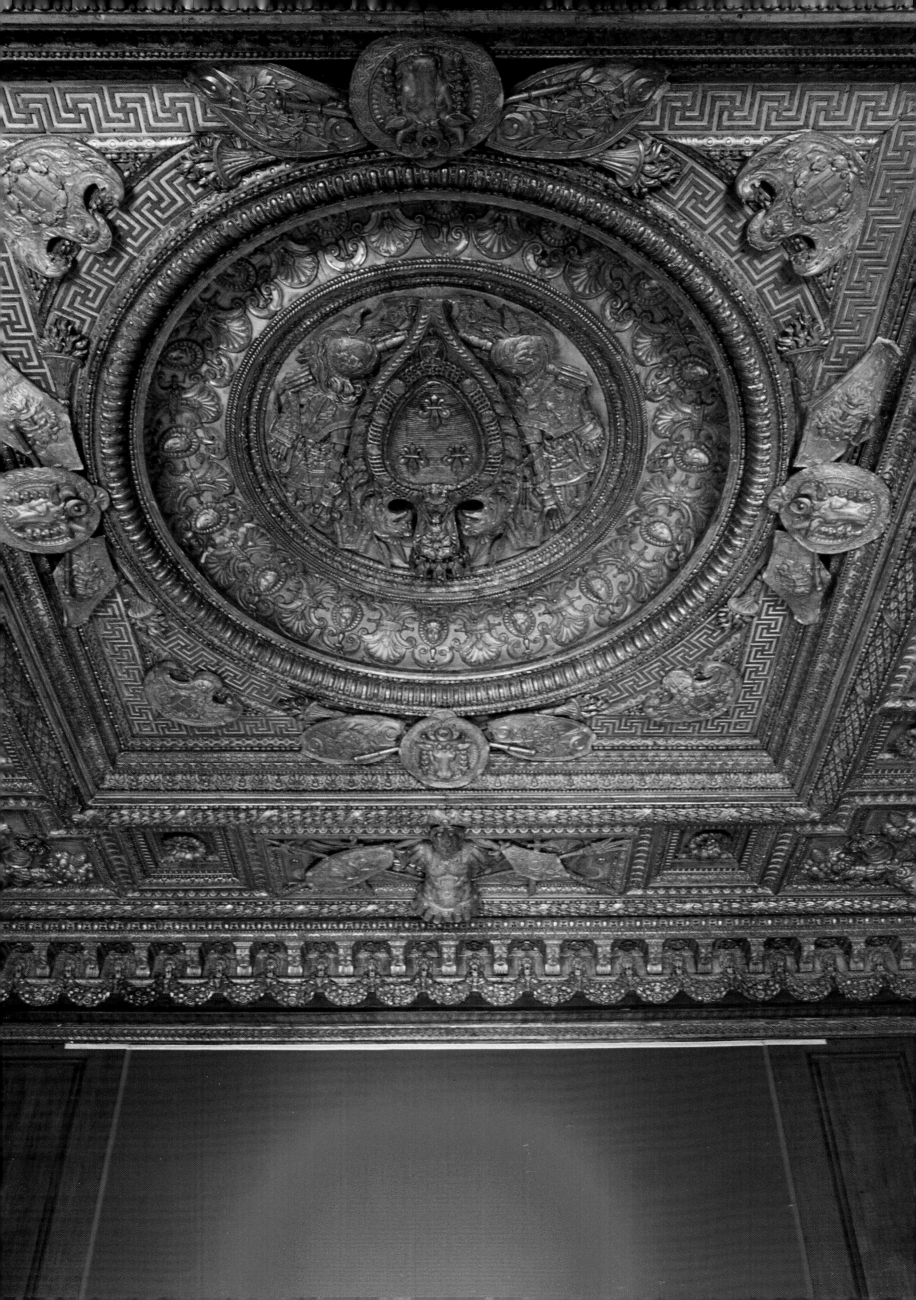

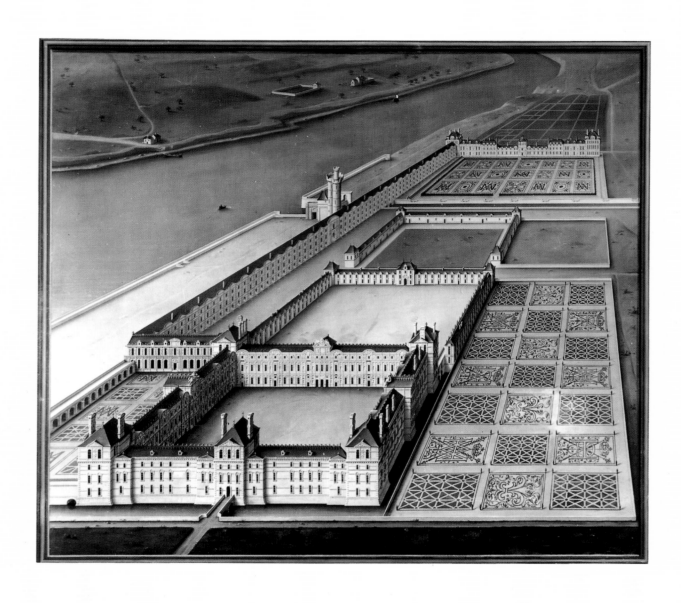

Henri IV's 'Grand Design', as depicted in a wall-painting in the château of Fontainebleau.
It envisaged a Cour Carrée the size it is today (in the foreground) and further courtyards extending
towards the Tuileries as far as the city walls. The two palaces were to be linked, via the Petite Galerie,
by the Grande Galerie along the Seine. Of the proposed new work, only the latter was executed in the King's lifetime.

The Bourbons' Grand Design

1594–1610: Henri IV builds a vast Parisian palace

Henri IV entered Paris on 22 March 1594 after defeating his opponents there, and though he was to engage in lengthy works of improvement at Saint-Germain-en-Laye and Fontainebleau, he determined on making the Louvre his chief residence. The long civil and religious war was at an end: the Protestant King of Navarre, now Catholic King of France, was concerned to establish the legitimacy of his dynasty, the Bourbons, and to make the authority of the king, who ruled by divine right, felt in the city whose sympathies for the Catholic League were not yet extinguished. The popular image of Henri IV as a jovial, high-living monarch with a string of mistresses, promoting popular prosperity and promising a chicken in the pot every Sunday, overlooks his political acumen. He was the chief administrator, with the task of rebuilding the kingdom on the ruins of war, and his main concern was to lay the foundations of a modern state. This was the spirit in which he decided to make the Louvre – and the Tuileries – into a great symbolic palace, in the capital, at the heart of the kingdom, where the various branches of power would be brought together with the royal collections behind walls whose decorative symbolism, carried out by official artists, would proclaim the monarchy.

He ordered first the completion of the Tuileries, then that of the southern range of the old Louvre, then the heightening and completion of the Petite Galerie, and finally in 1595 the building of the Grande Galerie to link the Petite Galerie with the Tuileries along the river.

Henri IV had a great vision: he wanted to quadruple the size of the small courtyard of the old Louvre, and to link the Louvre and the Tuileries by two long wings and a system of courtyards. His architects were Louis Métézeau and Jacques II Androuet du Cerceau. But the scheme was not to be completed, for the King was struck down by the dagger of Ravaillac in the Rue de la Ferronnerie on 14 May 1610 and died at the Louvre a few hours later. All work ceased on what was henceforth known as the *grand dessein* or 'Grand Design'.

The royal architects had been extraordinarily active on the vast project. In 1596 the Petite Galerie was completed, and in 1602 its west façade was ornamented with figures of captives in chains by the sculptor Pierre Biard. Inside, on the first floor, the painter Jacob Bunel decorated the walls with a series of portraits of the kings and queens of France and of famous men; only the portrait of Marie de Médicis by Frans Pourbus survives today (in the Department of Paintings of the Louvre). In 1595 work had begun on the Grande Galerie, extending some 500 metres (1640 feet) along the river; the shell of the building was completed in 1608. It joined up with a new pavilion attached to the southern end of the Tuileries, which was to become known as the Pavillon de Flore after a ballet performed in 1669 under Louis XIV. The eastern section of the Grande Galerie had a complex three-storeyed elevation, with alternating triangular and segmental pediments and prominent rustication and aedicules. Moving westward, there followed a higher pavilion containing an entrance – the predecessor of the Pavillon Lesdiguières – and then the western extension of the gallery, marked by a giant order of coupled composite pilasters supporting large pediments.

Overleaf The river front of the Grande Galerie, recorded by Edouard Baldus *c.* 1857 before the destruction of its western part. At the left are two units of Du Cerceau's elevation, with its giant order; at the right, part of Métézeau's eastern half. There, a pavilion matching the end of the Petite Galerie at the eastern extremity of the range is followed by a five-bay composition (later heightened by a storey) copying the design of the Salle des Antiques; on the right we see part of the standard elevation of the east gallery, with its rich carved decoration (renewed in 1850).

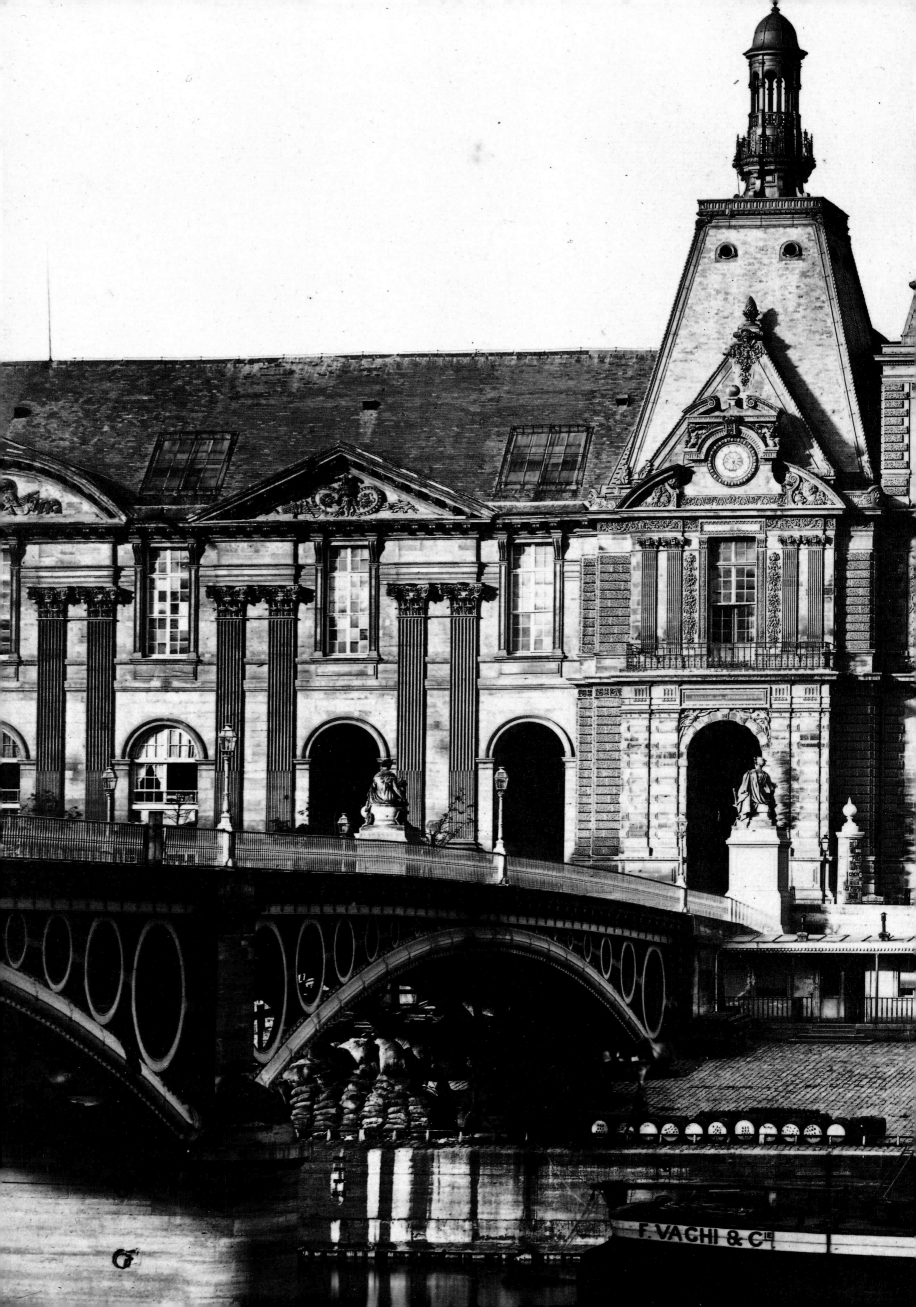

F. VACHI & C.

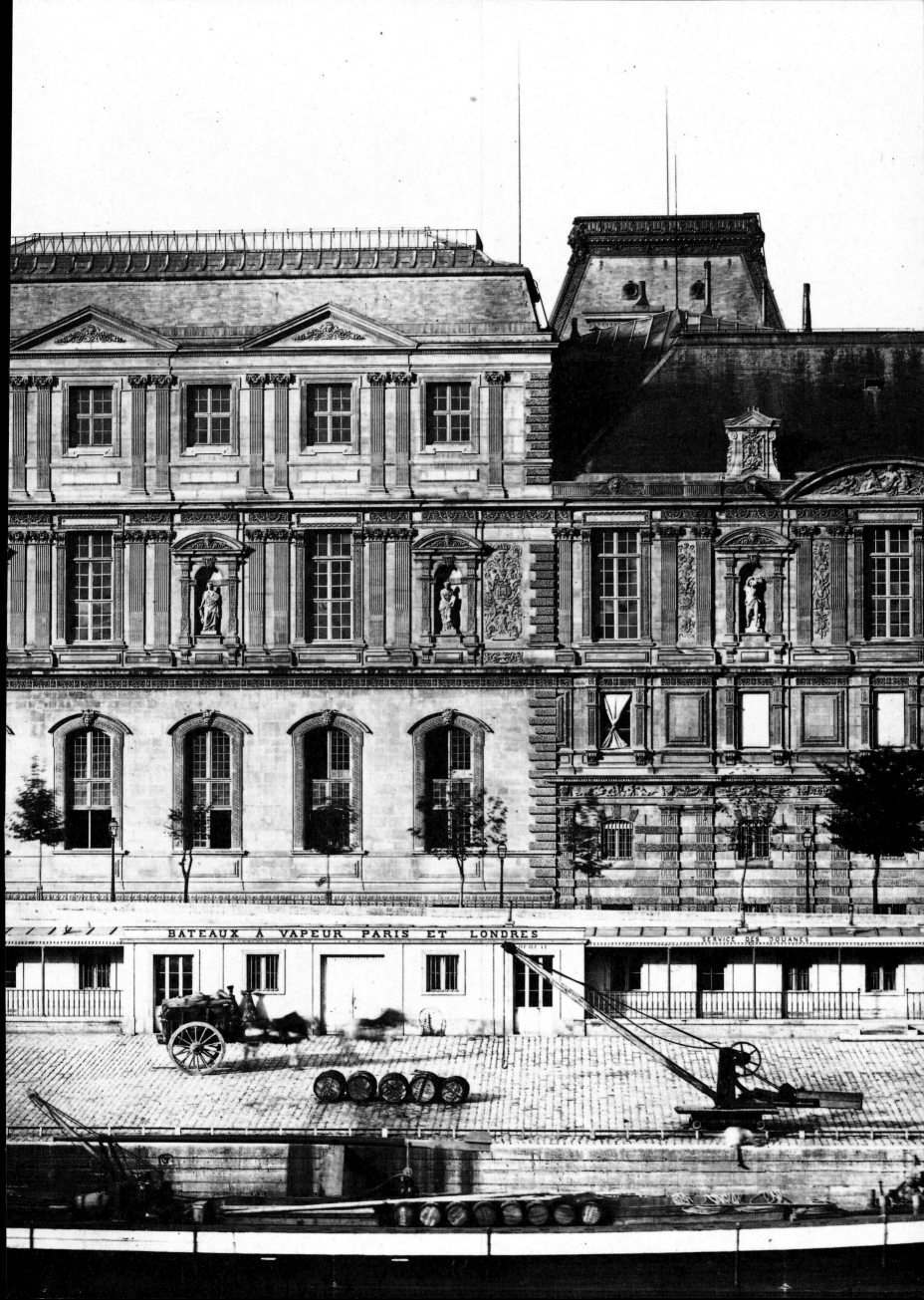

BATEAUX À VAPEUR PARIS ET LONDRES

SERVICE DES DOUANES

The latter were alternately triangular and segmental. The eastern part is attributed to Métézeau, on the grounds that he had decorated the Salle des Antiques at its east end; the western part to Du Cerceau.

Both the Petite Galerie and the Grande Galerie were much altered over the centuries. Napoleon III went so far as to destroy and rebuild the entire western part of the Grande Galerie, but the appearance of its original elevation can still be seen on the wing north of the Cour du Carrousel, where Napoleon I's architects, Percier and Fontaine, had faithfully replicated Du Cerceau's design. On the river front of the eastern part of the Grande Galerie the charming frieze of putti playing with nets and other props alluding to water survives, though it was restored in 1850. That frieze, ascribed to the brothers Pierre and François Lheureux since the seventeenth century, forms part of a decorative scheme which also contains a profusion of emblematic allusions to Henri IV – not only dolphins, symbolizing the birth of the heir (the *dauphin*), but also royal sceptres and crowns, scales of justice, and wheat, signifying abundance. The cipher 'HG' must stand for Henri and Gabrielle, an allusion placed here in 1599 to the beautiful Gabrielle d'Estrées, the King's mistress, whom he was preparing to marry at the time of his assassination.

Henri IV had introduced into the Louvre two features that were to have a great future. A room lined with coloured marbles from the Pyrenees was created in 1604–9 to display the finest antique sculptures from the royal collections – including the *Diane à la Biche*, now shown in the Salle des Cariatides – as well as some contemporary works, such as a statue by the Florentine Baccio Bandinelli. Known as the Salle des Antiques, it was the beginning of the Louvre as museum. Then, by letters patent of 22 December 1608, he ordered the installation on the ground floor and mezzanine of the Grande Galerie of a series of studios and workshops for artists and craftsmen under royal patronage; the document mentions artificers and masters in painting, sculpture, goldsmiths' work, clockmaking, lapidaries, and 'others' – armourers, perfumers, and especially tapestry weavers, who were to move to the Gobelins and set up the royal manufactory there in 1671. These artists, supported and lodged at the king's expense, were free from the authority of the guilds, and could devote themselves entirely to royal commissions.

Henri IV followed the Valois in making his Louvre a centre of power (here the Council met, and ambassadors were received) and of the display of power. It was the setting for jousts, festivals, ballets and mascarades. The Grande Galerie was also the scene of the ceremony of touching for the King's Evil: the descendant of Clovis and St Louis could, it was believed, heal scrofula merely by touching the swollen tubercular gland in the sufferer's neck. The 'miracle' was carefully managed as political propaganda, since it was a sign that the Bourbons ruled by God's will.

The King was active at the Tuileries as well. The great gardens were altered by Claude Mollet, who was both a theorist of garden design and a practical gardener: he laid out an extensive walk covered with *berceaux*, created pools, and devised *parterres*. And in 1600 he created a new garden east of the palace, with compartments of *broderies* (complex decorative patterns) set in containing hedges of box and juniper. This garden overlooked the moat of Charles V's town wall, and its retaining wall, of fine ashlar masonry, can be seen today in the underground complex of the Carrousel. The most striking features of all this work, however, were the planting in the Tuileries Gardens of white mulberry trees all along the northern boundary, and the construction by the architect Etienne Du Pérac of an orangery which was transformed into a silk-worm farm. Under the influence of Olivier de Serres, the royal garden became a model for the budding French silk industry.

The Louvre of Louis XIII

The funeral of Henri IV, whose body had lain in state for twelve days in the Salle des Cariatides, marked the end of the great plans for the Louvre. It was still the scene of court intrigues, as Marie de Médicis ruled as regent for her son; on assuming power, in 1617, Louis XIII ordered the assassination of his mother's favourite and grand counsellor, the Florentine Concino Concini, at the very entrance to the Louvre.

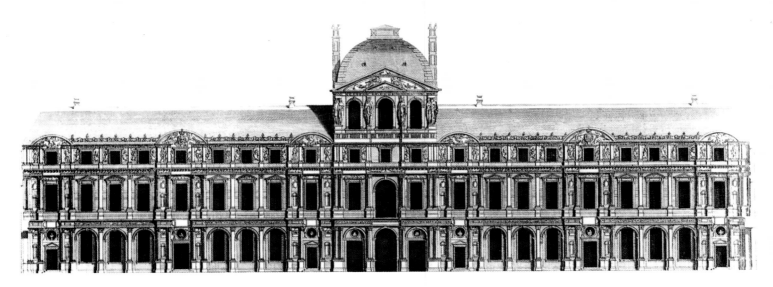

Little was done during the regency or the early years of Louis XIII's reign except for the creation in 1611 of a new garden along the river, known now as the Jardin de l'Infante but then as the Queen's Garden. Again designed by Claude Mollet, it was a pleasant space between the Petite Galerie and the quayside, with arbours and an ornamental pool. A little bridge over the medieval moat linked it to the Queen Mother's Apartment on the ground floor of the southern range of the Louvre proper; scandalmongers whispered that Concini used this when he went to see the Queen, and christened it the 'bridge of love'.

What the Louvre looked like at this stage was an abandoned building site. The main courtyard was small, and it was still enclosed on two sides by medieval buildings, with Charles V's Grande Vis corbelled out into the space, further encroached on by the *châtelet*; at roof level there were towers, and outside there were stinking moats, and the kitchen court to the west.

A long interval elapsed before the King began to take up the ideas of his father. Once his power was securely established, as Classicism was taking hold in France, he decided to make the Louvre into an experimental laboratory for the new style. In that experiment he called upon three artists, all of them trained in Rome, the artistic capital of Europe: a great architect, Jacques Lemercier; the man who introduced classical sculpture to France, Jacques Sarazin; and a painter of genius, Nicolas Poussin.

In 1624, almost certainly on the initiative of Richelieu, Louis XIII decided to reactivate his father's Grand Design: he issued an edict forbidding the construction of any new building in the area planned for the future palace, and continued the demolition of the old fortress. The north wing of the medieval Louvre, the Library Tower and the Grande Vis all came down, and in July 1624 the King laid the first stone of a new pavilion at the north end of the Lescot wing. Completed and decorated in 1639–40, under the direction of Lemercier, this became known as the Pavillon de l'Horloge (clock pavilion) and eventually, in the nineteenth century, received the name of Pavillon Sully. (The two names are best applied to its eastern and western faces.) Henri Sauval, one of the first historians of the Louvre, who saw Lemercier at work, described him as 'rather slow, weighty, and ponderous, but to make up for it shrewd, judicious, profound, solid – in a word, the outstanding architect of our century'. Lemercier came from a family of master masons from Pontoise, near Paris. After a long stay in Rome, he combined familiarity with traditional building techniques with a profound knowledge of stylistic developments. The new pavilion, and the new wing designed to rise on the other side of it, carried on Lescot's elevations. At the top of the pavilion, however, Lemercier introduced something quite new. Here there were three openings – the architect had originally intended to have a monumental figure of the King in the centre – framed by pairs of sensuously modelled caryatids; and these caryatids support a particularly complex crowning feature.

Above The west side of the Cour Carrée: left, the Lescot wing; centre and right, the Pavillon de l'Horloge and wing built by Lemercier in continuation of the earlier design.

Pages 44–45 Looking west in the Cour Carrée. Lescot's work is on the left at the end, Lemercier's on the right.

Pages 46–47 Sculpture of the Pavillon de l'Horloge, carved in 1639–40 under the direction of Jacques Sarazin by Philippe De Buyster and Gilles Guérin.

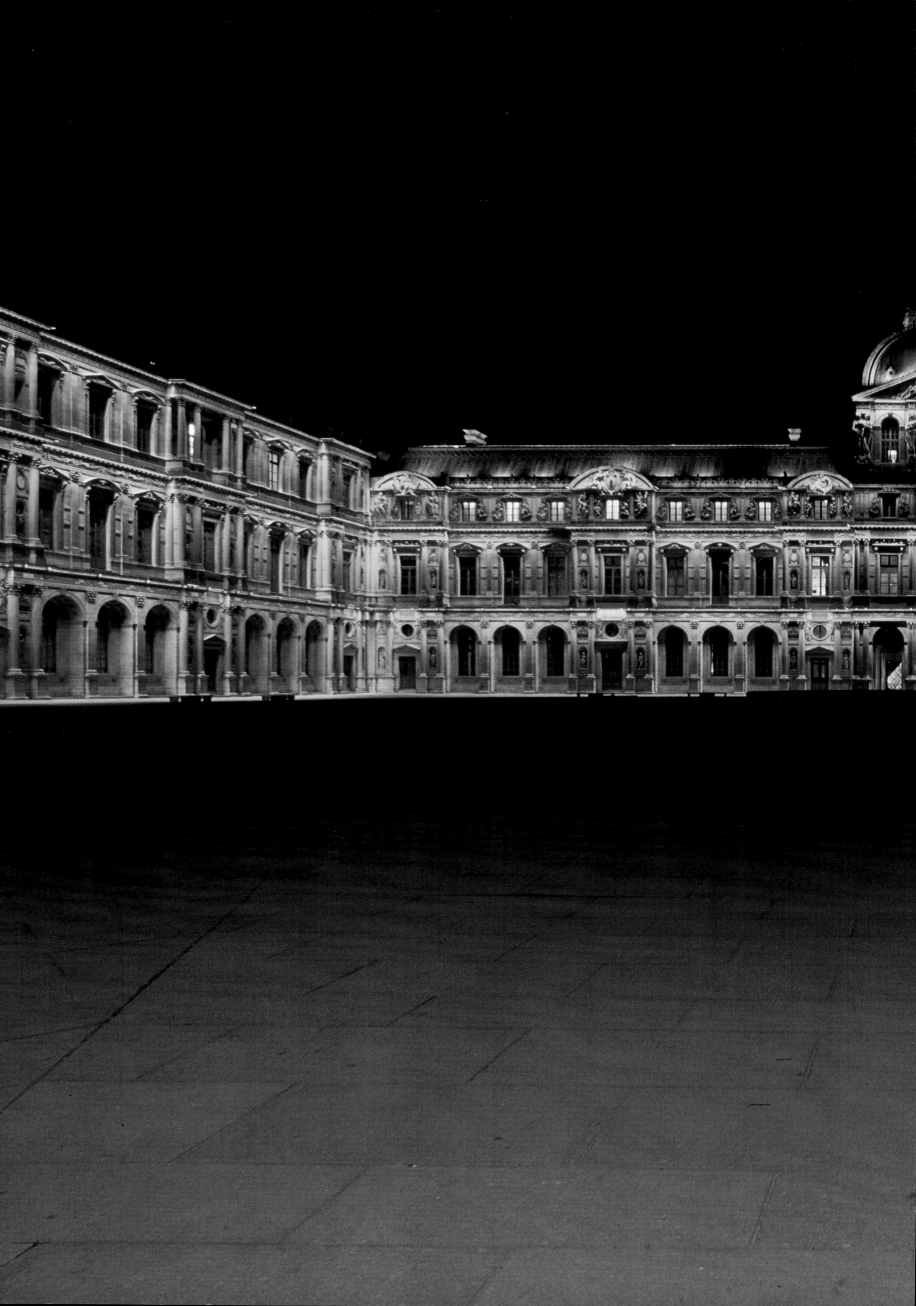

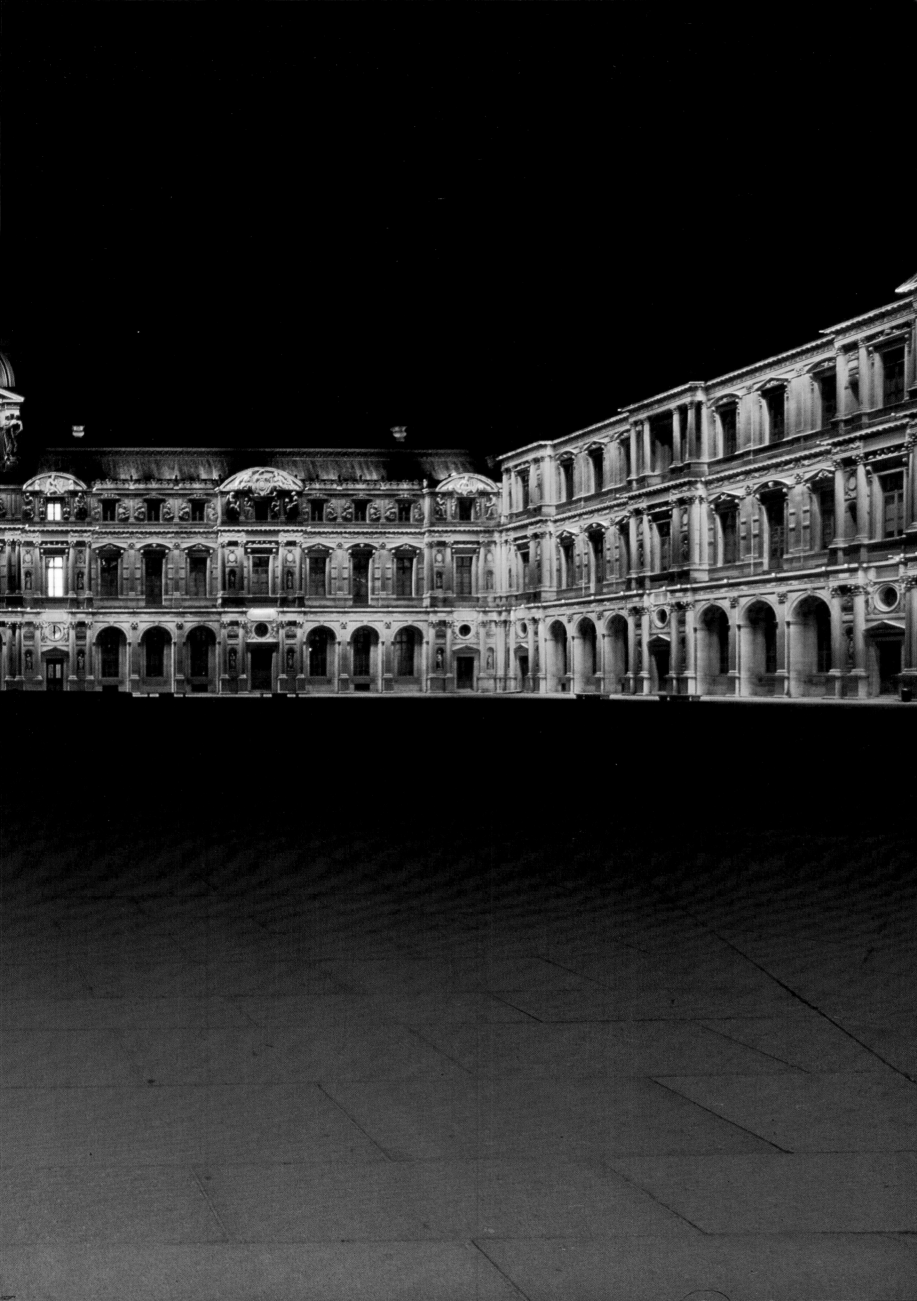

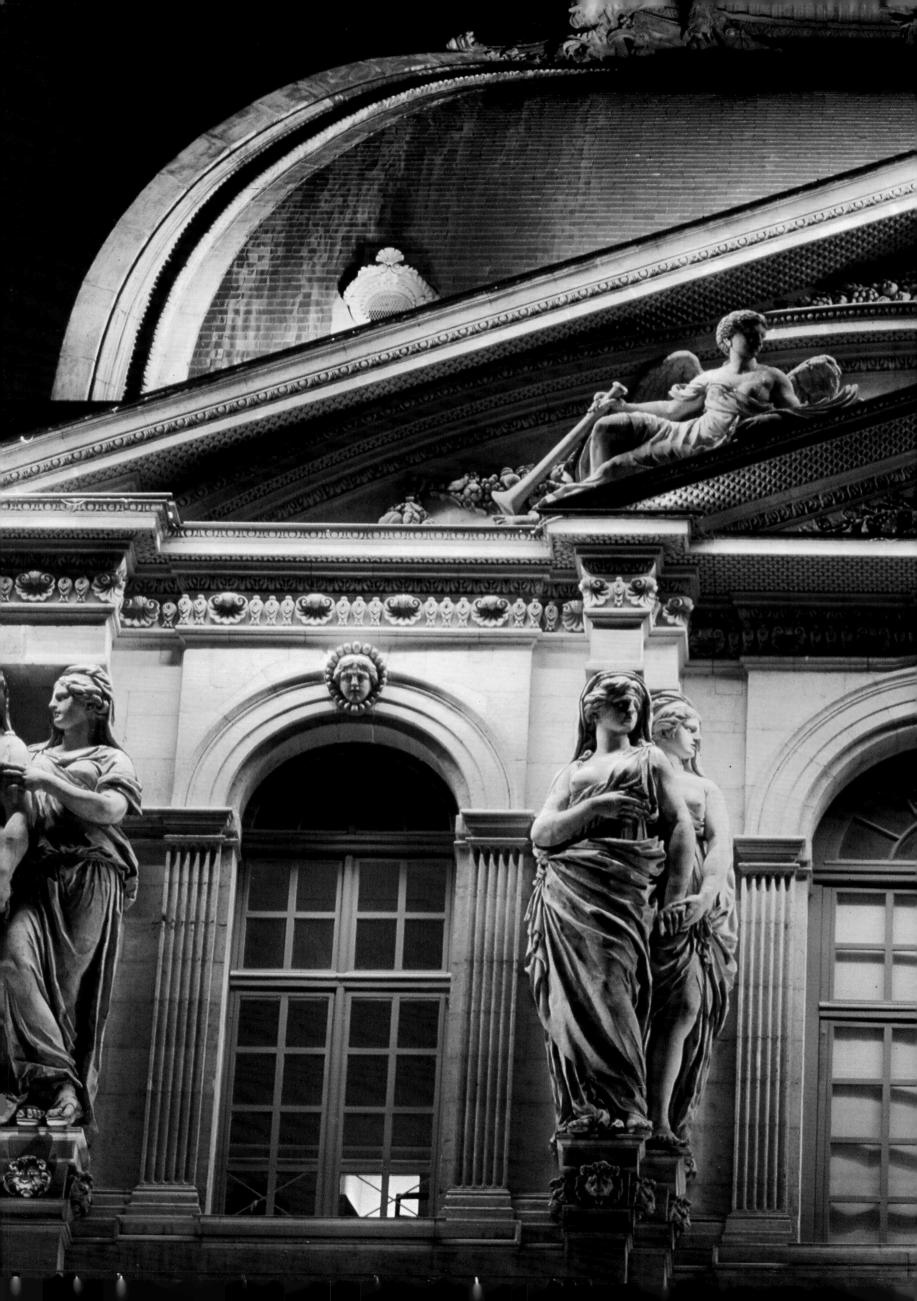

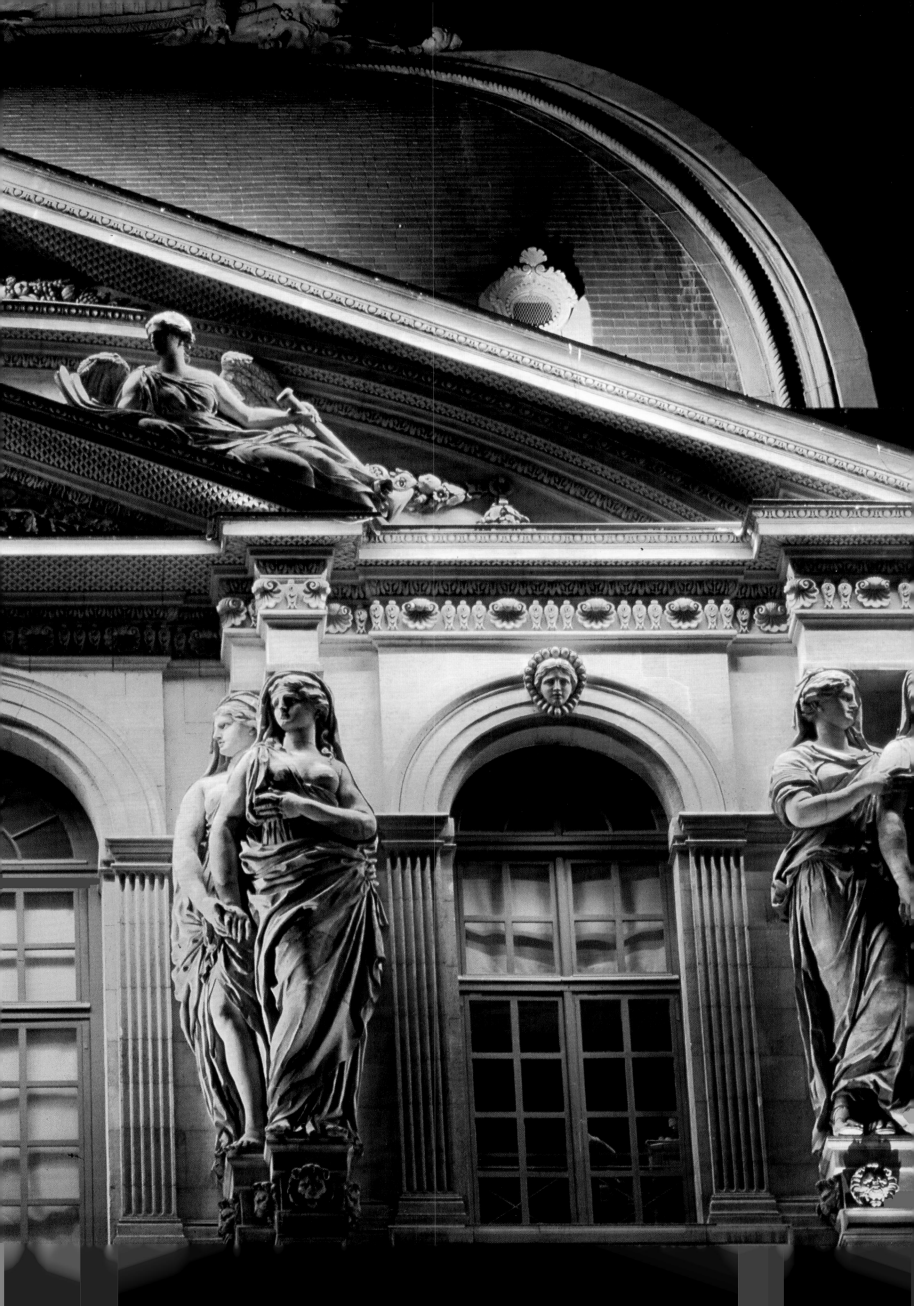

First there is a small triangular pediment; then a segmental pediment containing reclining allegorical figures; and finally, enclosing the whole, another triangular pediment. Above this came an elegant square dome, which provided the model for all subsequent pavilion roofs at the Louvre. Alterations in 1856 left it with a silhouette encrusted with ornament.

The caryatids were carved by Philippe De Buyster and Gilles Guérin, under the direction of Jacques Sarazin: their pleasure in the task is plain to see in these figures which are based on antique models but whose rounded bodies and vivacious poses are full of life. Holding hands, arms intertwined, turning to one another, they are a world away from the columnar women sculpted by Jean Goujon for the neighbouring Salle des Cariatides. The same feeling of life radiates from the friezes of laughing putti playing among garlands of leaves, in which we can make out the royal cipher, with a *lambda* for Louis and an A for Anne of Austria. Sarazin, who designed all this sculpture, had been trained in the Roman studio of Alessandro Algardi just as the early Baroque style was coming into being, and its influence can be felt in the delight that Sarazin's own studio took in depicting children, in all their vulnerable, chubby vitality.

Louis XIII commissioned alterations to the inside of the palace as well. The timber ceiling of the Salle des Cariatides was replaced by a stone vault, and the new Surintendant des Bâtiments du Roi, Sublet de Noyers, proposed to decorate the Grande Galerie, which had hitherto remained bare, even though it was the setting for the ceremony of touching for the King's Evil. In 1639 Nicolas Poussin was requested to come to Paris and undertake the sort of grand decorative scheme that existed in great Italian palaces.

Poussin was celebrated in Rome and comfortably settled there, and it eventually proved necessary to send a special emissary to force his decision. This was Fréart de Chantelou. Now, under the painter's direction, Chantelou obtained casts of the finest antique reliefs – those of Trajan's Column and the Arch of Constantine, and the famous Borghese Dancers – which were to be reproduced in bronze for the Grande Galerie. At last Poussin arrived in Paris, where he was lodged in a pavilion in the Tuileries Gardens and named Premier Peintre du Roi. He began work in 1641, with the grudging assistance of the landscape painter Jacques Fouquières, whose task was to produce views of ninety-six French towns. Poussin soon began to weary, however: he was exasperated by all the orders he received, and infuriated by having to work in a setting imposed by Lemercier, without a studio, and surrounded by jealousy and hostility. In November 1642 he returned to Rome. The ceiling in which he planned to depict the Labours of Hercules was left unfinished, and though in 1643 he fulfilled his grudging promise to send drawings for it from Rome, all that survives of the grand scheme is a few sketches and two bronze reliefs, cast in 1643 by the founder Henri Perlan, which are adaptations of the Borghese Dancers by the sculptor François Anguier (now in the Salles d'Histoire du Louvre and the Wallace Collection in London).

The first campaigns under Louis XIV

Louis XIII died on 14 May 1643. Again, the heir was not of age and a period of regency followed, during which the authority of the State was weakened. The new King was four years old, and his mother, Anne of Austria, was a foreigner: it was a situation that various noblemen sought to exploit. By the end of the year, the Queen had abandoned the Louvre in favour of the Palais Cardinal (bequeathed to the King by Cardinal Richelieu), known henceforth as the Palais Royal. Here she was close to the Palais Mazarin, home of her beloved minister the Cardinal, who was the new power at court. The Tuileries had since 1637 been occupied by Mademoiselle, daughter of the Duc d'Orléans and cousin of the young King, who built a splendid new formal garden to the east, known as the Parterre de Mademoiselle. As to the Louvre, it became a refuge for the English royal family.

Pages 49–51 Stucco by Michel Anguier in the former Summer Apartment of Anne of Austria: details of the Salle des Saisons (*opposite* and *page 51*) and Grand Cabinet (*page 50*).

Pages 52–53 Mucius Scaevola by Romanelli in the Grand Cabinet.

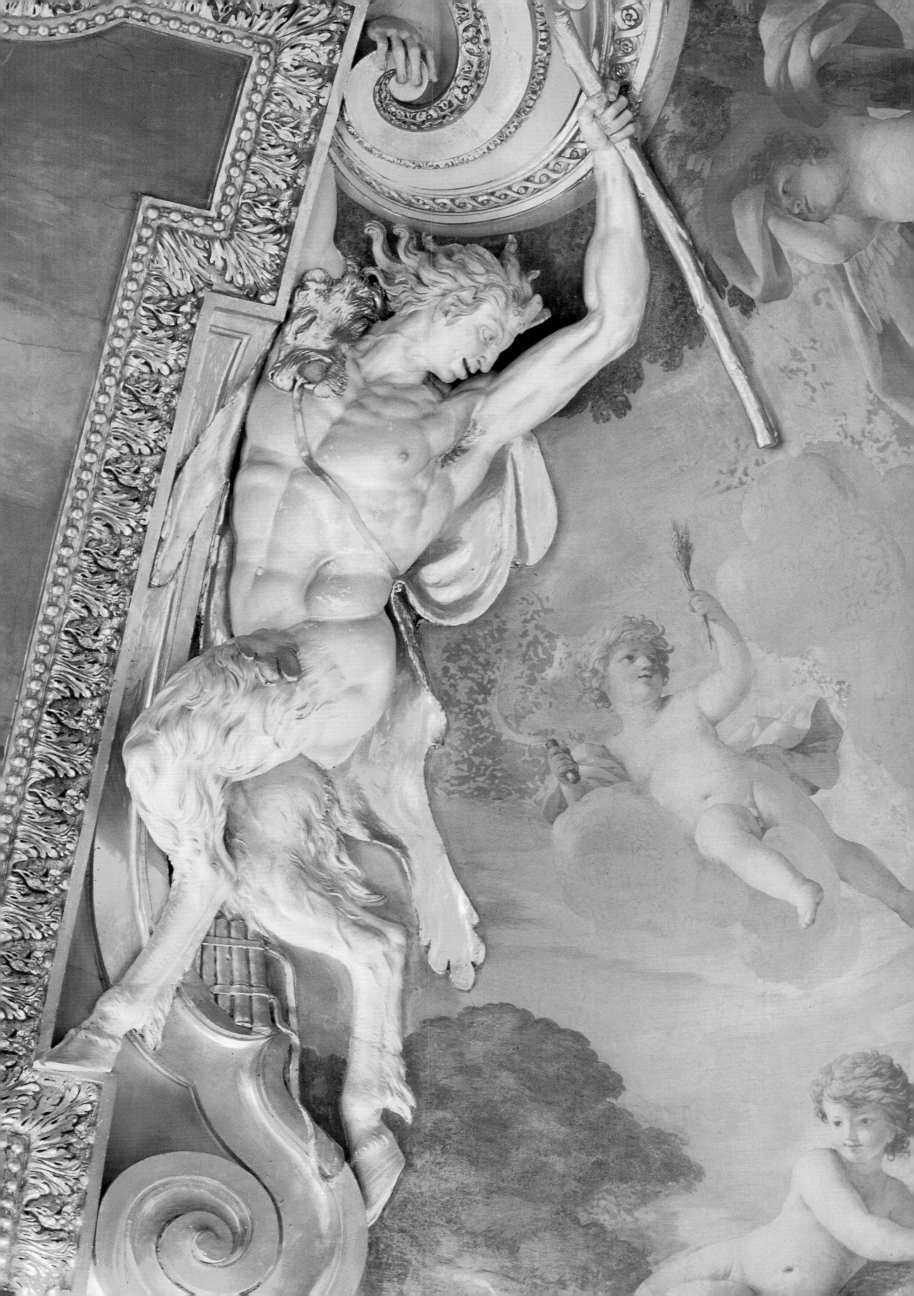

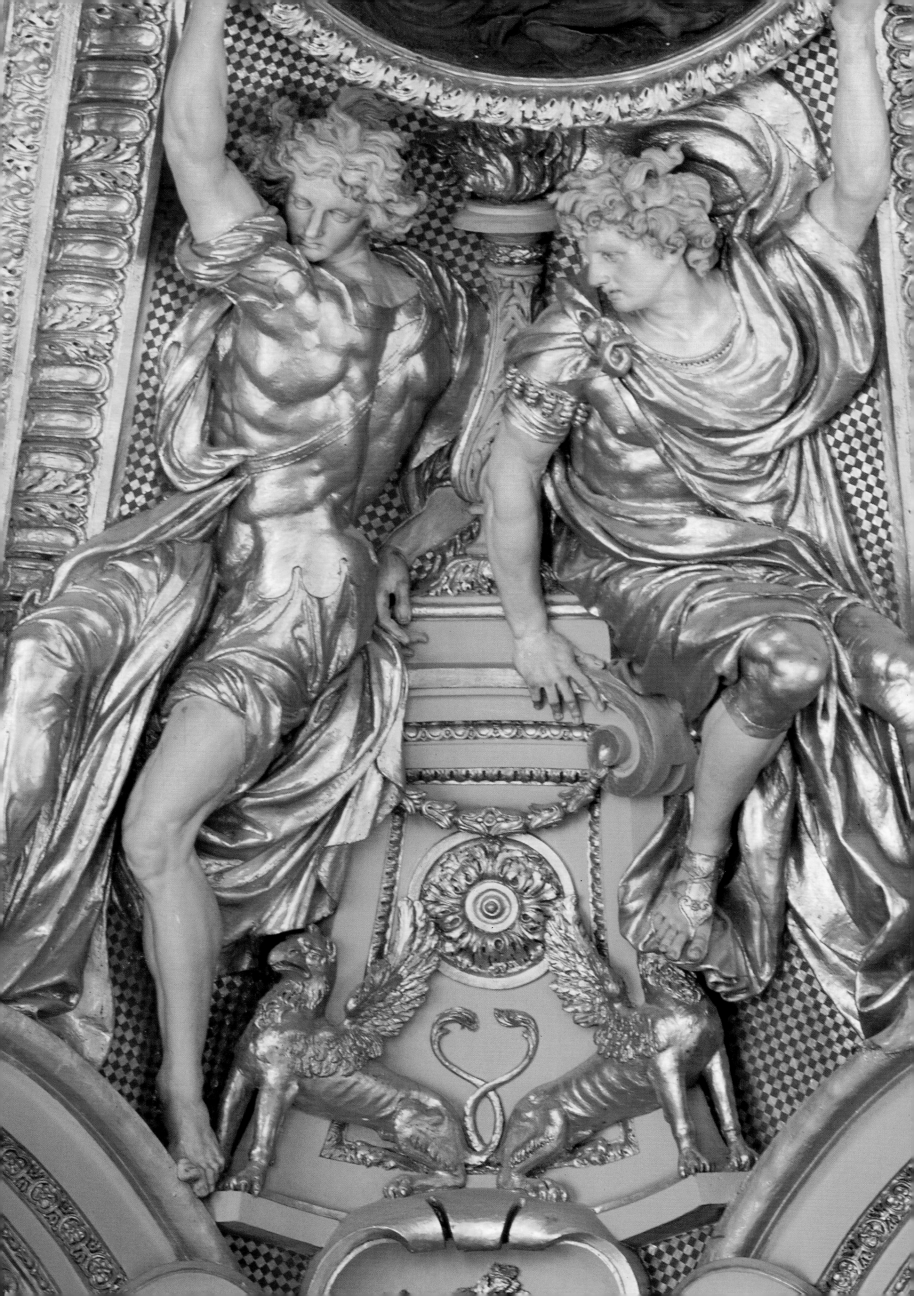

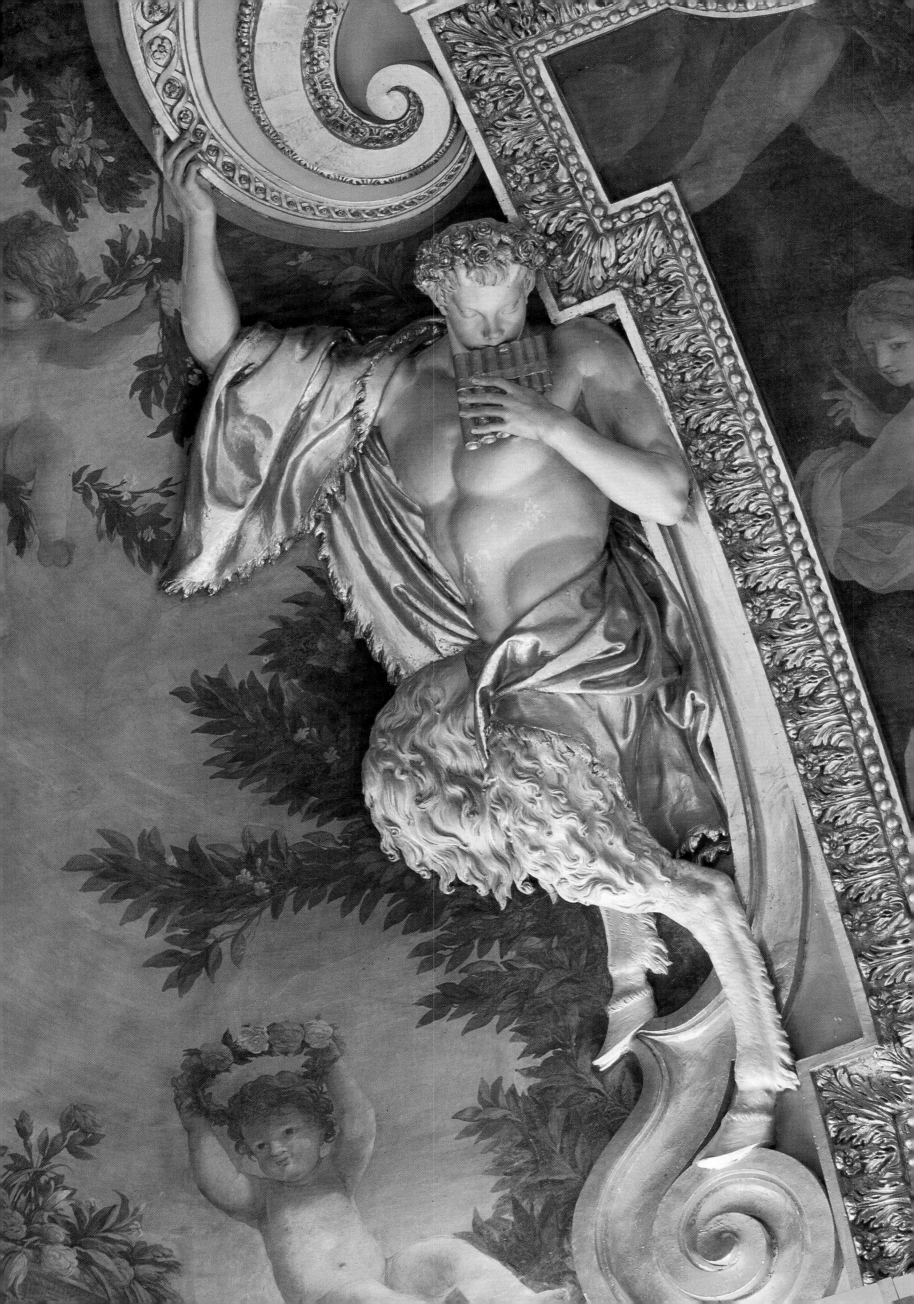

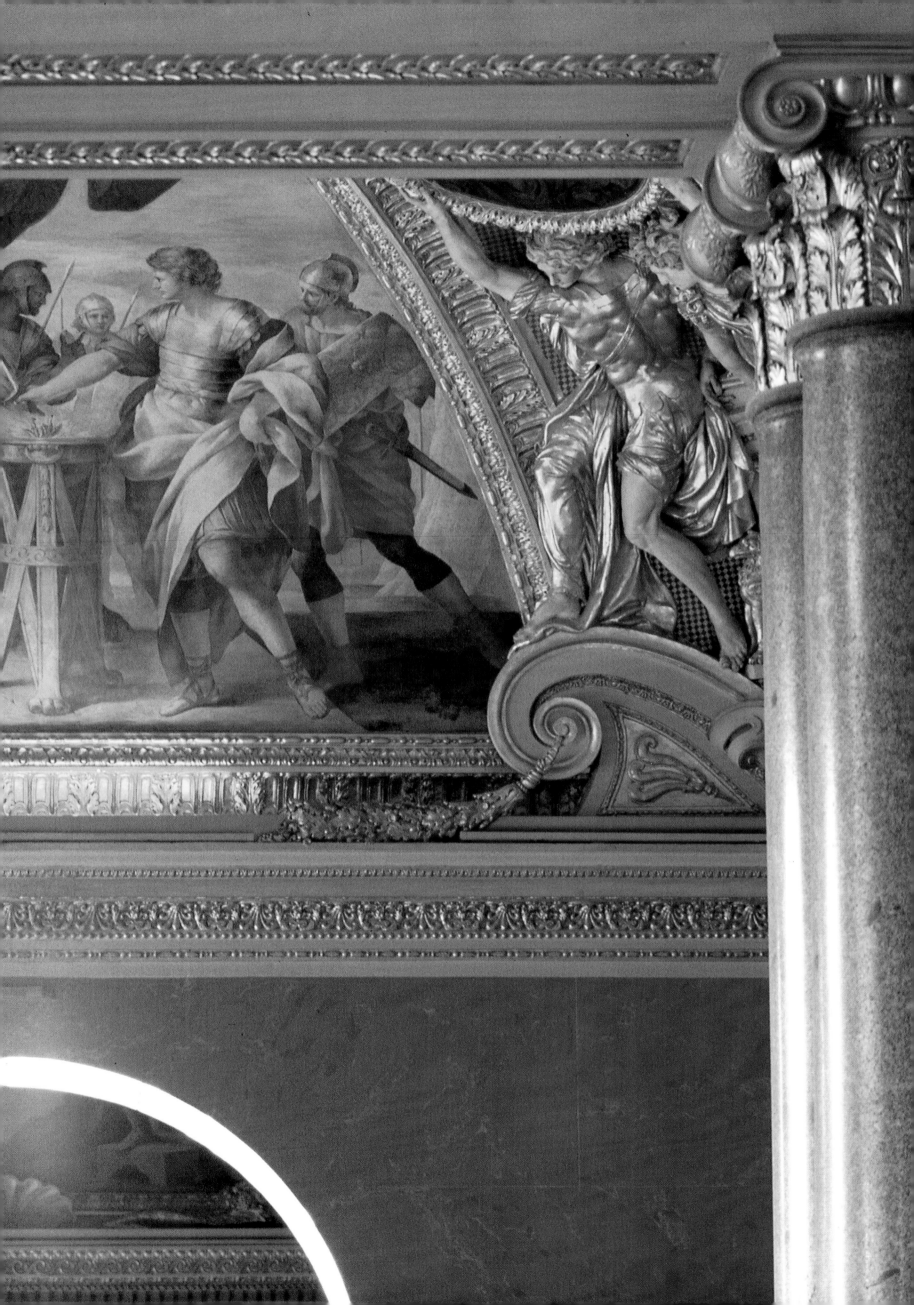

Henrietta Maria – daughter of Henri IV and aunt of Louis XIV – had fled England with her children in 1648 to escape the Civil War. Her daughter Henrietta, much loved by Louis XIV, was to marry the Duc d'Orléans and to become one of the tragic heroines of the seventeenth century in France, her early death immortalized by Madame de Sévigné's account of its circumstances, culminating in the anguished cry: '*Madame se meurt, Madame est morte*' (Madame is dying, Madame is dead).

In 1648, the civil war known as the Fronde spurred the King and his mother to flee the city. When they returned in 1652, it was not to the Palais Royal but to the Louvre, whose moats still offered protection. Mademoiselle, who had taken part in the plot, was expelled from the Tuileries.

The regency was at last on a firm footing, thanks to Mazarin's political acumen. He himself lived in the Louvre, and he had installed his sister and his pretty nieces in the attic story of the Lescot wing: now, with his encouragement, works of improvement resumed. The Queen Mother's lodgings – both the Winter Apartment on the ground floor of the south range and the Summer Apartment in the Petite Galerie – were sumptuously redecorated. The former, known also as the Appartement des Bains, was realized under the direction of Lemercier in 1653–54. It was subsequently completely destroyed, and the painted decoration by Eustache Le Sueur is known now only from preparatory sketches. A few of the paintings from the frieze survive, such as the *Crucifix with Angels* by Charles Le Brun from the private oratory and the *Infanta Maria Margarita* by Velasquez, a little picture from a series of family portraits sent from Spain for reasons both sentimental and political.

If the Winter Apartment is lost, the ambitious interiors of the Summer Apartment of Anne of Austria, created in 1655–59, survive in almost all their splendour. The wall panelling decorated by Jean Daret and Etienne Carel has disappeared, but the ceilings still proclaim the grand message of Roman Baroque, with their frescoes by Giovanni Francesco Romanelli set within white and gold stucco by Michel Anguier. Romanelli here displays the vibrant colour and delicate touch that had already brought him success at the Palais Mazarin during his first stay in Paris. Anguier had been trained under Algardi at the heart of Roman Classicism, and a long stay in Italy had left him with a love of monumentality, of energy conveyed through volume, which is reflected in works where the most striking movements and contortions may be juxtaposed with calmer compositions.

The Summer Apartment consisted of an antechamber, the Salle des Saisons; a vestibule, the Salon de la Paix; the Grand Cabinet; and finally the Queen's Bedchamber with the Petit Cabinet opening off it towards the river (in the 1790s these two rooms were made into one). Throughout, the decoration reflects a complex iconographic programme, devised with great ingenuity and carried out with great skill.

The Salle des Saisons, of 1657, has Time as its theme, and presents a cosmic vision which prefigures that of the Galerie d'Apollon. Sun and moon, and day and night, are alluded to in frescoed scenes of myths associated with Apollo (*Apollo and Marsyas, Apollo with the Muses*) and Diana (*Diana and Endymion, Diana and Actaeon*). The Seasons are depicted in the corners of the room, while the Elements are represented by stucco figures of gods – *Vulcan* (fire), *Juno* (air), *Neptune* (water) and *Cybele* (earth). In the vault, the theme of transience is evoked by depictions of Time with the zodiac and the Hour with a clepsydra or water-clock.

The name of the Salon de la Paix alludes to the Treaty of the Pyrenees, signed with Spain in 1659. Here it is the richness of Nature that is celebrated, in frescoes by Romanelli of *Peace* and *Agriculture*, and in modelled stucco figures by Anguier of *France* and *Navarre*, whose lithe female forms contrast with the robust male figures of the rivers of France – the *Garonne* reclining under a vine, the *Rhone* resting on the lion of Lyons, the *Seine* and the *Loire*.

The Grand Cabinet featured notable episodes from Roman history, typically displaying heroic virtues: *The Rape of the Sabines, Mucius Scaevola, The Continence of Scipio* and *Cincinnatus* by Romanelli, and *Romulus and Remus, Marcus Curtius leaping into the Abyss, The Innocence of the Vestal Virgin Tuccia*, and a *Sacrifice* by Anguier (1655). The overdoors held portraits of Louis XIII by Juste d'Egmont and of Anne of Austria by Jean Nocret, which are now at Versailles.

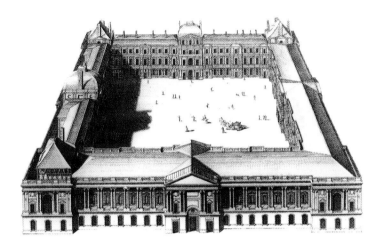

The subjects chosen for the Queen's Bedchamber were great women of history (*Judith and Holophernes* and *Esther and Ahasuerus*, by Romanelli) and the virtues of the Queen (*Liberality, Majesty, Felicity* and *Magnificence*, by Anguier), again executed in 1655. The Petit Cabinet was decorated by paintings on canvas of the story of Moses by Romanelli (now in the Salles d'Histoire du Louvre), set in wooden panelling (now in the Senate).

Beyond the northern end of the Queen's Summer Apartment a setting was created for the King's Council, with decoration commissioned in 1658 from the painter Charles Errard and the sculptor Thibaut Poissant, who had been a pupil of Poussin in Rome. Nothing of this survives except for some stucco figures in what is known as the Rotonde de Mars. From here the Council moved to the new Lemercier wing, which was now ready, where they occupied a handsome suite consisting of a great chamber, small chamber, cabinet and chapel.

The King's Apartment, in the Pavillon du Roy, was also given entirely new decoration in 1654–56. The centrepiece was the King's Bedchamber, where he received privileged guests. The fittings of this splendid room are dispersed or lost. Most notable among them was the great ceiling, moved in the nineteenth century to a room in the Colonnade wing (as had been the fate of the ceiling of Henri II's State Bedchamber). Composed around a large oval of carved and gilded wood, it is the work of the sculptor Gilles Guérin assisted by François Girardon, Laurent Magnier, Thomas Regnaudin and Nicolas Legendre; figures of chained captives in its composition take up the theme first stated in Jean Goujon's carvings on the Lescot wing and reiterated in a pediment of Henri IV's Petite Galerie. The bed alcove is by Louis Barois, with two putti holding up the curtains also carved by Guérin. The fireplace by Guérin and Pierre Bordoni, on which three putti represented Authority, Faith and Justice, has disappeared altogether. The paintings by Le Sueur, now known only from drawings, included a large-scale *Triumph of the French Monarchy* and *Justice and Valour putting France's Enemies to Flight*. Rooms were also created around the King's Bedchamber, most notably the small antechamber, of which the ceiling was painted by Le Sueur and Le Brun.

A new architect had followed Lemercier on the scene in 1654: Louis Le Vau. In response to a request from the King for a wider passage between his apartment and the Petite Galerie, Le Vau created the Salon du Dôme above the Rotonde de Mars – a rotunda similar to the great oval room he had built for Fouquet at Vaux-le-Vicomte – and the Grand Cabinet. (These rooms are now the Rotonde d'Apollon and Salle des Bijoux.) The Salon du Dôme, decorated with stucco by Francesco Caccia, was intended as a chapel. Eventually, however, in 1659, the first floor of the Pavillon de l'Horloge was converted into a chapel dedicated to Our Lady of Peace and St Louis; this too was intended to be domed, but the dome was never built.

In the Grand Cabinet the King received foreign ambassadors. To decorate this room, in 1658 a ceiling-painting by Poussin of 1641 was brought from the Palais Royal. Should we see in this re-use of *Time rescuing Truth from Envy and Discord* (now in the Department of Paintings of the Louvre) a sign of respect for the great French artist, or merely thrift? The major alterations carried out at this time included the remodelling of the State Bedchamber (originally that of Henri II), given carved and gilded overdoors by Louis Hutinot and Laurent Magnier.

Above The Cour Carrée in the time of Louis XIV. Note the roof of the centrepiece of the Colonnade wing, later replaced by a flat terrace.

Pages 56–57 Elements of the Bedchamber of Louis XIV: we are looking out from the carved bed alcove to the sumptuous ceiling by Guérin.

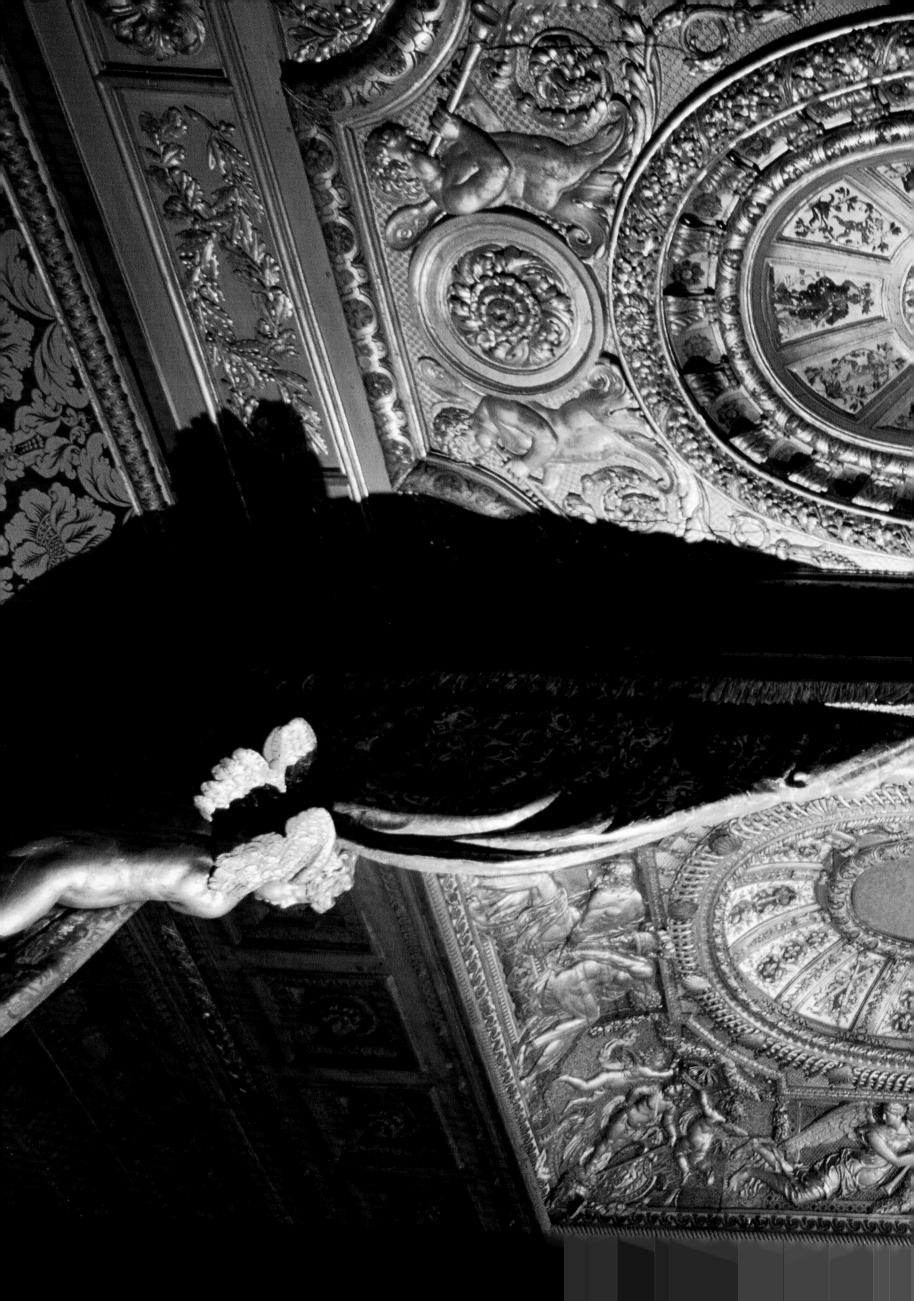

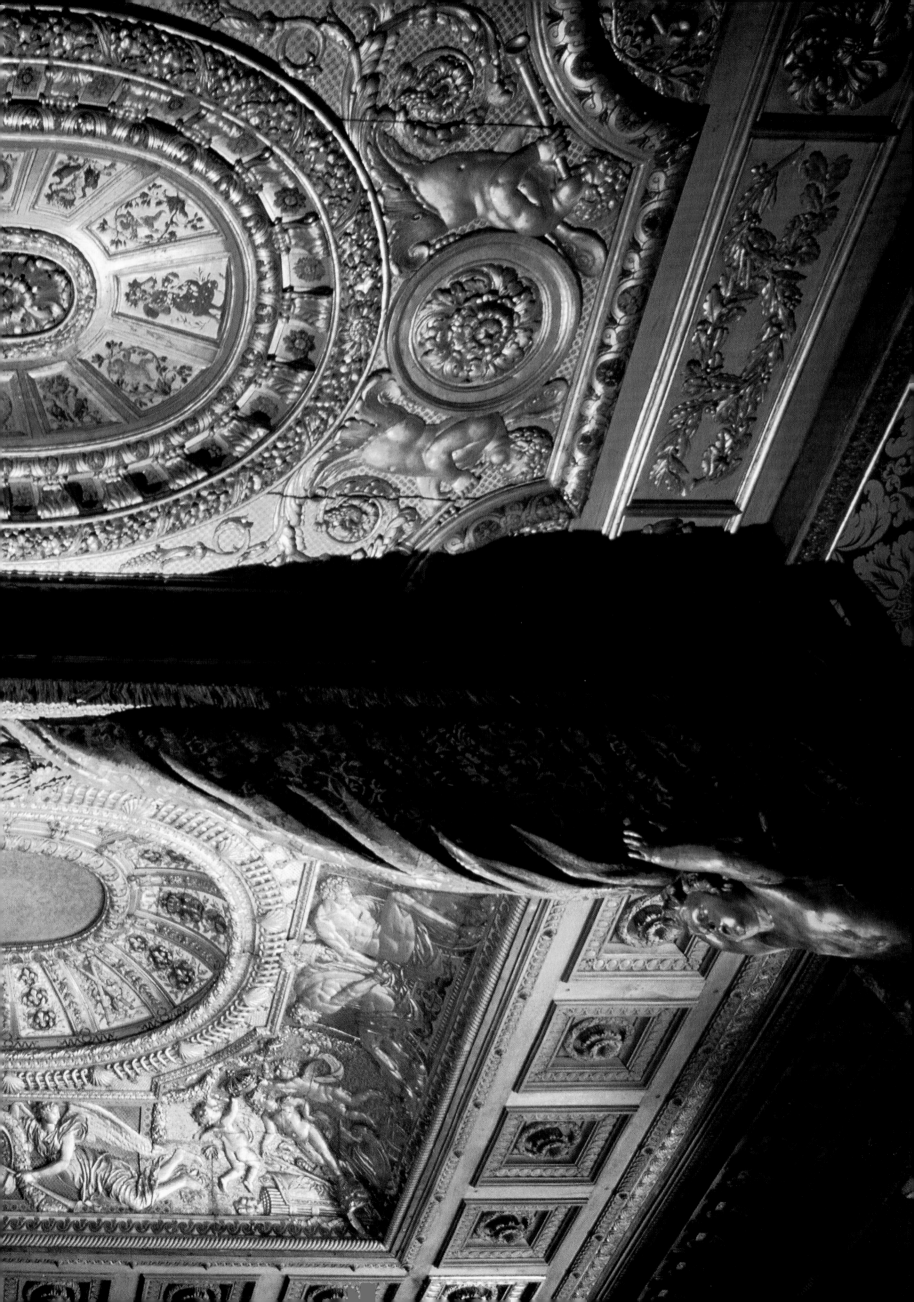

With the arrival in 1660 of a new queen, Louis XIV's wife Maria Teresa of Spain, the Queen's Apartment on the first floor of the southern wing was redecorated again, by Charles Errard and Noël Coypel. Nothing of this survives; the space was transformed in the early nineteenth century into the 'Musée Charles X'.

Amid all this work, Cardinal Mazarin did not neglect the Tuileries. Here he had a new wing built containing a theatre, the 'Salle des Machines', which was the ingenious design of Gaspard Vigarani, an architect who had come to Paris from Modena with his two sons, Charles and Louis. Charles Vigarani was to remain in France as the organizer of court entertainments for Louis XIV.

The Grand Design resurfaces

All the decoration so far was merely cosmetic: something grander would be needed for the future Sun King. After the signing of the Treaty of the Pyrenees in 1659 had given him more financial scope, Louis XIV turned once more to the Grand Design of his grandfather, Henri IV. The young King, not yet twenty-three, was noted for his charm and grace, and for his handsome presence; his taste for ballet and the arts was to transform the Louvre into a palace of feasts and festivals. But Louis XIV, that proud ruler who saw himself as the living embodiment of the absolutist State, and insatiably promoted the power of the monarchy, was motivated above all else by a desire for 'glory'. This was the vision that prompted all his political actions, and from 1662 onwards it was also promoted with conviction by his minister, Jean-Baptiste Colbert. The Louvre was to be the first setting for his glory, the stage for the ritual of kingship, before Versailles was created to provide an even grander context.

Louis Le Vau presented a new scheme to realize the Grand Design in 1660. Another project, by Léonor Houdin, was set aside, and all energies were focused on the business in hand: all private building work was forbidden so as not to deflect workmen from the site; and within the area covered by the Grand Design, a plan was drawn up to expropriate existing buildings, to forbid any new construction, and to prevent the repair of standing structures. Le Vau was thus enabled to undertake the shaping of the west façade of the palace, which looked out on the kitchen court, now ennobled as the 'Place du Louvre'. Of his design there survives the 'Mur Le Vau', the boldly rusticated footing of a bridge leading to the Pavillon de l'Horloge, which was discovered during the 1985 excavations in the Cour Napoléon. The dream of quadrupling the size of the courtyard of the Louvre was finally realized. The last remains of the medieval Louvre were demolished, together with all the neighbouring houses with the exception of a few in the Rue d'Autriche, which survived as an eyesore in the middle of the new courtyard right up to the mid-eighteenth century. First to be completed was part of the north wing, with the Pavillon de Beauvais at the north-west corner, and then attention turned to the extension of the south wing (1661–63), which received as a centrepiece a large pavilion similar to Lemercier's Pavillon de l'Horloge.

The upper storey of the Petite Galerie had been destroyed by fire in 1661: Le Vau reconstructed it, and doubled it in width to the west by the addition of a parallel range of which the façade can be seen today in the Cour du Sphinx, formerly the Cour de la Reine. The elevation is curiously unclassical, with two doors and two windows embraced by a single pediment, in which Lespagnandelle carved representations of the Arts and Sciences (1663). The ground floor was intended to house a theatre, a new room for antique sculptures, and an oratory; on the first floor were the Cabinet des Tableaux du Roi, for the King's pictures, and a great reception room, known to this day as the Salon Carré (though it is in fact rectangular, not square), which opened into the Galerie d'Apollon. The great height of this room necessitated the heightening and remodelling of the river front of the Petite Galerie, which received a new decorative pediment by Etienne Le Hongre. Now too the fourteen pediments of the Grande Galerie, left unfinished at the death of Henri IV, were carved by the brothers Gaspard and Balthazar Marsy.

The Galerie d'Apollon (opposite), of 1662, is the first great decorative essay in the Louis XIV style.
The stucco work includes figures of Terpsichore and Polyhymnia by Balthazar Marsy (pages 60–61).
Castor or The Morning Star, by Renou, was set into the original ceiling in 1781 (pages 62–63).

58

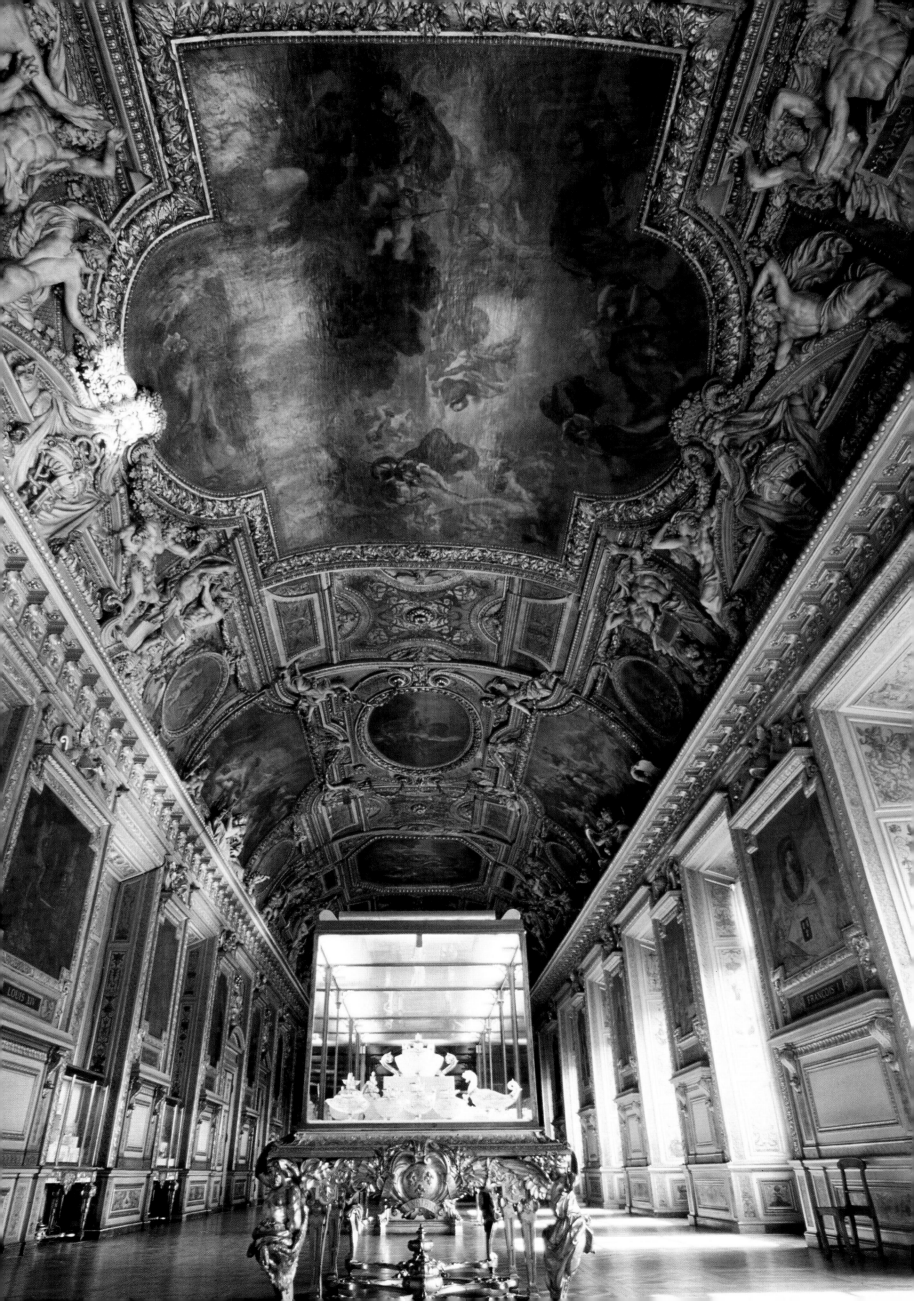

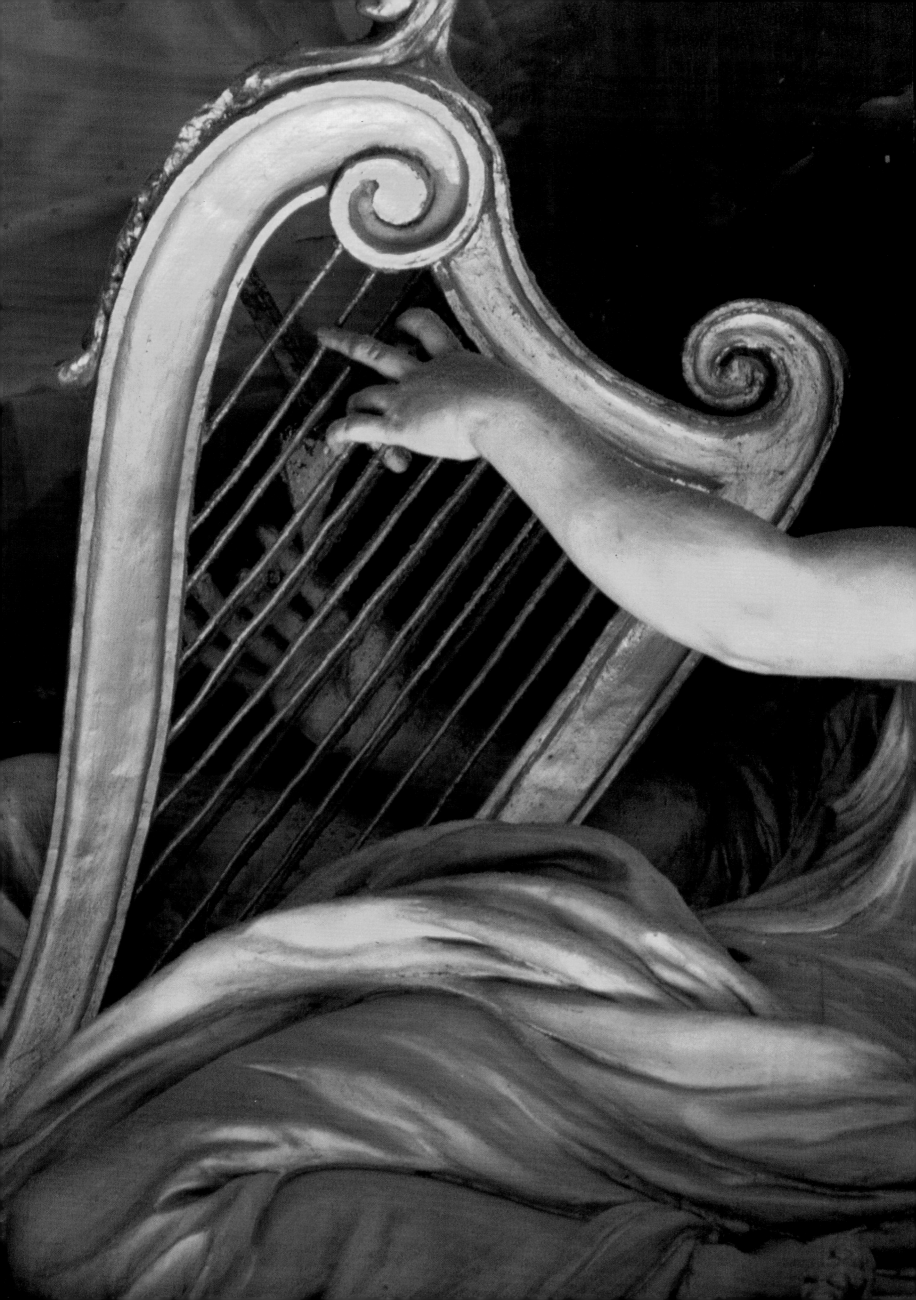

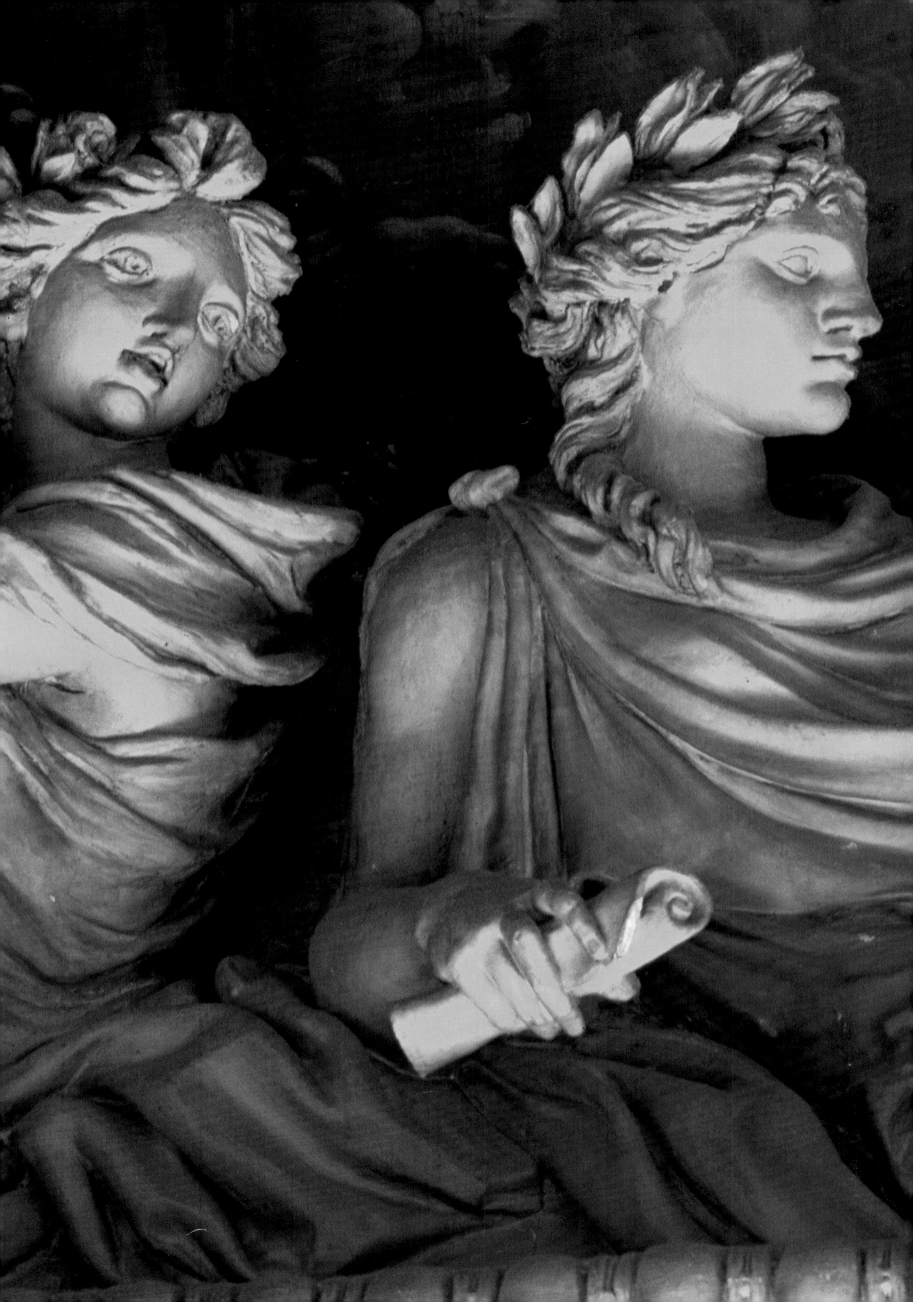

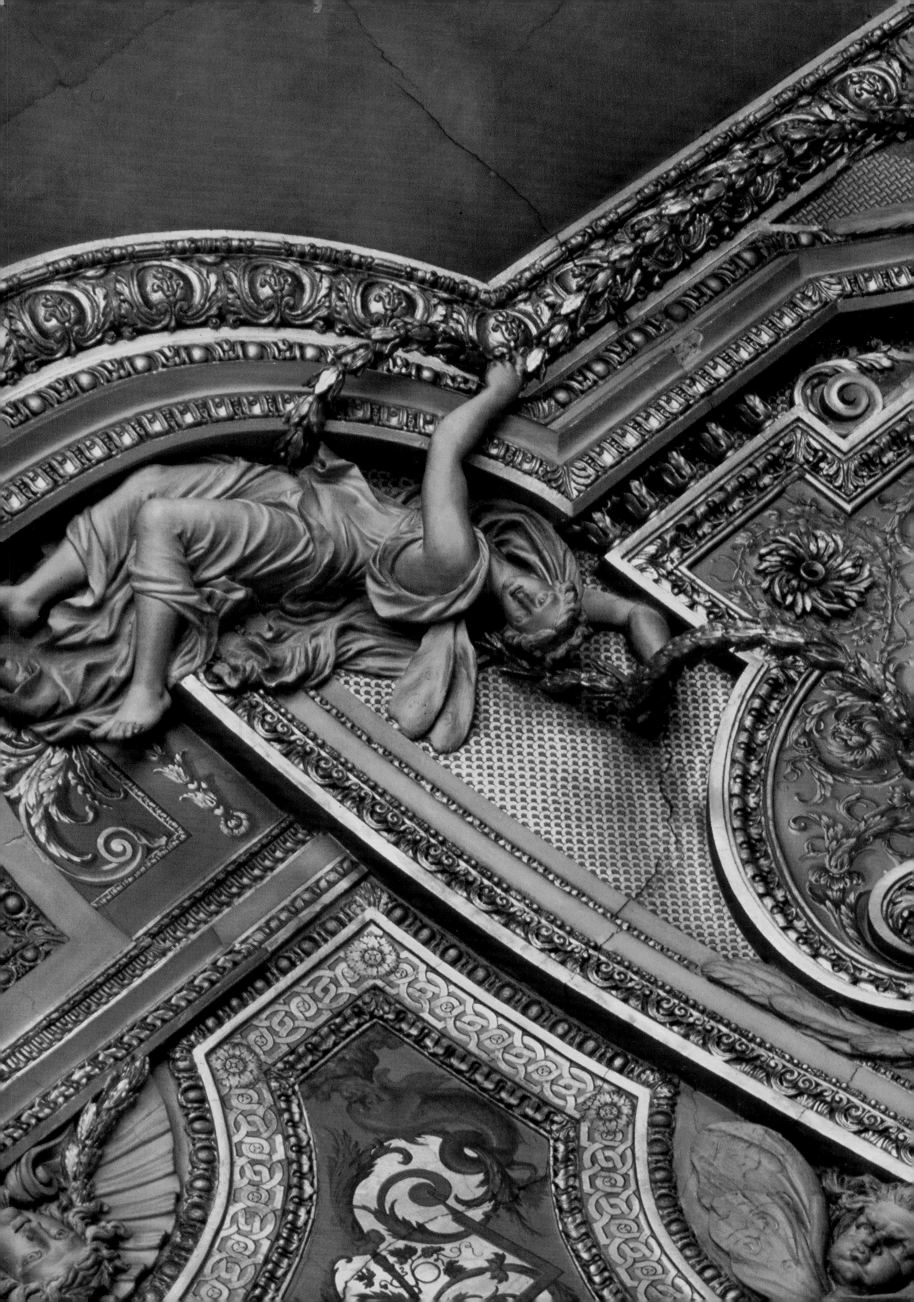

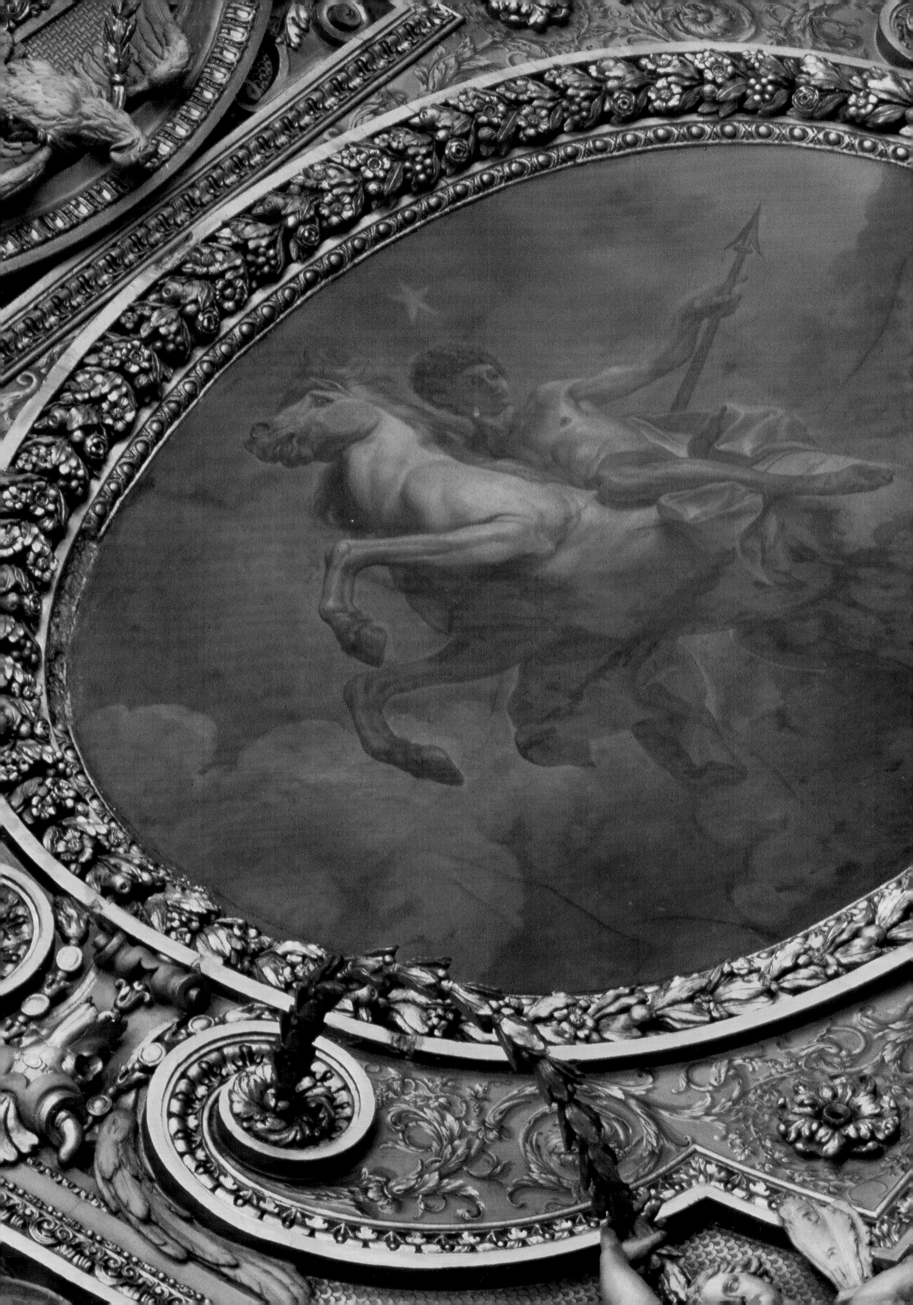

The decorators' greatest energies were focused on the interiors. Here, for the upper storey of the Petite Galerie the painter Charles Le Brun conceived a scheme in painting and sculpture on the theme of the Sun, the Muses, and the Sun's movement through space and time. The result was the Galerie d'Apollon, the first manifestation of a decorative manner that was to flower at Versailles. Le Brun began work on the paintings at the southern end (*The Triumph of the Waters*) and in a few compartments of the ceiling (*Dawn, Evening, Night*), but the project was soon stopped and only fragments survive. The lunette at the end was painted directly on the wall: while it is very damaged, the vigour of Le Brun's handling is still apparent in the heads of the fiery horses and in the playful nymphs. On the ceiling, where the paintings are on canvas, an oval compartment shows *Evening* under the guise of Morpheus, god of sleep and begetter of monsters (one of his offspring appears to his right), reclining on clouds with poppies in his hand. Further on, in an octagonal compartment, *Night* is represented by Diana in her chariot drawn by two does; above is Phoebe, pulling back the curtain of darkness. The rest of the ceiling paintings date from the eighteenth and nineteenth centuries.

While the painted scheme remained unfinished, the stucco decoration was completed. The work of Girardon, the Marsy brothers and Regnaudin is unique among the decorative schemes of the age of Louis XIV in its breathtaking monumentality combined with gaiety and supple movement. The groups of captives in chains at the four corners of the room (captives again, as in the King's Bedchamber), who represent the four parts of the world, are admittedly not joyful, but they are powerful and expressive. The greatest animation appears in the groups representing the zodiac, where lively putti tease the relevant animals – ram, bull, lion, scorpion, etc. – while elsewhere handsome athletes show off their muscles to smiling Muses. Between these groups are six compositions of grotesques separating the major compartments, executed by the ornament painter Léonard Gontier in 1666. In 1666–70 Jacques Gervaise produced eight medallions from a cycle of the labours of the months in the tradition of French Gothic cathedral portals (March–June are absent); each medallion was surrounded by a floral garland, the work of the flower-painter Jean-Baptiste Monnoyer.

The decoration of the Galerie d'Apollon also included Savonnerie carpets specially commissioned by the King, which survive to this day as the most magnificent examples of their kind. But lost are the great cabinets by Domenico Cucci and Golle, and lost too is the original decoration of the lower part of the room, comprising shutters and panelling on which the Lemoine brothers had painted arabesques and flowers. Their wealth of ornament was recorded in several series of black-and-white line engravings, which were used as models by the restorers in the mid-nineteenth century.

At the other end of the palace, the façade of the Tuileries was completely remodelled by Le Vau and his assistant, François d'Orbay. The central pavilion was widened, and decorated with large stone figures sculpted under the direction of Philippe De Buyster and Thibaut Poissant. The overall composition, which had hitherto been an assemblage of disparate elements, was at last given some symmetry by the erection of a pavilion to the north, known then as the Pavillon de Pomone and eventually rebuilt as the present Pavillon de Marsan. In the centre, the architects created a new staircase, where on the instructions of Colbert – placed in charge of royal building works in January 1664, as Surintendant des Bâtiments du Roi – the balusters were carved with a sun, emblematic of the King, and a grass snake (*colubra* in Latin), his own device. Some sixteen of these stone balusters, perhaps the work of the sculptor Jacques Houzeau, survived the building's demolition in the nineteenth century and are now in the Department of Sculpture of the Louvre.

The State Apartments, where Louis XIV lived while work on the Louvre was in progress (1667–74), were themselves luxuriously decorated, with stucco by Girardon, Jean-Baptiste Tuby and Louis Lerambert, and paintings by Noël Coypel, the brothers Jean-Baptiste and Philippe de Champaigne, Nicolas Loir and Bertholet Flemalle. Here again a few elements survive, notably two large paintings: *Apollo* by Coypel (Salles d'Histoire du Louvre) and *The Education of Achilles*, on a gold ground, by Jean-Baptiste Champaigne

One of the signs of the Zodiac modelled in stucco by Gaspard Marsy in the Galerie d'Apollon.

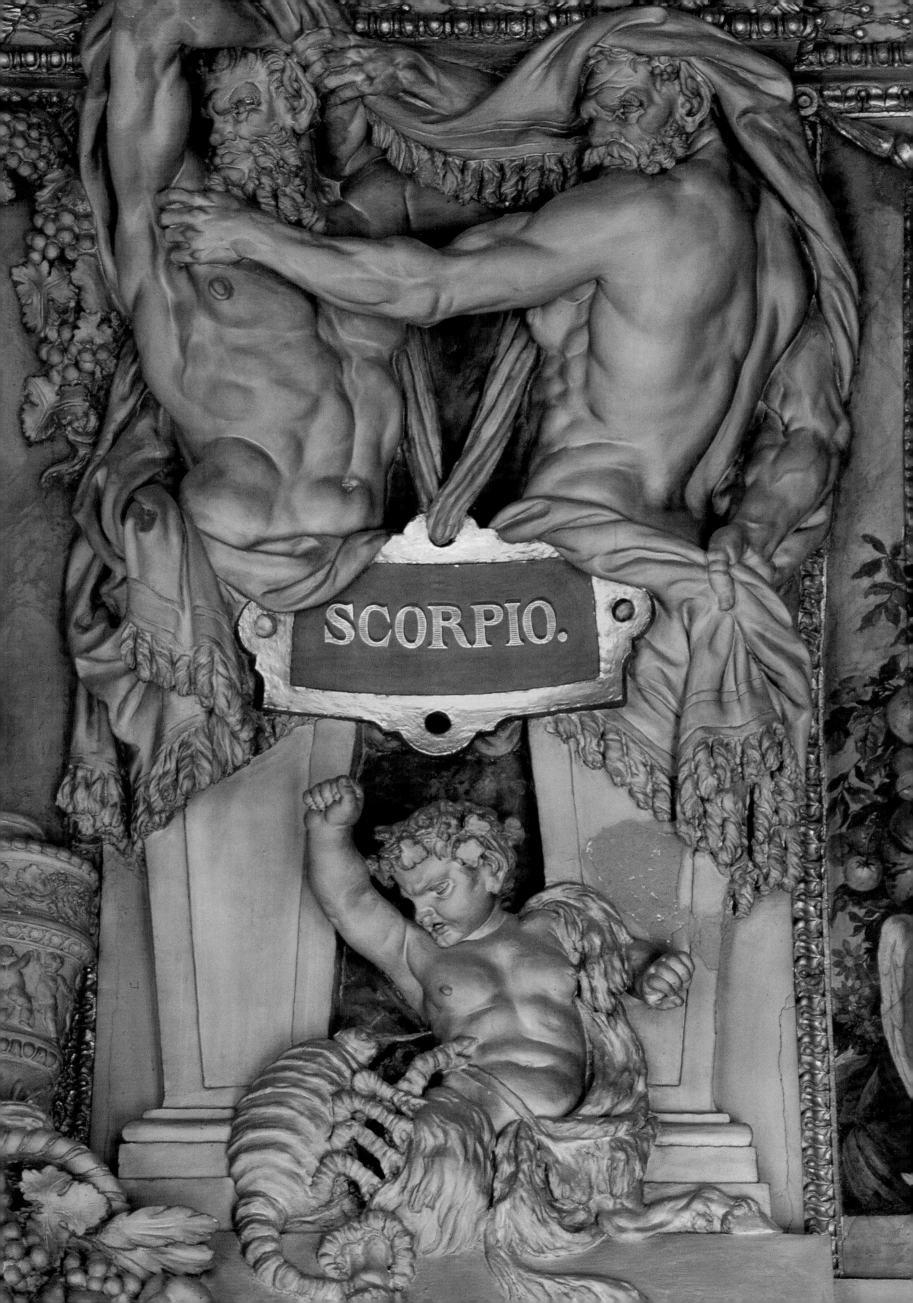

(Department of Paintings). In the great Galerie des Ambassadeurs, the ceiling was ornamented with copies of the Carracci frescoes in the Palazzo Farnese, executed on Colbert's orders by the *pensionnaires* of the French Academy in Rome.

Outside the windows of the Tuileries Palace, to the west, a new garden was begun for the King in 1664. Its deviser was André Le Nôtre, himself born in the Tuileries, son and grandson of the royal gardeners who had laid out the first garden on the site. Here, before the days of his fame as the creator of the park at Versailles, and of many others such as those of Chantilly, Saint-Cloud, Sceaux and Meudon, he first demonstrated his abilities. He tamed nature, sculpted space, and laid out a vast vista that extended to the horizon. First came a great *parterre*, like a coloured mirror below the palace, then leafy woods with concealed *bosquets*. Through it all ran the axis of the central *allée*, providing a long perspective as the land rose, its effect enhanced by a large theatre on a segmental plan laid out at the far end of the park.

What the King and Colbert were chiefly interested in, however, was the east wing of the Louvre, which was to be the setting of the new royal apartments. This range, the fourth side of the courtyard, looked out towards the city, and it was to be given a dramatic façade that would express the power of the King and proclaim the notions of royal glory and grandeur which the court was concerned to cultivate. Le Vau had already begun the substructure of this façade (his work was rediscovered first in 1850, and then fully exposed in 1964 when André Malraux ordered the creation of the moat in front of the Colonnade), but the Bâtiments du Roi decided to look again for a prestigious architect worthy of the project. Proposals came from a number of Frenchmen, including Le Vau himself, François Mansart and Louis Marot. Colbert was not satisfied with any of them, and invited designs from leading Italians, such as Pietro da Cortona and Carlo Rainaldi, and Candiani, an amateur. Gianlorenzo Bernini, then at the height of his fame both as architect and as sculptor, produced the grandest palace design in June 1664, but Colbert found it too vulnerable to 'damage by the elements'. Bernini followed this with a more sober design in January 1665. His successive projects, for a building with a great central rotunda and then for a monumental four-square palazzo in the Roman manner, were conceived as part of a radical reorganization of the space between the Louvre and the Tuileries, which he already proposed to transform into a vast composition of royal courtyards. Bernini was invited to Paris in 1665, the Pope being officially solicited to lend his architect to the King of France. We know a good deal about his stay from the journal of Chantelou, who describes the visits and experiences of the great Baroque architect. Well lodged, entertained and pampered, he set to work, refining his project for the Louvre and sculpting a marble bust of the King (now at Versailles). On 17 June 1665 the first stone of the new façade was laid amid great ceremony by Louis XIV himself. Three days later Bernini departed, laden with honours, with the guarantee of a pension of twelve thousand *livres* and a commission for a marble equestrian statue of the King. He reached Rome; and the Bâtiments du Roi shelved the whole project. Finally in July 1667 Colbert wrote to extricate himself from his commitments, claiming that the scheme had had to be abandoned for lack of funds.

The truth of the matter is that the French architects had resented the intruder from the south, and Colbert, for his part, looked on the project with the eyes of a scrupulous civil servant, more concerned with function and display than with architectural innovation. Moreover, he was prejudiced against Bernini by his deputy in the Bâtiments du Roi, Charles Perrault (famed as the author of *Puss in Boots*). An architectural commission was set up in the same year, 1667: its members were the painter Charles Le Brun, the architects Louis Le Vau (who was to die soon) and Le Vau's son-in-law François d'Orbay, who had done a great deal of designing for him, and the moving spirit, Claude Perrault, who was the brother of Colbert's factotum Charles. By training a doctor, Claude Perrault was in fact interested in everything. He was an anatomist, but he was also involved with technology: he had already designed the Observatory, and his consuming interest was in technical feats.

Opposite Detail of the colonnade on the east front of the Louvre.

Pages 68–69 Projects for the east front – left, by Houdin, Mansart, Cottart and Marot; right, by Bernini (first project, and façade and section through the courtyard of the second project) and Rainaldi.

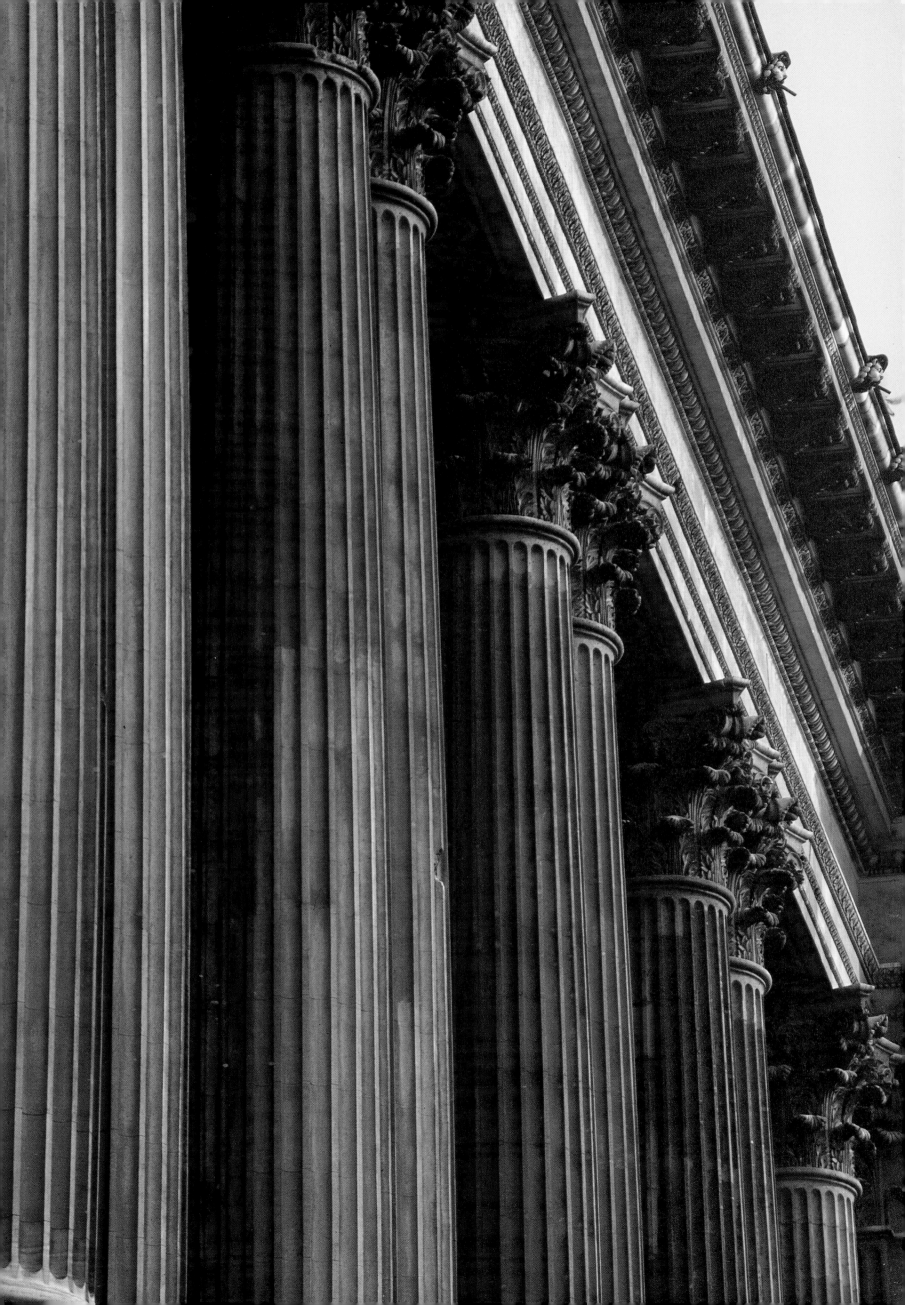

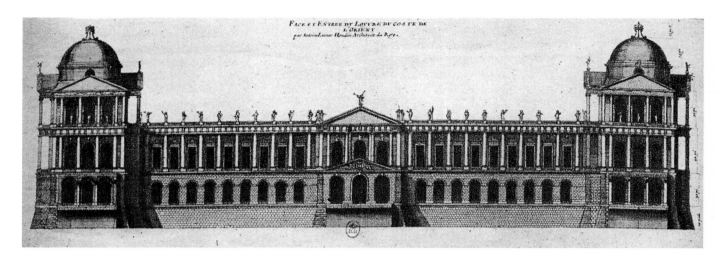

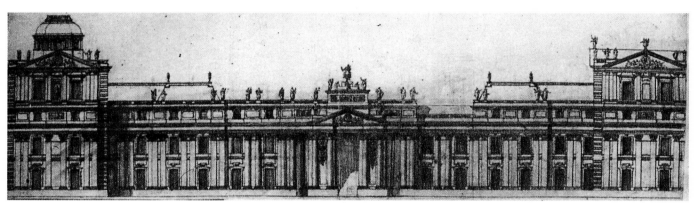

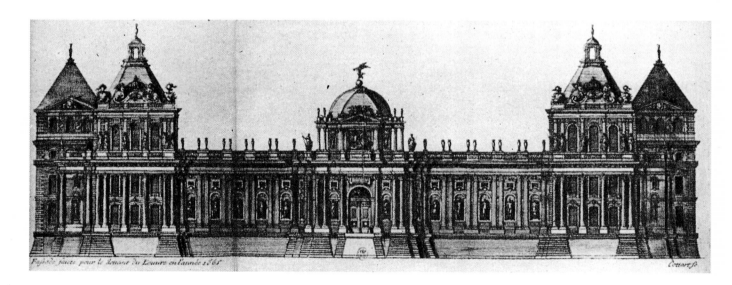

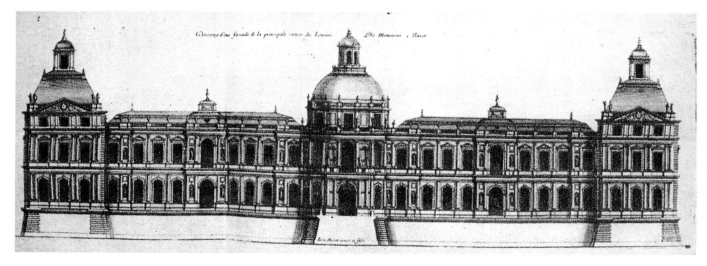

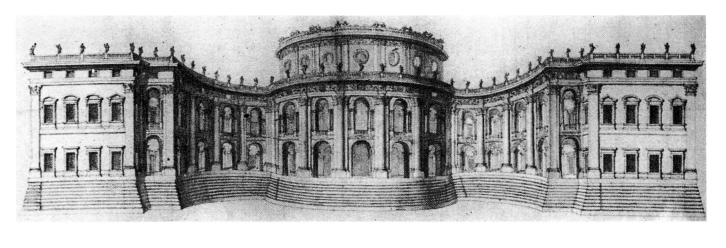

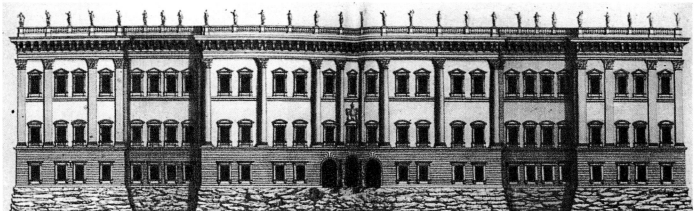

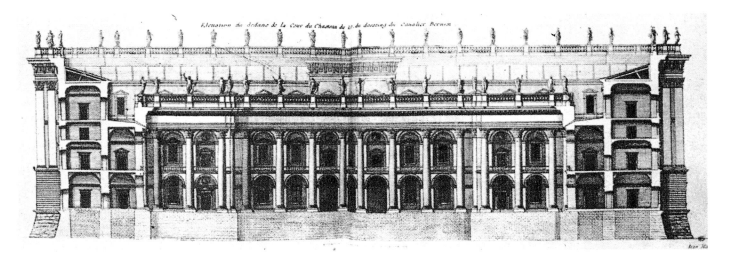

Elevation du dedans de la Cour du Chasteau de et du dessein du Cavalier Bernin

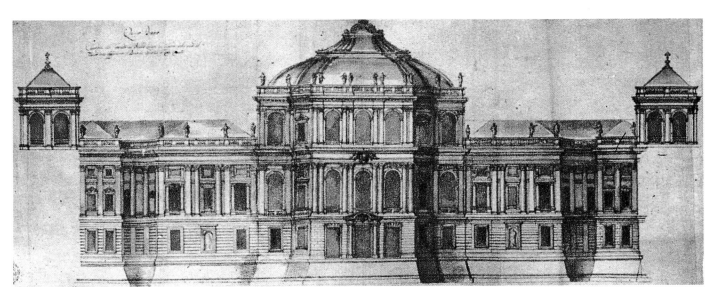

He was to design the machines which were used in 1672 to raise the two gigantic monoliths for the sides of the pediment of the east front of the Louvre, each of them 17 metres (56 feet) long and 2.5 metres (8 feet) thick, and was also responsible for the use of iron cramps sheathed with lead to fix the stones in the long lintels of the new façade, an innovation that was to prove costly when the iron rusted.

The commission turned again to the French projects put forward before Bernini's involvement, and in 1667 work began on the monumental front known as the 'Colonnade', in which the prestigious first floor is emphasized by a succession of paired columns flanking a pedimented central pavilion. The King, who wanted his new royal apartments along the river to be grand, decreed that the south wing should be thicker than the others around the Cour Carrée. The architect was thus compelled to erect a new façade only a short distance in front of the one that had so recently been built. The new east front thus had to be longer, and therefore also taller. This meant that on the inner face it outtopped the other sides of the Cour Carrée, forcing Perrault to abandon the design of the attic stage that had been followed since the days of Lescot in favour of a third storey. He chose to use columns to flank the projecting bays at this level, clashing with the other façades. Some projects, by Perrault and Le Brun, suggested a new 'French order' ornamented with lilies or cockerels, but in the end the order chosen was Corinthian.

While this vast campaign was under way, slow progress continued to be made on the decorative work. The grimacing masks which so strikingly ornament the keystones of the northern façade were carved in 1669 by a team made up of the best royal artists – Etienne Le Hongre, Jean-Baptiste Tuby, Nicolas Legendre and Benoît Massou. The same team had already, a year earlier, provided models for the capitals of the Cour Carrée and of the Colonnade. Inside, the decoration of the Grande Galerie was resumed: the stucco work was continued by Legendre, Laurent Magnier and Philibert Bernard (1668–71), while Jacques Prou, Philippe Caffieri the elder and Mathieu Lespagnandelle carved the panelling and others carried on with the wall-paintings; the carpets were supplied by the Savonnerie factory.

In 1674 the King and the court moved to Versailles, and work slowed down, eventually ceasing completely in 1678. The new Louvre was left unfinished, its roofs incomplete. The square that Le Brun had conceived to the east of the palace, which was to have had a magnificent royal monument, never got beyond the stage of a drawing. The exterior decoration was far from complete on the Colonnade front, with only the capitals and the medallions carved; the rest of the stones were still rough, waiting to be sculpted, as were those in the pediments of the attic facing the Cour Carrée and of the end pavilions facing out.

Even in its unfinished, abandoned state, Louis XIV's palace had an immense influence. The vast Colonnade, 183 metres (600 feet) long, was conceived to stand on a high basement (exposed during the excavation works of the 1960s). It is composed of a central pavilion flanked by two colonnades which stand a long way forward from the wall. The paired columns are echoed on the rear wall of the gallery by pilasters which originally framed niches (transformed into windows under Napoleon I). Unified and compact, with its perfect rhythm and marked contrasts of light and shade, the Colonnade is a quintessential embodiment of Classical architecture, and it is the prototype of a long list of major works, from Gabriel's twin buildings in the Place de la Concorde to a host of Neoclassical successors.

A palace for academies

Louis XIV had spent much of his life at the Louvre, and it had been the scene of a variety of royal entertainments: in the Salle des Cariatides in 1658 Molière had performed *Le Docteur Amoureux*, followed later by *L'Etourdi* and *Les Précieuses Ridicules*; the Salle des Machines in the Tuileries, built by Vigarani, had served for magnificent spectacles; in 1662 the King himself had been the moving spirit in a splendid *carrousel* or tournament, staged to celebrate the birth of the Dauphin, which saw the entire nobility performing the most elaborate equestrian feats in exotic costume.

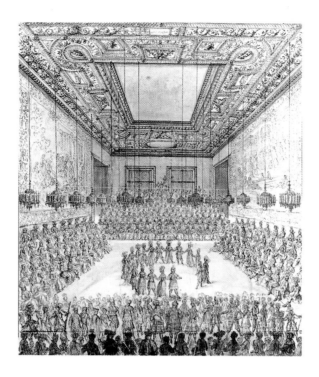

In 1669, when he had withdrawn to the Tuileries, the King organized a lavish ballet in the 'great pavilion on the river' at the end of the Grande Galerie: known as the 'Ballet de Flore', it was to bequeath its name to the pavilion itself, which retains it to this day.

Nevertheless, the King decided to quit Paris. Despite the grand vista of his garden at the Tuileries, he felt confined. Hunting, his favourite sport, was impossible here; the Louvre carried painful memories of his mother, who had died there in 1666; and Paris reminded him of the rebellious citizenry that had opposed him with the Fronde. Although Colbert considered it essential to have a great royal palace in the capital city, Louis XIV opted for isolation at Versailles, surrounded by his court and the immense park.

Part of Louis XIV's Louvre was left as an empty shell, while all the areas that were habitable were taken over by royal administration, by courtiers, and particularly by academies and artists. The finest apartments were used for academic sessions. The Académie Française was installed in the palace in 1672, on the ground floor of the Pavillon du Roi, while the King was still nominally in residence. In 1685 the Académie des Inscriptions et Belles Lettres moved into the ground floor of the Lemercier wing, on the west side of the Cour Carrée. The Academy of Painting and Sculpture joined them in 1692, the year when the King's antique sculptures were moved to the Salle des Cariatides, which became the new Salle des Antiques: the Academy occupied the Salon Carré and the neighbouring rooms (now the Salle Duchâtel and Salles Percier et Fontaine), next door to the King's picture collection, which was housed in the Galerie d'Apollon and the Rotonde de Mars. Also in 1692, the Academy of Architecture moved into the Queen's Apartment. The Academy of Science took up residence in the King's Apartment. Books and collections piled up. The Louvre housed the Imprimerie Royale (for letterpress printing), the Chalcographie (for the intaglio printing of images), the Salle des Antiques, the Cabinet des Tableaux du Roi (the King's picture collection), the Naval and Mechanical Cabinets, the Political Academy (in the Pavillon de l'Horloge), and a set of relief plans of French strongholds, displayed in the Grande Galerie as an aid to the teaching of military strategy.

The Academy of Painting and Sculpture was a learned association of artists, who met together and listened to lectures in which artistic theory was formulated; but its primary function was as a teaching institution, for the training of future royal artists. In the 'model' room drawing was taught. A carefully chosen collection of works served to form the students' eye: there were casts of famous works of antique sculpture, portraits of academicians, and the academicians' reception pieces. It was already in essence a little museum, supplemented by the neighbouring Salle des Antiques and Cabinet des Tableaux.

A ballet in what is now the Henri II Vestibule, recorded in a drawing by Israël Silvestre (Louvre).

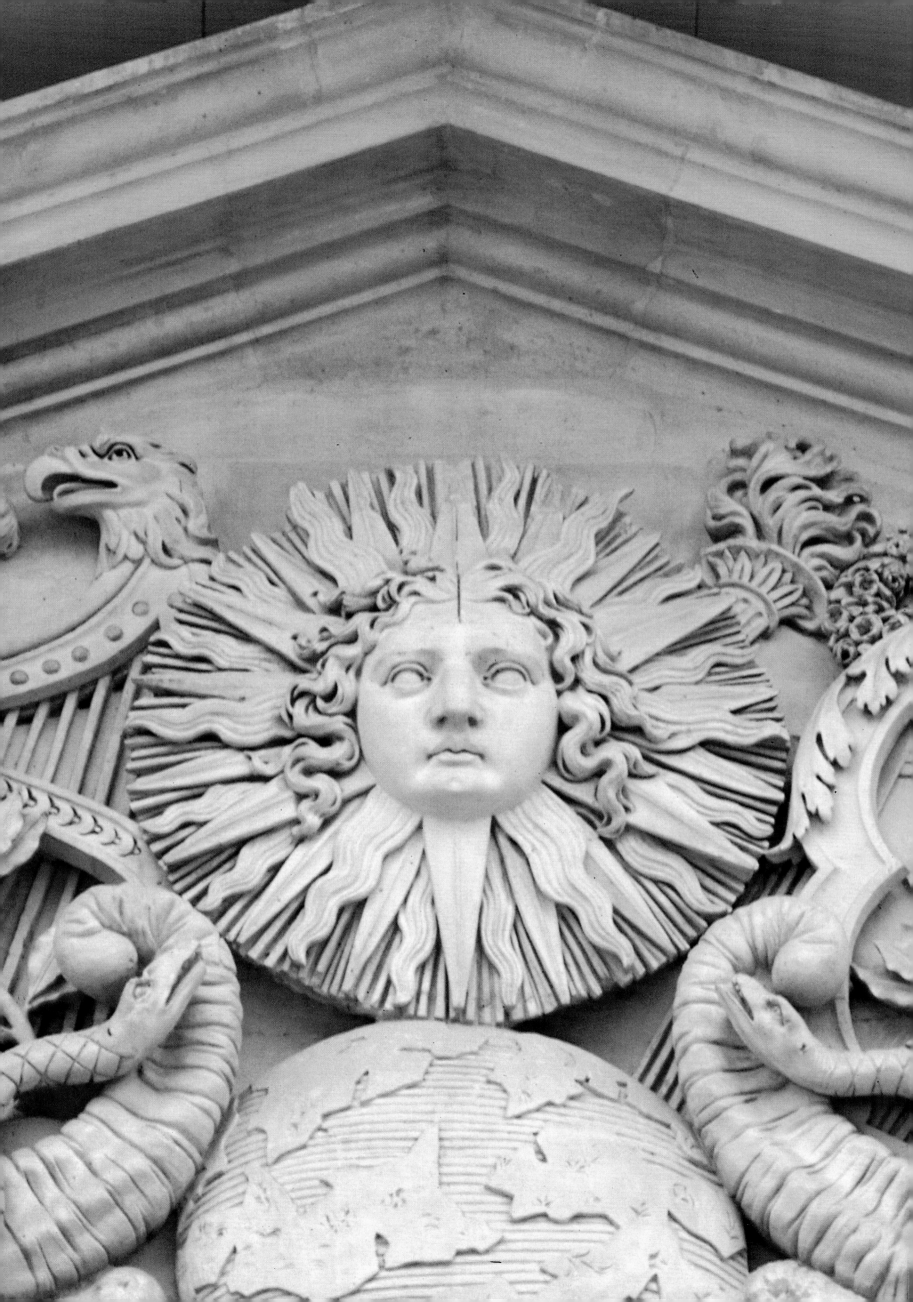

Contemporary art was actively present in the form of periodic exhibitions by members of the Academy. Held at first in the Palais Royal, the display moved to the Grande Galerie in 1699, and then to the adjacent Salon Carré – hence the use of the name 'Salon' for the biennial exhibitions of academic work held on the Feast of St Louis (25 August), which in the eighteenth century became the high points of Parisian artistic life. Pictures by Gabriel de Saint-Aubin record the Salon Carré filled with pictures hung so close they almost touch, with sculptures displayed on long tables in the centre. The difficult task of hanging the pictures fell to an artist (Chardin held the post for a time), who had to behave with great diplomacy faced with touchy artists each determined to get the best position for his work. Pride of place went to royal commissions, to reception pieces, and to a selection of the best works of each Academician. The critics or *salonniers* had a field day, damning or praising, making and unmaking reputations, and using the occasion as a pretext to voice their theories of art. From Diderot in the age of Enlightenment to Baudelaire in the following century, reviews of the Salon were to provide the most prestigious platform for art theory.

Modest progress during the Régence

The eighteenth century was not a good time for improvements to the Louvre. When Louis XIV died in 1715 the new king, Louis XV, was a child. The Regent, the Duc d'Orléans, brought him back from Versailles to Paris, and from 1716 he was in residence at the Tuileries. In 1719 he spent a few months at the Louvre, which was partly occupied by various royal councils. Philippe d'Orléans wanted to re-establish Paris as the centre of power, but his success was short-lived, for in 1722 the King returned to Versailles.

For Paris, the regency or Régence (which gave its name to the age) meant liberation from the grand formality of the age of Louis XIV. The city experienced a new sense of freedom, a light and festive decorative style, and the rapid rise of a class determined to enjoy themselves (all too soon to be ruined by the financial system introduced by John Law). Parisian social life was now centred in the *salons* of houses built in the new aristocratic suburbs. At the Louvre there was very little activity, though this period did see the enrichment of the Tuileries Gardens by statues brought from Versailles and Marly (which is how the great royal statues eventually came to be sheltered in the Louvre museum), and the construction of a great Manège or Riding School there by the architect Robert de Cotte in 1720.

In 1722 the Queen Mother's Apartment was used to lodge the little Infanta of Spain, Maria Ana Victoria, who had been betrothed to Louis XV at the age of four. The marriage was never consummated and she eventually returned home, leaving her name to the riverside garden – the Jardin de l'Infante – which the Bâtiments du Roi redesigned and filled with a set of statues of the attendants of the goddess Diana, originally intended for the park at Marly.

The Louvre was now a sort of vast caravanserai, housing the academies and the 'Tribunal de la Garenne du Louvre' (concerned with the royal rabbit warren), and the archives of Foreign Affairs, the Royal Council and the Finance Council. The apartments were subdivided, with some rooms even floored across, to produce lodgings for courtiers and artists receiving pensions, and sometimes for their widows as well. There was even a proposal to find space in the Louvre for the royal library, then housed in inadequate premises in the Rue de Richelieu: Robert de Cotte worked on the project for two years (1720–22) before it was finally abandoned.

Detail of the pediment of the Cour de la Reine, now Cour du Sphinx, carved by Mathieu Lespagnandelle.

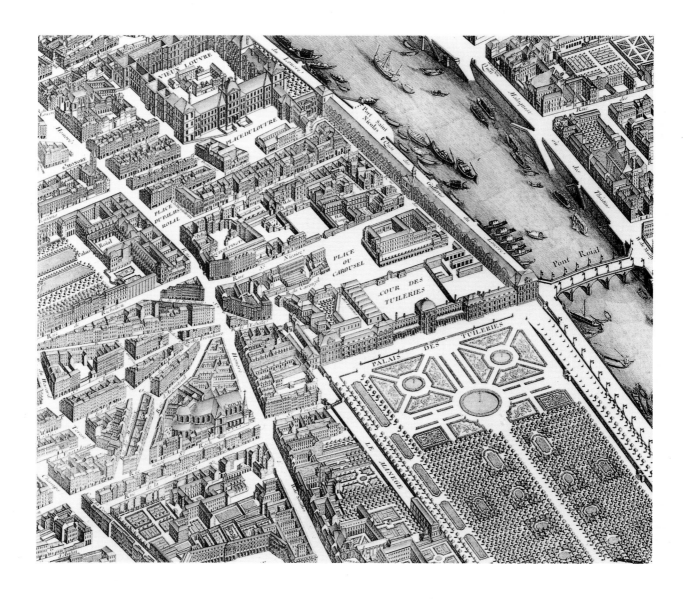

The Louvre and Tuileries in their setting at the beginning of the eighteenth century, from the Turgot plan of Paris. Note the complete neighbourhood that lay between the two palaces, and the houses in the middle of the Cour Carrée.

The Museum:
From Idea to Creation

Louis XV now spent all his time at Versailles and his other well-wooded estates at Marly, Fontainebleau and Compiègne, and the Louvre, that palace of the arts, was abandoned by the court. Paris itself, however, had become an intellectual capital and a centre of the Enlightenment. The city of Diderot and d'Alembert's *Encyclopédie* (1751-80) and of the *philosophes*, whose artists set the pattern for the rest of Europe, was less concerned than it had been with royalty. The new intellectual movement had its home in the salons of Paris, particularly in the neighbourhood of the Louvre, notably those of Madame Geoffrin in the Rue Saint-Honoré and of Helvetius in the Rue Saint-Anne. The Louvre district and the palace itself, home to academicians and artists, were a centre of the new culture, and it was here that the future belonged.

Steps towards a museum

Inside the Louvre, courtiers kept house in rooms designed for greater things, as rival administrations fought each other for power; the palace was also divided up into dozens of artists' studios. It was completely surrounded by houses, and a cluster of houses still occupied the middle of the Cour Carrée; stables were built on to the façades of the Colonnade wing. Now, fired by Lafont de Saint-Yenne, who in a pamphlet imagined 'the shade of the great Colbert' returning to lament the unfinished state of his work, there was a swell of feeling against the building's state of neglect. Architects produced new projects for completing it, and writers – including Voltaire in 1749 – lent the movement their support.

In 1753 the Bâtiments du Roi noticed that the iron rods used by Perrault to hold the enormous stones of the Colonnade lintels together had rusted, splitting the surrounding stone. Urgent repairs were called for, the more so because the King now chose the Louvre to house the Grand Conseil, a political weapon against the rebellious parliament. The Marquis de Marigny, brother of Madame de Pompadour and director of the Bâtiments du Roi, took charge. A modest campaign of improvement was put in hand, under the architect Ange-Jacques Gabriel, assisted by Jacques-Germain Soufflot. The north wing of the Cour Carrée was refurbished for the Grand Conseil, the unsightly houses in the courtyard were demolished, houses crowding around the Colonnade were removed (1756), a passage was created leading out of the courtyard on the north (where handsome columns by Soufflot can still be seen today), and the Colonnade front towards the city was restored.

It also proved necessary to rebuild the upper storey of the Colonnade wing facing the courtyard. Gabriel eventually followed Perrault in his choice of the Corinthian order, but altered the design, effectively destroying it. In 1757 Soufflot presented models of capitals to the Academy of Architecture for their final decision. Work began, and the sculpture of the west-facing pediment was at last executed, by Guillaume II Coustou, in 1758-59. But the Seven Years War now took priority for funding, and work soon came to a halt.

Marigny managed nevertheless to accomplish a smaller project, the conversion of the former Salle des Machines in the Tuileries. The new theatre was to house the Opera (1763-70), then the Comédie Française (1770-82); here Beaumarchais' *Barber of Seville* received its first performance. The position of the stage, between the courtyard of the Tuileries and the gardens, gave rise to the expressions still used by actors in France today to designate the two sides of the stage, '*côté cour*' and '*côté jardin*'.

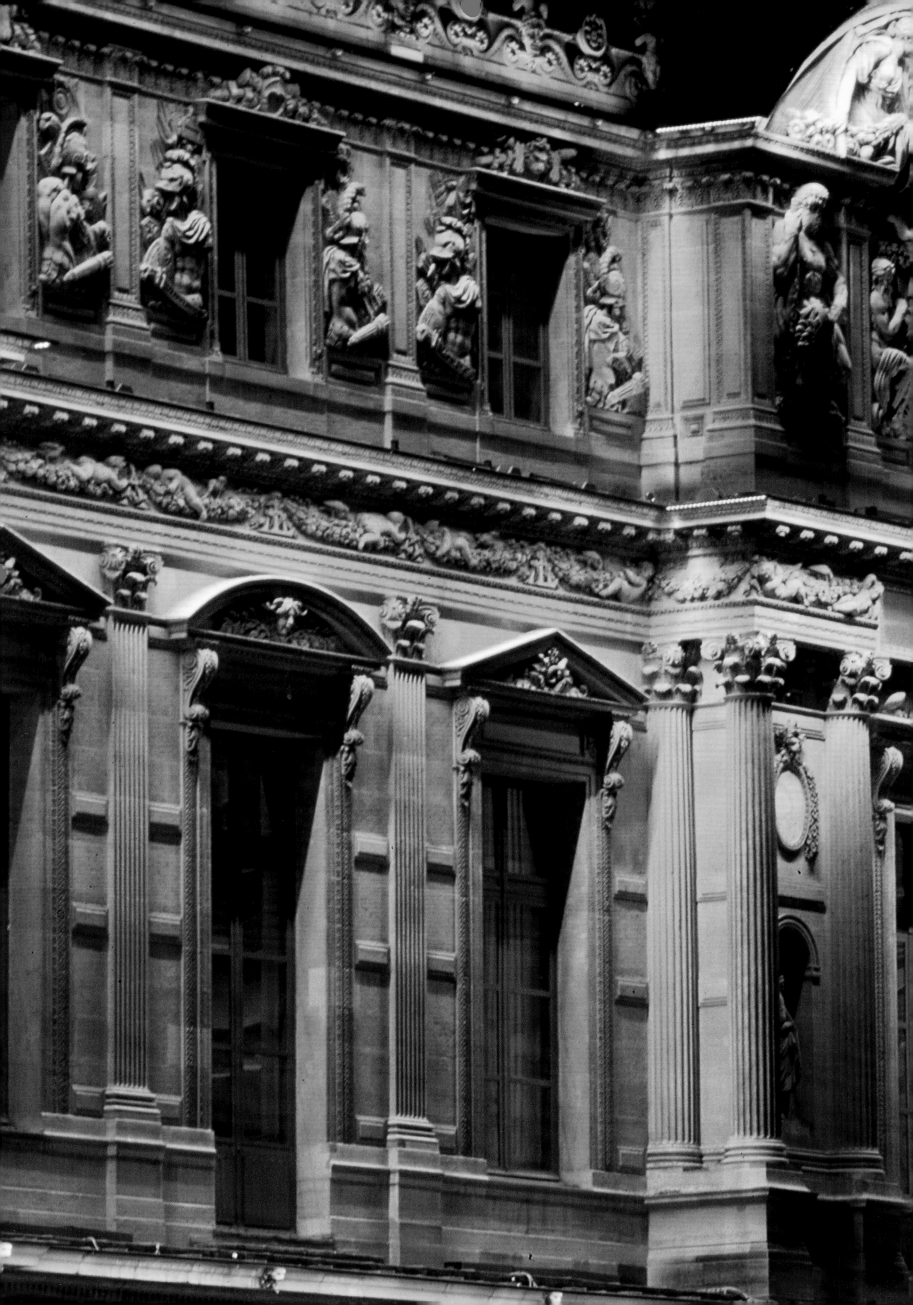

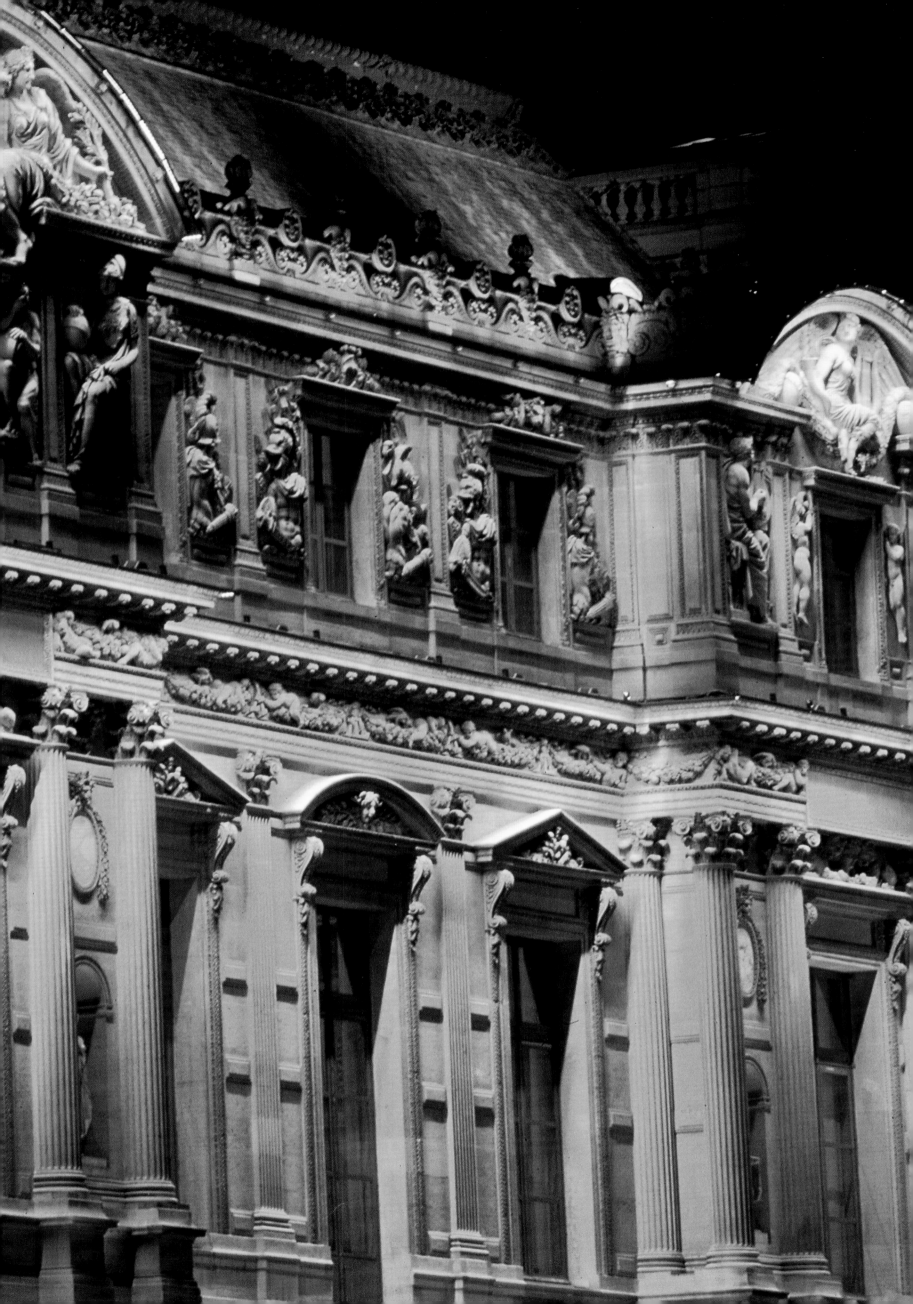

But an altogether grander idea was in the air, in which Soufflot took an interest. In 1767 he presented plans for a complete remodelling of the buildings surrounding the Cour Carrée, where the Grand Conseil occupied a prime site. He proposed moving the academies into the north and west wings, while the east wing was designated as the home of the royal library, which was to be reached by a monumental staircase (for which magnificent drawings survive) and to have storage space in the south wing. This first scheme for a 'palace of the intellect' at the Louvre foundered for lack of funds, despite Marigny's support.

Public opinion was most excited by the idea of a 'museum' in the Louvre, where the royal collections could be displayed. Feelings were the more intense because in Rome the papal collections had long been accessible in a 'museum' or temple of the Muses, a novel institution, which was open to the public. In 1750 a selection of 110 paintings from the French royal collections had been put on display in the Luxembourg Palace. Their removal had allowed the Academy of Painting to claim the space liberated by the Cabinet des Tableaux du Roi in 1747; in 1764, it took over the adjacent Galerie d'Apollon.

In 1768, Marigny proposed that the collections of paintings, medals and prints should be moved to the Grande Galerie and the Salon Carré. His successor as director of the Bâtiments du Roi, the Comte d'Angiviller, took the idea much further: he had studies made of how the pictures should be presented, had some restored, and even made new purchases. A series of large marble statues were commissioned, four per year, to decorate the rooms with images of famous Frenchmen – not only politicians and military men but also artists and writers. The work of the greatest sculptors of the time, including Augustin Pajou, Jean-Jacques Caffieri, Pierre Julien and Clodion, they are now housed in the Louvre's Department of Sculpture.

To create a worthy approach to the new museum, a staircase leading to the Salon Carré and Grande Galerie was built by the architect Maximilien Brébion. It lay in Le Vau's wing parallel to the Petite Galerie: the new main entrance was in the façade of that wing, fronting on what was then named the Cour du Musée (now the Cour du Sphinx). Brébion also realized Soufflot's design for a new opening in the south range of the Cour Carrée, giving access to the court from the river front (1780).

Work on the new museum soon progressed to matters of detail. In 1776, the relief plans of French towns housed in the Grande Galerie had been moved to the Invalides, leaving the space free. Top-lighting was considered best for pictures, and various alternative schemes were proposed: Soufflot suggested an additional attic storey (1778), then dormers in the roof (1779); Hubert Robert, who was in charge of the King's pictures, suggested large skylights to provide bright overhead lighting, supplementing the windows in the side walls.

The Academy of Painting and Sculpture made its own contribution by prescribing that prospective members should submit as their reception work a painting for one of the ceiling compartments of the Galerie d'Apollon, of which the decoration had never been completed. From 1770 onwards the director of the Academy was Jean-Baptiste Pierre, himself a key figure in the revival of grand ceiling painting. The scheme was filled out by *Autumn*, or *The Triumph of Bacchus* by Hughes Taraval (1769), *Summer*, or *Ceres and her Companions invoking the Sun* by Louis-Jacques Durameau (1774), *Winter*, or *Eolus unleashing the Winds that Cover the Mountains with Snow* by Jean-Jacques Lagrenée the younger (1775), *Spring*, or *Zephyr and Flora crowning Cybele with Flowers*, by Antoine Callet (1780), and finally *Castor* or *The Morning Star* by Antoine Renou (1781).

Louis XVI, who had come to the throne in 1774, had not completely ruled out the possibility of returning to Paris. Marie-Antoinette made frequent stays at the Tuileries between 1773 and 1785 to enjoy the entertainments the city had to offer. When the Opera was destroyed by fire in 1781 every architect turned to his drawing board, and the most visionary among them revived the idea of the Grand Design, producing extremely ambitious projects for works at the Louvre and Tuileries palaces to enable them to house not only the museum and the Opera but the machinery of royal power. Grandiose projects came from the pens of Boullée, Bélanger,

Pages 76–77 Detail of the west façade of the Colonnade wing, with the pediment carved by Guillaume II Coustou.

Opposite Upper storeys of the Lemercier wing, on the west side of the Cour Carrée.

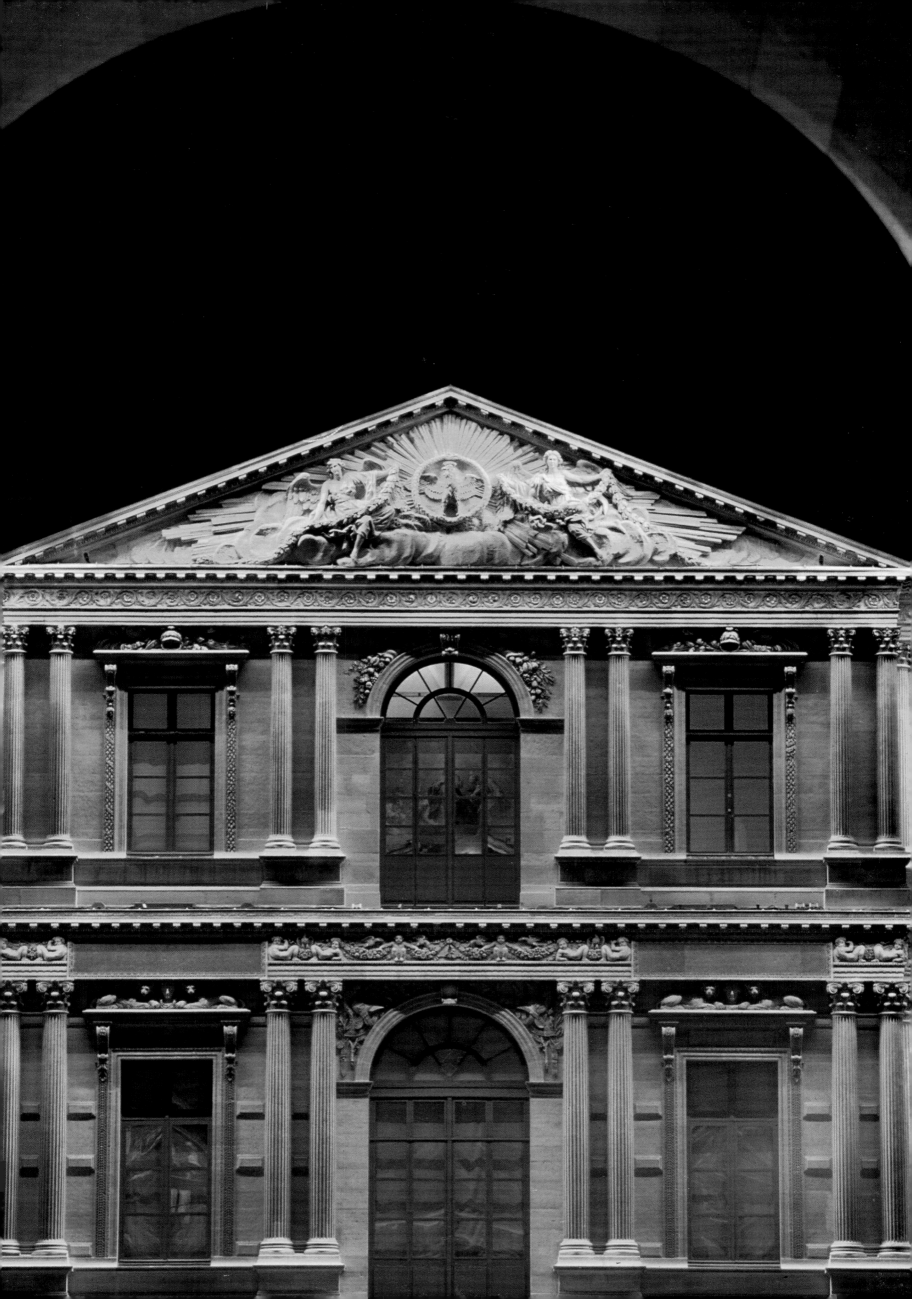

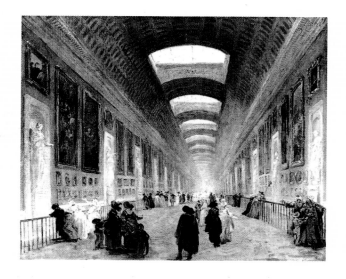

Brébion and Lenoir, but none received the necessary funding. New schemes were put forward, in 1790-91 and even in the troubled days of 1794, by Antoine, Legrand and Molinos, Poyet, De Wailly and others.

The National Museum

The Revolution started in Paris, and the district of the Louvre became the focus of power. Government was centred on the Tuileries; the King was housed in the palace, to which he had been brought from Versailles on 6 October 1789, and the Assembly met in the Manège in the Tuileries Gardens. On 10 August 1792 the people of Paris attacked the Tuileries Palace: the King took refuge under the protection of the Assembly in the Manège, and from then his fate was sealed. With the end of the monarchy, the new Assembly and revolutionary committees moved into the Louvre itself, which was renamed the Palais National. In 1793 the former Salle des Machines was remodelled to accommodate the Convention, followed by the Cinq Cents.

      With the victory of the Revolution, the plans for a museum at the Louvre were at last implemented. The decision was taken in 1792, and the inauguration of the new public museum of the arts took place on 10 August 1793, the anniversary of the capitulation the King: visitors saw both the national collection of paintings (with a few objets d'art and busts) and a 'Salon' of works by living artists. In November this arrangement became a permanent institution. The revolutionary government divided time not into weeks but into 'decades' of ten days, and the museum's 'decades' were divided into six open days for artists and strangers, three for the general public, and one day for cleaning.

      Both necessary works and political upheavals affecting the museum's administrators led to closures, such as that of the Grande Galerie, which was inaccessible between 1796 and 1798, but the Salon Carré continued to be used for the display of paintings. The Galerie d'Apollon was transformed into a discrete display space by the installation of large wrought-iron gates brought from the château of Maisons, and here in August 1797 a selection of the finest drawings went on view. Part of the ground floor was given over to antiquities.

      The new museum became richer, as the revolutionary government decreed its province to cover all the arts. Other institutions given similarly specific roles were the Museum of Natural History and the Conservatoire des Arts et Métiers (devoted to arts and crafts). Two other new bodies were concerned with the arts, but only with those of France: the Musée des Monuments Français, set up in the former convent of the Petits-Augustins in 1795, and the special museum devoted to the French School in the château of Versailles, which was planned in 1798 and opened in 1802.

Above Hubert Robert's vision of the Grande Galerie lit by skylights (Louvre).

Opposite *The Union of the Three Arts*, stucco medallion by Chaudet in the Rotonde de Mars.

Page 82 Wrought-iron grille installed at the entrance to the Galerie d'Apollon in 1797.

Page 83 The Summer Apartment of Anne of Austria, transformed into the Musée des Antiques in 1799.

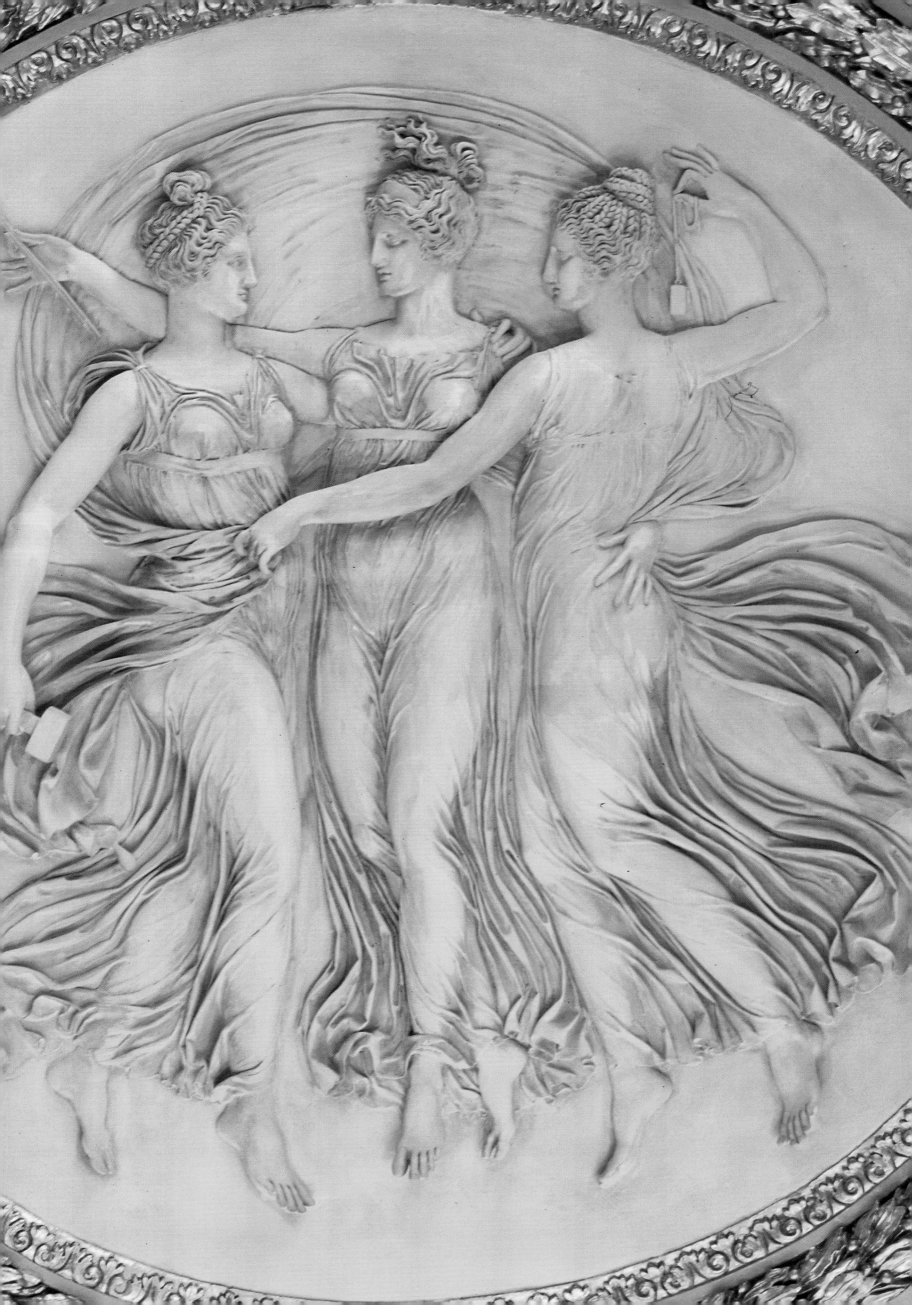

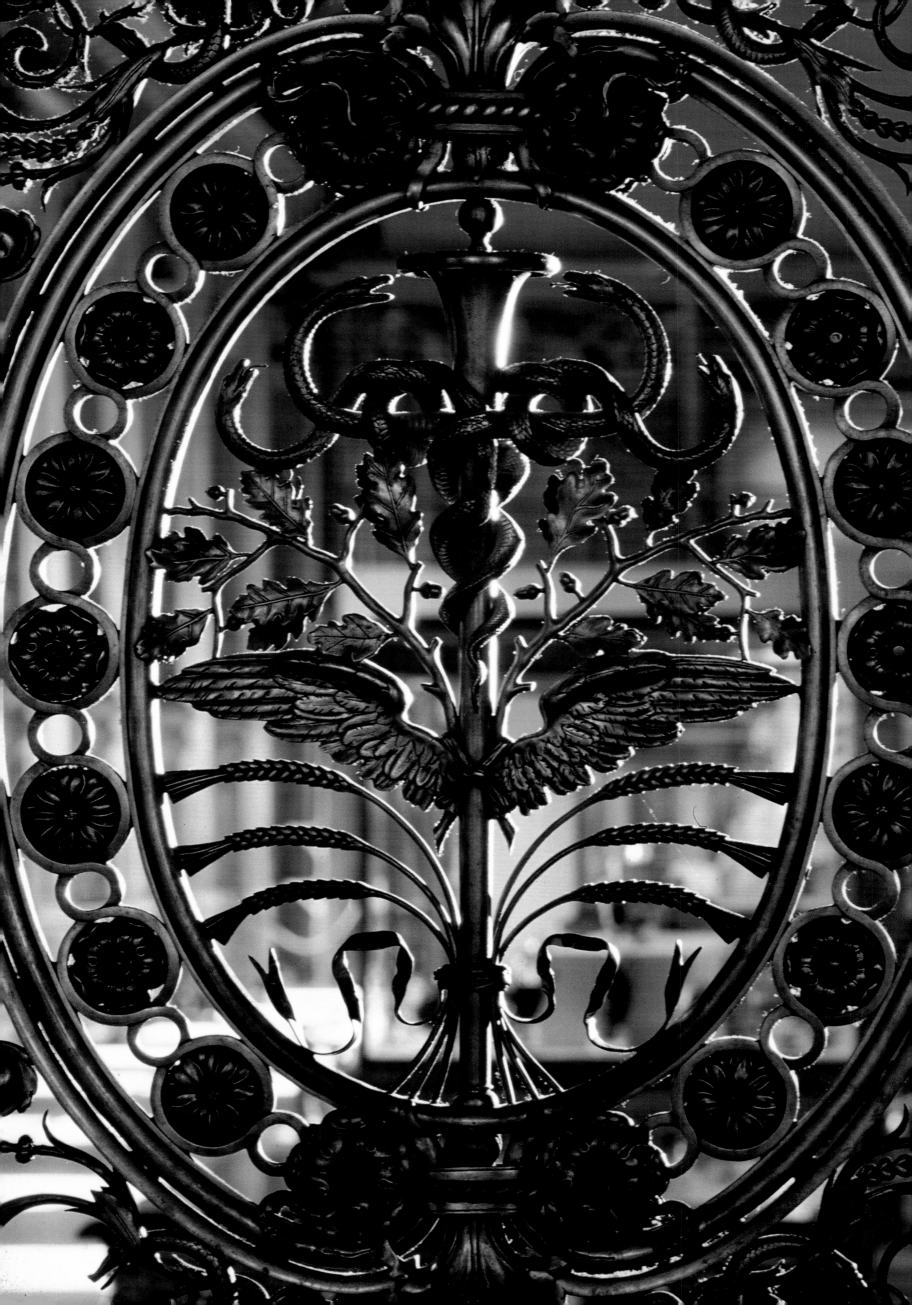

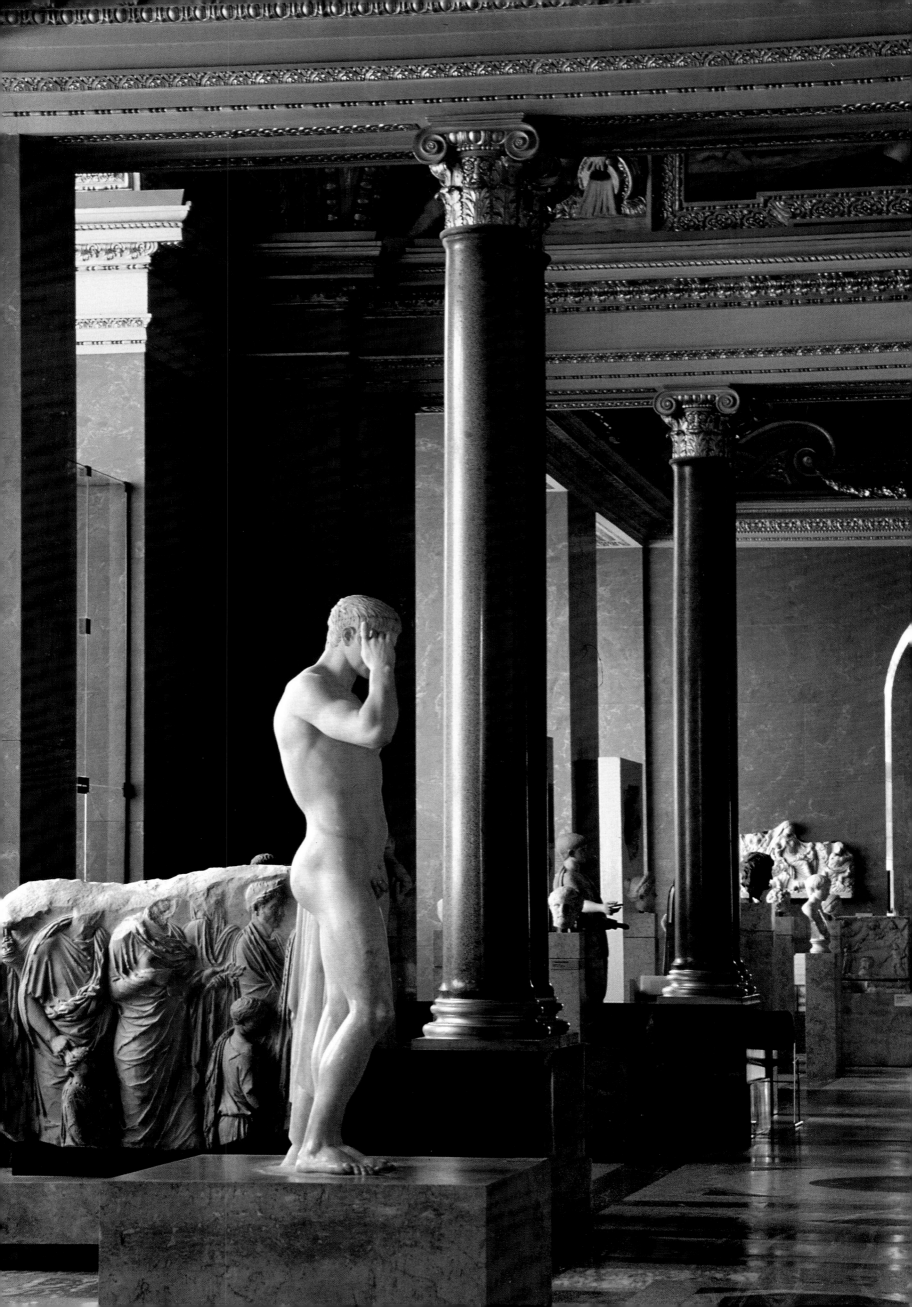

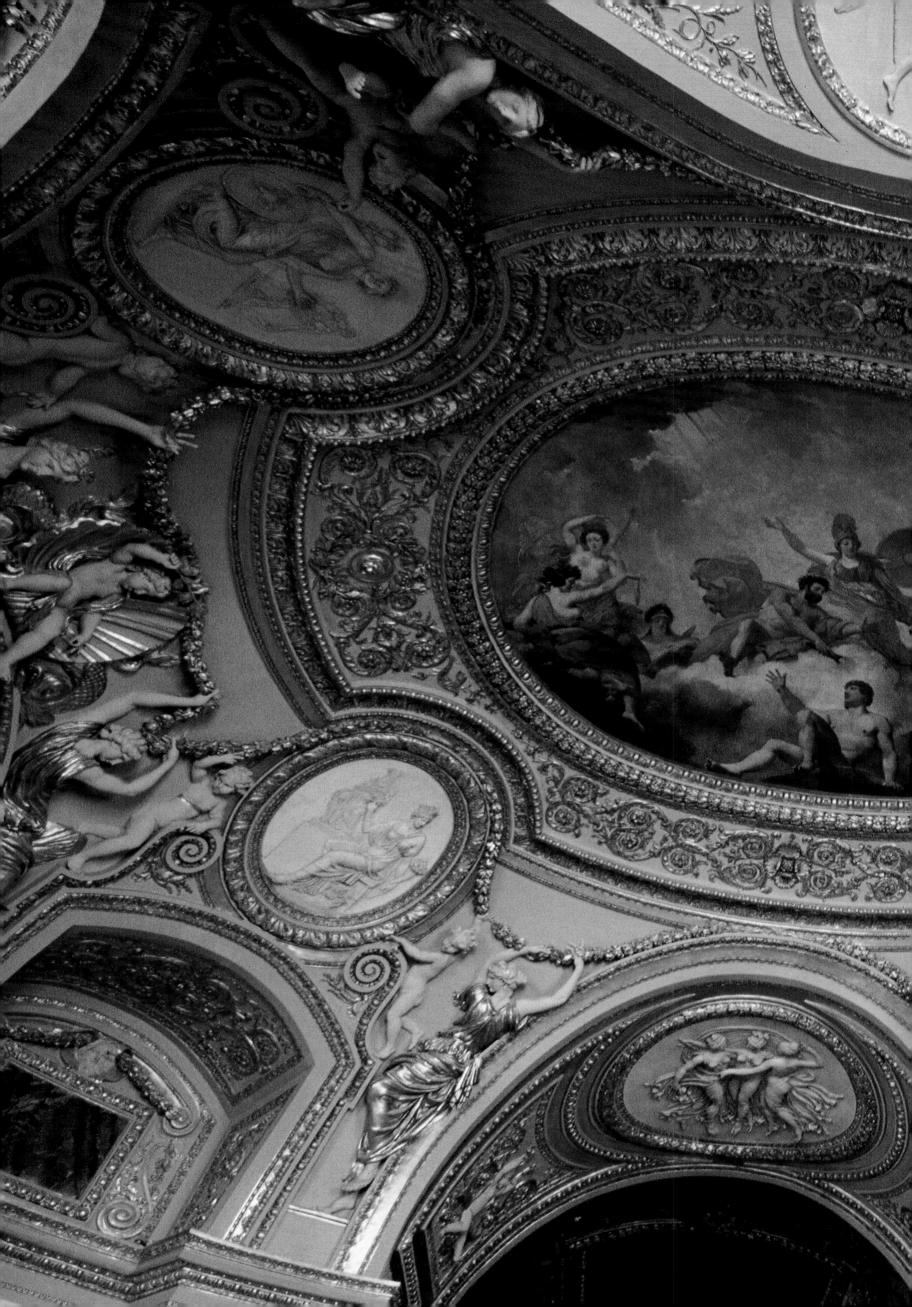

This first public museum at the Louvre was above all a museum of painting. From 1793 onwards, the royal collections were supplemented by a large number of pictures belonging to people who had fled the country and to the Church. Their presentation did not follow any chronological system: rather, in the words of the artists now in charge, it looked like a colourful flower-bed. In addition to the paintings there were a few antique busts, two Egyptian statues from the Petits-Pères, some objects made of hardstone, porcelain, and clocks, soon joined by Michelangelo's *Slaves* and by the contents of the Sainte-Chapelle.

The revolutionary armies unleashed across Europe added a spectacular haul of artworks, from Belgium, Germany and above all from Italy. Under the terms of the Treaty of Tolentino (19 February 1797), the Pope agreed for masterpieces from the Vatican to be sent to the Louvre – not only paintings by Raphael but also the most famous among the papal collection of antique sculptures, including the statues of the *Nile* and the *Tiber*, the *Laocoön* and the Belvedere *Apollo*. The works arrived in Paris in a train of waggons on 27 July 1798 and were ceremonially paraded from the Champ de Mars to the Louvre before taking their place in the museum.

The Summer Apartment of Anne of Austria was transformed into a new Musée des Antiques, completed in 1799. An initial design by Cheval de Saint-Hubert, brother-in-law of the painter Jacques-Louis David, was taken up by the official Louvre architect Jean-Arnaud Raymond, and the walls separating the rooms were replaced by columns taken from Charlemagne's Palatine Chapel at Aachen. New decoration in painting and sculpture was commissioned. The Rotonde de Mars became the entrance vestibule: here part of the seventeenth-century stucco was retained, but new plaster medallions by the sculptor Antoine-Denis Chaudet were introduced in the soffits of the arches, representing *The Genius of the Arts* and *The Union of the Three Arts*, where Painting, Sculpture and Architecture appeared as the Three Graces with arms intertwined. In the spandrels of the dome, stucco reliefs by Bernard Lange and Jean-Pierre Lorta illustrated Egyptian, Greek, Italian and French art, in the form of allegories each featuring a statue: there was Egypt displaying the Colossus of Memmon, Greece with the Belvedere *Apollo*, Italy with Michelangelo's *Moses*, and France with Puget's *Milo of Crotona*. The ceiling in the centre was painted by Jean-Simon Berthélemy in 1802 with the subject of *Man, formed by Prometheus, brought to Life by Minerva*. This was repainted by Jean-Baptiste Mauzaisse in 1826.

From this Rotunda the visitor entered the Salle des Empereurs Romains, decorated in 1796-99 with large imitation bronze medallions of rivers (*Nile, Tiber, Eridanus* and *Rhine*, by Bridan the younger, Gois the younger, Barthélemy Blaise and Jacques-Philippe Le Sueur) and a composition by Philippe-Laurent Roland (*The Germans grant Peace to Marcus Aurelius*). Charles Meynier contributed two subjects in grisaille and the ceiling (*The Emperors Hadrian and Justinian presenting to the World the Codes of Roman Law*).

At the far end, beyond the Salle des Saisons, the vestibule and the Grand Cabinet de la Reine, whose decoration was left untouched, Raymond transformed the Queen Mother's Bedchamber and the Petit Cabinet next to the river into a single space. It was a remarkable technical feat, for the southern tympanum of the Bedchamber, complete with its fresco by Romanelli and stucco by Anguier, was taken down and moved to the end wall. The vault was then completed and the spandrels decorated with new work: Dejoux created stucco in the spirit of Anguier, Philippe-Auguste Hennequin depicted *The French Hercules* in the centre, and the medallions and tympana were completed by Guillaume Guillon-Lethière, Pierre Peyron, Narcisse Guérin and Pierre-Paul Prud'hon. Nothing of the old Cabinet went to waste: the paintings by Romanelli became part of the Louvre collections, and the painted panelling was recently identified by Olivier Meslay, carefully re-used by Chalgrin in the Luxembourg Palace. The new galleries opened on 9 November 1800, the anniversary of the *coup d'état* of 18 brumaire, and were enthusiastically recorded by the painter Hubert Robert.

Pages 84–85 Dome of the Rotonde de Mars. The stucco putti and allegorical figures were executed in 1685 by the Marsy brothers, working under the direction of Errard. The medallions by Lange, Lorta and Chaudet were commissioned in 1801. The ceiling fresco depicts *Man, created by Prometheus, brought to Life by Minerva*; it is a repainting by Mauzaisse of the original composition of 1802.

Opposite Looking from the Rotonde de Mars through the rest of the former Summer Apartment of Anne of Austria (cf. page 83). The next room is the Salle des Empereurs Romains.

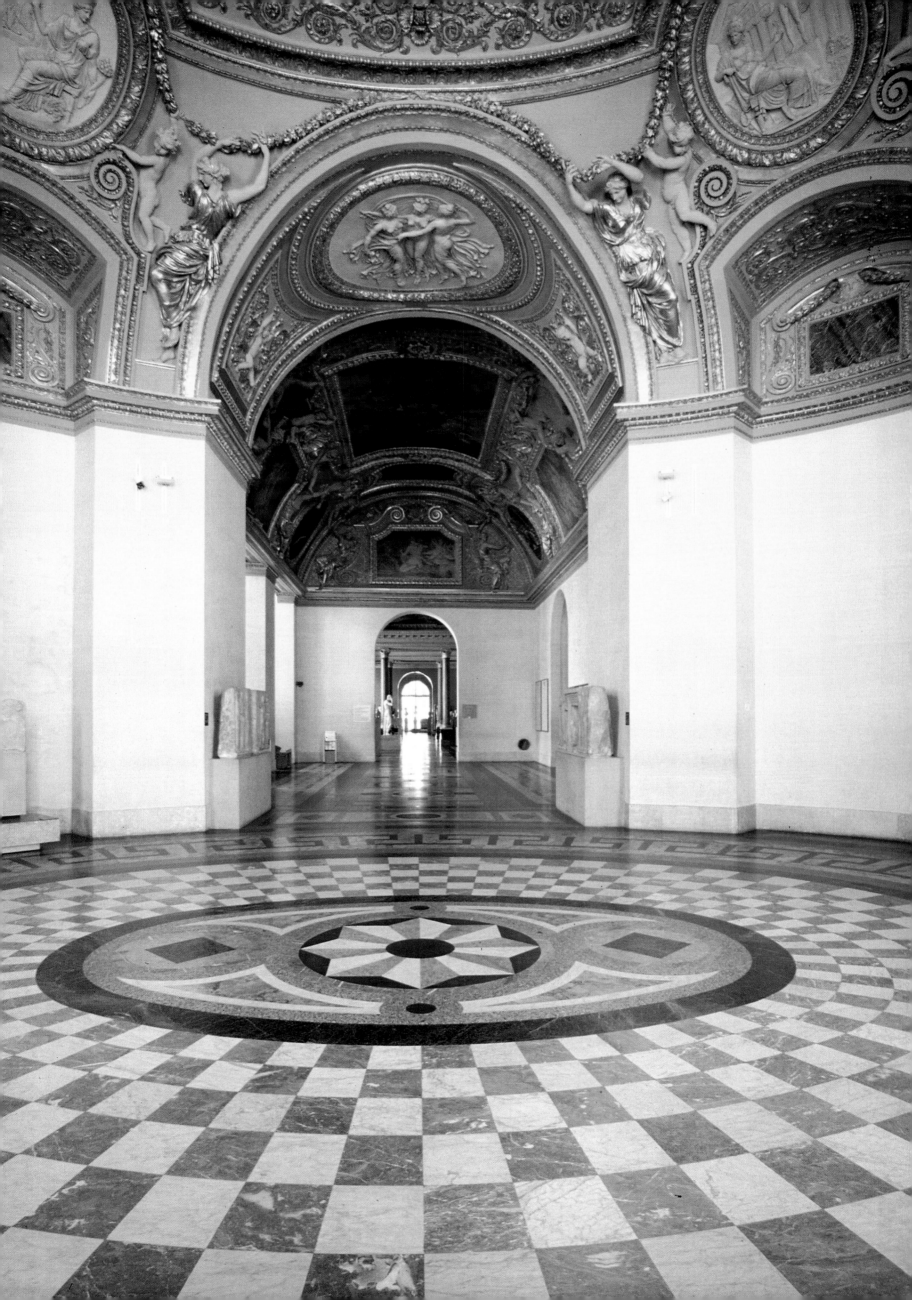

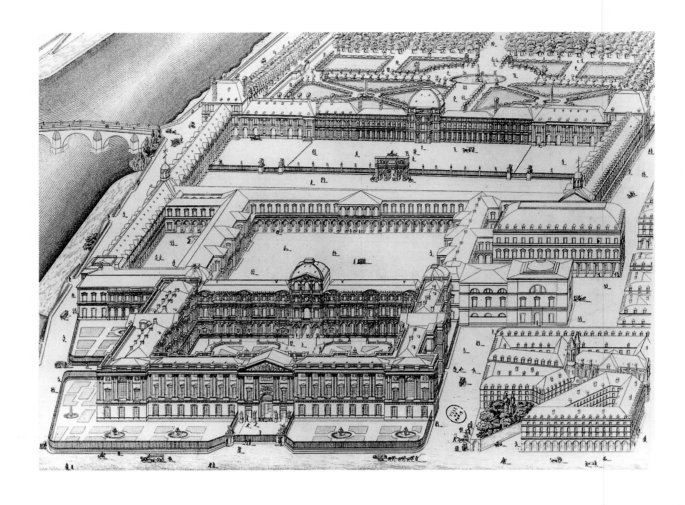

Percier and Fontaine's plan for linking the Louvre and the Tuileries. Of this scheme, with its enclosed courtyards
(in the centre) and perpendicular ranges (at the right), they built only the Rohan Wing, along the Rue de Rivoli (top right).

Showcase of the State: Museum and Palace

Napoleon Bonaparte's rise to power meant that the politics of monarchy resumed its course. He had lived in the Tuileries since his appointment as First Consul. Now he was to take up the Grand Design for the Louvre, to impress a subjugated Europe. Keen to make people forget his humble origins and to establish his own dynasty, the Emperor revived all the rituals of monarchy: court etiquette, ceremony, and above all an abundant use of emblems and iconography, marking with his N, his eagles and his bees the ancient palace that he intended to adorn. But he was also to be a protector of the arts and a benefactor of the museum to which he had given his name in 1803, even before he had become Emperor.

Musée Napoléon and imperial palace

Napoleon watched jealously over his museum. Above its entrance he placed a colossal bust – nearly 2 metres or 6 feet high – representing himself in classical costume, by the Florentine Lorenzo Bartolini (now in the Salles d'Histoire du Louvre). He revived the idea of joining the Louvre to the Tuileries, and this meant expelling all the undesirables, courtiers, artists and the Institut de France who had rooms there. In 1808 overall plans for the project were submitted by a number of architects. The Emperor chose to entrust the Grand Design to a partnership who had already worked for him at the Louvre, Pierre Fontaine and Charles Percier. Preparations started at once. A road was driven through to connect the Louvre with the Tuileries, running from the Pavillon de l'Horloge to the Carrousel and cutting through the congested and dangerous district where an attempt had been made on Napoleon's life in 1800. A new wing was begun at the north along the recently created Rue de Rivoli, and two blocks, intended to join up, were begun. The point where work on the western part stopped is clear on the south façade, where the elevation reproduces the design of Du Cerceau's part of the Grande Galerie of Henri IV, which then stood opposite; at the east end, however, the circular chapel of St Napoleon, begun near the Pavillon de Beauvais to balance the projection containing Le Vau's rotunda of the Salon du Dôme, disappeared under the Second Empire.

The most visible sign of Napoleon's great work was its exterior decoration. The Arc de Triomphe du Carrousel was raised in honour of the Grande Armée on the model of Roman triumphal arches (1806). It cost a fortune: a million francs were paid by the Grande Armée, despite the saving achieved by finding the columns of red marble from the Languedoc in the Louvre's marble store, among building materials abandoned ever since the reign of Louis XIV. The arch functioned as the ceremonial entrance to the Tuileries courtyard. Large marble reliefs evoked the treaties and campaigns of Napoleon. The best sculptors of the age – Clodion, Pierre Cartellier, Louis-Pierre Deseine and Jacques-Philippe Lesueur – carried out the work to the designs of the painter Charles Meynier. Higher up, statues of soldiers from the different corps (dragoons, grenadiers, sappers) honoured the 'other ranks' of the victorious army. On the top stood the Horses of St Mark's, looted from Venice in 1798, flanked by two Victories in gilt lead by François-Fréderic Lemot.

Overleaf The Arc de Triomphe du Carrousel, erected in 1806 in honour of the Grande Armée. On the left is *History*, by Gérard (1809).

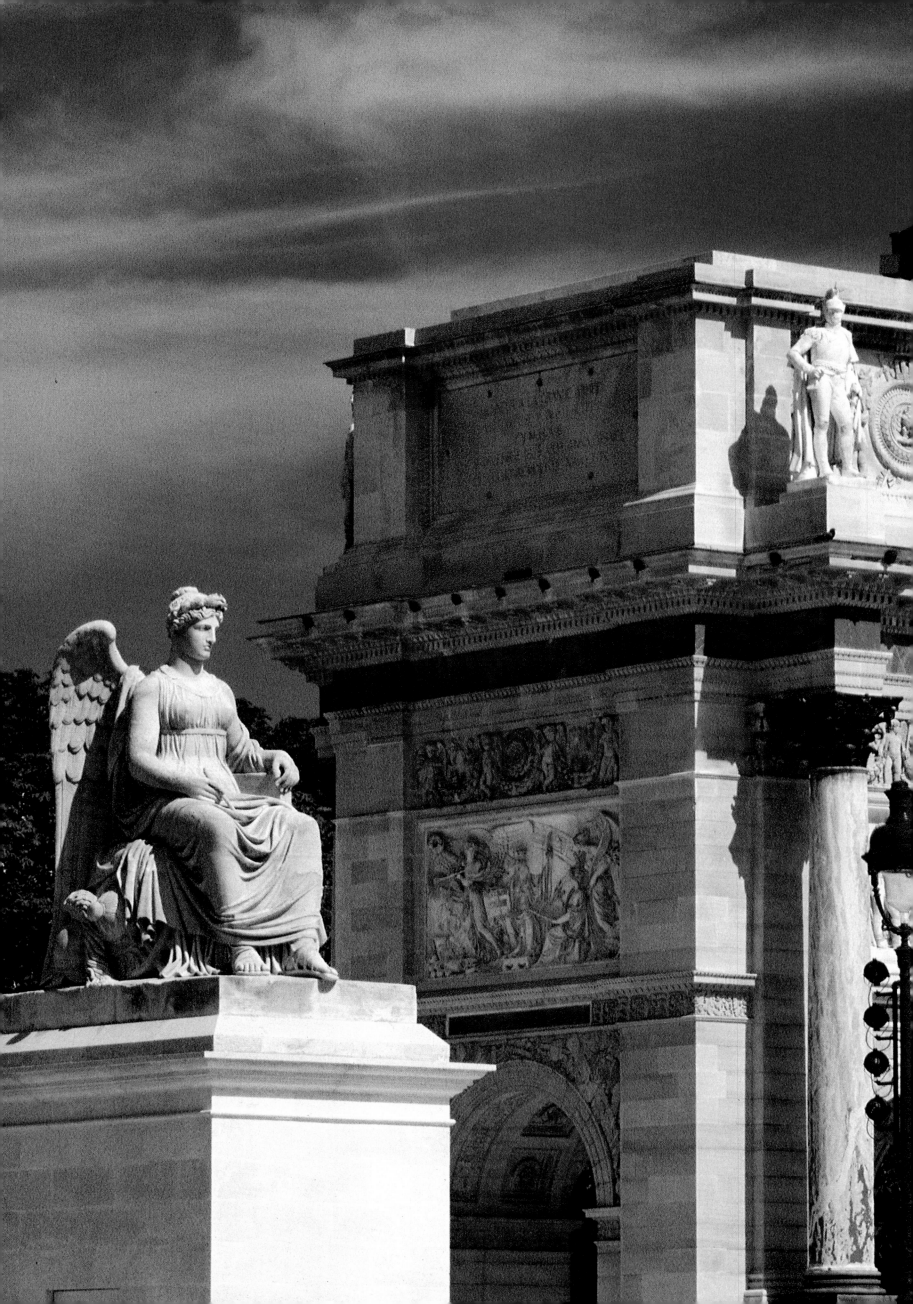

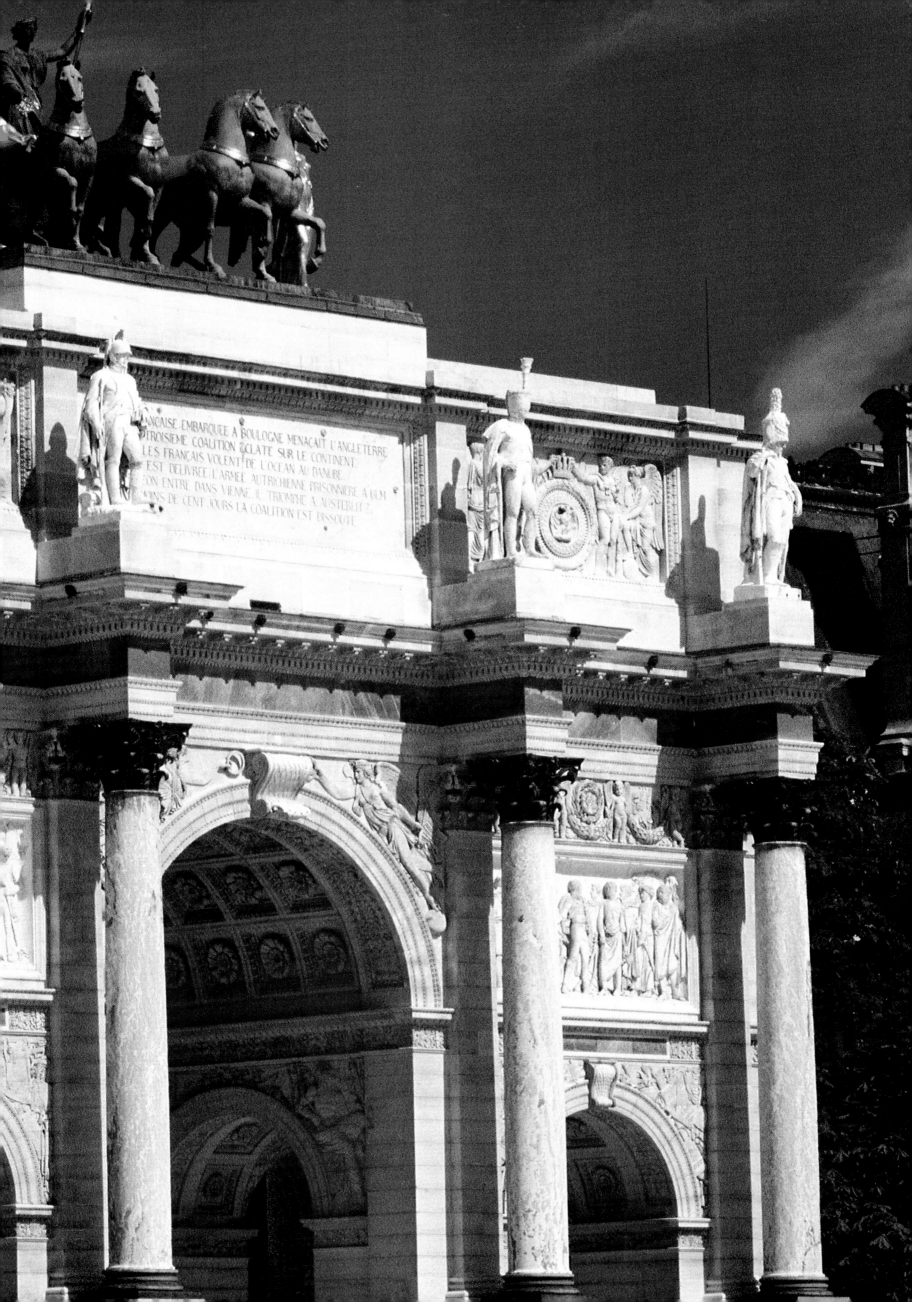

Behind the arch a grille closed the courtyard of the Tuileries. This was punctuated by four stone sentry-boxes which served as pedestals for immense stone statues, of which two survive, *France* and *History* by François-Antoine Gérard; those carved by L.-M.-L. Petitot the elder have disappeared.

In 1805, Percier and Fontaine revived Gabriel's project for unifying the façades of the Cour Carrée. They proposed to demolish all the attic storeys, including those of the Lescot wing sculpted by Goujon. Napoleon would not agree. 'The architects wish to adopt a single order', he said, 'and change everything. Economy, common sense and good taste are opposed to this; we should leave to each of the parts that exist the character of its own age, and for the new work adopt the most economical style.' Nevertheless, in 1806 a commission agreed to the alteration of all the attics except those on the west side to conform to Gabriel's design. Percier and Fontaine accordingly demolished the attic storeys on the north and south sides, and replaced them by a Corinthian order on the model of the inner elevation of the Colonnade wing. The reliefs on the part of the south wing that had been completed in the sixteenth century were taken down but preserved, as we have seen. The architects also undertook the completion of the sculptural decoration of the Cour Carrée. The three projecting features of the attic of the Lemercier wing were provided with sculptures by Roland, Jean-Guillaume Moitte and Antoine-Denis Chaudet (1807). As in Goujon's compositions, the principal figures are accompanied by secondary ones which clarify their meaning. On the central bay, imperial victories are represented in the tympanum by the figures of Victory and Plenty; Hercules and Minerva stand for strength and wisdom, and the allegorical figures of the Nile and the Danube for the extent of Napoleon's conquests. On the left-hand projecting bay Law is enthroned; she rests on the tradition of Thucydides and Herodotus, and introduces the great religious leaders – Numa Pompilius, Isis, Moses and Manco Capac – in a highly exotic kind of ecumenism. More traditionally, on the right-hand bay, Heroic Poetry, with the genii of Love and War, introduces Homer and Virgil. The central pediments of the north and south wings were sculpted with large reliefs in honour of the ruler as protector of the arts: on the north the Genius of France in the guise of Napoleon evokes the Gods of Peace and Law-giving (by Lesueur, 1814), while on the south is Minerva accompanied by the Arts and Sciences (by Claude Ramey, 1811). On the exterior, the most important façade, to the south, has a pediment by Augustin-Félix Fortin (1808–9) and lower down genii supporting a bust of Napoleon. On the exterior of the Colonnade wing, Lemot in 1808 filled the pediment with a bust of Napoleon surrounded by figures of Minerva, the Muses and Victory, and Cartellier designed a huge winged figure of Glory in a quadriga, holding crowns, for the space above the entrance arch.

After they had transformed the interior of the Tuileries, most notably creating a monumental room called the Salle des Maréchaux, adorned with a tribune supported on caryatids inspired by that of Lescot, Percier and Fontaine were commissioned to prepare state apartments on the *piano nobile* of the Colonnade wing. To reach them they provided grand staircases in the north and south pavilions of the wing. The design includes those groups of free-standing columns the architects were so fond of, and at the top of the walls, lunettes with allegorical figures, antique gods and virtues sculpted by the best artists: Barthélemy-François Chardigny (who was killed falling from the scaffolding), Gérard, Callamard and Fortin (1811–14). This campaign ran concurrently with the decoration of a lower room in the Colonnade wing, the present Grande Salle Egyptienne, whose ends were richly adorned with reliefs by Petitot the elder. As this room was dedicated to 'great men', official rhetoric was given a free hand on the set theme: Victory on Land and Victory on Sea were to 'gaze upon the generals thanks to whom France had so often been victorious on land and on sea and appear proud of the favours that they had lavished upon them'. It is in details like these that one can understand the part played by the Louvre and its décor in imperial ritual, and the use of art in promoting extreme claims of propaganda.

The museum too benefited from the work of the two architects, although Percier officially resigned in 1812. A new Museum Staircase was built to the north of Brébion's in the same wing, opening off the Rotonde de Mars. It was subsequently removed, its function taken by the new Daru Staircase further west.

Opposite Looking south through the Arc de Triomphe du Carrousel towards the Pavillon des Etats.

Pages 94–95 Glory in a quadriga, distributing crowns, carved by Cartellier over the main arch of the Colonnade wing.

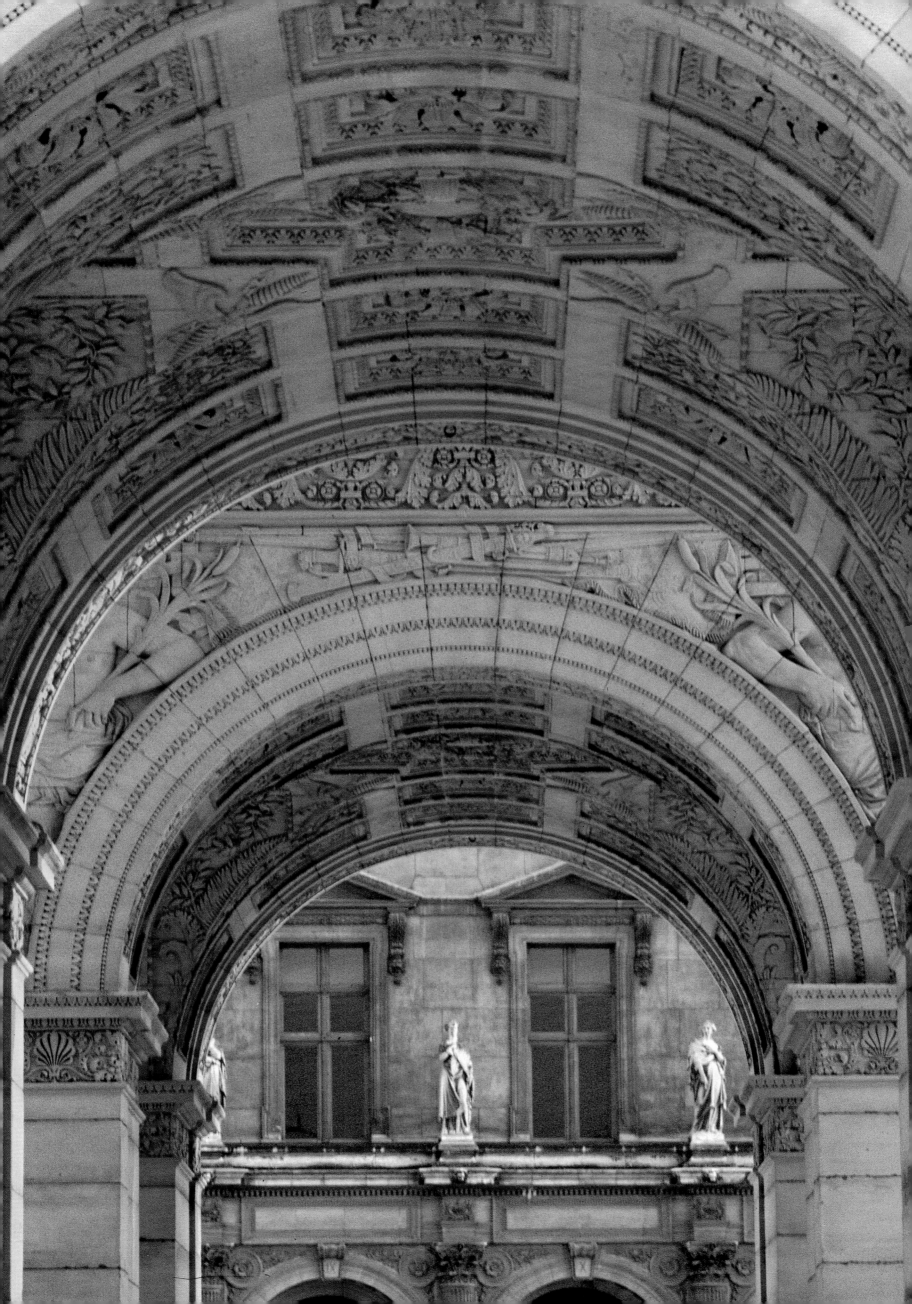

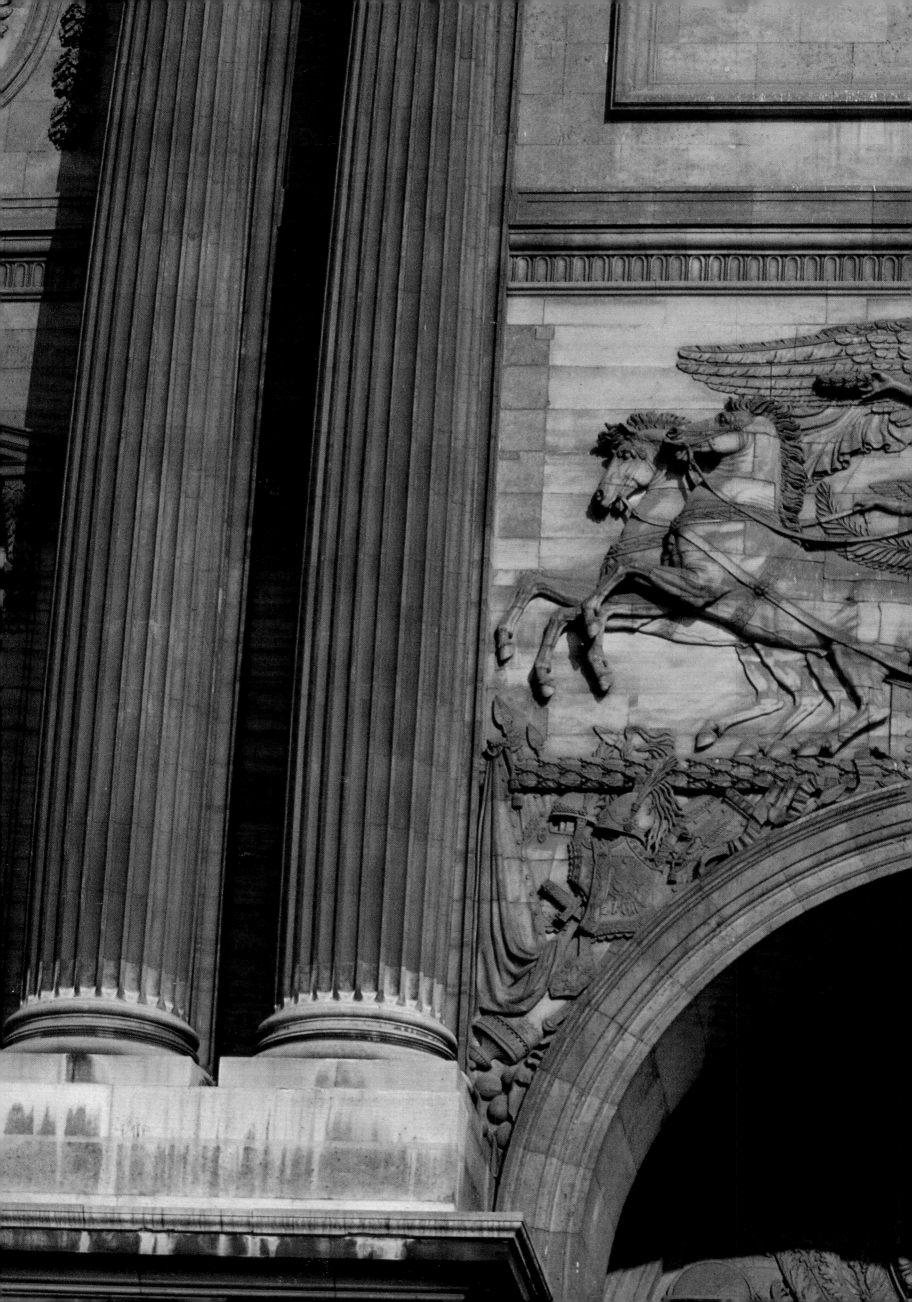

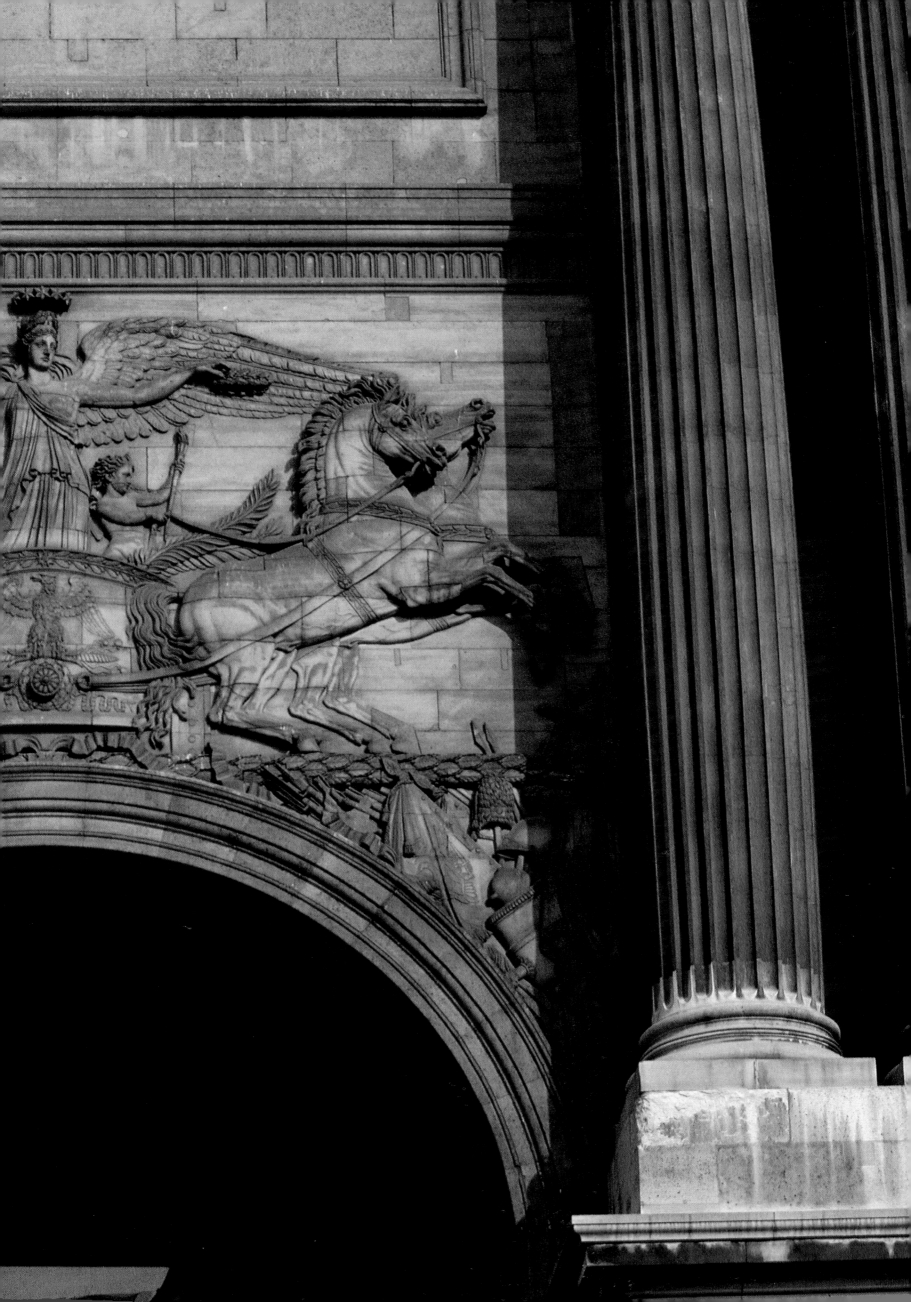

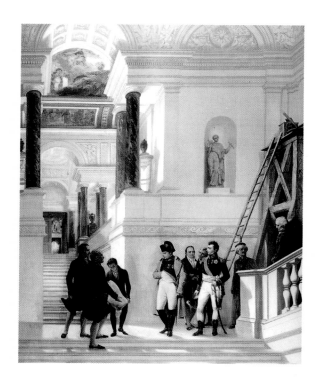

The space that had contained an upper flight leading south survives, however, as what is now called the Salles Percier et Fontaine, and there one can still see the marble columns and opulent sculpted decoration. The Grande Galerie was also furnished with columns and a richly coffered ceiling. The Salle des Cariatides, after being the setting for the meetings of the Institut de France until 1806, was made part of the museum. The architects remodelled the vault and the walls, providing fluted columns, a marble fireplace by Paride Belloni incorporating two statues by Jean Goujon, and over the musicians' gallery a large bronze relief of the *Nymph of Fontainebleau* made for François I by Benvenuto Cellini. The ground-floor rooms of the south wing followed, fitted up with columns, red marble cladding on the walls, and inlaid pavements by Belloni.

The Salle de Diane on the left of the entrance vestibule, begun by Raymond and finished by Percier and Fontaine, is one of the few to make painting the principal medium of decoration. It has a ceiling and tympana by Prud'hon, Etienne-Barthélemy Garnier and J.-F.-L. Mérimée, and bas-reliefs along the walls by Cartellier, Jean-Joseph Foucou and Jean-Joseph Espercieux (1808), evoking the cult of Diana in tribute to the antique *Diana* in the Louvre collections.

In this palace in flux, with the museum at the height of its splendour, the Emperor chose to celebrate his marriage to Marie-Louise of Austria in the most spectacular way on 2 April 1810. The procession began in the Tuileries, moved through the Grande Galerie and reached the Salon Carré, where the religious ceremony took place. Art joined with politics to make the museum the privileged setting for an imperial liturgy. Everything was organized to exalt Napoleon's conquests. The works of art were his spoils of war, to be redistributed to the nation – nay, to the human race itself. The museum taught an aesthetic and historical lesson: it was public, open, exemplary.

The collections under the Restoration

After the final fall of the Empire in 1815, the return of the Bourbons, which politically speaking meant a complete break with the revolutionary and imperial period, did not mean any great change for the Louvre. True, the director, Vivant Denon, was dismissed, and the museum lost the masterpieces which it had acquired by the conquest of Europe and which the Allies now restored to their countries of origin. But museum politics did not alter fundamentally. Louis XVIII established himself in the Tuileries, and certain prestige functions were carried

The appearance of Percier and Fontaine's destroyed Museum Staircase can be judged from Couder's painting of 1833, which imagines a meeting between Napoleon I and his architects (*above*), and from its upper landing – at the back in the painting – which survives as the Salles Percier et Fontaine (*opposite*).

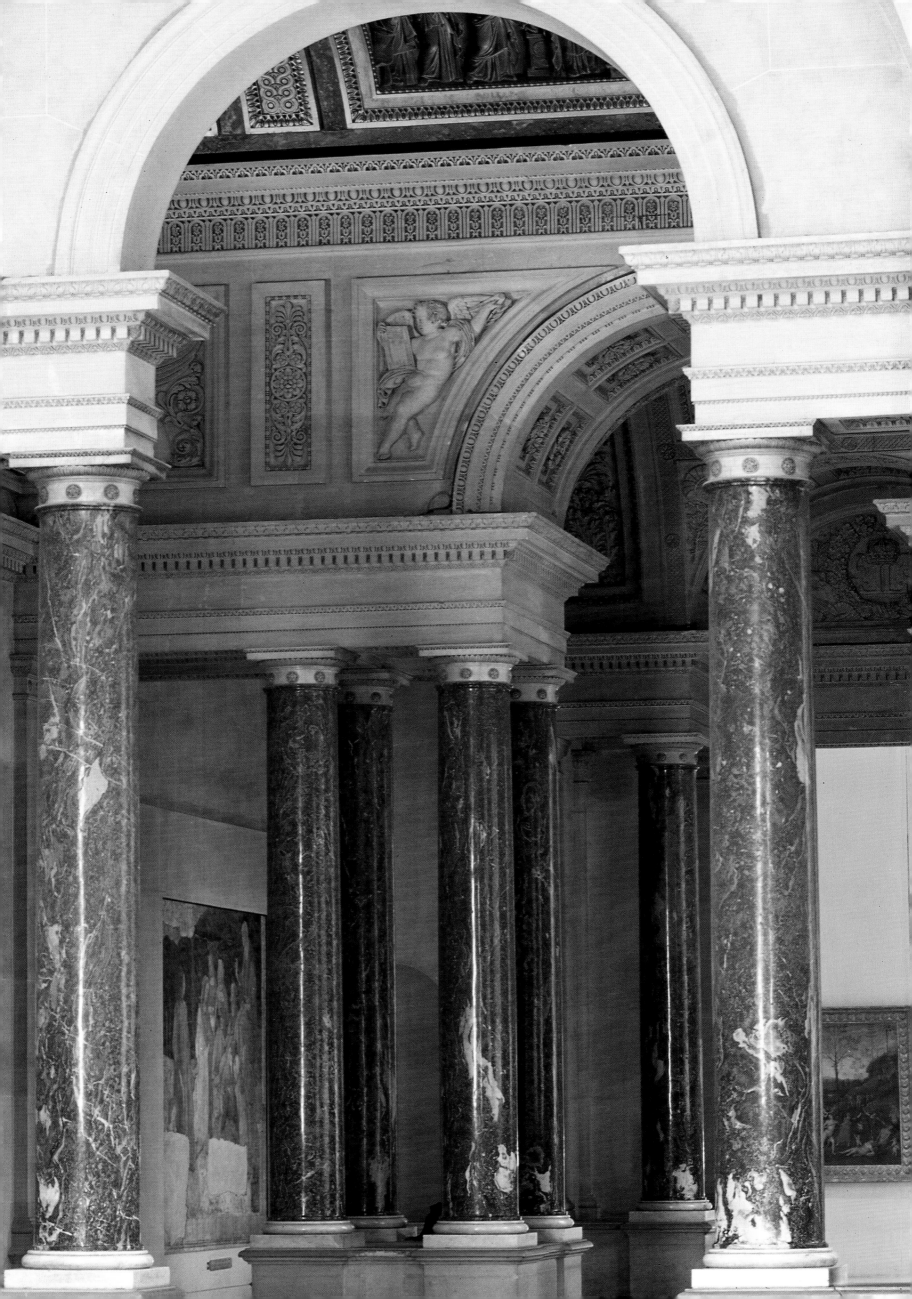

out in the Louvre (Salle des Séances Royales, Conseil d'Etat). But the museum was not forgotten: the royal administrators bought works of art and commissioned painted and sculpted decoration; new sections were opened, and even the Grand Design was – however hesitantly – revived.

Very soon the architect Fontaine was able to complete the projects that had been begun under the Empire. The Museum Staircase had not been give its decoration: its ceilings were now painted, that of the stair-hall itself by Alexandre-Denis Abel de Pujol, that of the first landing (the present Salles Percier et Fontaine) by Meynier, with *France protecting the Arts* (1819). In the adjoining room, now called the Salle Duchâtel, Meynier created *The Triumph of French Painting* (1822), a hymn to Poussin. Marble reliefs were also executed, of which two celebrating Apollo and Minerva (by Petitot the younger) can still be seen in the Salles Percier et Fontaine.

Next came new decoration for the Rotonde d'Apollon (1818–22), which leads to the Galerie d'Apollon. The central composition here featured the myth of Apollo: with his *Fall of Icarus*, Merry-Joseph Blondel sought to revive the panache of Le Brun. In the compartments of the dome, Auguste Couder and Blondel placed mythological scenes representing the four elements, while Jean-Baptiste Mauzaisse painted oval grisailles.

When the museum's redecoration was finished, the collections, diminished by the restitutions, had to be reorganized. The gaps were filled by works brought from other sites, such as Rubens' series of the life of Marie de Médicis, transferred from the Luxembourg. The Department of Antiquities was enriched by Greek vases and some new acquisitions, including the *Venus de Milo* which had been discovered on one of the Cycladic islands and presented to Louis XVIII. The gouty old King, who travelled from the Tuileries to the Salle des Séances Royales in a small carriage, used to admire it on the way, in the Rotonde d'Apollon.

It was above all under Charles X that new displays, virtually separate museums, were arranged in the palace. Further sections were opened, greatly enlarging the space available for sculpture, Egyptian antiquities, Greek vases and naval collections.

On 8 July 1824 a gallery of Renaissance and modern sculpture, called the Galerie d'Angoulême, in honour of the heir to the throne, was opened. It occupied rooms on the ground floor of the Lemercier wing, remodelled by Fontaine (now the setting for Oriental antiquities). The exhibits came mostly from the former Musée des Monuments Français, set up at the Revolution in the convent of the Petits-Augustins (now part of the Ecole des Beaux-Arts) and suppressed in 1816. To them were added some outstanding pieces from Versailles, including the *Milo of Croton*a by Pierre Puget. Medieval objets d'art were collected together in a room devoted to small precious objects, the Salle des Bijoux, formerly the Cabinet of Louis XIV. Here Mauzaisse painted the canvases of the overdoors and of the ceiling, where the figure of Time is shown revealing the recently acquired *Venus de Milo* (1822–28).

The most important development was the establishment of the Egyptian Museum, created in 1826 under the direction of Jean-François Champollion, who had deciphered hieroglyphics four years earlier. He managed to acquire several collections of objects and sculptures assembled in Egypt, particularly those of the British consul Henry Salt and the Italian Bernardino Drovetti. It was in this way that the great pink sandstone sphinx from Tanis arrived and was placed in the Cour du Musée, which came to be called the 'Cour du Sphinx'.

For the small-scale Egyptian and Roman antiquities, and Renaissance objets d'art, Charles X had the 'Musée Charles X' fitted up on the first floor of the south wing of the Cour Carrée. This was opened on 15 December 1827. Here, beneath ceilings painted by the best artists of the time, amid rich stucco decoration and fireplaces set with bronze, in tall mahogany showcases by the furniture-maker Jacob-Desmalter, the collections were displayed to the best possible advantage. Throughout, the decoration was planned to be in harmony with the objects on exhibition. The large ceiling canvases in the nine rooms were realized in record time in 1826–27. They are set in painted covings which frequently include scenes in grisaille. The complex décor can be appreciated more easily in the charming small sketches made by the artists for the various ceilings, some of which are shown in the Salles d'Histoire du Louvre.

Detail of the Cour Carrée showing one of the oculi decorated during the Restoration period with *Sculpture* and *Painting*, carved by Matte (1822)

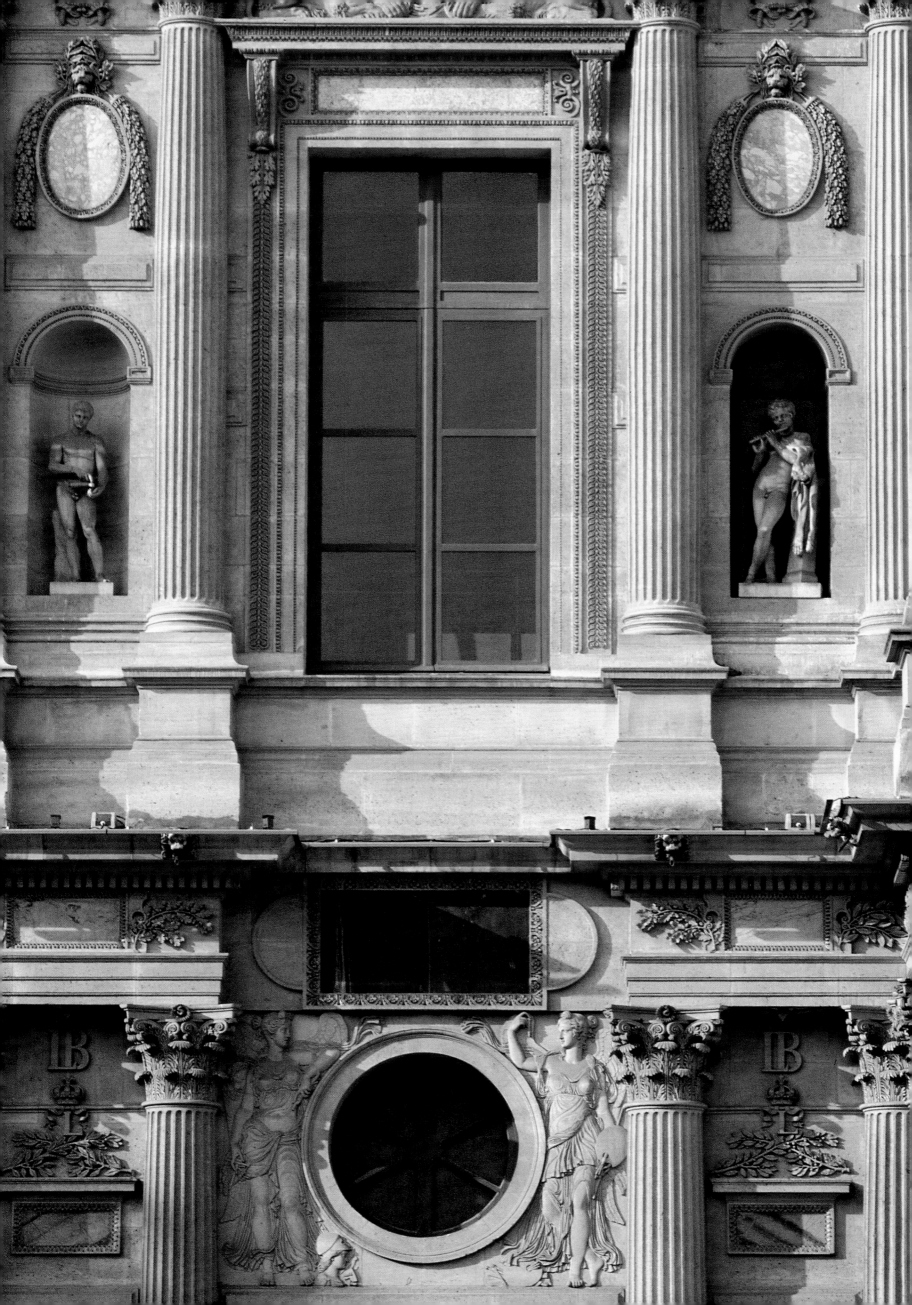

For the ceiling of the first room in the Musée Charles X Ingres painted *The Apotheosis of Homer* (now exhibited with other easel-paintings and replaced by a copy). Next comes *The Nymphs of Parthenope, bearing their Penates, are led to the Banks of the Seine* (by Meynier) and *The Personification of Vesuvius receiving from Jupiter the Fire which was to consume Herculaneum, Pompeii and Stabiae, despite the Intercession of Minerva on behalf of the Weeping Towns* (by François-Joseph Heim), and finally *Cybele protecting the Towns of Stabiae, Herculaneum and Pompeii from Vesuvius* (by François-Edouard Picot). Beyond the Salle des Colonnes, decorated by Baron Gros with heroic allegories (*Fame and Virtue, Mars and Victory, Time and Truth*), the themes evoked Egypt, with *Study and Genius revealing Ancient Egypt to Greece* (by Picot) and *Egypt saved by Joseph* (by Abel de Pujol), while Horace Vernet decorated the penultimate room, devoted to the Renaissance, with a depiction of Pope Julius II commissioning works at the Vatican from Bramante, Michelangelo and Raphael.

At the same time, preparations began on a second enfilade of rooms parallel and to the south of the Musée Charles X, to be used for the display of collections of objets d'art (in particular those which had been acquired from the southern painter Pierre-Henri Révoil) and of earlier French painting. (They later became the Campana Gallery.) In 1828 the first decorative canvases were inserted in the ceilings and surrounded by painted covings, as in the Musée Charles X. The iconography centred on the role of the French kings as patrons: there was Louis XII, father of the people; François I armed as a knight, by Alexandre-Evariste Fragonard, son of the famous Honoré Fragonard; and Louis XIV receiving Puget's great *Milo of Crotona* from the artist, by Eugène Devéria.

A naval museum, known then as the Musée Dauphin, was inaugurated on 22 December 1827. Part of its collection consisted of models of ships assembled in the eighteenth century by the Inspector General of the Navy, Henri-Louis Duhamel de Monceau. But there was also ethnographic and archaeological material (the nucleus of a future American section) and even a pyramid raised to the honour of La Pérouse's discoveries, consisting of objects brought back from his expedition to the Pacific.

The French kings did not, however, forget the royal character of the Louvre, which formed a single entity with the Tuileries where they lived. Louis XVIII actually died in the Tuileries (the only monarch to do so), in 1824, and received the homage of the people as he lay in state in what continued to be called his 'château' rather than his palace. The outward signs of Napoleon's reign had been removed: the bees and the eagles had disappeared (though a few isolated examples remained in the oval paterae of the Colonnade), and busts of Napoleon had been transformed into Louis XIV on the Colonnade, and into a helmeted Minerva on the south front. Everywhere the lilies and the 'L's of Louis reappeared on the façade. On the Arc de Triomphe du Carrousel, from which the Horses of St Mark's had been returned to Venice, the sculptor François-Joseph Bosio placed a personification of the Restoration driving a quadriga.

Fontaine continued to be employed as Royal Architect. In the Tuileries he designed a new staircase with a gilt bronze handrail by Delafontaine, and a reception room (1833). His alterations meant the disappearance, in 1836, of one of the terraces along the western front of the palace. But his main task was the completion of the great works at the Louvre: the north wing along the Rue de Rivoli was well under way; Montpellier had carved the pediment of the north front of the Cour Carrée facing the Oratory (1815), and the oculi that had not yet been finished in the Cour Carrée had been decorated on the model of those by Goujon (1820–25) – one of them by the sculptor David d'Angers, although he was not sympathetic to the monarchy. Two further royal set-pieces were also created: the Salle des Séances Royales for the meeting of the two houses, above the Salle des Cariatides (1821–24; now the Greek bronzes room); and, from 1825 onwards, an enfilade of rooms beyond it for the Conseil d'Etat (now occupied by the Department of Objets d'Art). The panelling from the royal bedchambers was re-used in the large rooms of the Colonnade wing.

Opposite and *pages 102–3* Looking up in the Rotonde d'Apollon. In the centre is *The Fall of Icarus* by Blondel, and in the surrounding compartments allegories of the elements by Couder, alternating with grisailles by Mauzaisse. The ceiling of the adjacent Salle des Bijoux (visible on *page 102*), by Mauzaisse, depicts Time disclosing antiquities among which is the *Venus de Milo*.

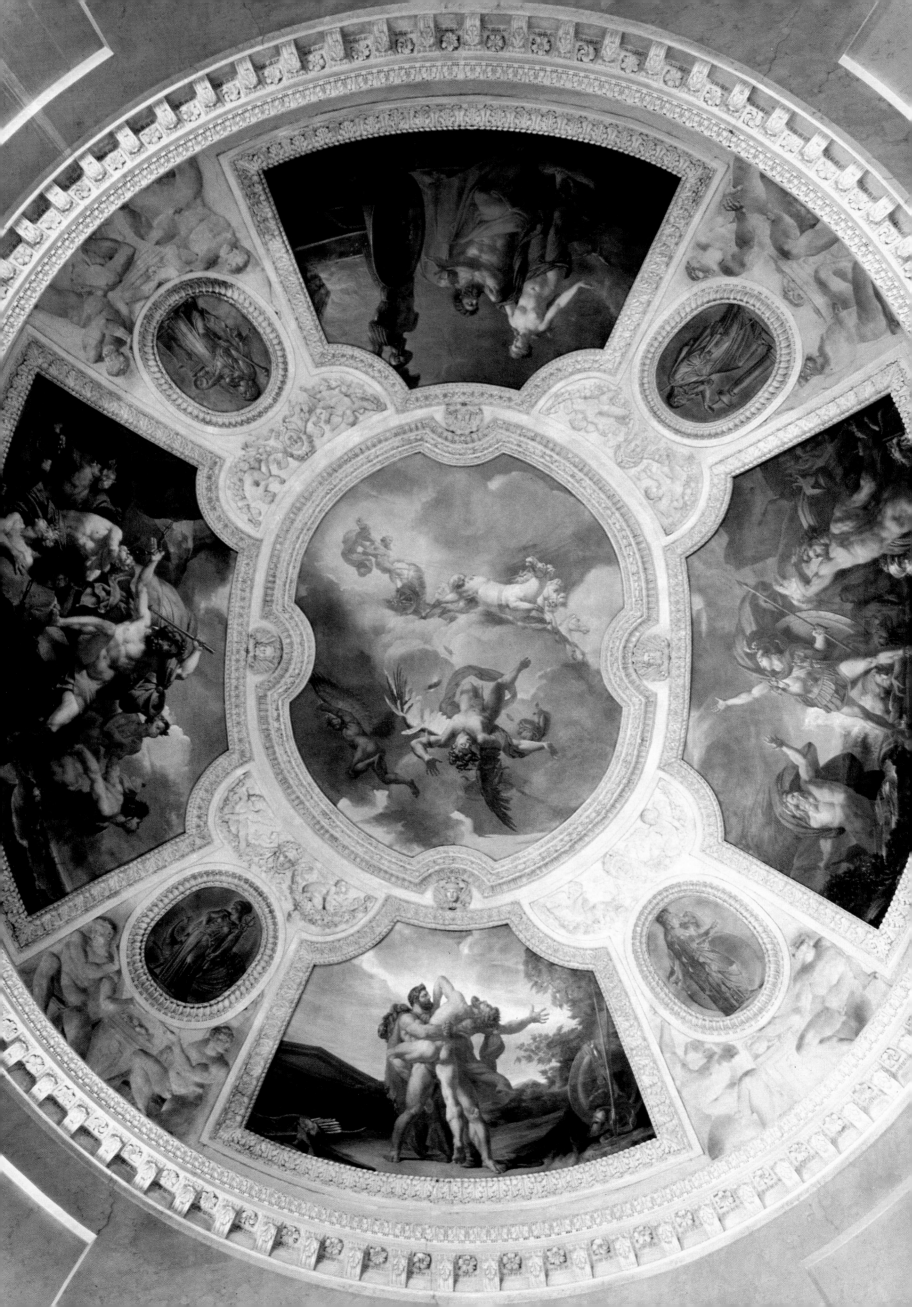

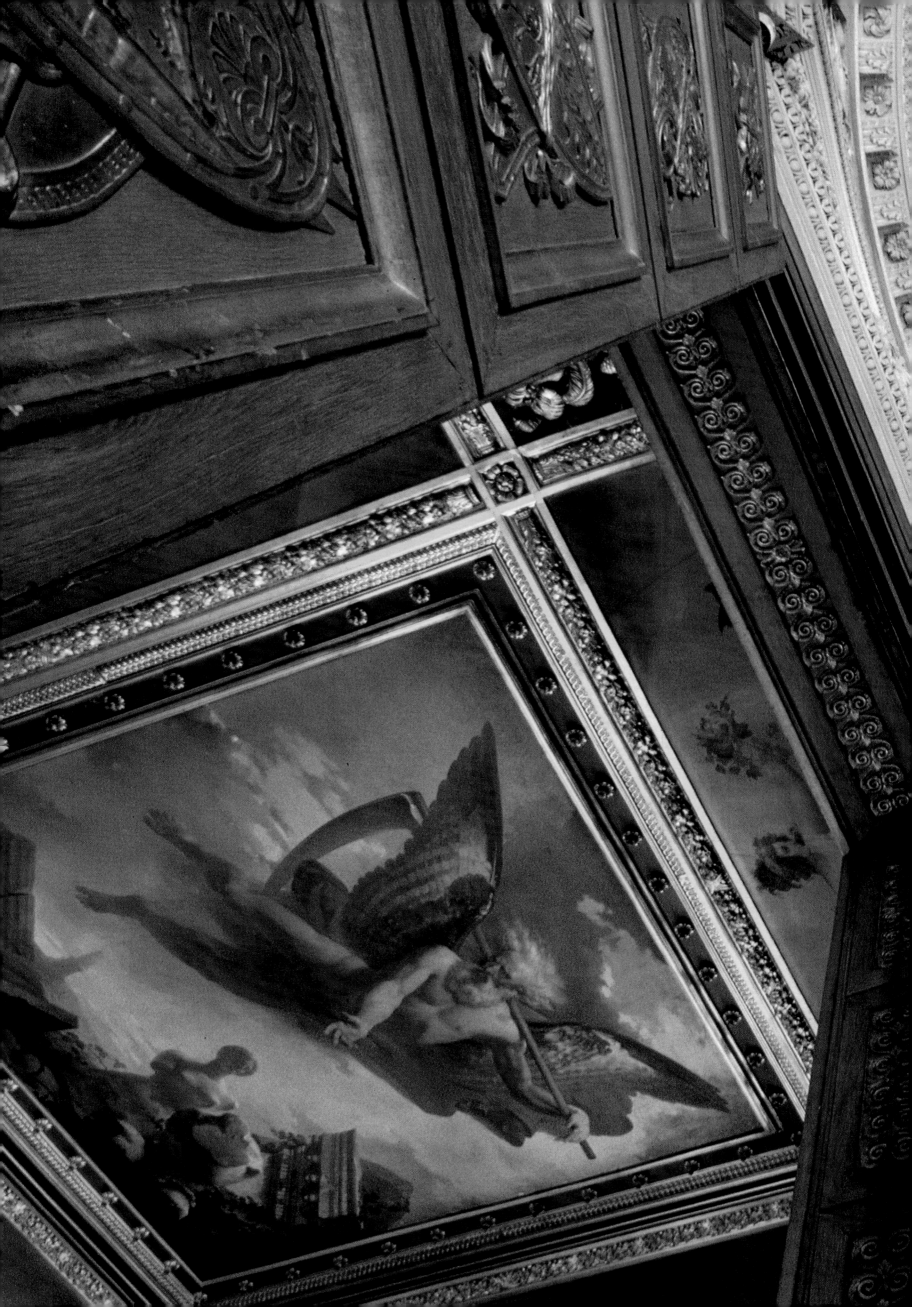

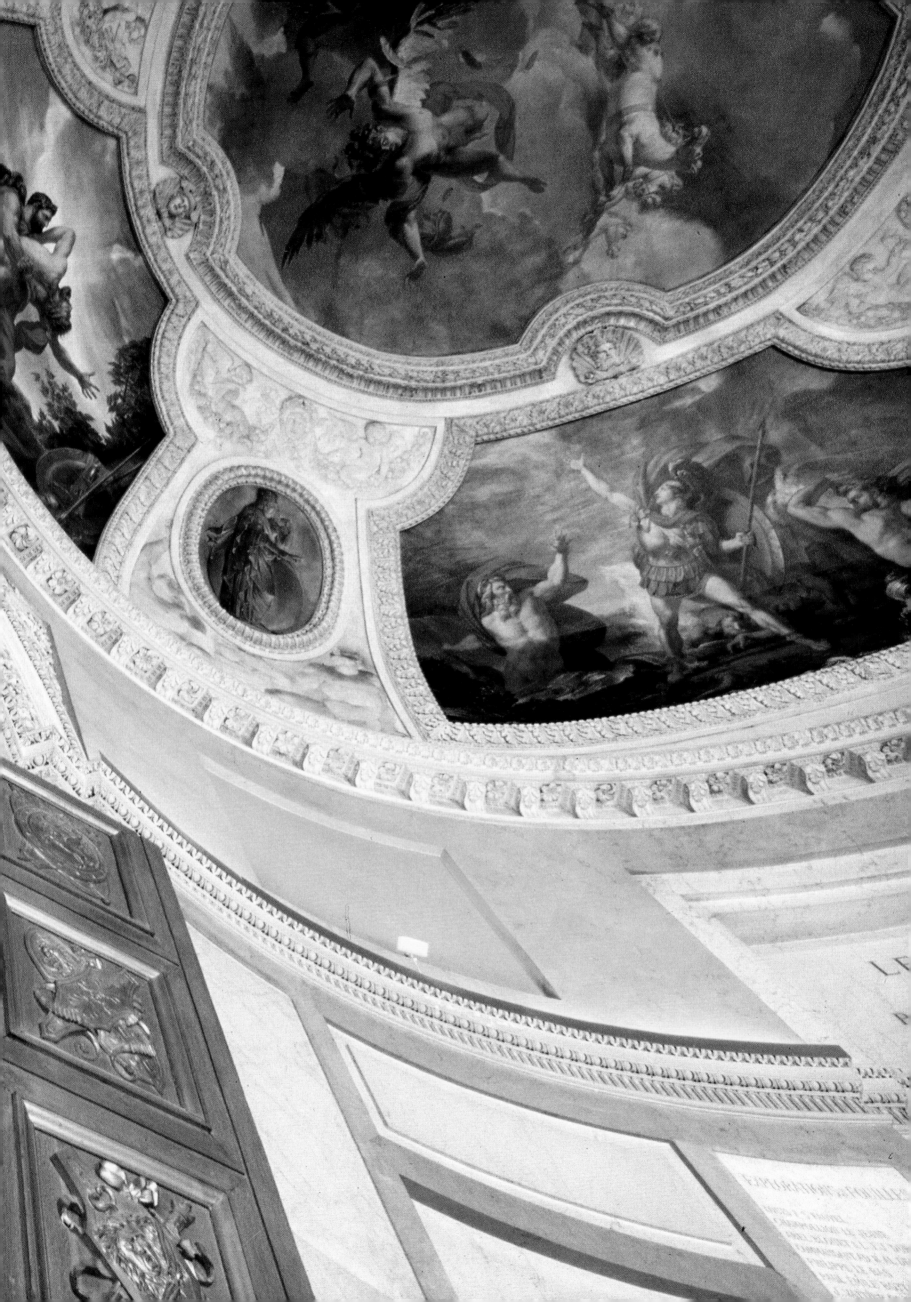

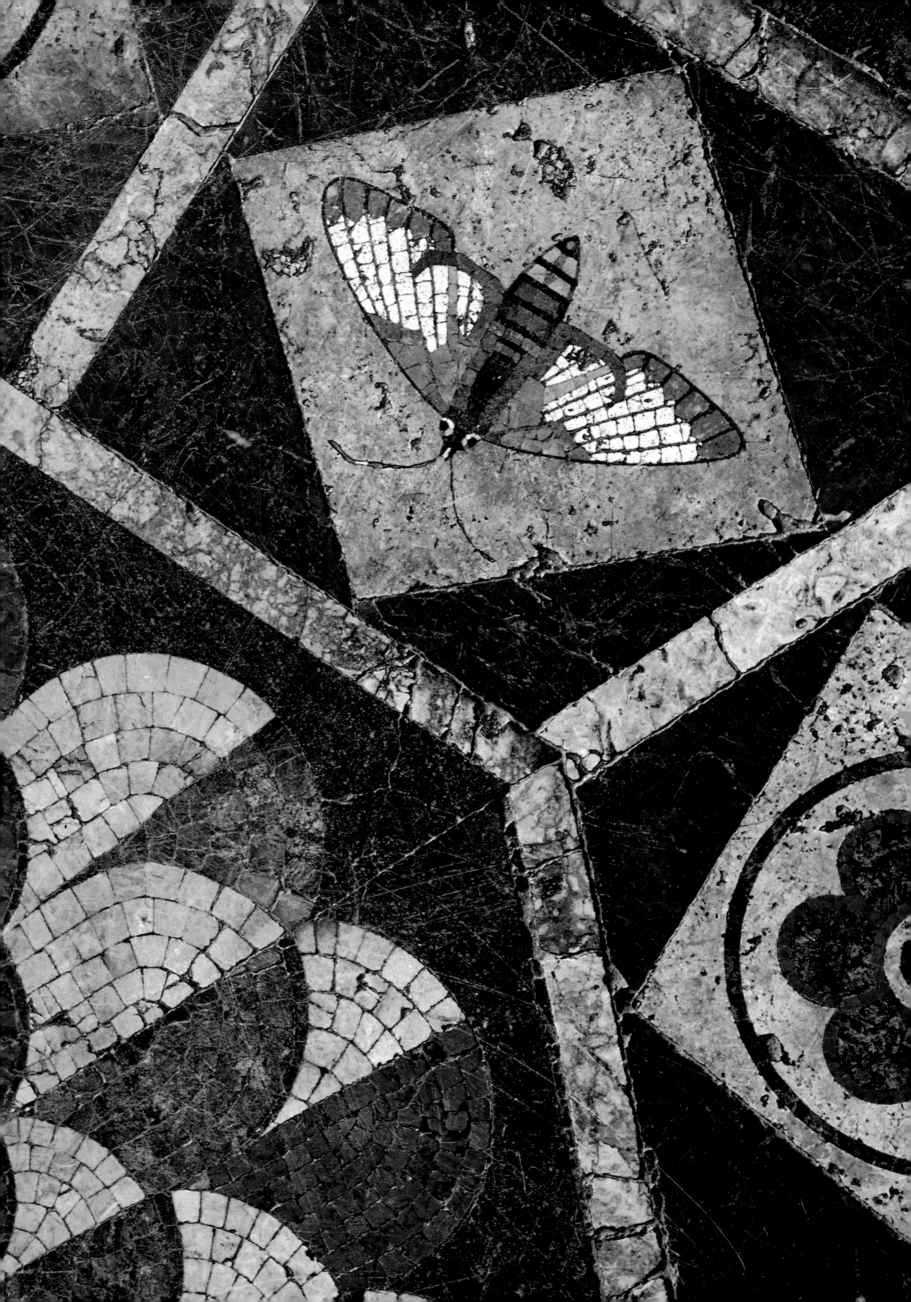

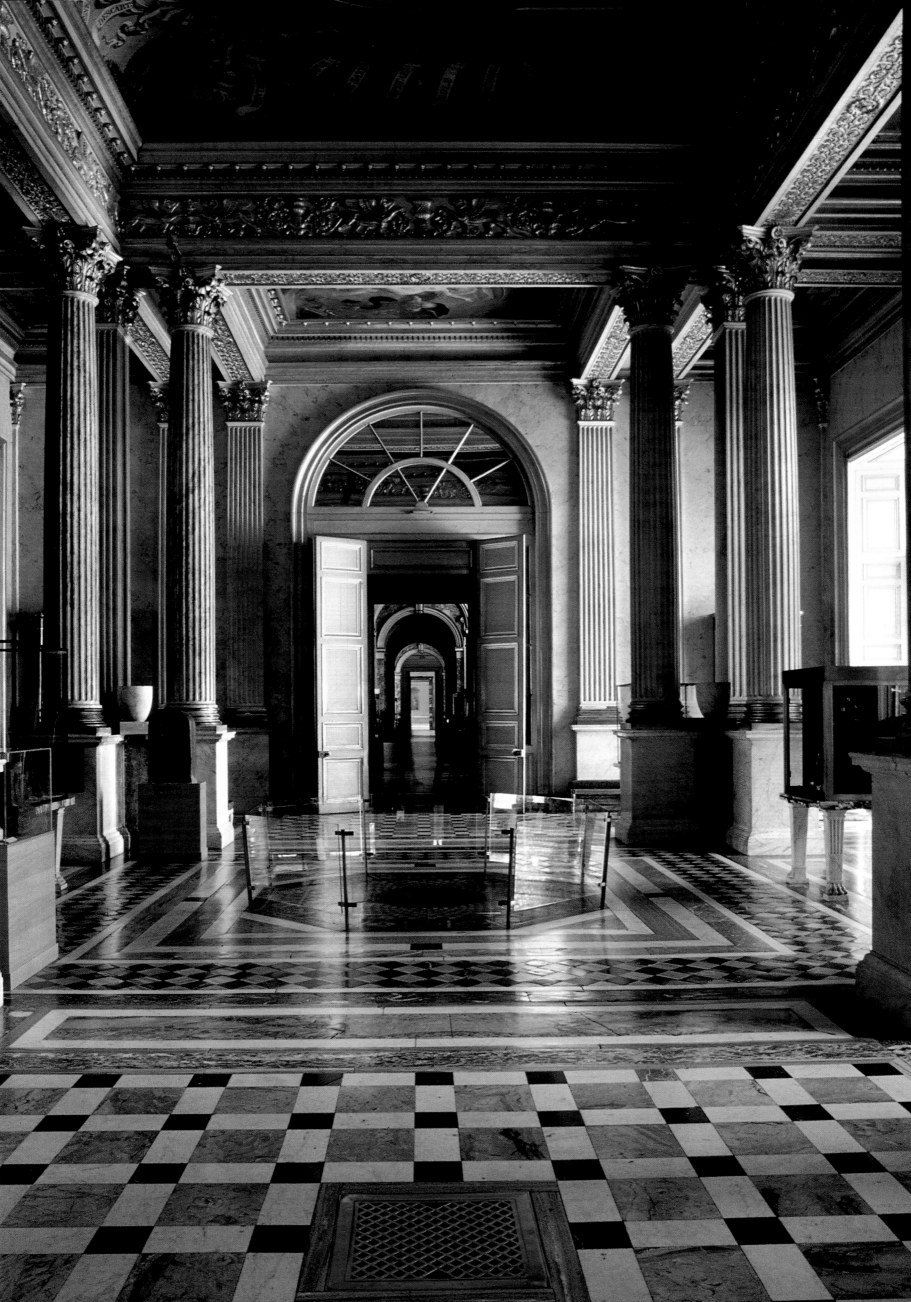

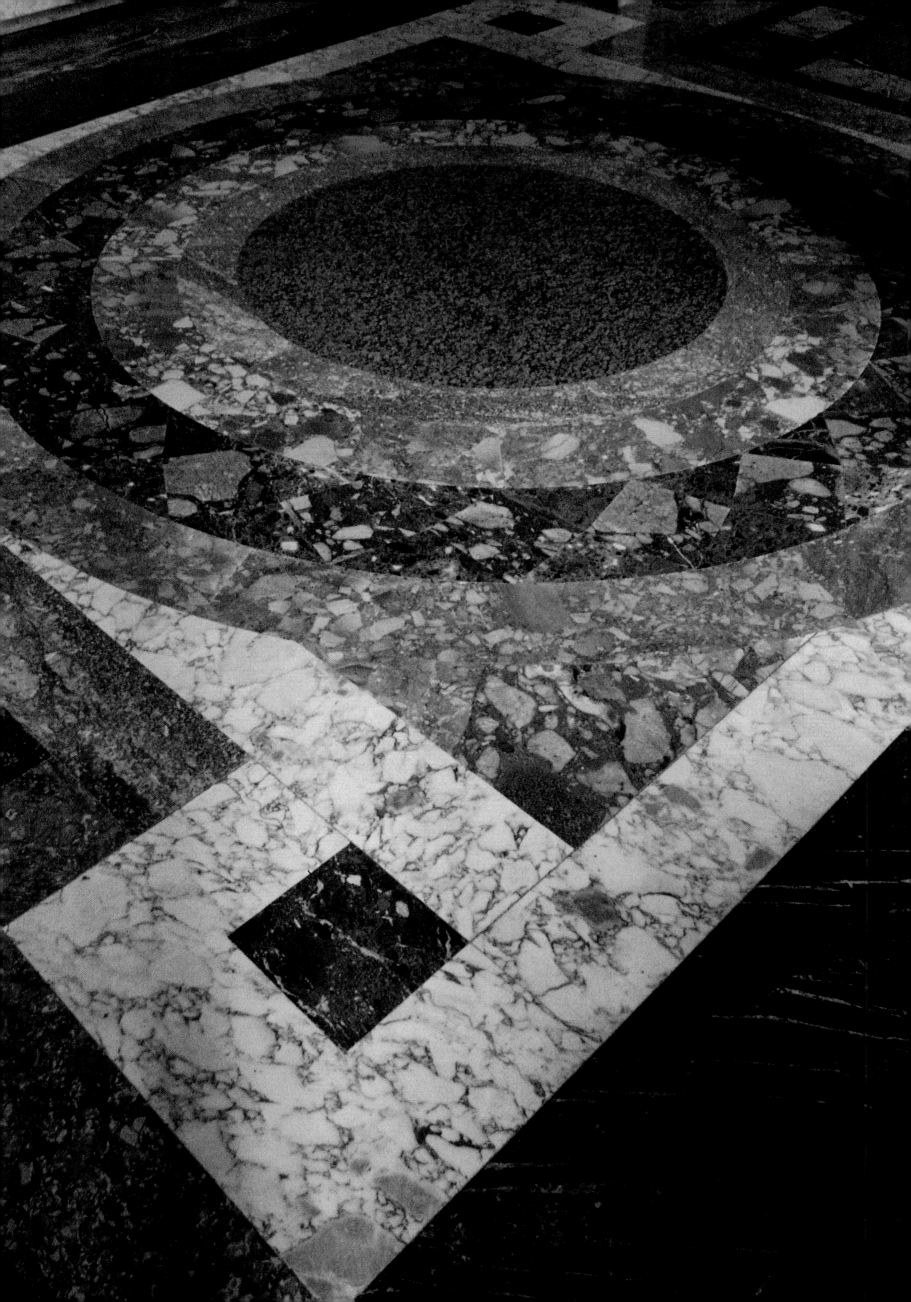

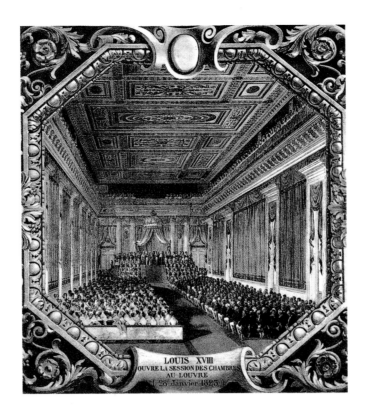

All this architectural activity was accompanied by commissions to artists. The former antechamber or Henri II Vestibule, which lay just before the Salle des Séances, was altered in 1822 by the insertion of large canvases by Blondel (*The Dispute between Minerva and Neptune*, *War* and *Peace* – since replaced by Braque's *Birds*) into the ceiling by Scibecq de Carpi. On the other hand, the Salle des Séances was left much plainer because of lack of money; the ceiling was simply an expanse of painted canvas, while the columns which flanked the royal throne were of stucco. But a sumptuous balustrade with gilt bronze ornaments enclosed a gallery which ran round the upper level, giving the public a space from which to view proceedings below. It was re-erected in 1935 in the reading room of the Bibliothèque des Musées Nationaux.

Everywhere appropriate iconography informed the works of art commissioned by the Royal Household. In the Cour Carrée Gérard sculpted *France* and *The Charter*. In the enfilade south of the Musée Charles X one could follow pictorially the benefits conferred by the kings of France. In the suite of rooms for the Conseil d'Etat, historic and legal themes unfolded, chosen in 1826 by the representative of the Beaux-Arts, Vicomte Sosthène de La Rochefoucauld, with the following ringing titles: *France victorious at Bouvines*, by Blondel; *Law coming down to Earth, establishing her Empire and spreading her Benefits*, by Michel-Martin Drölling; *Divine Wisdom giving Laws to Kings and Legislators*, by Mauzaisse; and *France, surrounded by French Law-Making Kings and Jurists, receiving the Constitutional Charter from Louis XVIII*, again by Blondel, the leading decorative painter in all genres for the monarchy at the Louvre. Eugène Delacroix received a commission for only one small picture, *The Pandects of Justinian*, in the third room. For besides the large compositions of the ceilings, official propaganda was completed in the covings, where great historical figures (Charlemagne, Numa Pompilius, Justinian) competed for space with scenes from national history suggested by the nascent discipline of historical research (the freeing of the serfs by Louis VI, the creation of the Cour des Comptes by Philippe le Bel, etc.), and the never-ending allegories characteristic of royal decorative schemes (Fidelity, Piety, Hope, Constancy, and so on). At a lower level, painted overdoors completed this apotheosis of visual rhetoric.

Charles X even intended to transform the large hall called the Salle des Sept Cheminées into a coronation room, and his painter Baron Gérard executed some immense canvases to decorate its walls. Louis-Philippe changed the programme, and in the end the paintings were sent to the Musée de Versailles.

Pages 104–6 The Salle des Colonnes, created by Fontaine. The enfilade continues as the Musée Charles X.

Above Louis XVIII opens the session in the Salle des Séances Royales.

Pages 108–9 A room in the Musée Charles X. The ceiling, by Picot, depicts *Study and Genius revealing Ancient Egypt to Greece*.

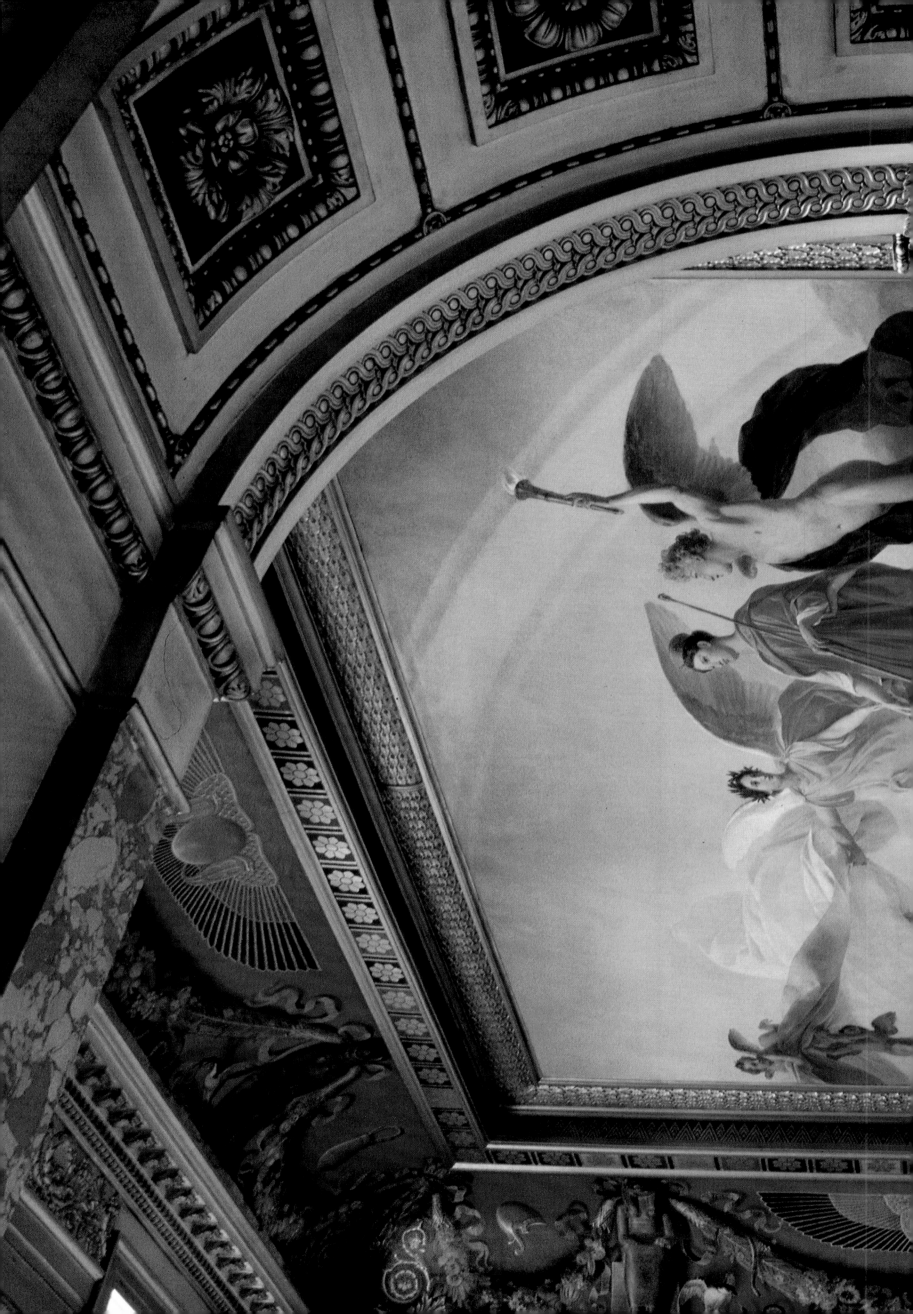

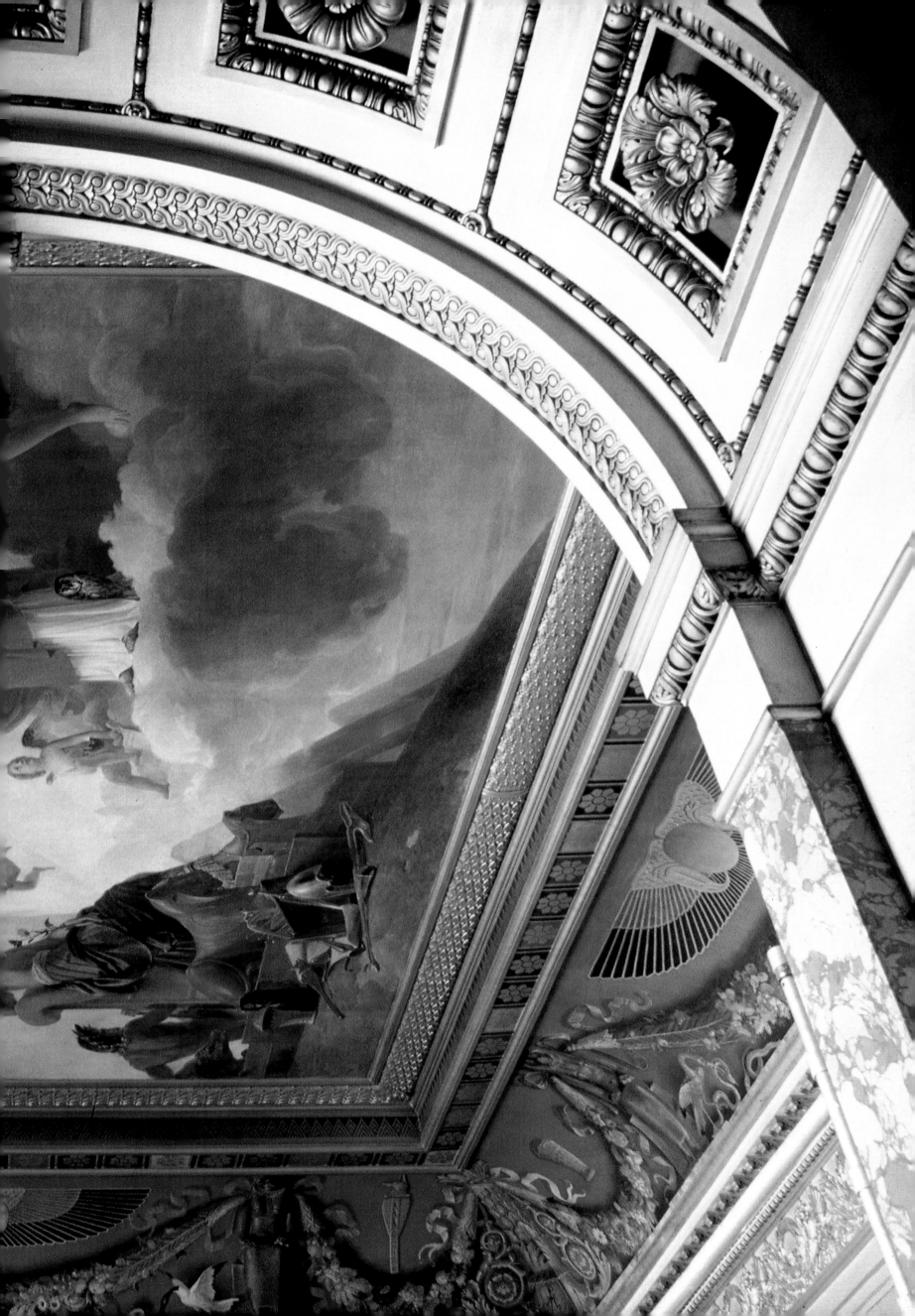

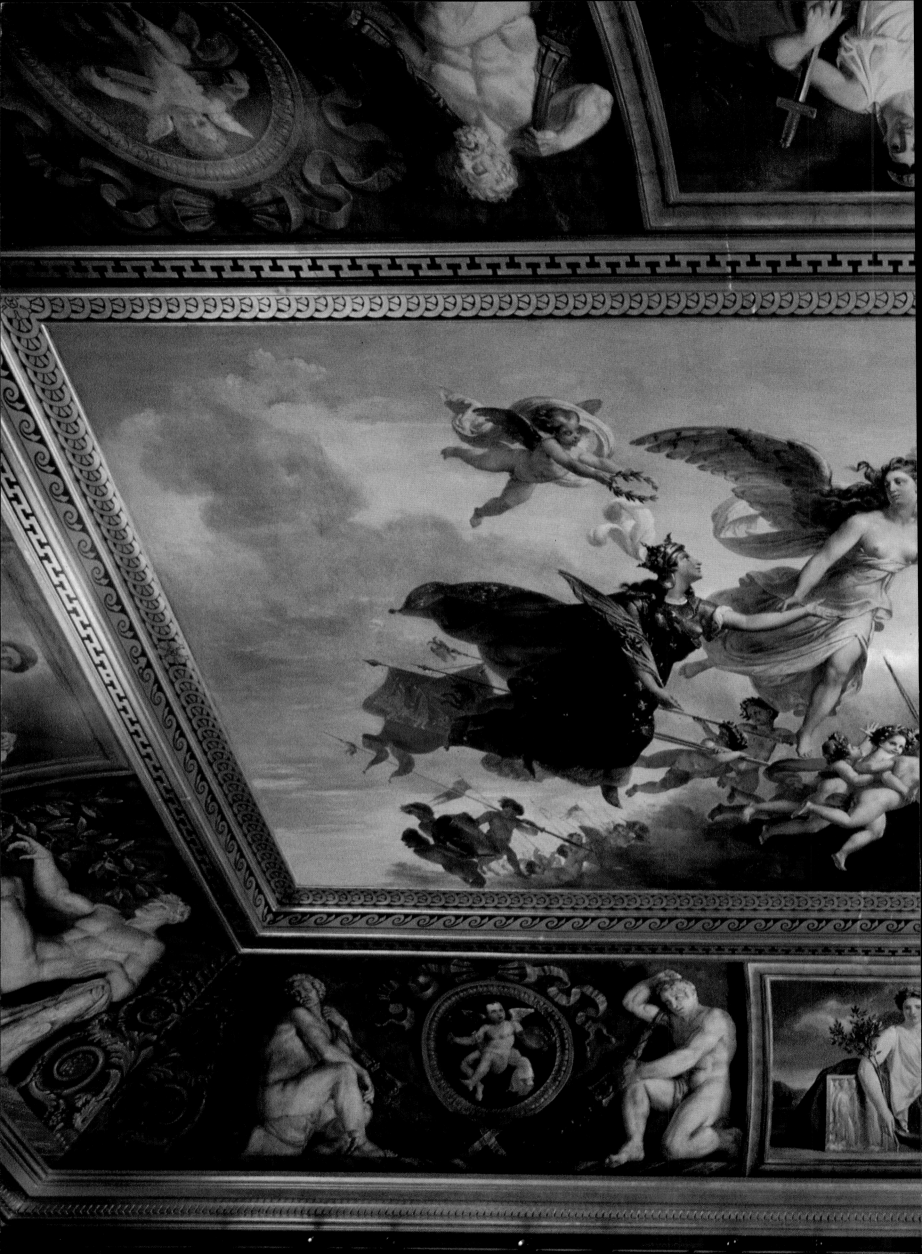

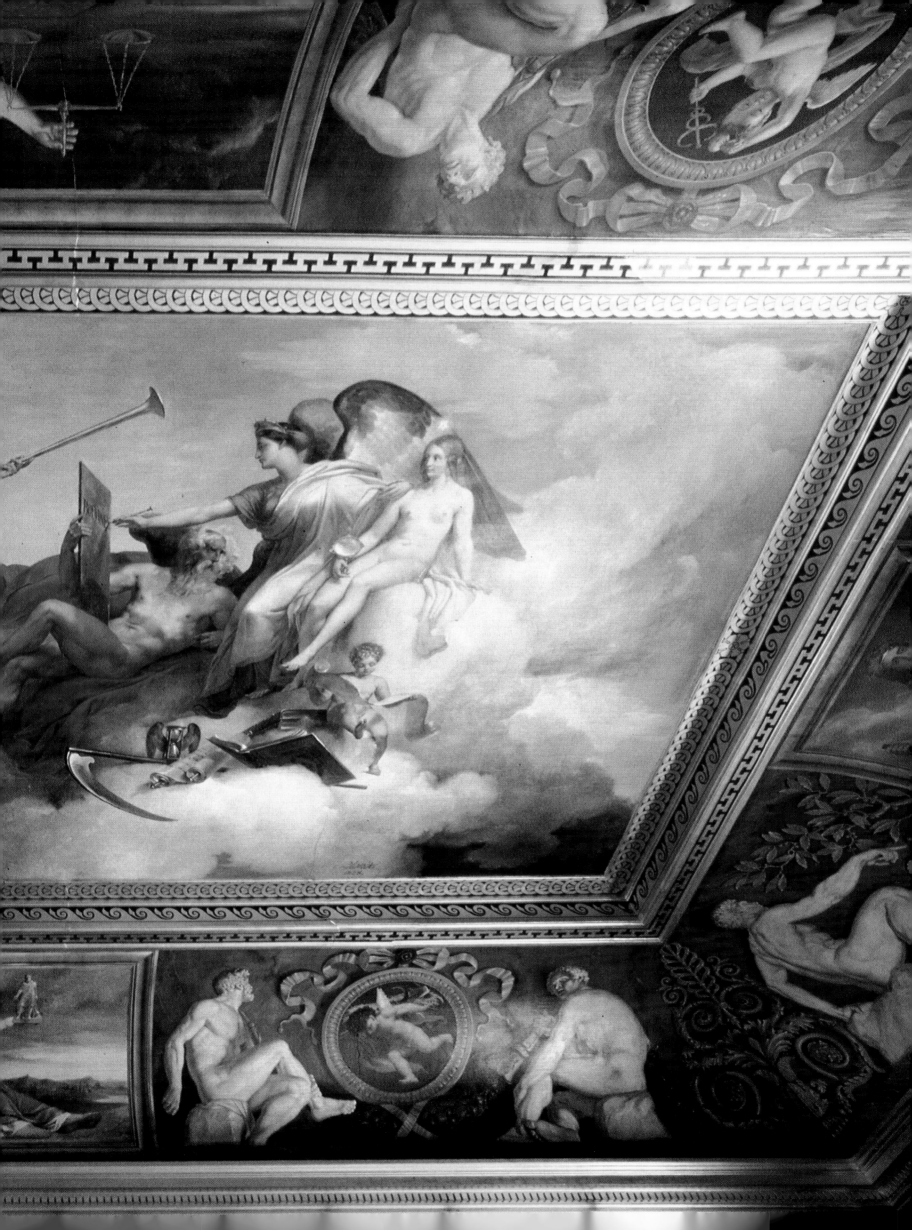

During the Revolution of 1830 the Louvre was attacked from the east. There were some nasty moments for the museum when the rioters destroyed images of the deposed king, Charles X. The new monarch, Louis-Philippe – king 'of the French' rather than 'of France', and popularly known as the 'Citizen King' – owed his throne to a complex political balance. He was afraid of Paris. Resignedly and without enthusiasm, he moved into the Tuileries, and had a substantial ditch dug to mark off his private garden, a haven of peace and if necessary of defence. Lacking both means and motives, he carried on the work of his predecessors at a very reduced pace. He completed certain decorative schemes, such as Leon Cogniet's ceiling celebrating the Egyptian campaign; he had a ceiling in the Musée Charles X, which included a portrait of his predecessor, taken down, and replaced it in 1833 by a more generalized *Genius of France giving Life to the Arts and protecting Humanity* (by Gros); and he commissioned a series of pictures telling the story of the Louvre, destined for the Galerie d'Apollon. But this last of the kings of France was relatively uninterested in the Louvre museum. He definitely preferred his own museum of French history at Versailles.

Nevertheless, it was in the Louvre, on the first floor of the Colonnade wing, that the King arranged the Spanish museum, constituting of 450 pictures from his personal collection – which were later returned to him after his deposition and departure into exile. This fleeting exhibition of Spanish paintings had a profound influence on contemporary artists, who were able to discover the darkness and realism of a school only sparsely represented in the museum's collection.

But independently of who was in power, the museum pursued its policy of acquisition. Under Louis-Philippe, the first Assyrian antiquities, discovered at Khorsabad by the French consul at Mosul, Paul-Emile Botta, entered the Louvre. The first two winged bulls from the palace of Sargon were placed in a little 'Assyrian Museum' in the north wing of the Cour Carrée in 1847.

Thus it was that in 1848 the Louvre presented the spectacle of a great idea that was still unrealized. The Chamber of Deputies had refused to vote the funds necessary to complete the Grand Design, although it had won the support of Thiers in 1833 and of his successor in 1840. Balzac in *La Cousine Bette* (1846) described with horror the district in which 'the houses are plunged into perpetual gloom by the tall galleries of the Louvre, blackened on this side by the north wind. Darkness, silence, chill, the cavernous depth of the ground level, all combine to make of these houses a sort of crypt, living tombs' – intensified by the fact that they were surrounded by 'a marsh in the direction of the Rue de Richelieu, an ocean of uneven paving-stones in the direction of the Tuileries, little gardens and similar shacks in the direction of the galleries, and expanses of hewn stones and rubble in the direction of the old Louvre'.

Pages 110–11 The ceiling of one of the Conseil d'Etat rooms in the west range of the Cour Carrée. The main subject is *France victorious at Bouvines*, by Blondel (1828); the paintings in the coving are by Gassiès.

Opposite Detail of another of the Conseil d'Etat rooms. In the coving is *Abundance*, by Blondel. The mirror reflects the central composition of the ceiling – *France, surrounded by French Law-Making Kings and Jurists, receiving the Constitutional Charter from Louis XVIII*.

Pages 114–15 One of the Conseil d'Etat rooms, now part of the Department of Objets d'Art, houses elements of Louis XVIII's Bedchamber from the Tuileries.

Pages 116–17 The quadriga on the Arc de Triomphe du Carrousel, by Bosio, cast in bronze by Crozatier in the Restoration period, replaced the Horses of St Mark's. Flanking it are Napoleonic gilt lead statues by Lemot.

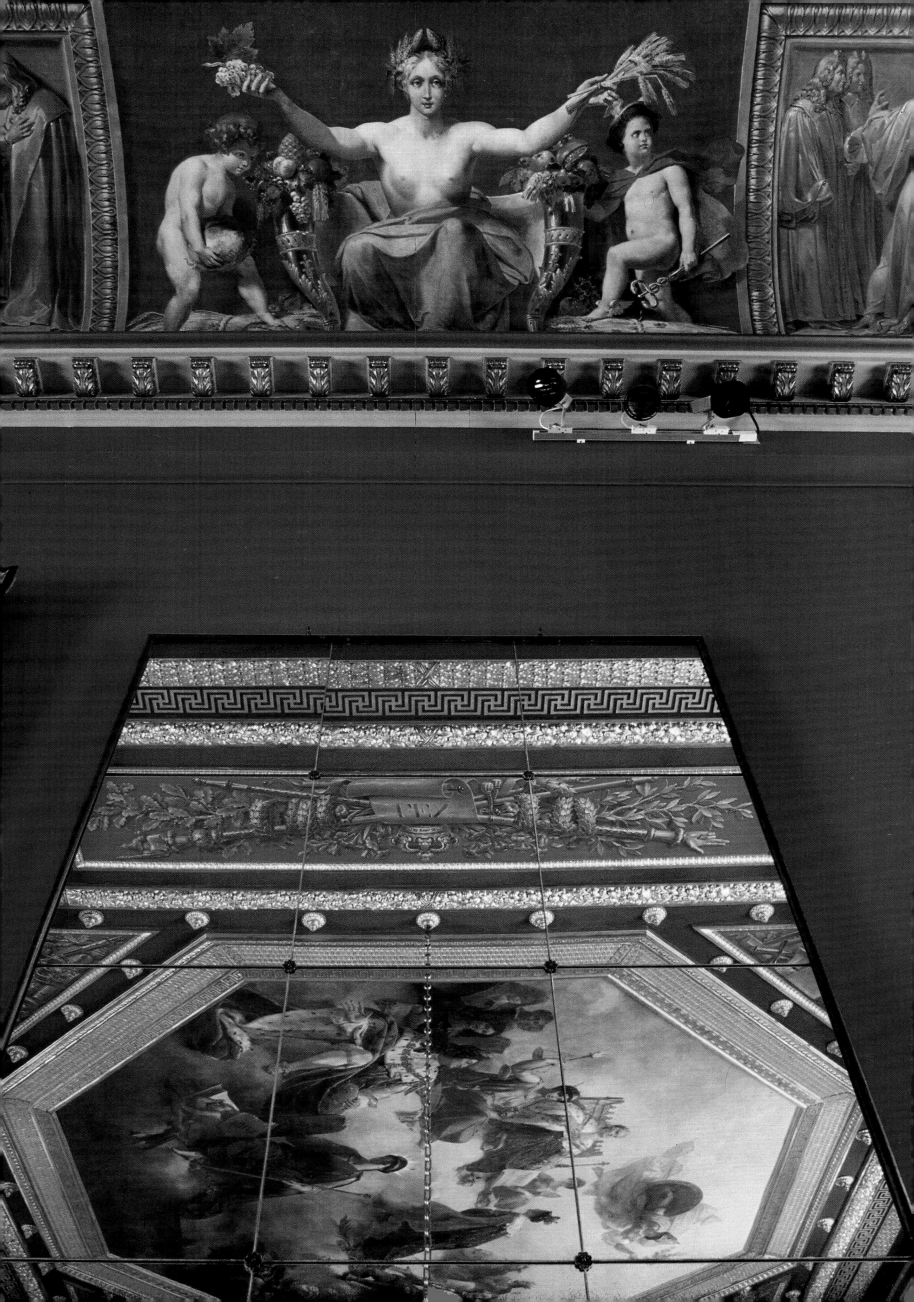

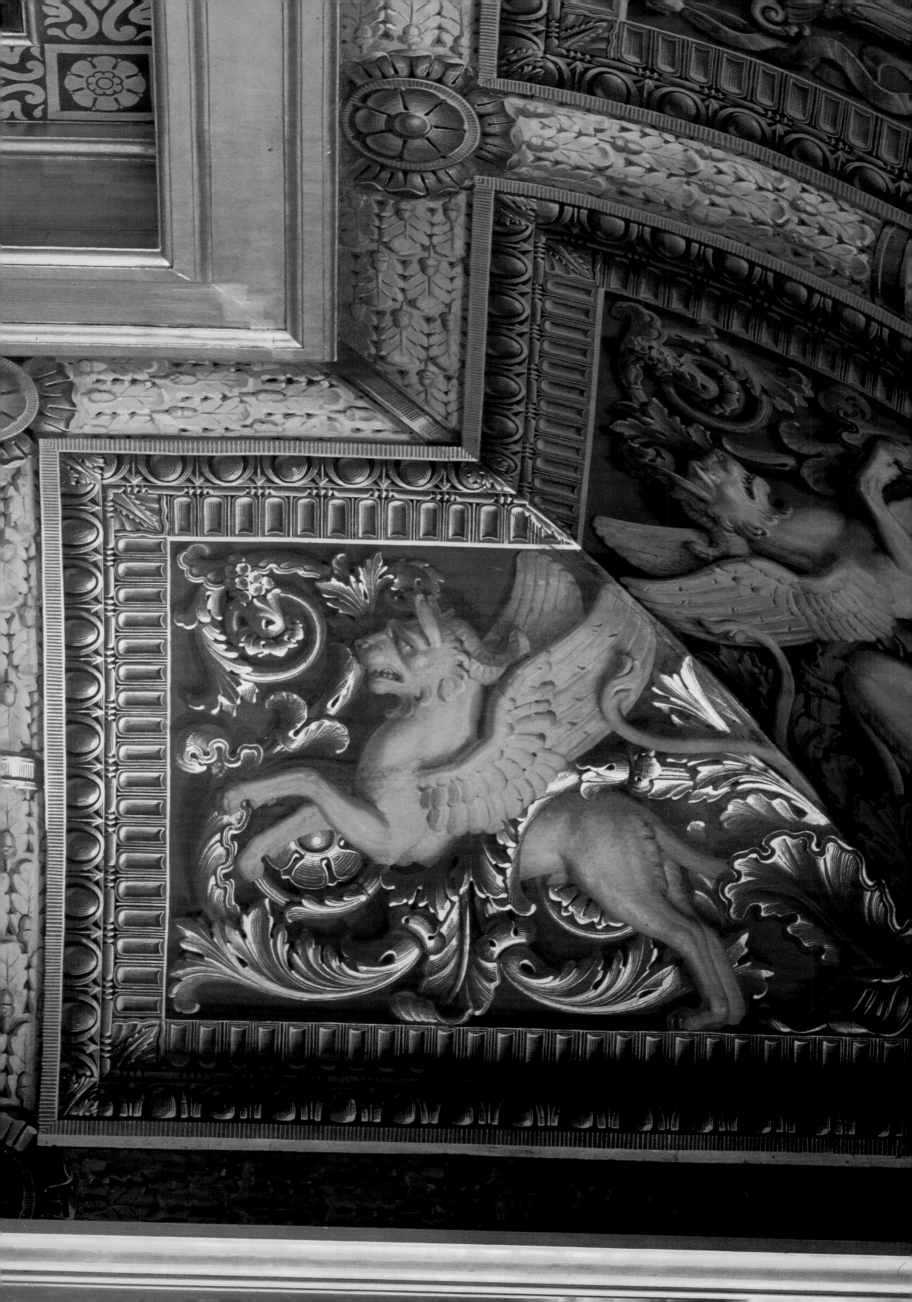

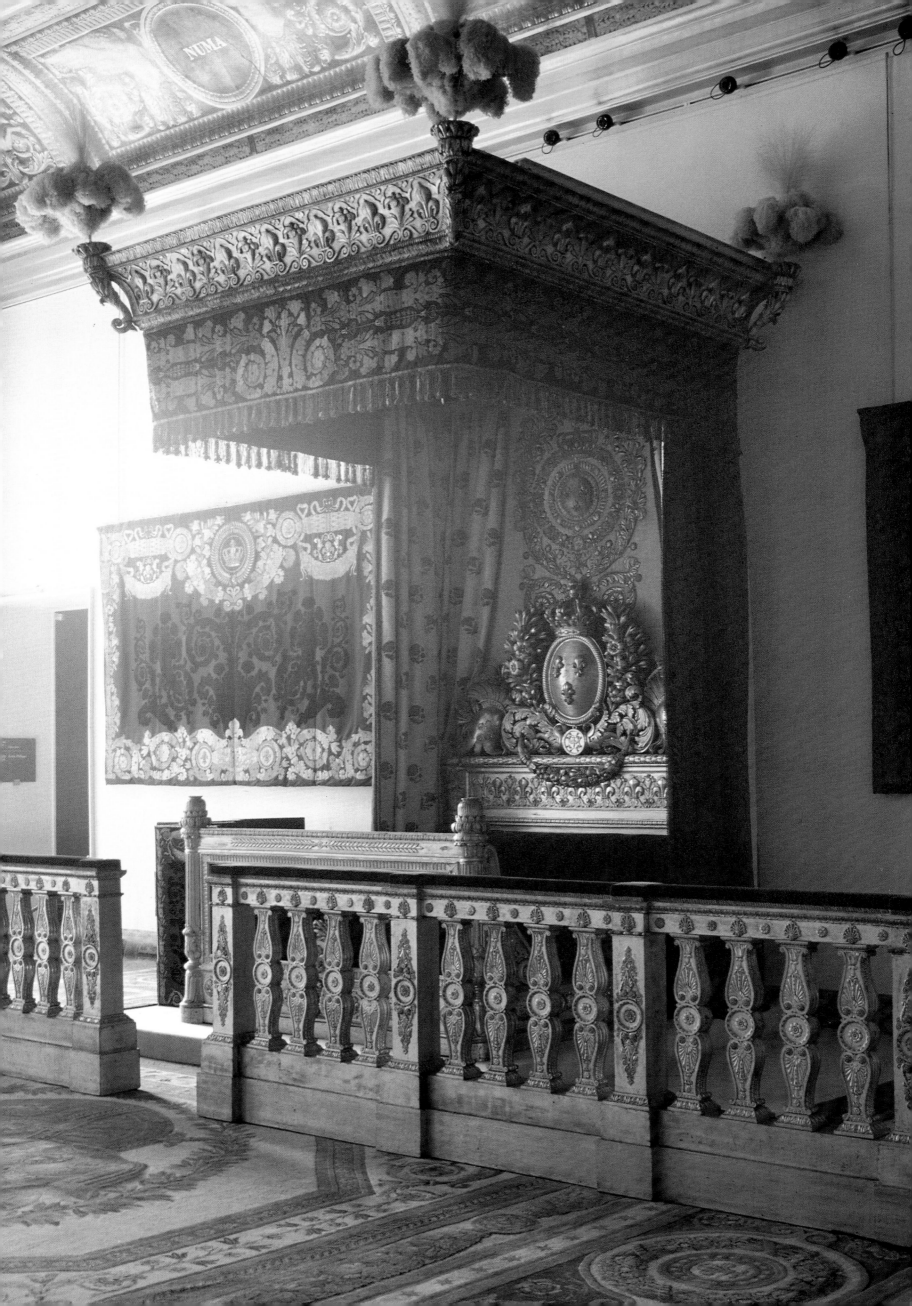

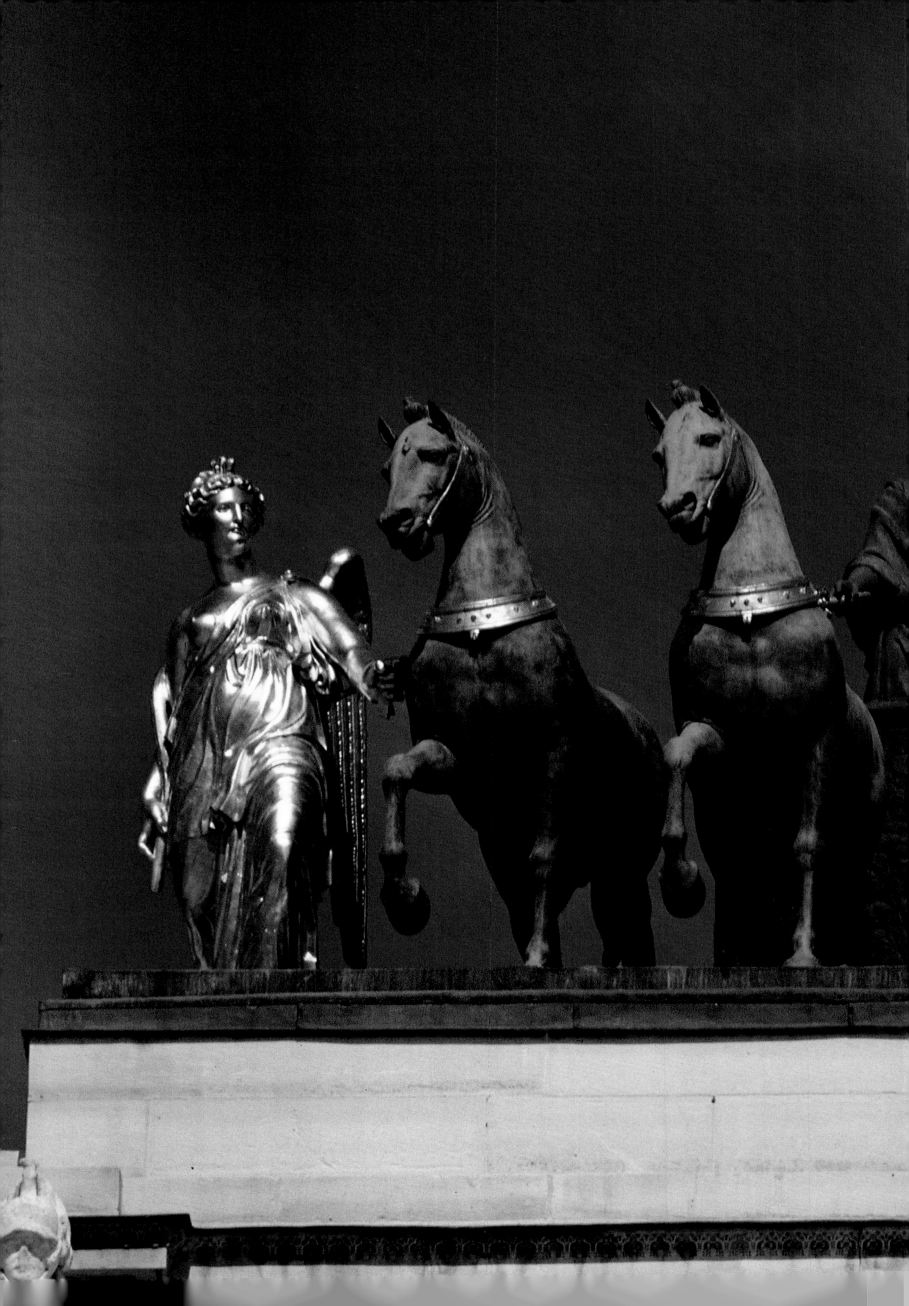

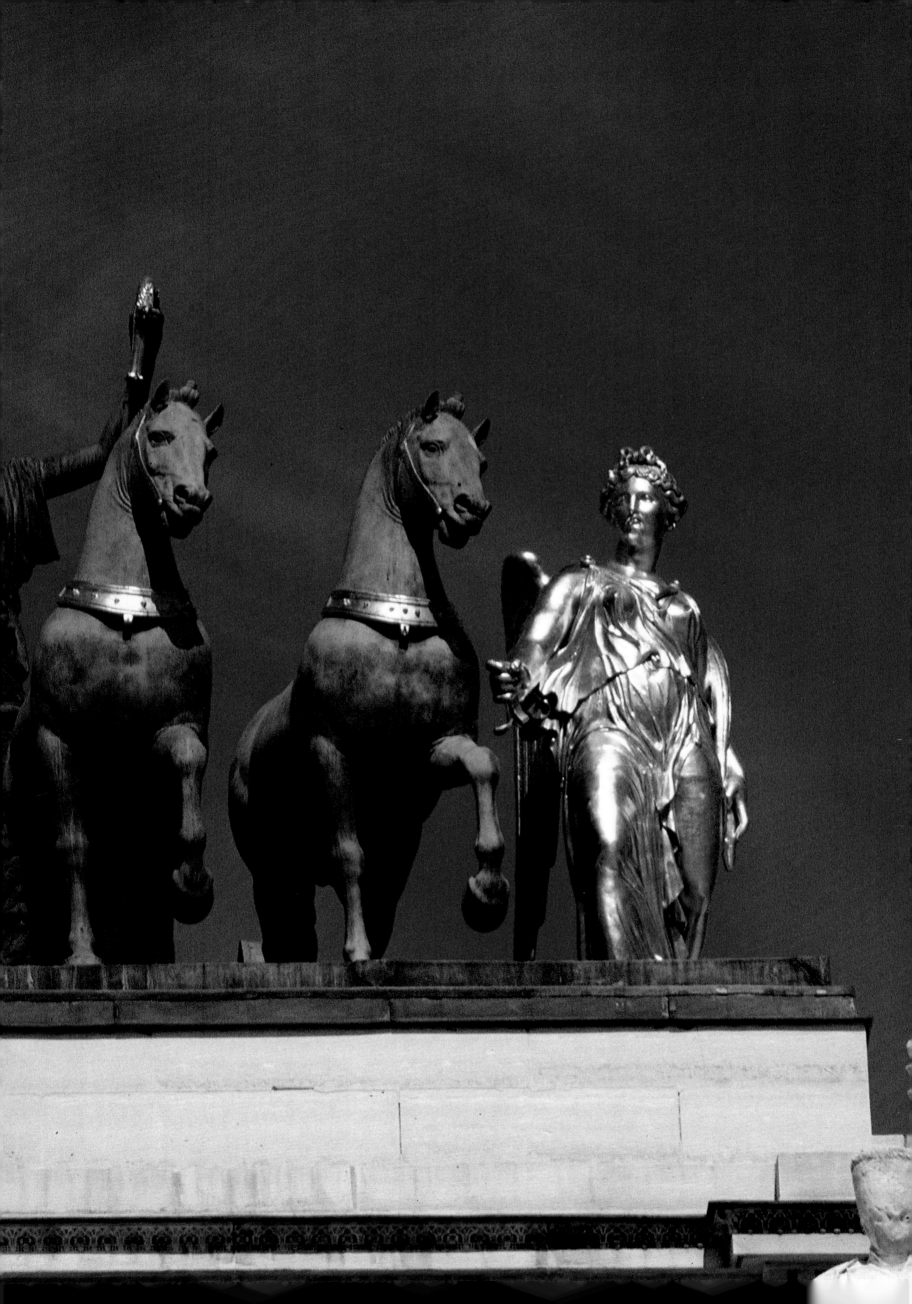

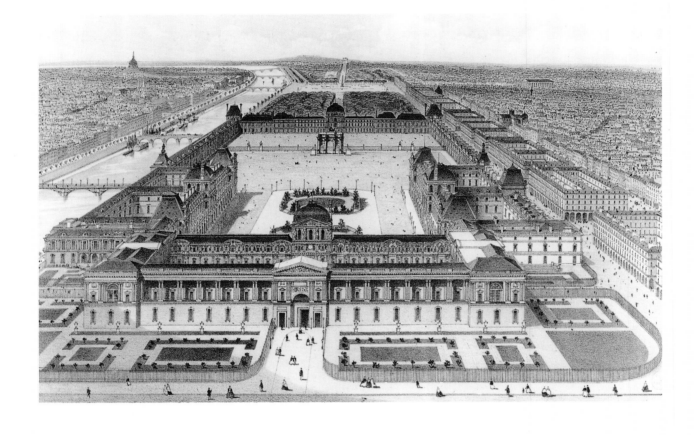

The 'New Louvre' of Napoleon III, as it looked from the east in 1857. A vast open space, composed of the Cour Napoléon and the Cour du Carrousel, extends from the Louvre to the Tuileries. The Rue de Rivoli can be seen at the right.

The 'New Louvre'

'The Mecca of the intellect'

The Louvre was now exposed to the shock-waves of the Revolution of 1848, that radical social explosion that rocked Europe. Popular feeling was chiefly directed against the two strongholds of the Orléans family, the Palais Royal and the Tuileries. The Louvre museum, regarded as the property of the nation, was spared; had it not been, a volunteer committee made up of artists was on guard to protect the collections. With the republican victory, the Louvre became a major stake in the game of cultural politics. A new director of the museum was appointed, Philippe-Auguste Jeanron, whose simple and effective principles laid the foundations of modern museum practice: 'inventorize, conserve, describe, classify, communicate, display'. During his short but critical time in office, the spotlight was turned on to new areas of interest – archaic Greek art, Early Christian art, medieval art, and ethnography.

The future of the palace itself was a central issue. With the support of the Assembly, the Government decreed on 24 March 1848 that the Louvre was to be completed, and proclaimed it as 'the palace of the people'. Victor Hugo supported this noble aim, declaring in the Assembly that it should become 'the Mecca of the intellect'. A number of projects to link the Louvre and the Tuileries were drawn up, but all foundered for lack of money and political will. In October 1848 Fontaine, by now aged 86, retired and yielded the post of architect to Félix Duban. Duban had proved his ability in the restoration of the Gothic Sainte-Chapelle and the Renaissance château of Blois; his own eclectic style, in the Classical tradition, appears in his building for the Ecole des Beaux-Arts in Paris and in the château of Dampierre which he designed for the Duc de Luynes. A supporter of the senior branch of the royal family rather than Louis-Philippe and his son the Duc d'Orléans, he seemed to come to terms with the great social upheaval of the Revolution: the rise to power of Louis-Napoleon Bonaparte, on the other hand, was to prove a constant source of irritation. Incompatibility between the architect and the interfering Prince-President, who presumed to pronounce on matters of taste, became open hostility in 1851.

In 1849, efforts were focused on the restoration of the Grande Galerie and Petite Galerie, both of which were in a dangerous state of disrepair. The façades were cleaned, worn stones were replaced, and the pediments, whose sculpture had never been completed, were carved in 1850–52. As part of the social programme of the new Republic, sixteen sculpture workshops were set up to provide employment for ornamental carvers, and these now undertook the decoration of the river front of the Grande Galerie. At the same time, Pierre-Jules Cavelier sculpted an allegorical figure for the newly recreated pediment of the Petite Galerie facing the Jardin de l'Infante (1850), and two ornamental sculptors, Victor Pyanet and Henri Duvieux, restored the exterior of the Petite Galerie and provided new decoration for the river front, including the pediment and the so-called 'Balcony of Charles X', which became a sort of tribune glittering with gold.

Duban also worked on the open spaces of the palace. In front of the Petite Galerie he redesigned the Jardin de l'Infante, providing a marble exedra-like structure with a pavement in brilliant colours. His greatest concern was for the Cour Carrée. When the Revolution of 1848 broke out, the courtyard housed a recently erected statue of the Duc d'Orléans. This was hastily removed to the château of Eu in Normandy, and Duban began to make plans to give the empty space an architectural character. His first thought was to re-erect Jean Goujon's Fontaine des Innocents in the centre, where it would echo Goujon's work on the Lescot wing.

Overleaf The Salon des Sept Cheminées, decorated under the direction of Duban by the sculptor Duret, assisted by Pyanet.

119

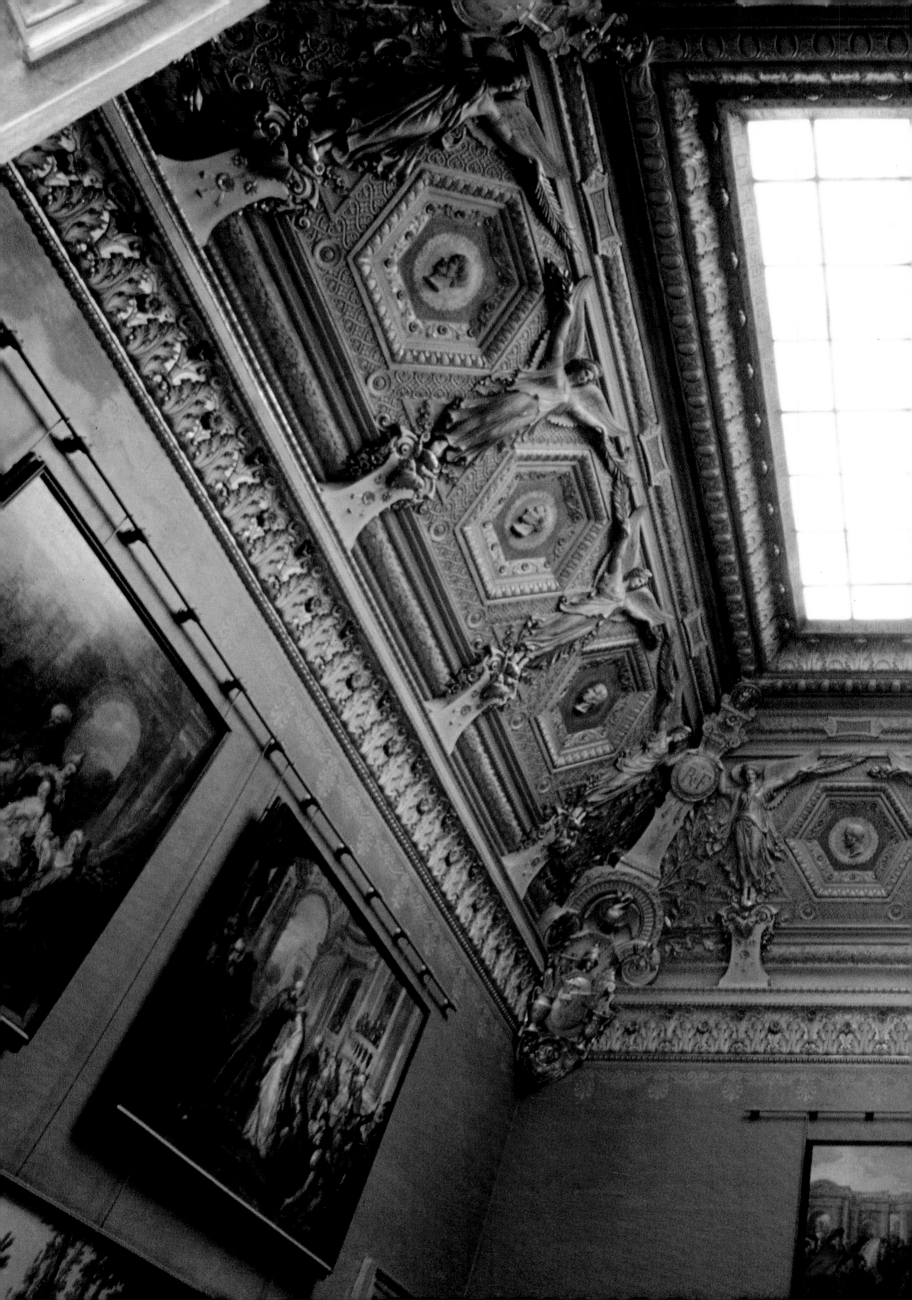

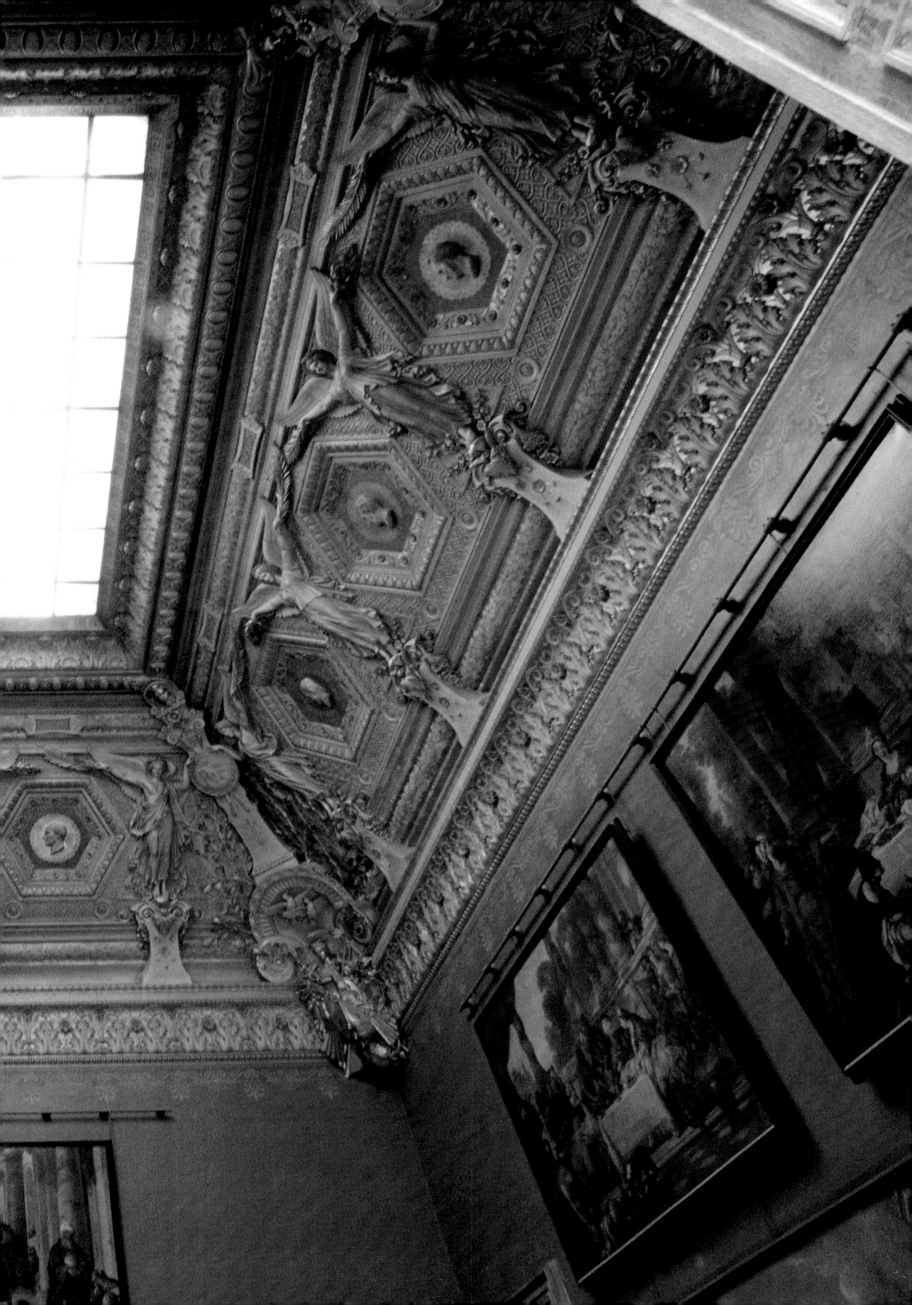

Nothing came of that scheme, and he turned to other ideas; for the centre he proposed a fountain, and for the corners marble exedras with railings, vases, ornamental lamp-posts and lawns, transforming the stony courtyard into a garden square. Louis-Napoleon had his own opinions, however, and after much discussion and many revisions what was finally executed was a simplified version of the scheme, which survived until 1984.

Work went on inside the museum as well. The Galerie d'Apollon was now completely restored, after decades of neglect when it was shored up and concealed behind canvas, and entered only at the risk of being hit by a piece of falling plaster. Duban had the vault taken down by the stuccoist Desachy, strengthened the roof timbers, inserted tie-rods to hold the structure together, and then in 1850 began the work of redecoration. The vault was re-erected, Le Brun's *Triumph of the Waters* was restored, and the decision was taken to complete the decorative ensemble. The central compartment was now filled with a dazzling composition by Delacroix of *Apollo Vanquishing the Python*, in which the great Romantic artist played with light in the spirit of the seventeenth century. At the northern end of the gallery, a painting by Guichard of *Earth* now formed a pendant to Le Brun's lunette on the southern wall. In a more self-effacing vein, Charles-Louis Müller produced a painting of *Aurora* for one of the ceiling compartments based on an engraving of 1695 by Saint-André which recorded Le Brun's original composition.

The walls of the gallery at this stage were bare. Duban reconstructed the seventeenth-century scheme on the basis of engravings, and a team of specialized decorators recreated the consoles with gilded fleurs-de-lis, moulded panelling, gilt capitals, and painted doors and shutters. The intermediate panels were to be filled by portraits of famous men, to stress the historical continuity of the room, and Duban commissioned their execution in tapestry at the Gobelins, but work was delayed after a change in programme, and eventually in the late 1860s the spaces were filled by portraits of the architects, painters and sculptors who had worked at the Louvre, together with large-scale compositions alluding to royal patrons.

Jeanron, with the help of the curator of Paintings, Villot, had decided to reorganize the hang of the pictures. First, he had banished the 'Salon' from the museum, on the grounds that contemporary paintings were shown at the expense of great works of art, which had to be manhandled and put into reserve; moreover the last Salon, in 1848, had been 'democratic', resulting in a particularly vast and miscellaneous display. To solve the problem, there were to be two great complementary exhibition spaces: the Salon Carré, like the Tribuna of the Uffizi in Florence, was to display the great masterpieces of the collection, drawn from all periods and all schools; the Salon des Sept Cheminées was to be the province of modern French art. Suitably palatial decoration was needed for both rooms, and Duban opted for a scheme that involved only sculpture, so as to avoid any clash between a painted ceiling and paintings hung on the walls. In the tradition of the Galerie d'Apollon, the sculptors Pierre-Charles Simart and Francisque-Joseph Duret produced white figures standing out against gold grounds. In Duret's Salon des Sept Cheminées, lithe winged Victories fill the vault and at the corners flank the 'RF' monogram of the Republic. In the Salon Carré, Simart placed atlantes bearing the 'RF' monogram in the corners and immense classical female figures, wrapped in antique drapery and pensive in mood, at the centre of the sides, accompanied by medallions representing the four major arts. That theme was a recurrent one in the decoration of the Louvre, appearing for instance in the Rotonde de Mars and on the Museum Staircase, but here it was treated with a difference, for instead of an allegorical figure each art was incarnated by a great French proponent – Jean Goujon for sculpture, Philibert Delorme for architecture, Nicolas Poussin for painting, and Jean Pesne for engraving.

The ceilings are still in place today, but below them the appearance of the rooms was very different from what it is now. The side windows were blocked up, and relatively little light came in.

Opposite Atlas figure in a corner of the ceiling of the Salon Carré, modelled in stucco by Simart (1850–51).

Page 124 Victories in a corner of the ceiling of the Salon des Sept Cheminées, by Duret.

Page 125 Detail of the panelling in the Galerie d'Apollon, executed under the direction of Duban. The portrait is of the architect Lemercier.

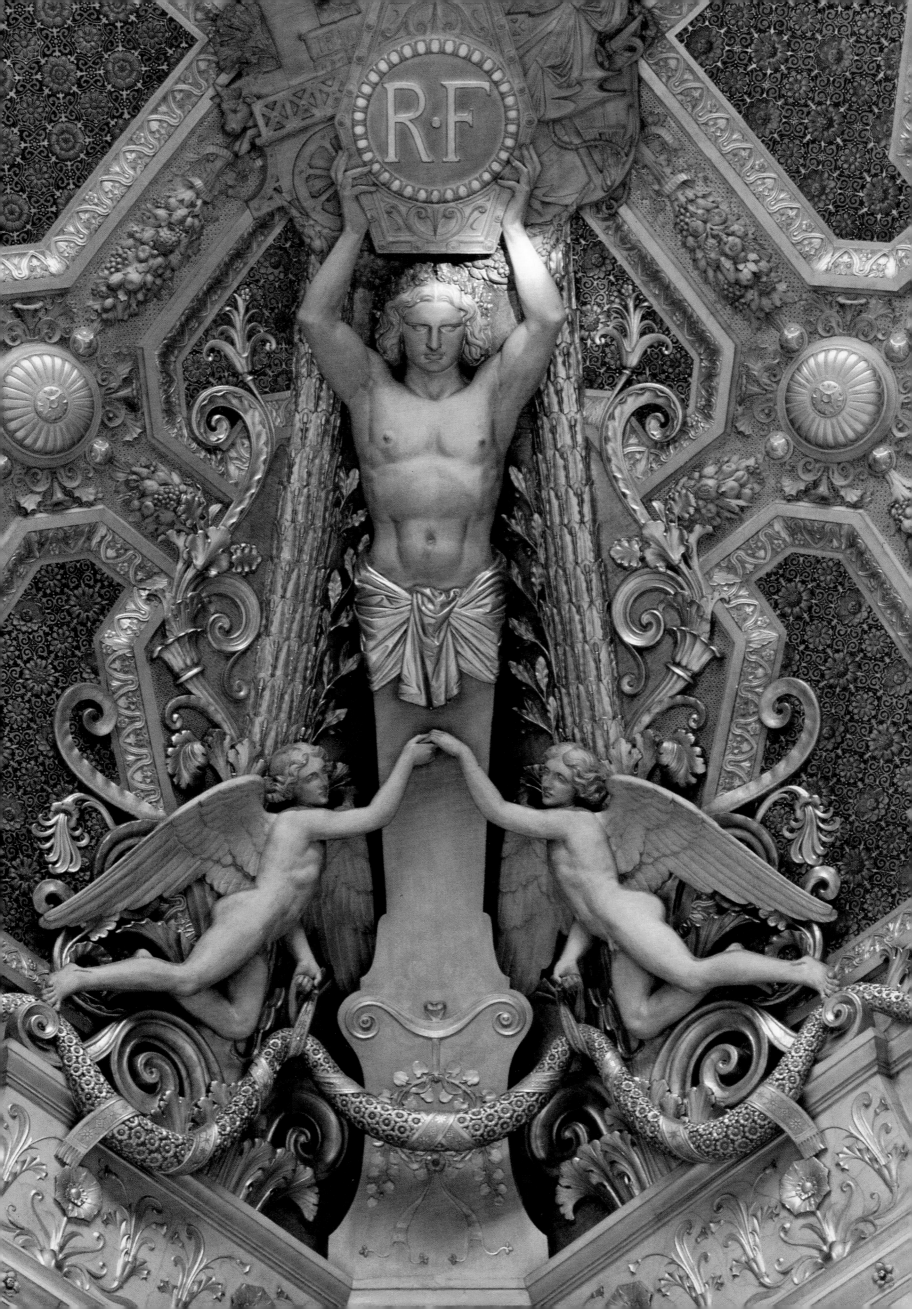

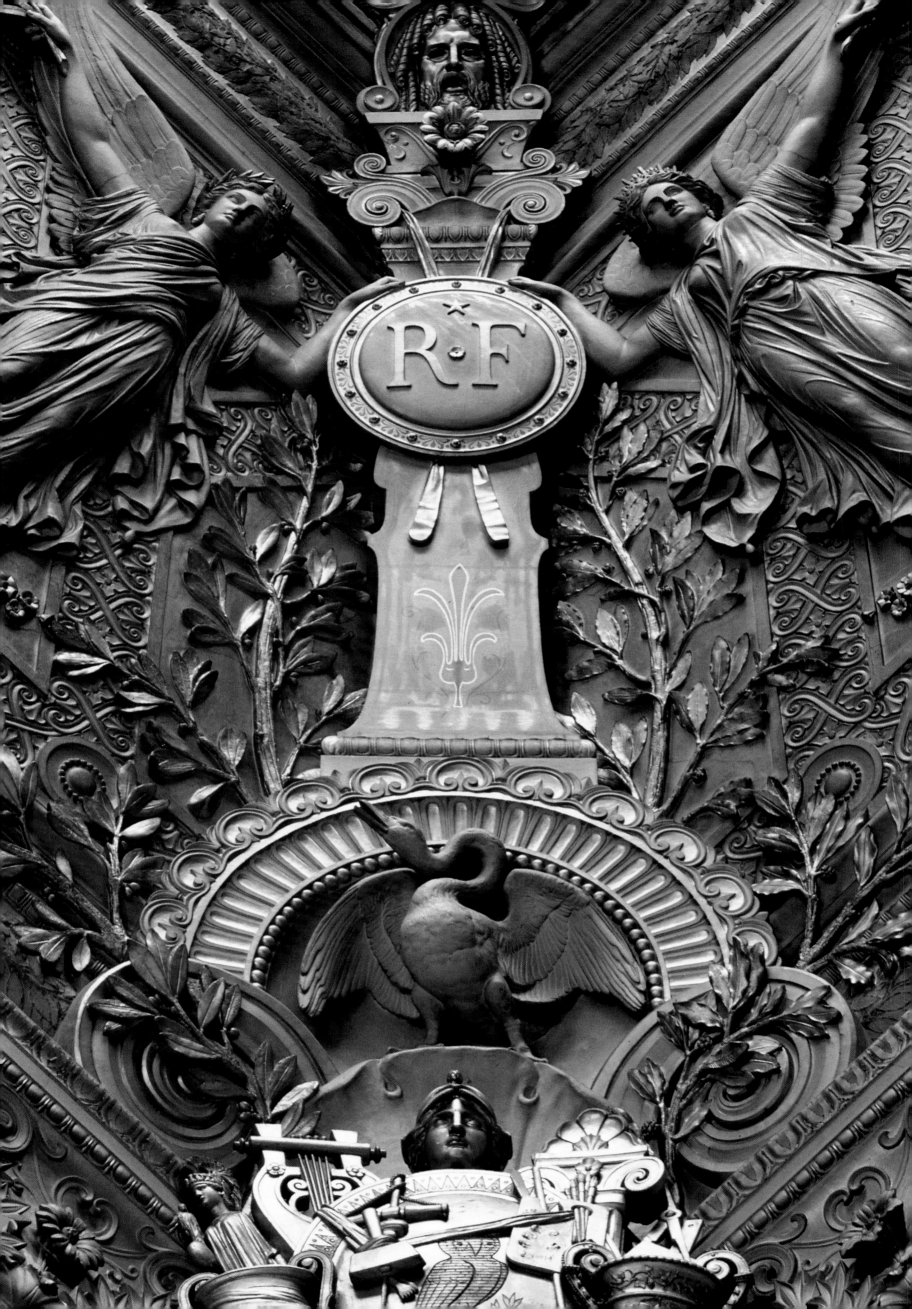

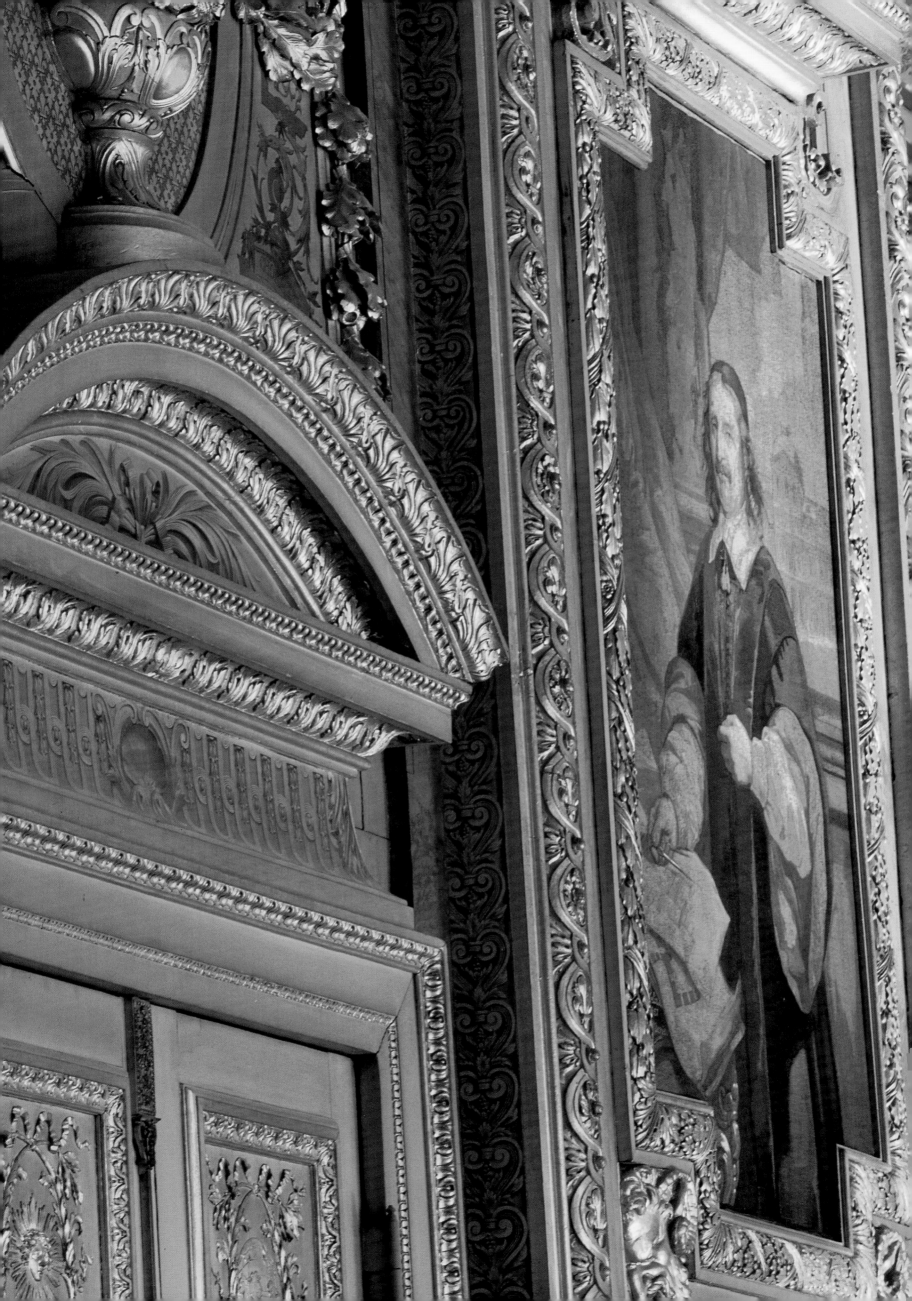

High panelled dados, dark colours on the walls, finely detailed railings keeping the visitors well back from the pictures, and painted doors combined to create a dim religious atmosphere of silence, concentration and richness that can be glimpsed in paintings and especially in prints of the time.

The two Salons, the Galerie d'Apollon and the Cour Carrée were officially opened by the Prince-President on 5 June 1851. Far greater transformations were in store.

The 'New Louvre' of Napoleon III

The political climate had changed. France was becoming an industrial nation, and to the rising bourgeoisie, dreaming of progress, mechanization and wealth, the Republic seemed to pose a threat, whereas a new imperial régime promised stability and protection. Louis-Napoleon Bonaparte's coup d'état on 2 December 1851 marked the end of liberal government. Now, as Napoleon III, he wanted to enjoy his uncle's inheritance in peace. At his official residence in the Tuileries Palace he gave splendid entertainments and surrounded himself with a glittering court, and he determined to transform the vast ensemble of the Tuileries and the Louvre into an imperial enclave.

The new Emperor had been a *carbonaro* and a man of progressive ideals, and it might have seemed at first that he was merely taking over projects put forward under the Republic; but in fact he now saw things from the point of view of a leader backed by strong political power, and the Louvre complex was to be not a 'Mecca of the intellect' but a palace of the State, housing the representative bodies of government, administrators, bustling imperial equerries, and troops. While amidst all this the Emperor did not lose sight of the museum, its primary importance for him seems to have been as a source of prestige. He gave orders for archaeological expeditions and entrusted the renovation of the museum to the sculptor Count Emilien Nieuwerkerke, who was a member of his private circle and a close friend of his cousin, the Princesse Mathilde. The Emperor was personally responsible for the acquisition of the vast collection of the Marchese Campana, and oversaw its display, together with objects from State-funded foreign excavations, in the 'Musée Napoléon III'. But he regarded the Louvre as his own private collection, and pictures that were on view to the public one week might be swept away to a palace the next, in an expression of thoughtless swagger that was bitterly criticized by opponents of the régime.

The great project of Napoleon III's reign was the final realization of the Grand Design with a northern link between the Louvre and the Tuileries. Louis-Tullius-Joachim Visconti presented a plan in February 1852 to the Conseil des Bâtiments Civils, who approved it, and in March he was appointed architect for the combined palaces. Visconti was the son of the former curator of antiquities at the Louvre, who had come to Paris in 1798 with the antique statues seized in Rome by the Revolutionary army. A classicist by training and by temperament, designer of the most beautiful fountains in Paris (that in front of Saint-Sulpice, and the Fontaine Molière), he combined a profound respect for the architecture of the past with a keen awareness of the needs of his own day.

The first stone of what was referred to as the 'New Louvre' was laid opposite the Palais Royal on 25 July 1852 by the Comte de Casablanca, Minister of State, accompanied by the clergy of Saint-Roch and Saint-Germain-l'Auxerrois, to whose parishes the Tuileries and the Louvre respectively belonged.

Duban disappeared from the scene in 1853. Visconti died in harness in December of the same year, and Hector-Martin Lefuel succeeded him in charge of an army of three thousand workmen. On 14 August 1857, the feast day of St Napoleon, the first phase was inaugurated: as the Emperor stressed in his speech at the ceremony, it was 'the realization of a grand design which the nation had instinctively desired for more than three hundred years'.

Opposite Wall panelling and shutters in the Galerie d'Apollon, re-created by Duban.

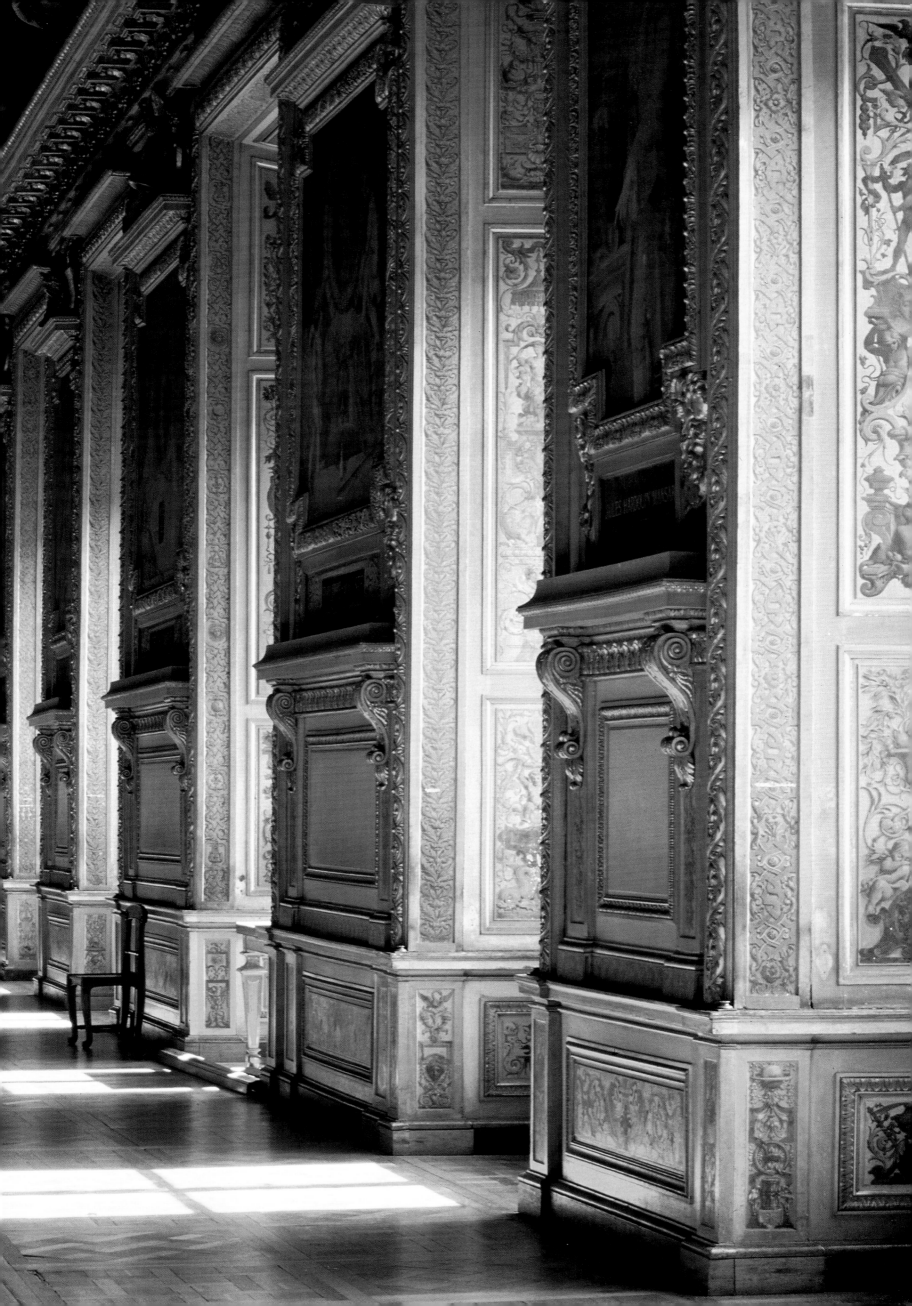

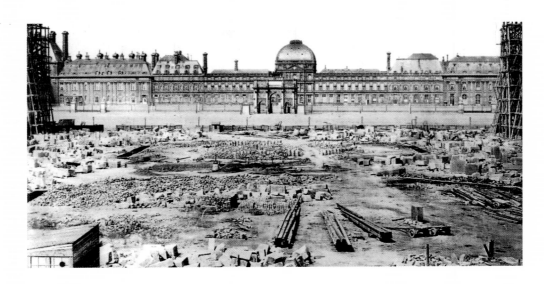

The linking of the Louvre and the Tuileries along the Rue de Rivoli in the years 1852–57 was an immense construction project. The first step was the demolition of all the houses – a complete little neighbourhood – that still survived between the two palaces: this was organized by Baron Haussmann, soon to put his stamp on Paris as a whole. Next came the building of the north wing along the street, between the Pavillon de Rohan and the Pavillon de Beauvais, which was designed by Visconti. Lefuel then continued the work, creating a whole ensemble of ranges and courts around a central space, the Cour Napoléon, punctuated by tall pavilions named after great servants of the State – Turgot, Richelieu, Colbert, Sully, Daru, Denon and Mollien. Visconti had strongly recommended that 'the general features of the architecture should be drawn religiously from the old Louvre'. Lefuel certainly used motifs from the earlier phases of the building, such as oculi flanked by allegorical figures, caryatids, trophies in the attic stage, and female heads surrounded by hounds; but perhaps from personal taste, or perhaps to please the imperial court, he exaggerated the decorative effects, and encrusted his façades with luxuriant sculpture.

The parts of the new building that most clearly reflect Visconti's more classical taste are the pediments of the Rohan wing (by Combettes), the Rivoli wing, with its keystones modelled on those carved in the time of Henri IV for the north façade of the Grande Galerie, the pavilion that faces the Palais Royal, and the Pavillon de Rohan, where the large figure of *France as an Artist* by Georges Diébolt (1854) recalls the composition of Visconti's Fontaine Molière.

From 1854 onwards, Lefuel was recruiting the services of the best sculptors of the day. The famous *animalier* Antoine-Louis Barye, by then already an old man, was responsible for the pediment of the Pavillon Sully (the east face of the Pavillon de l'Horloge) and the large groups on the Richelieu and Denon pavilions. The last of the Romantics, François Rude and Auguste Préault, more classically minded artists such as Cavelier, François Jouffroy, Duret and Simart, and the rising stars Jean-Baptiste Carpeaux and Eugène Guillaume formed the core of a group of more than three hundred sculptors. In the pediments of the Richelieu and Denon pavilions that faced each other across the Cour Napoléon, the imperial idea was exalted on the model of the pediments in the Cour Carrée: on one side was Napoleon III in coronation robes, while on the other the figure of France greeted personifications of the Arts and Commerce. On the terraces, the arts, literature, Church and State were represented by eighty-three gigantic statues 3.15 metres (10 feet) tall – the subjects all French, male, and civilians. The niches along the Rue de Rivoli were filled with eight statues of leaders of Napoleon I's armies. The treatment of the roofline sculpture, too, had no precedent in earlier work at the Louvre: here great seated statues were placed at the corners of the pavilions, while groups of putti (babies 1.80 metres or nearly 6 feet tall) concealed the bases of the roofs. The resources of official art were fully stretched to find identities for these vast cherubs and their attributes, such as the seasons, the continents, the arts (sculpture, painting, theatre...), trades and activities (hunting, fishing, industry, commerce...), and the sciences (astronomy, anatomy, mechanics...).

Work in progress on the Cour Napoléon, photographed by Baldus c. 1854–55. In the background are the Tuileries Palace and Arc de Triomphe du Carrousel.

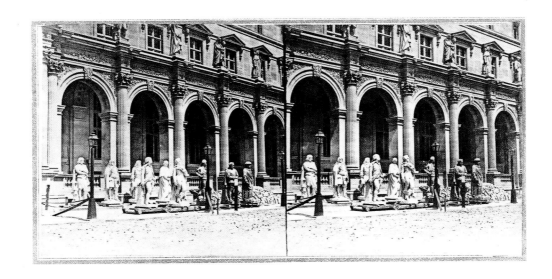

Building was already well advanced when early in 1856 it was decided to give a new face to the range of the old Louvre that stood at the end of the new Cour Napoléon, to bring into harmony with the rest its somewhat jumbled appearance. A visitor at the time would have seen there, from north to south, first a projection containing the rotunda of the chapel of St Napoleon (early nineteenth century), then Lemercier's wing and pavilion (mid-seventeenth century), then the Lescot wing (mid-sixteenth century), and finally another projection containing what had been Le Vau's Salon du Dôme. All this was skilfully masked by a new outer skin in 1856–57. Since there are no circulation galleries, there are no terraces here: the composition is linked to the rest by the row of statues of great men at first floor level, the groups of putti on the attic, and the fluted columns. To these decorative elements two immense sculptural groups were added at the corners, *Peace and War*, by Préault.

Further decoration appears on the inner courtyards, though only on those to the south, for Visconti's to the north have a classical austerity. Lefuel copied the elevation of the eastern half of the Grande Galerie with its carved pediments, statues in niches, and panels of trophies. Again we find a riot of allegorical themes, with here an emphasis on imagery connected with horses, in keeping with the purpose of these southern courtyards, off which the Manège (riding school) and imperial stables opened. The entrance to the Manège received a dynamic composition of galloping horses, by the fine animal sculptor Pierre Rouillard.

When all the work was finished, the masonry and sculpture were coated with a layer of calcium silicate, recommended by the engineer Kuhlmann to harden the surfaces – something it did too thoroughly, alas, for in many areas it formed a hard skin behind which the stone decayed in a slow process that was not addressed until the restoration work in 1990–91.

In 1861 Lefuel embarked on a new campaign, which involved the destruction of part of the old Louvre and its replacement by new, as ever ornately decorated, structures. The Pavillon de Flore and the western third of the Grande Galerie, said to be in dangerous condition, were demolished, and in their place rose a new Pavillon de Flore, a more richly decorated range to house the assemblies, and the 'Grands Guichets', three wide arches giving access to the quayside. The ornament was more elaborate than ever before. The elevations of the Grande Galerie and the south wing of the Tuileries, facing the gardens, played variations on themes from the Lescot wing. The Pavillon de Flore became a battleground between two great sculptors. On the south side, facing the river, Carpeaux presented his gigantic group of *Imperial France enlightening the World*, flanked by two allegorical male figures, *Science* and *Agriculture*, poised on the gable of the pediment in the manner of Michelangelo's Medici tombs. Lower down, Carpeaux managed to persuade Lefuel to commission a large relief full of sunny vitality, showing Flora bending down and smiling at a group of children who surround her – unquestionably the most famous work of sculpture on the whole exterior of the Louvre. On the west side, in 1863, Cavelier carved a colossal group of three figures at the top, two sentinels modelled on Donatello's *St George*, and friezes where putti play a prominent role.

Some of the statues of great men for the Cour Napoléon, photographed before their installation.

Opposite The columns of the Pavillon Denon, designed by Lefuel and built in 1854–57, reflected in one of the pools surrounding I. M. Pei's Pyramid.

Page 132 Five of the statues of great men on the terraces surrounding the Cour Napoléon, in the scheme devised by Lefuel: here, on the Turgot wing, they are from left to right *Boileau* by Seurre the younger, *Molière* by Seurre the elder, *Mézeray* by Daumas, *Pascal* by Lanno and *La Fontaine* by Jaley.

Page 133 The upper part of the Pavillon Daru, decorated by Brian. At the top are personifications of Sculpture and Painting.

Page 134 The wing at the end of the Cour Napoléon, refaced by Lefuel. At the top is *Peace*, by Préault. Lower down are statues of great men: from left to right, *Saint-Simon* by Hébert, *Joinville* by Marcellin, *Fléchier* by Lanno, *Commines* by Lequesne and *Amyot* by Travaux.

Pages 135, 136 The Guichet de l'Empereur, now known as the Porte des Lions. The ornate decoration copies that of Henri IV work at the Louvre. The lion on the right was created in 1847 by Barye.; in 1867 it was placed here with a mirror-image cast made specially for the new position.

Page 137 At the centre of the Grands Guichets the original equestrian statue of Napoleon II by Barye was replaced under the Third Republic by *The Genius of the Arts*, by Mercié. On the left is a figure of a river-god by Barye.

Page 138 *Bacchante* by Schoenewerk, in a niche of the Cour Carrée.

Page 139 The 'N' of Napoleon I on the door of the Colonnade wing was destroyed at the Restoration but replaced under Napoleon III.

Pages 140, 141 Façade of the western part of the Grande Galerie, rebuilt by Lefuel. The design is copied not from Du Cerceau's original, which Lefuel demolished, but from Métézeau's eastern part of the gallery.

Pages 142–43 Statues of famous men on the Turgot wing of the Cour Napoléon: left to right, *Colbert* by Gaurard, *Mazarin* by Hébert the elder, *Buffon* by Oudine, *Froissart* by Lemaire and *Jean-Jacques Rousseau* by Farochon.

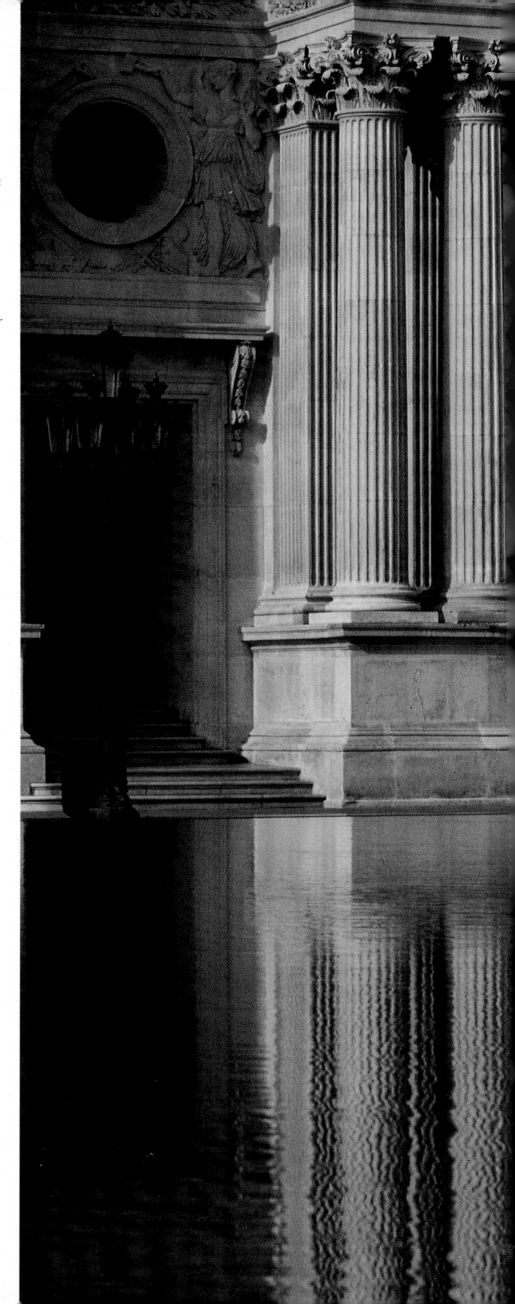

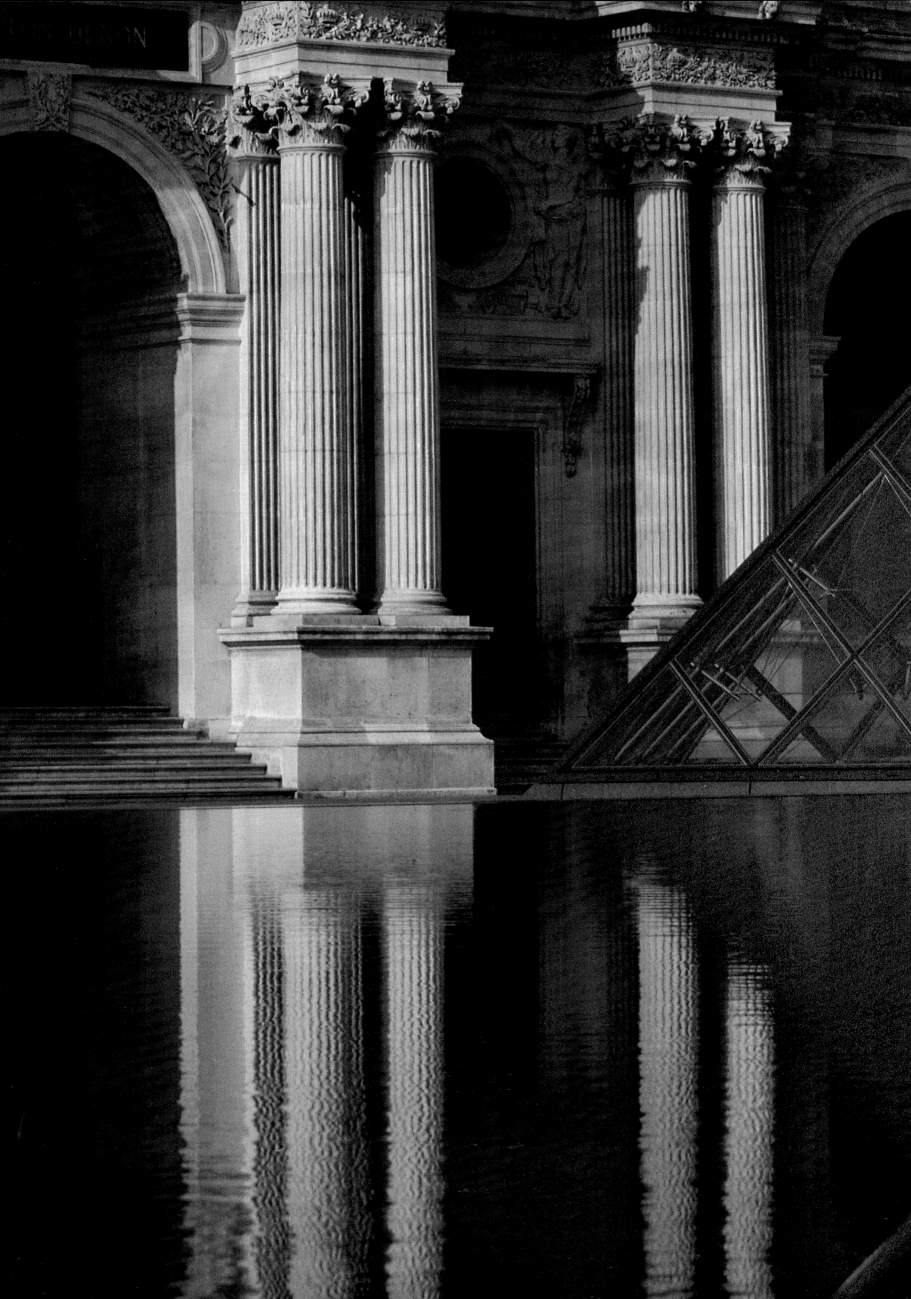

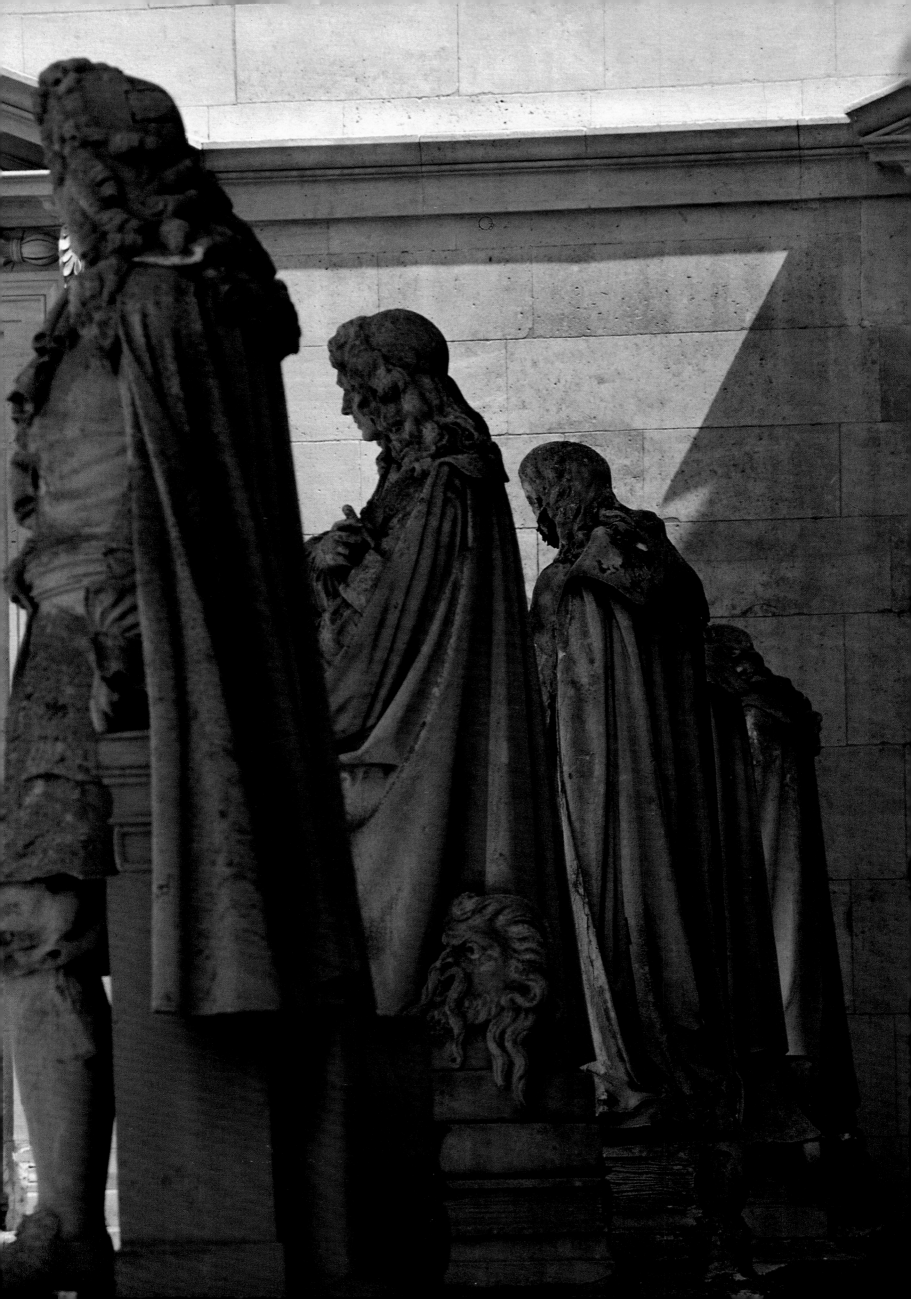

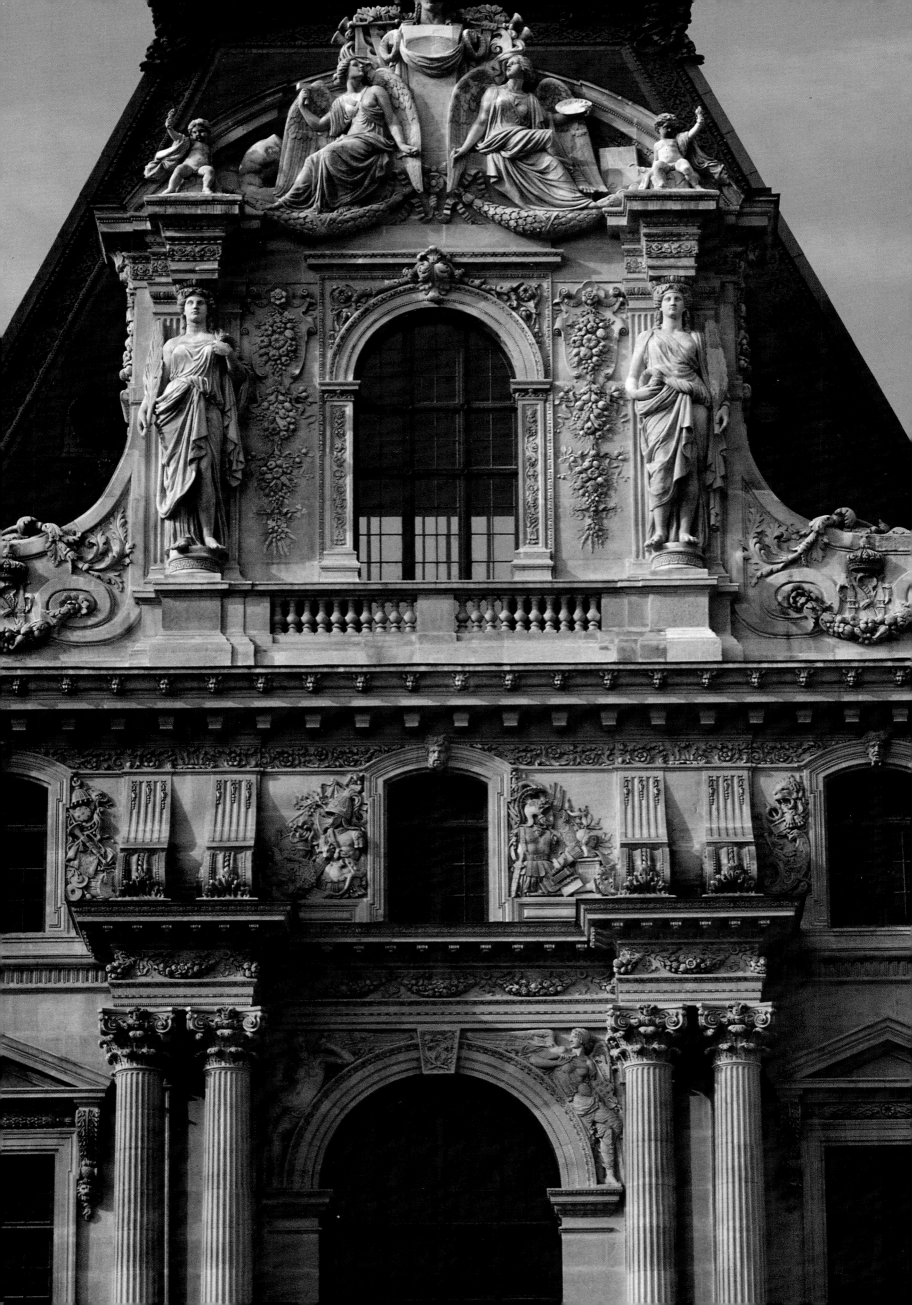

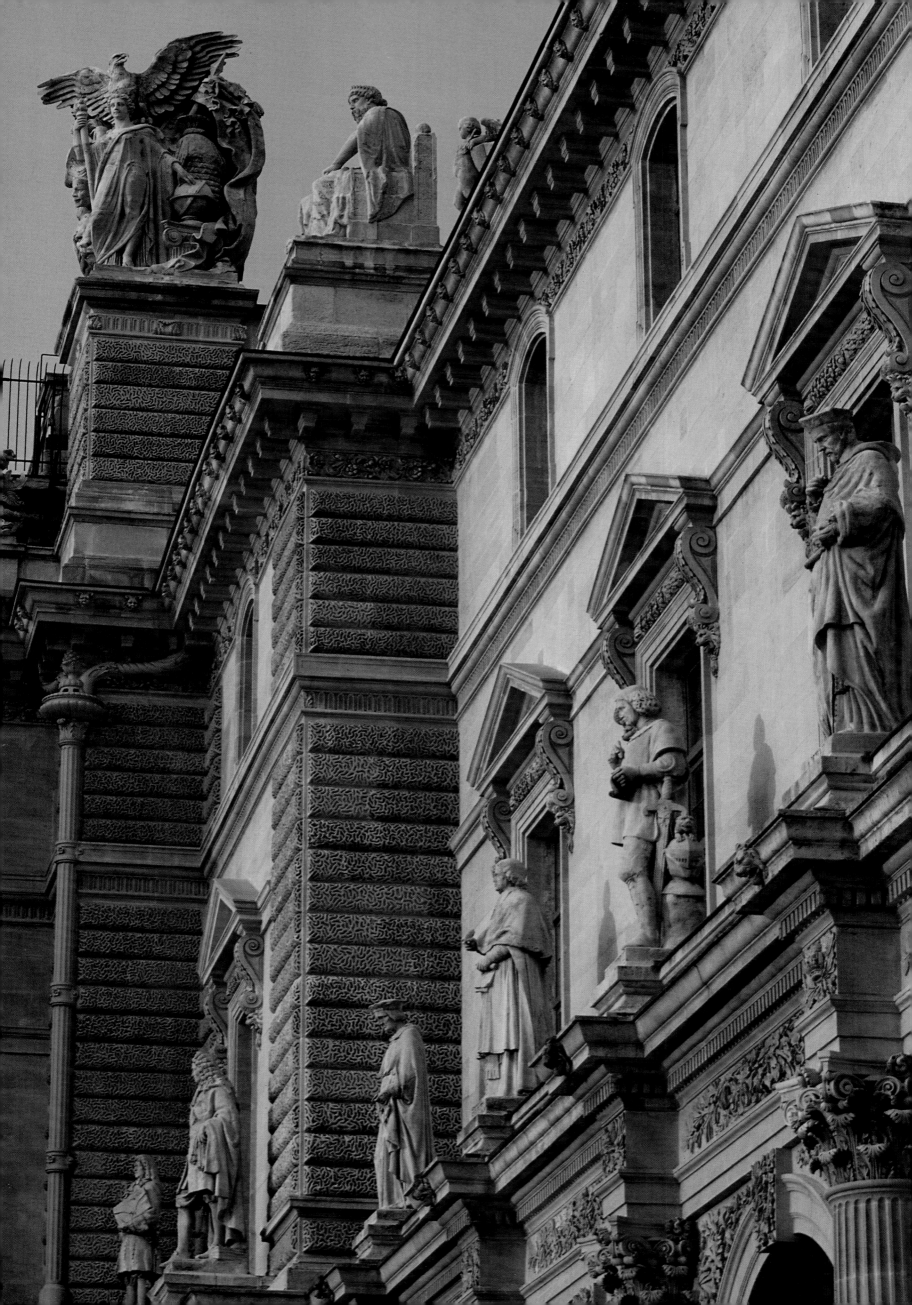

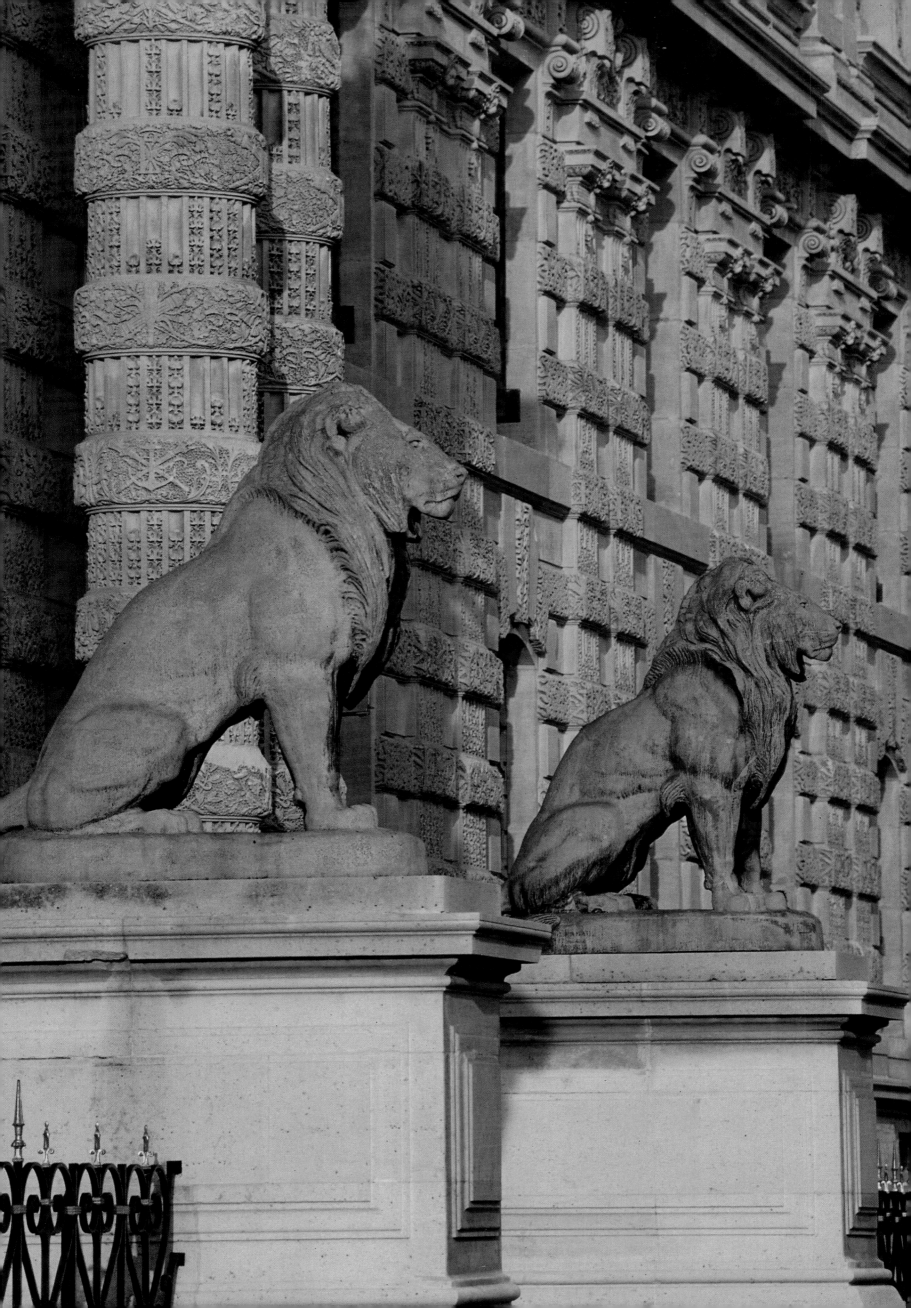

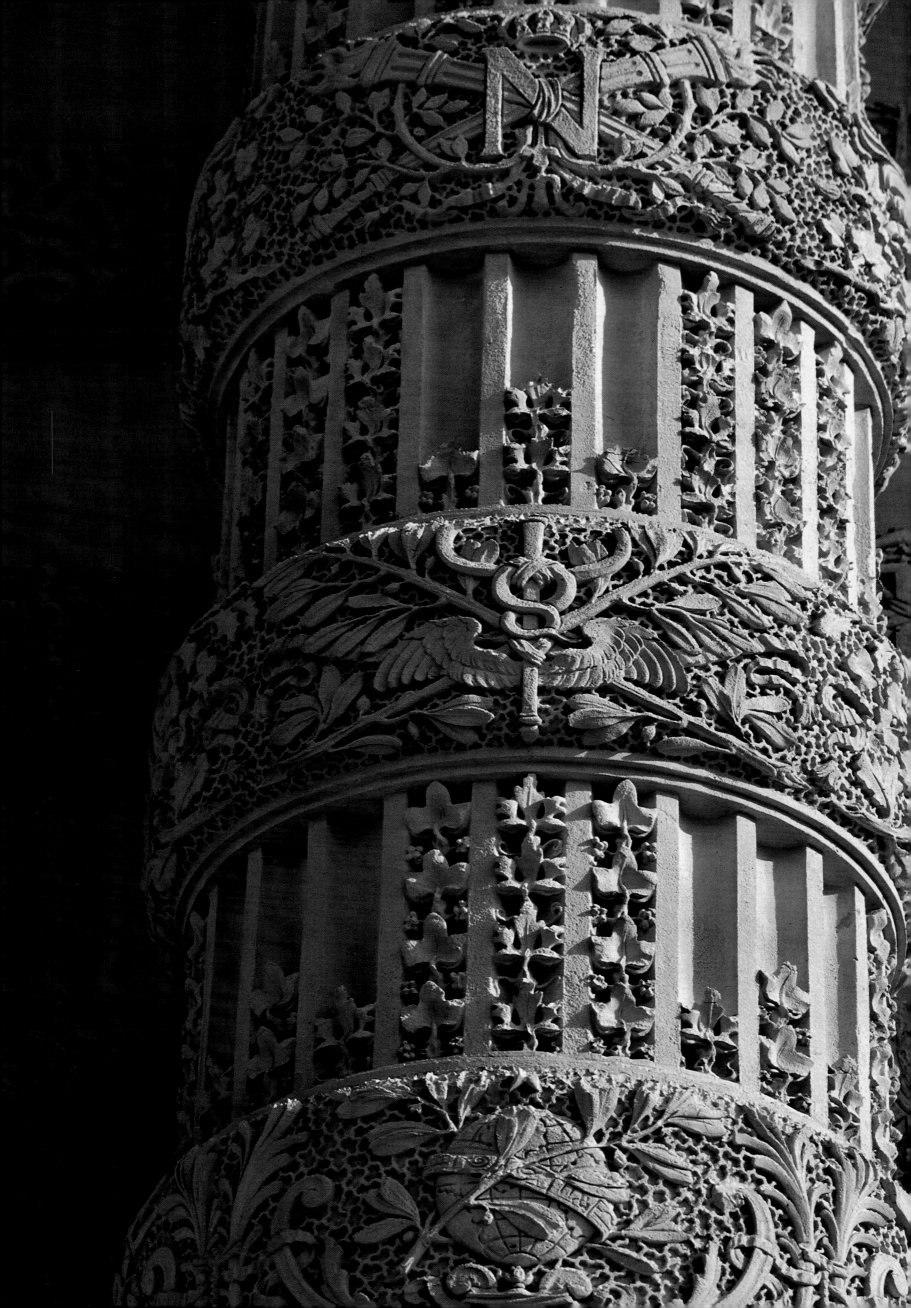

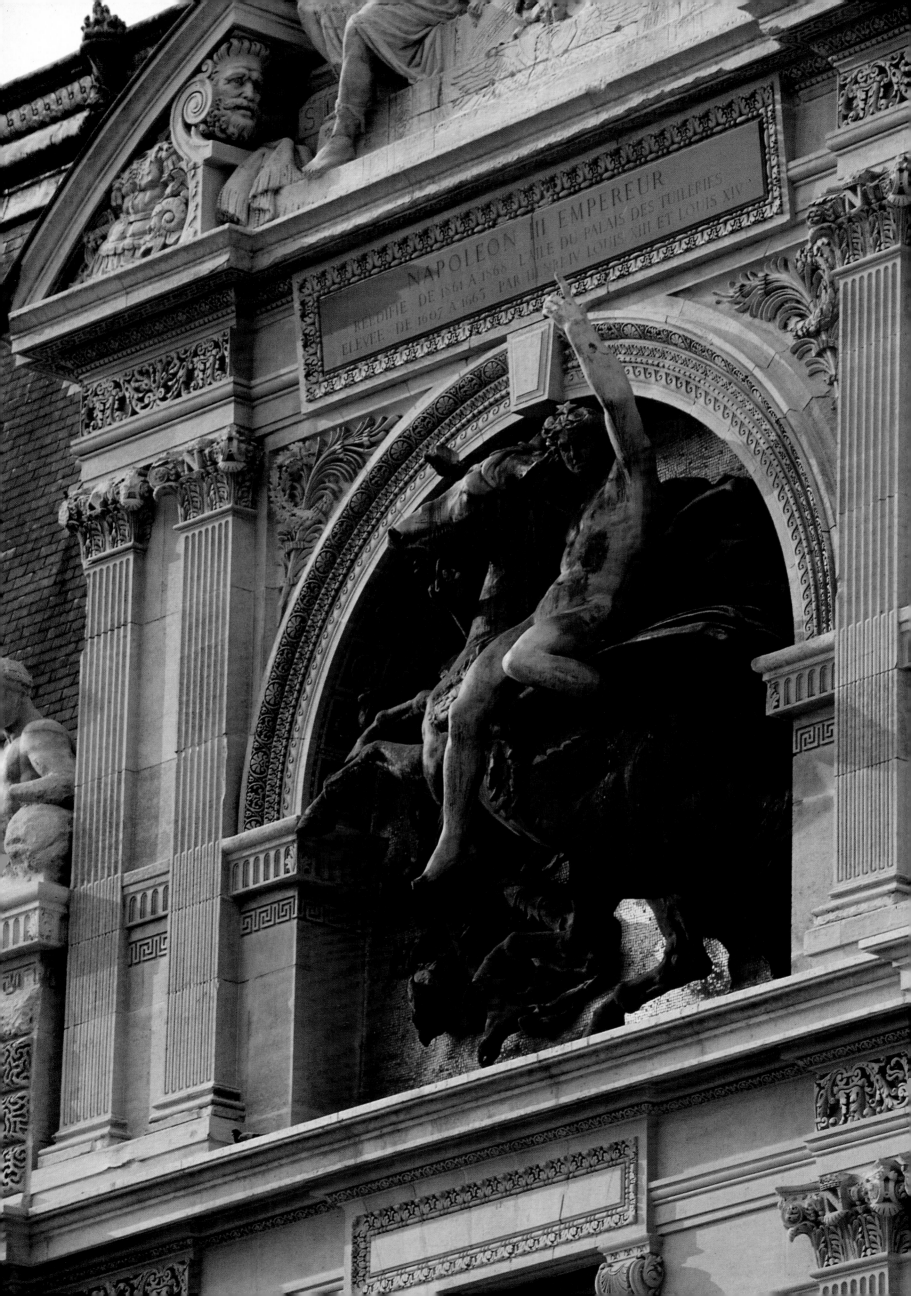

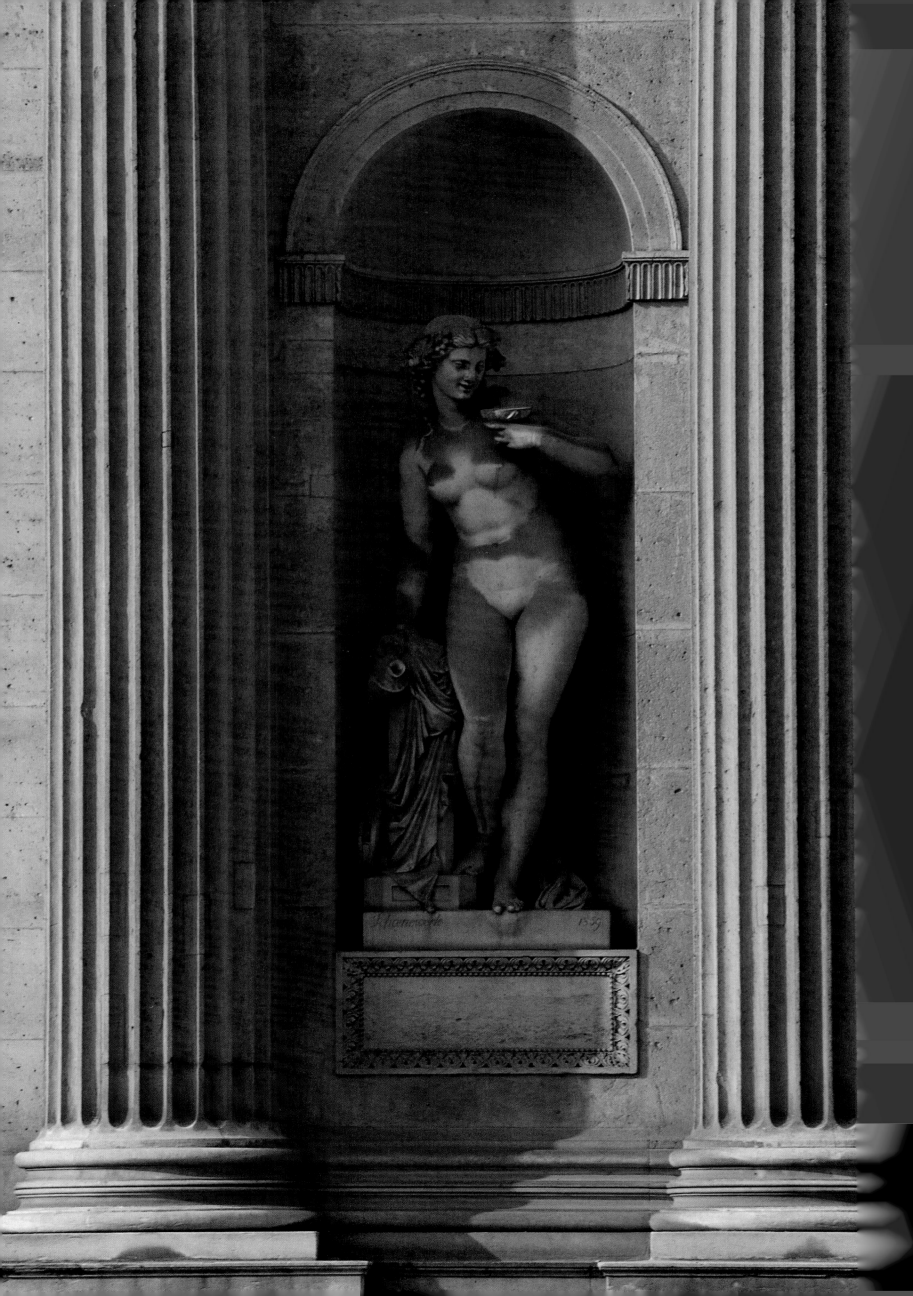

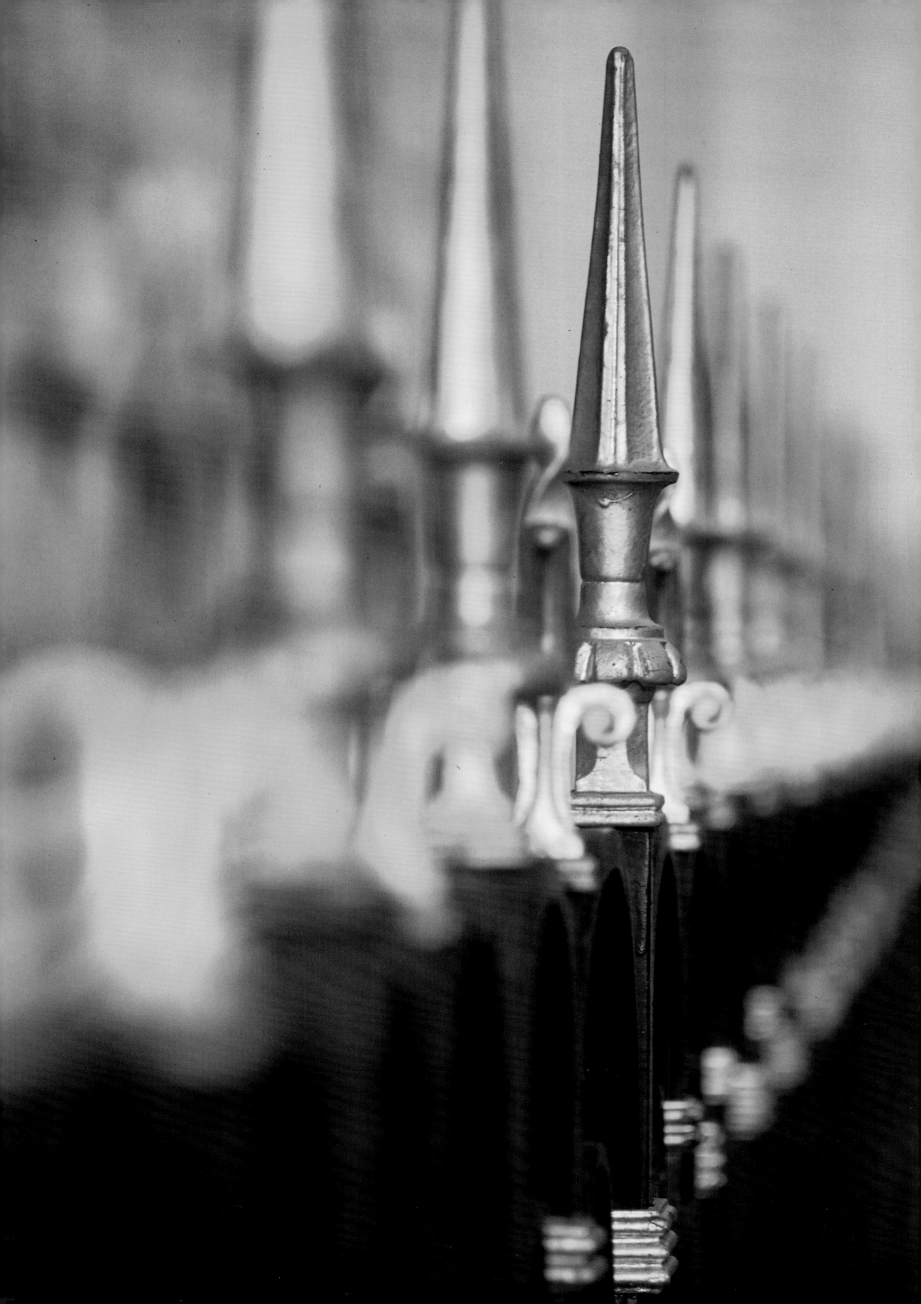

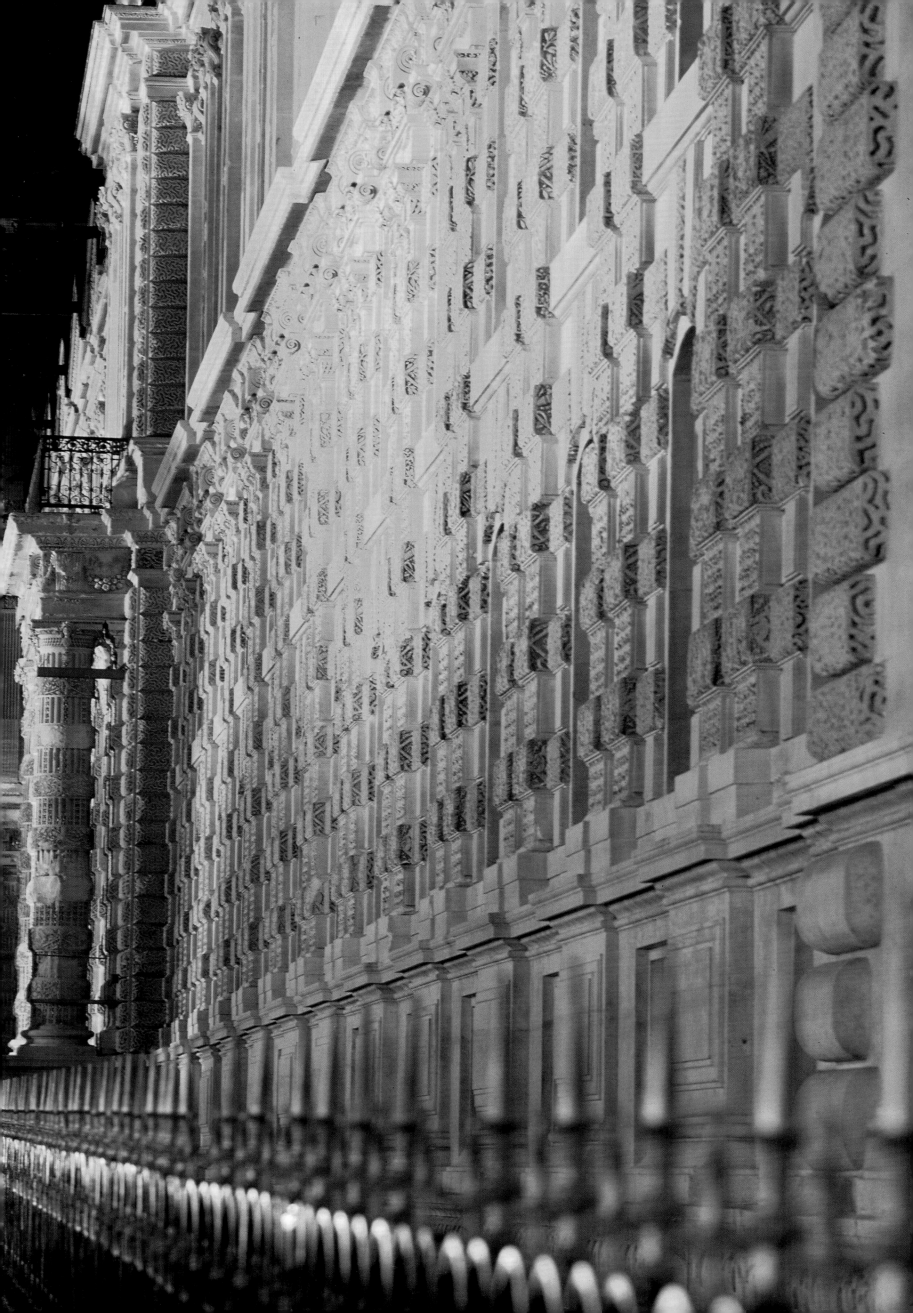

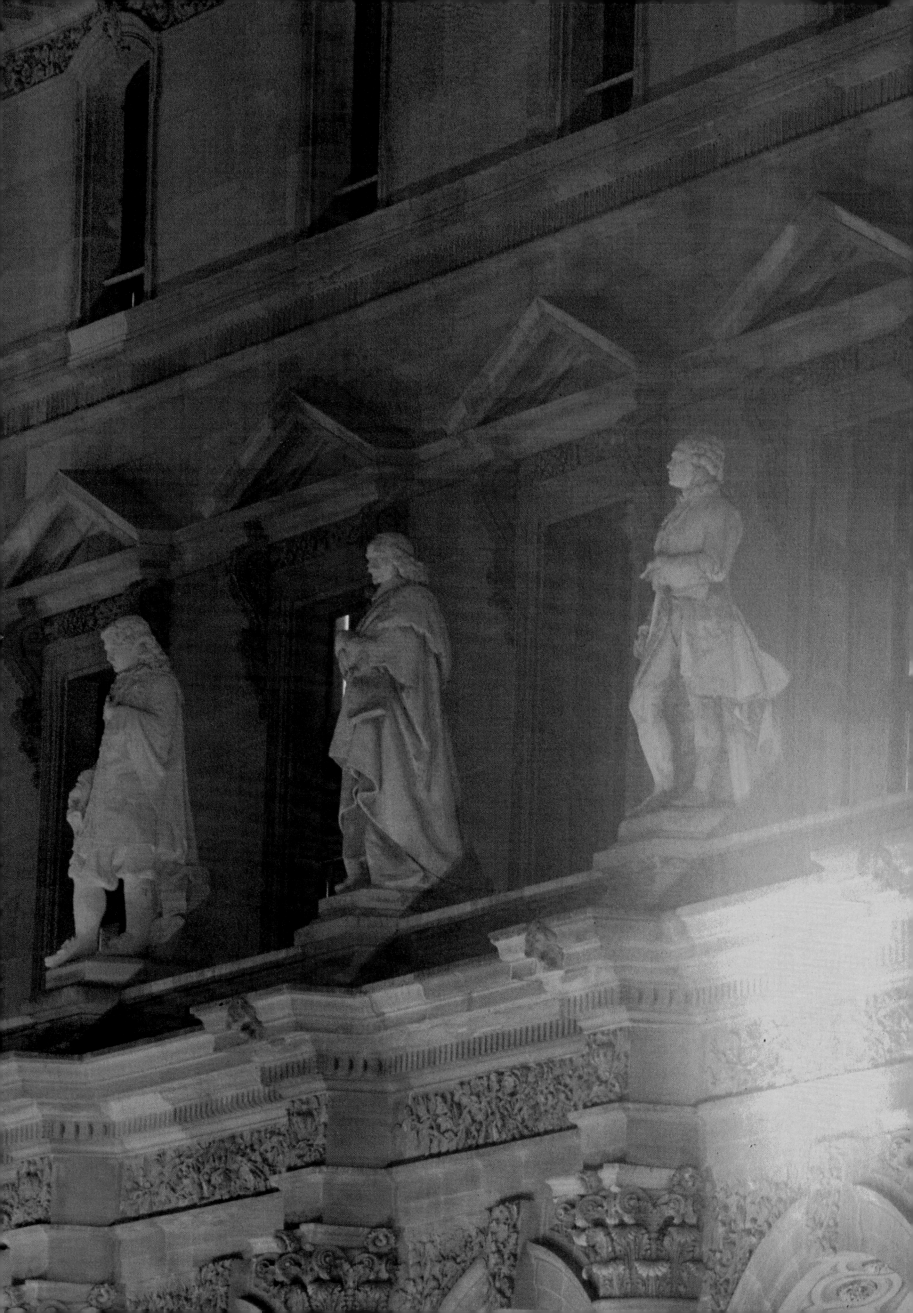

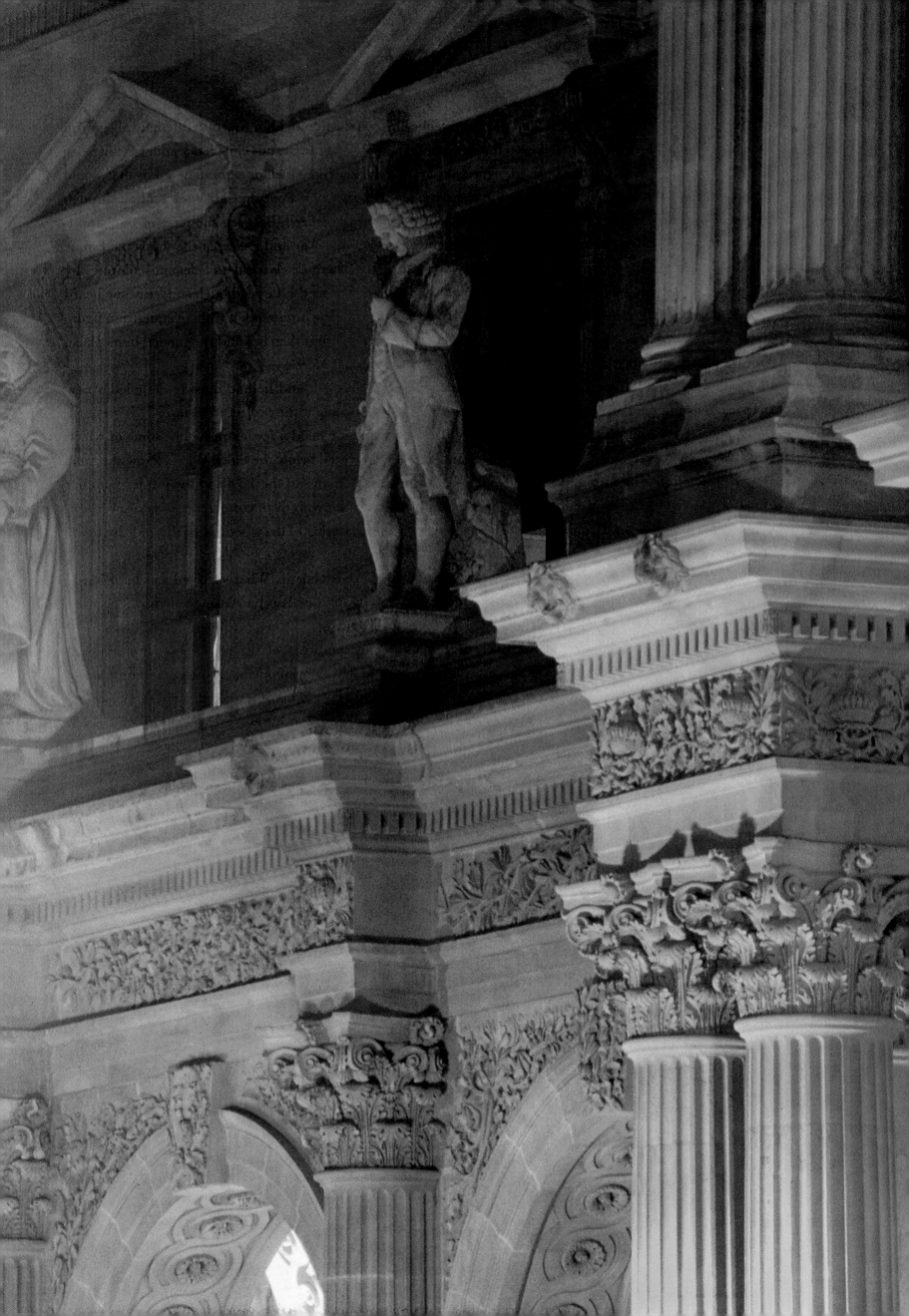

Next came the Pavillon des Etats, sober by comparison, with a row of ten female allegorical figures carved of marble. Then there followed the sculptural apotheosis of the Grands Guichets leading to the Seine (1868–69). This triple triumphal arch was designed as part of a scheme by Lefuel for a grand new axis that would cut across the city from the Opéra southward to the river, across a vast new Pont du Carrousel, and on through the left bank. Neither the bridge nor the southern extension was ever realized. Between the piers of the Grands Guichets Jouffroy provided two monumental female figures representing War and Peace; at the top is the throne of State displaying the imperial arms, surmounted by a giant eagle. Two more classical and elegant sculptures by Barye represent rivers, in the form of young men reclining crowned with reeds: it is as though suddenly one heard an individual voice in the midst of an official speech. Barye had also made a bronze relief with an equestrian figure of Napoleon III, but that was removed in 1870 and is known now only from sketches and fragments. In its place, the Third Republic provided an energetic *Genius of the Arts* by Antonin Mercié.

Even then, Lefuel did not consider his work finished, and he had already designed a new northern range containing a theatre when the Franco-Prussian War brought the project to a stop.

Within the new imperial enclave the museum had gained a few extra rooms, some of which were given splendid decoration. Another Salle des Empereurs was created below the Salon Carré. (Now the Salle d'Auguste, it should not be confused with the Salle des Empereurs Romains of the 1790s in the former Summer Apartment of Anne of Austria.) Designed to house antique sculpture, but with distinct reference to two successful modern emperors, Napoleon III and his uncle, it was given a ceiling painting of the assembly of the gods by Louis Matout, surrounded by medallions of imperial victories by Duchoiselle.

The museum had, however, lost part of the Grande Galerie. What survived was luxuriously dressed up in 1869 by two rotundas decorated with lively and voluptuous bacchanals modelled in stucco by Rodin's teacher, Albert Carrier-Belleuse.

Lefuel's greatest decorative energies went into the areas of the palace used for imperial ceremonial, such as staircases, ministries, and official halls. On the first floor of one of the new buildings, at the heart of the museum, a new Salle des Etats was opened in February 1859 to house extraordinary sessions of the assemblies presided over by the Emperor. Its decoration does not survive, but in the vestibule, or Salon Denon, the vault of 1863–66 is preserved: there, above great swags of fictive drapery, the painter Charles-Louis Müller depicted St Louis, François I, Louis XIV and Napoleon I as patrons, presiding over groups of artists in front of works of art.

On the ground floor below the Salle des Etats was the Salle du Manège, where the Prince Imperial could display his horsemanship. The vault is supported by twelve immense columns, with capitals incorporating heads of horses on the right and of bears and other animals on the left – alluding to the pleasures of riding and the hunt – carved in 1861 by Rouillard, Frémiet, Jacquemart, Demay and Houguenade. The extensive stables and quarters for grooms that originally surrounded the Manège were subsequently converted into exhibition spaces for the museum.

Amidst all the great official set-pieces in Lefuel's new buildings, the apartments of the Minister of State (now known as the 'Napoleon III Apartments') occupy a place of their own. The minister was one of the most powerful men at court, serving as a link between the Emperor and the assemblies and directing all the great building projects of the realm. The first holder of the post, Achille Fould, wanted the residence as the showcase of his power; in the event, it was inaugurated by his successor, Count Walewski (natural son of Napoleon I and Maria Walewska), with a magnificent reception in 1861.

Opposite The former Salle des Empereurs, now Salle d'Auguste, decorated under the direction of Lefuel (see also pages 157–59).
The Assembly of the Gods on the vault was painted by Matout; the tympanum at the end is by Biennoury.
Stucco compositions by Duchoiselle allude to victories of ancient, medieval and modern emperors.

(For captions to *pages 146–53*, see page 154.)

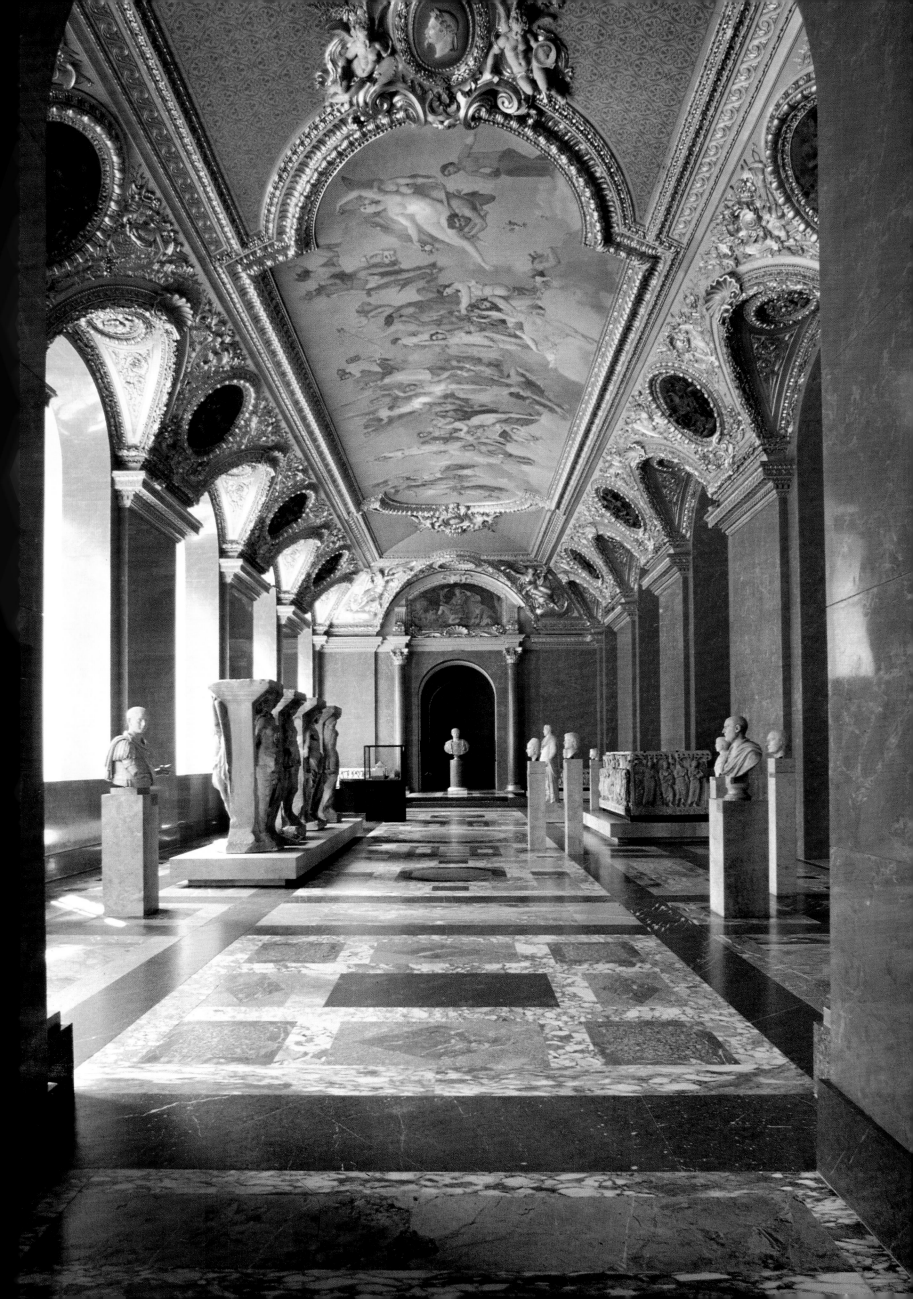

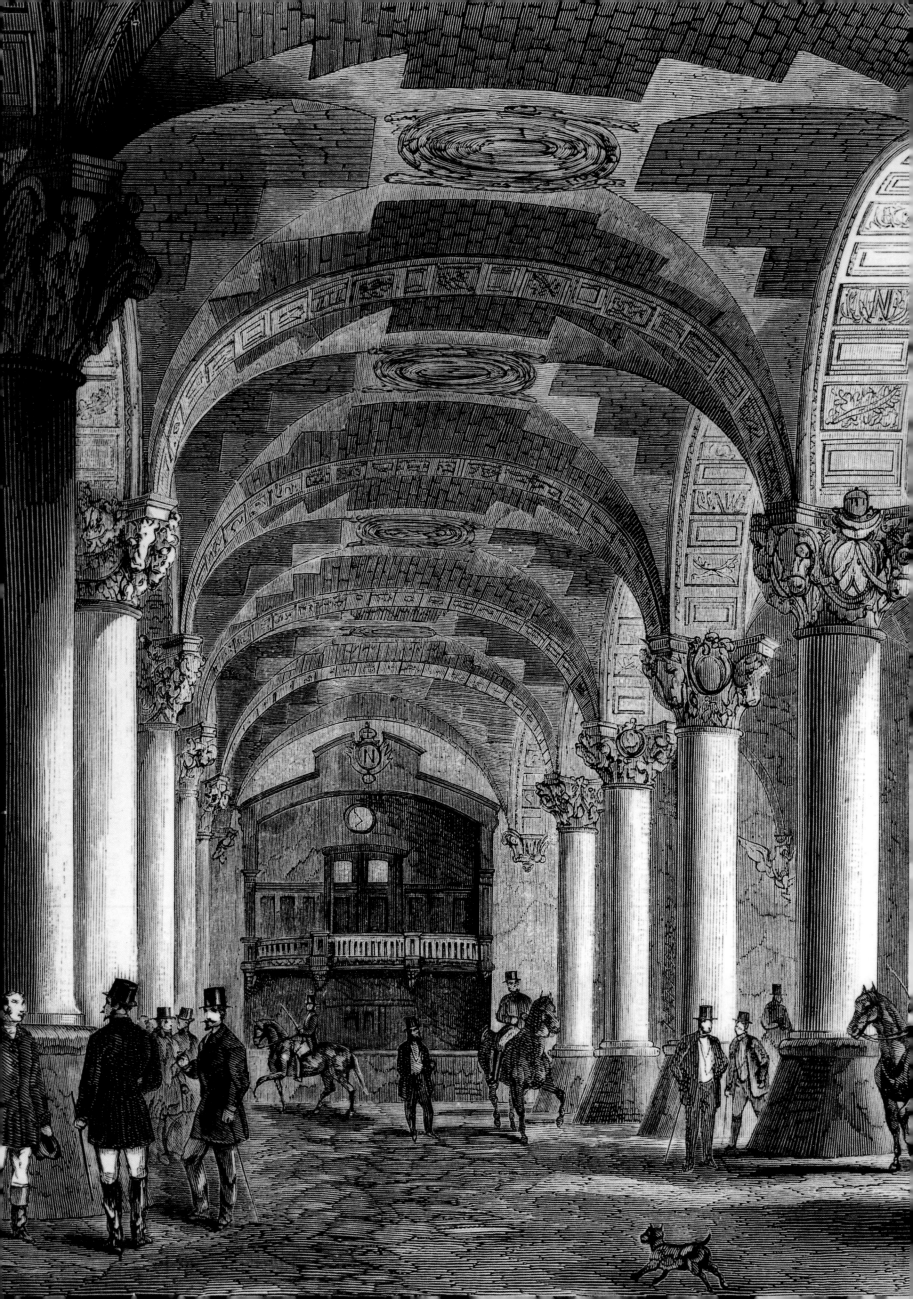

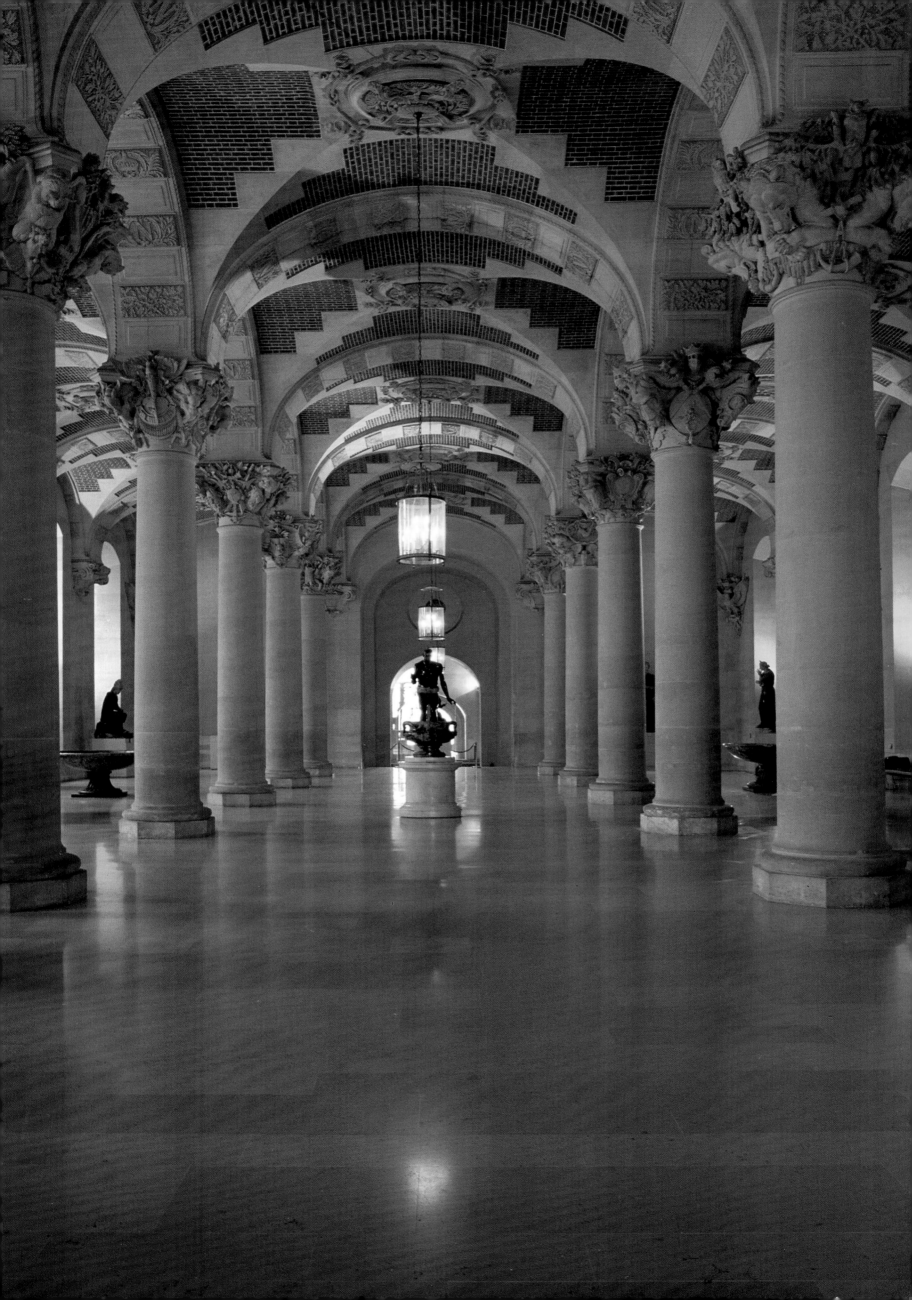

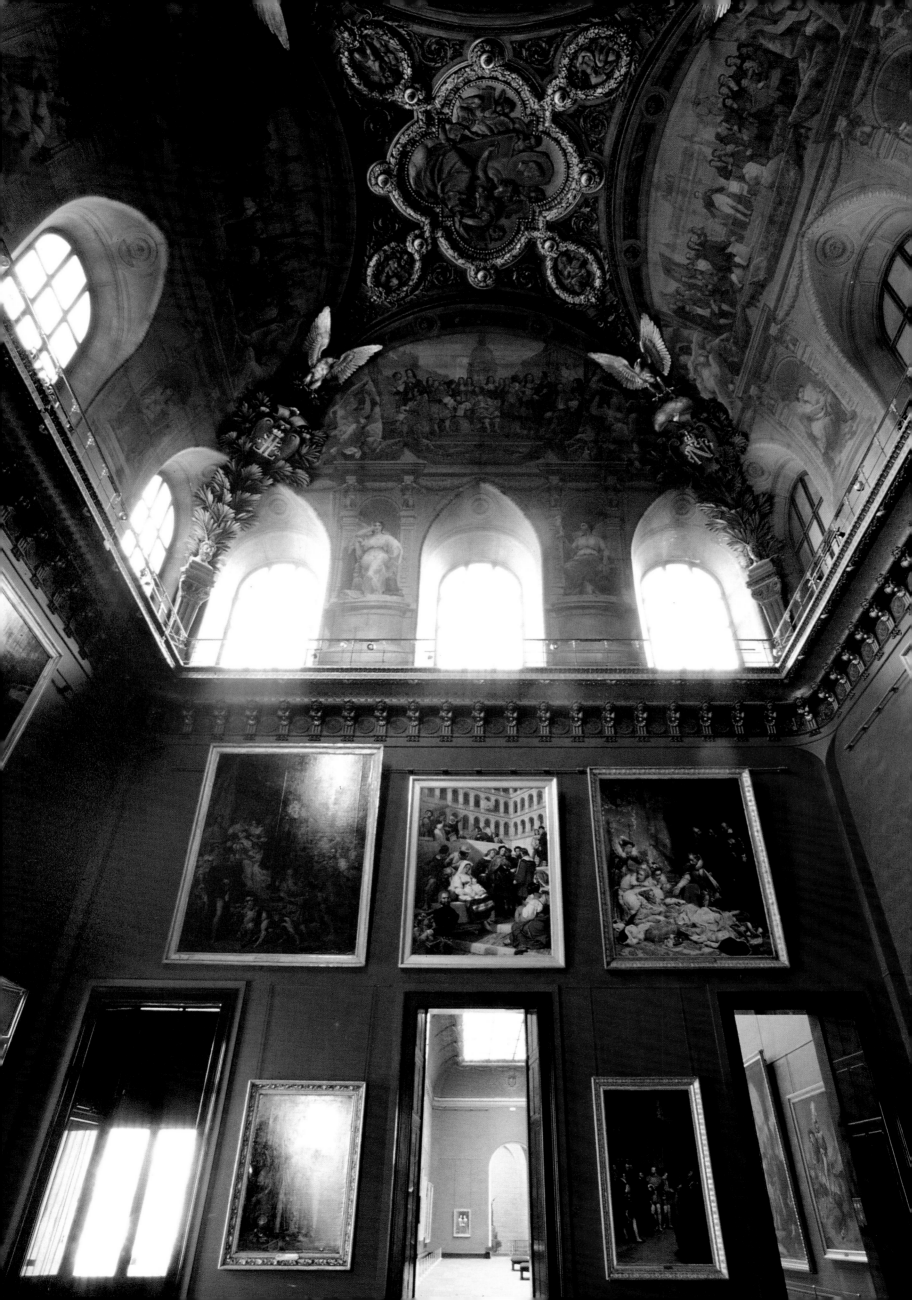

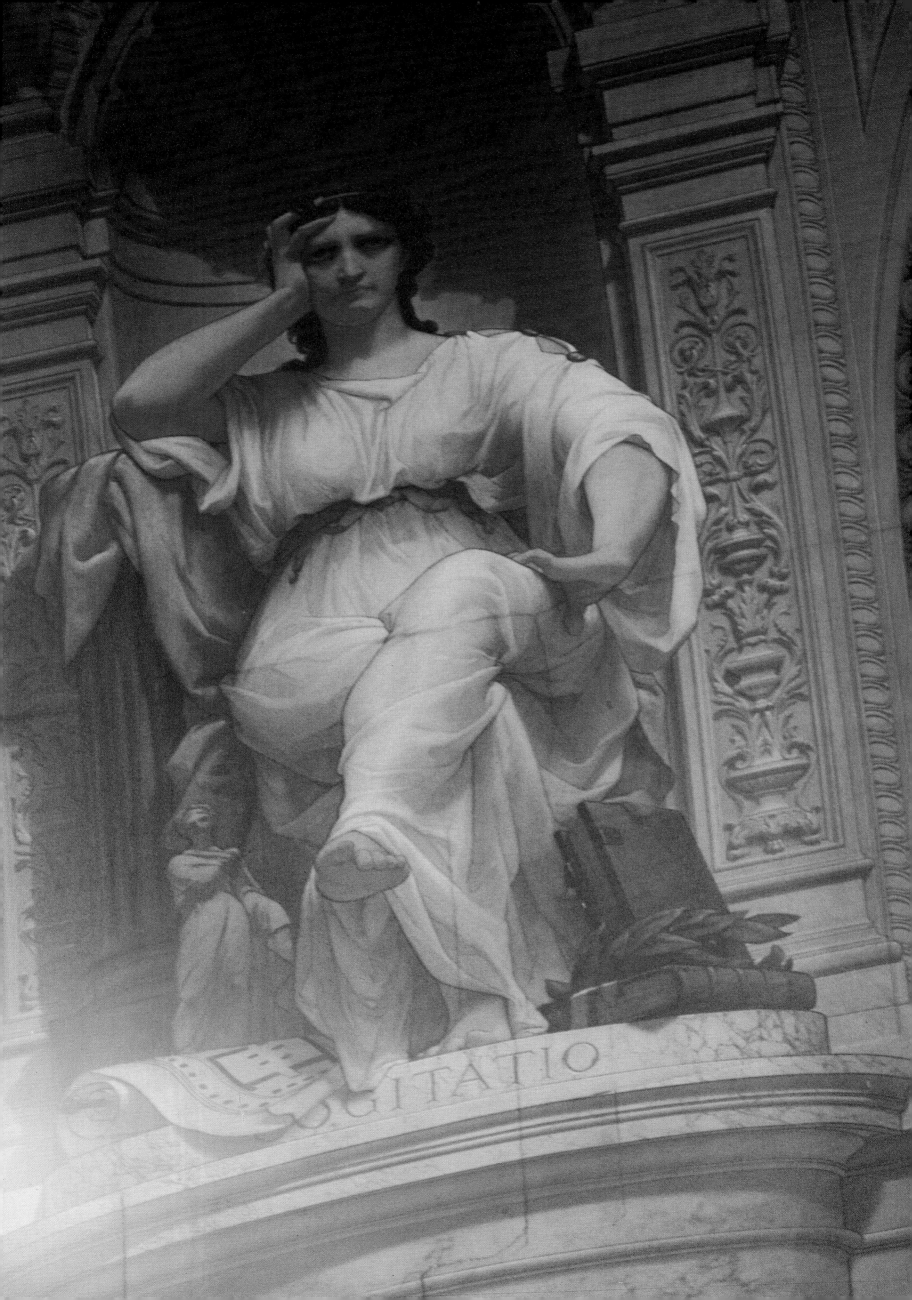

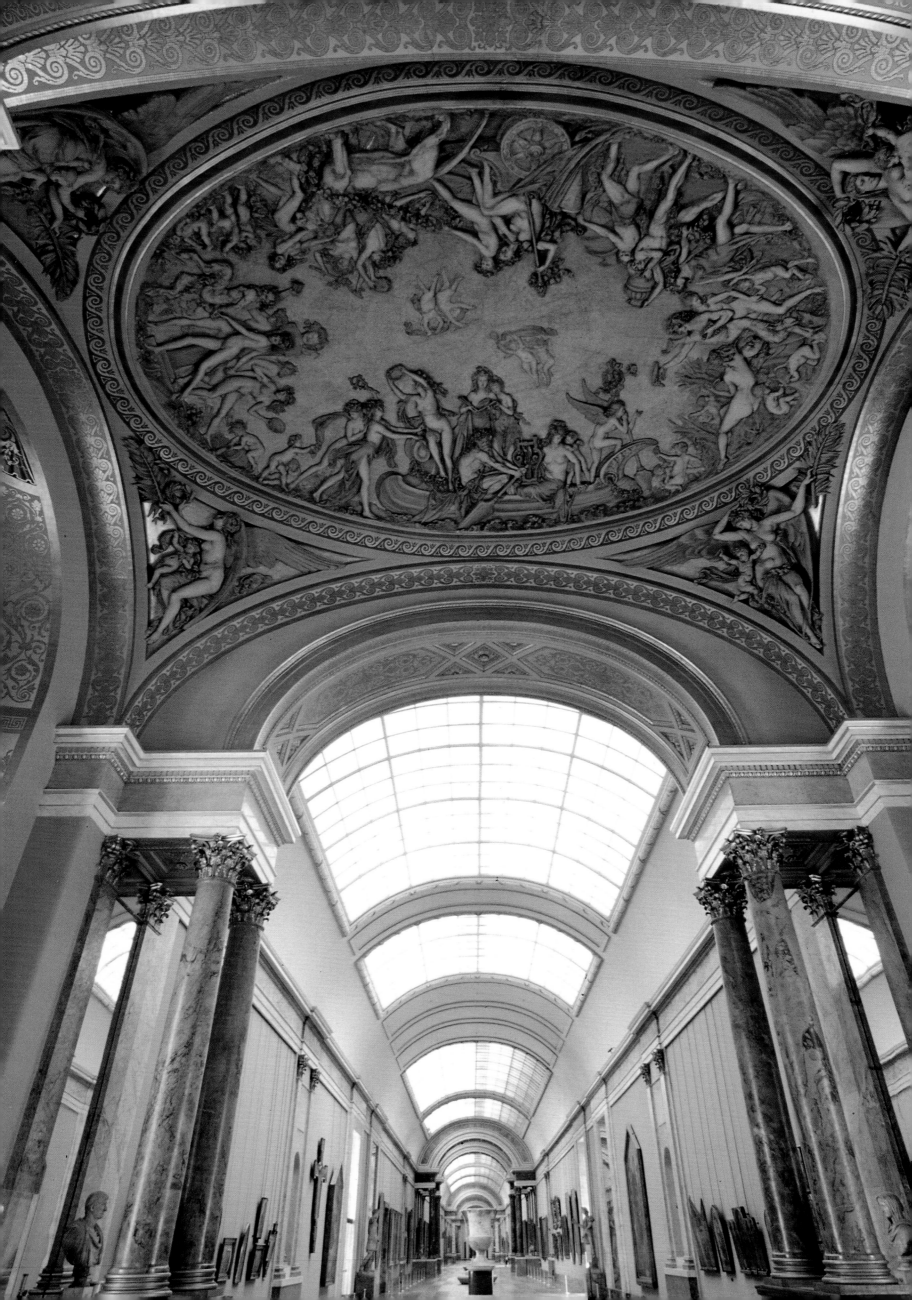

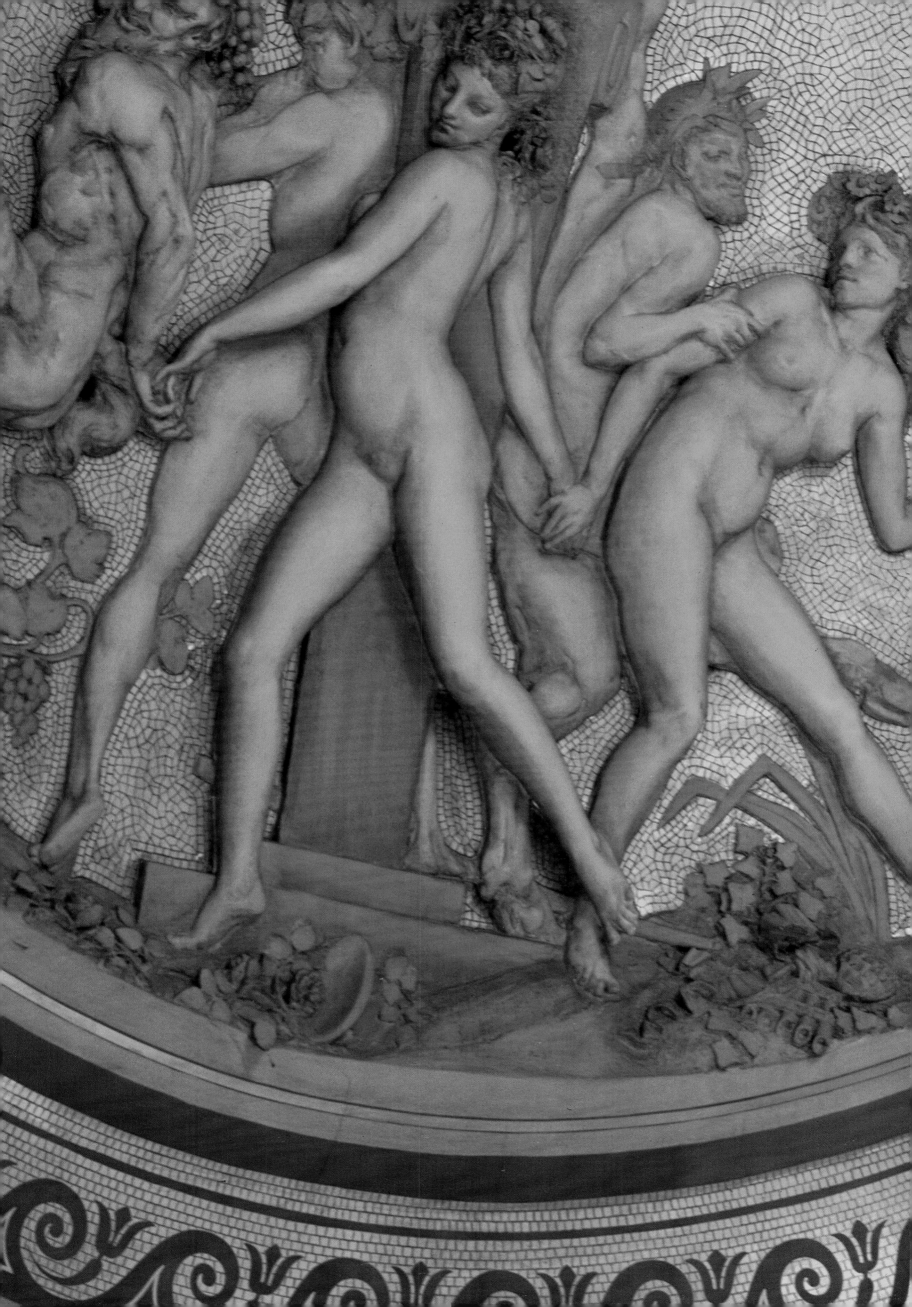

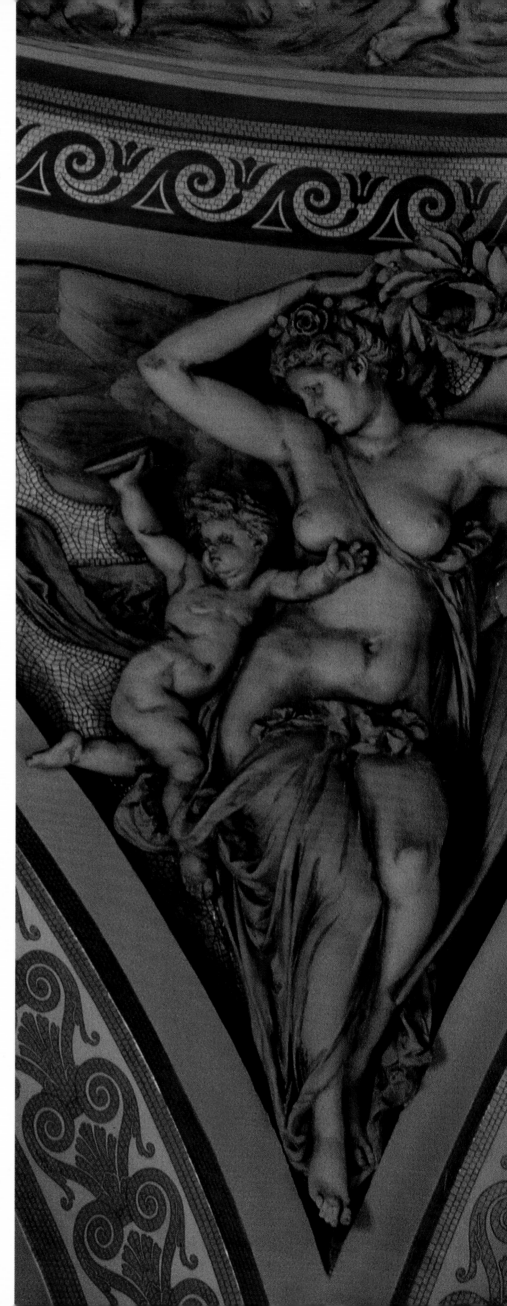

Pages 146, 147 The Salle du Manège, designed for schooling horses. The decoration, conceived by Lefuel and executed by Frémiet, Rouillard, Jacquemart, Demay and Houguenade, includes capitals with animal heads that allude to the hunt and to riding. The room now serves to display antique sculptures restored for great collectors in the seventeenth and eighteenth century, especially those incorporating coloured marble.

Pages 148–51 The Salon Denon, with decoration designed by Lefuel comprising paintings by Müller and stucco by Olivia. In the centre of the vault a trompe-l'oeil quatrefoil depicts the personification of France writing, below a portrait of Napoleon III. Surrounding it are painted tympana representing the patronage of French rulers – St Louis, François I, Louis XIV and Napoleon I (counter-clockwise from the left on *pages 150–51*). The figure of *Thought* (*page 149*) is placed below the scene of Louis XIV.

Pages 152, 153 and *opposite* The rotunda of the Pavillon Lesdiguières, rebuilt by Lefuel and given a dome decorated with white stucco on a gold ground by Carrier-Belleuse. The view on *page 152* shows the vista through to the Grande Galerie.

The years 1859–61 had seen teams of artists furiously at work – the painters Appert, Gendron, Charles-Raphaël Maréchal and even the landscapist Charles-François Daubigny, and the sculptors Tranchant and Knecht – and gold leaf shone in the suite of state rooms, from the Grand Salon, the Salon-Théâtre, the Small Dining Room and the Great Dining Room through to the small so-called 'family apartment', in what is one of the outstanding examples of the opulent decorative style of the Second Empire. In the manner of Müller in the Salon Denon, Maréchal painted the ceiling of the Grand Salon with a somewhat sketchy rendering of rulers surrounded by artists preparing the decorative style of the Louvre and the Tuileries.

The Louvre of Napoleon III was also a palace of staircases. The grand staircase of the museum – the Daru Staircase where the *Winged Victory* stands today – was never completed, and only its bold underlying structure is by Lefuel, but elsewhere the architect provided a dazzling array. There is the Mollien Staircase, which leads to the displays of painting; the staircase now known in its designer's honour as the Lefuel Staircase, whose ingenious unsupported flights and landings decorated with reliefs gave access to the Imperial Library; the Minister's Staircase, leading to the grand apartments, with its glittering chandeliers, gleaming columns, and landscapes by Daubigny; and finally the Escalier de Flore, designed to serve the reception rooms of visiting foreign rulers, of which only the upper part was decorated on Lefuel's instructions, after the fall of the Empire, with large reliefs by Eugène Guillaume. (It is now the students' room of the Department of Prints and Drawings.)

Opposite and *pages 158–59* Decoration of the Salle des Empereurs, now Salle d'Auguste (see page 145). The Victories in the corners are by Duchoiselle; the ceiling, depicting *The Assembly of the Gods*, by Matout.

(For captions to *pages 160–75*, see page 170.)

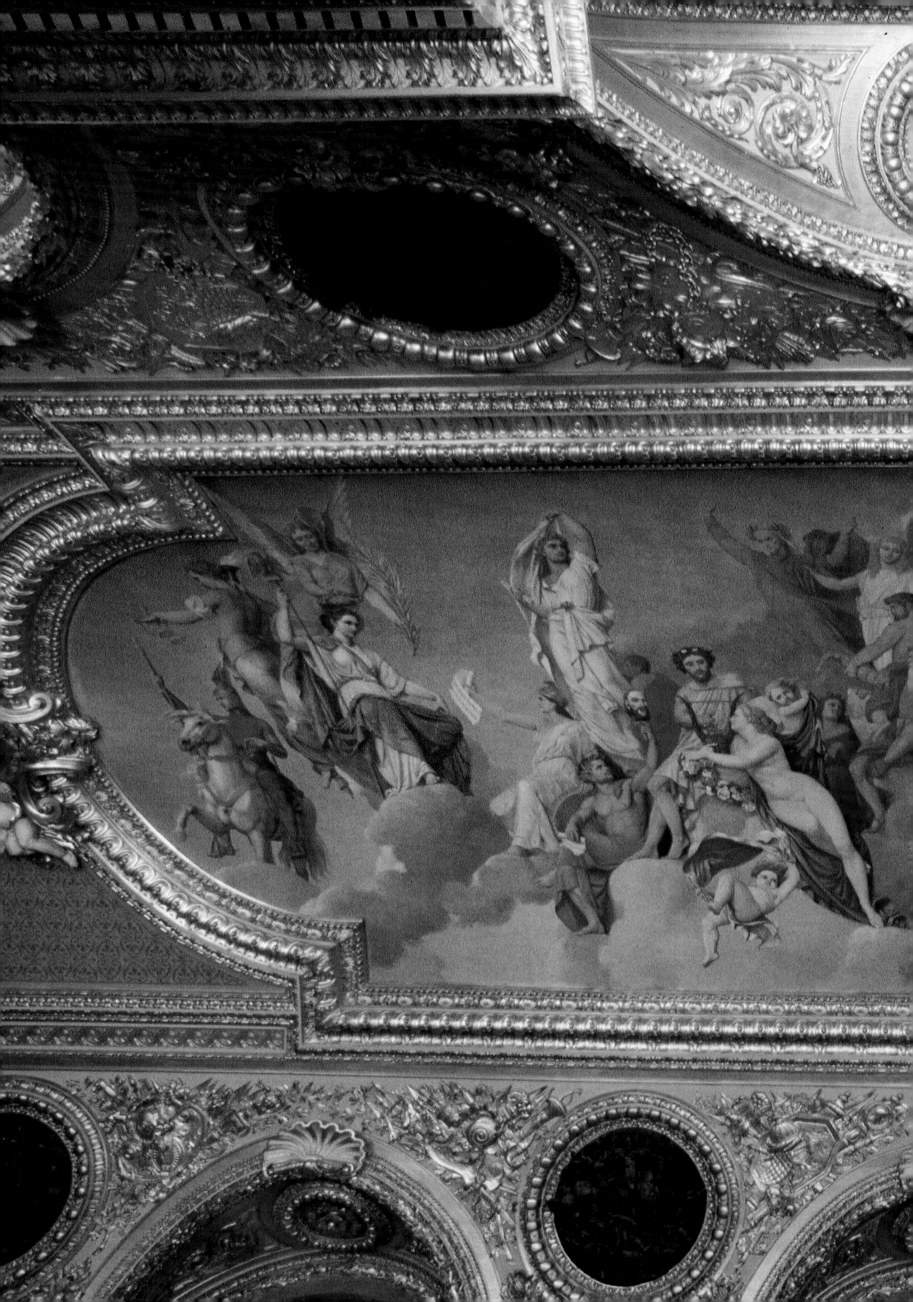

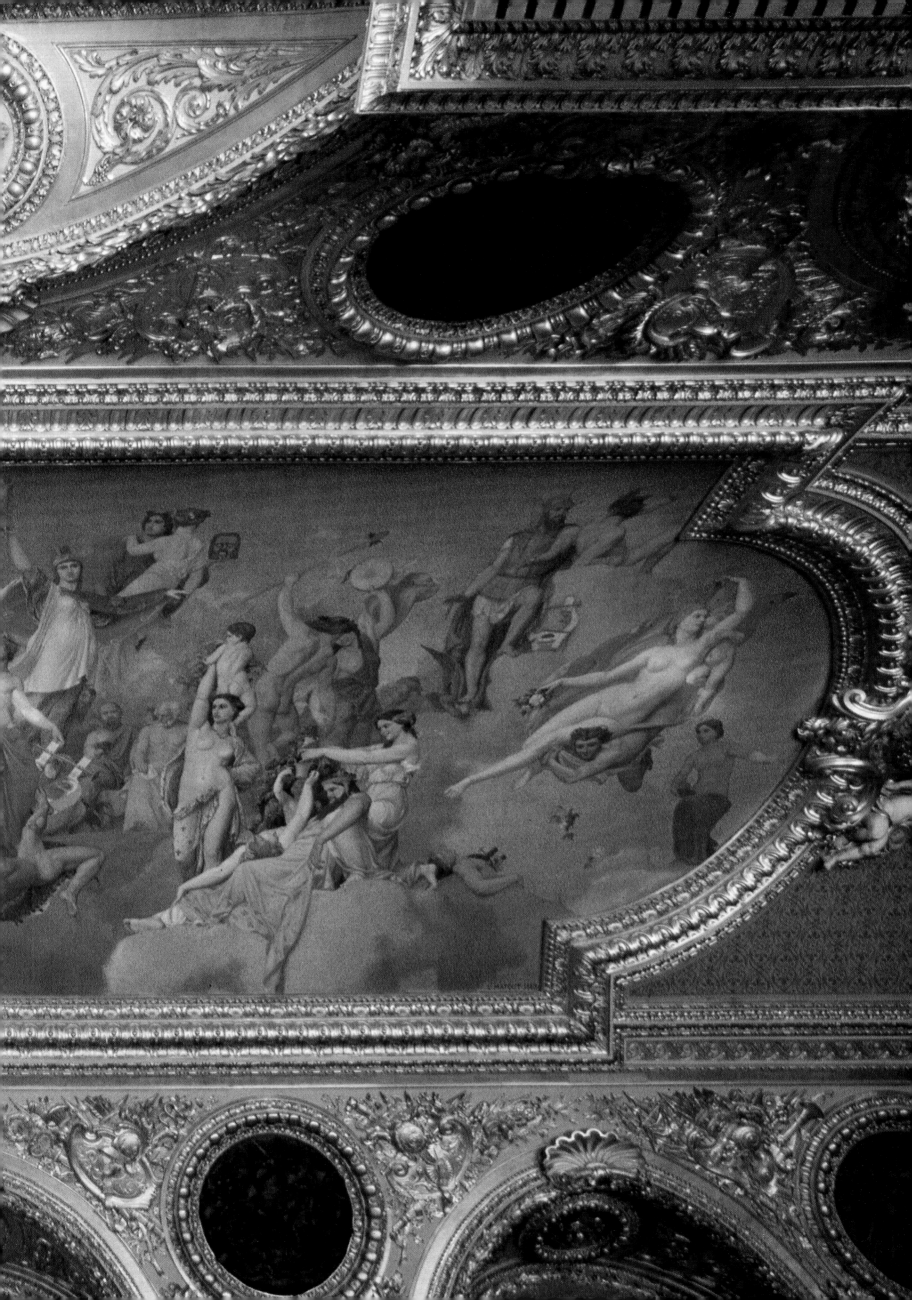

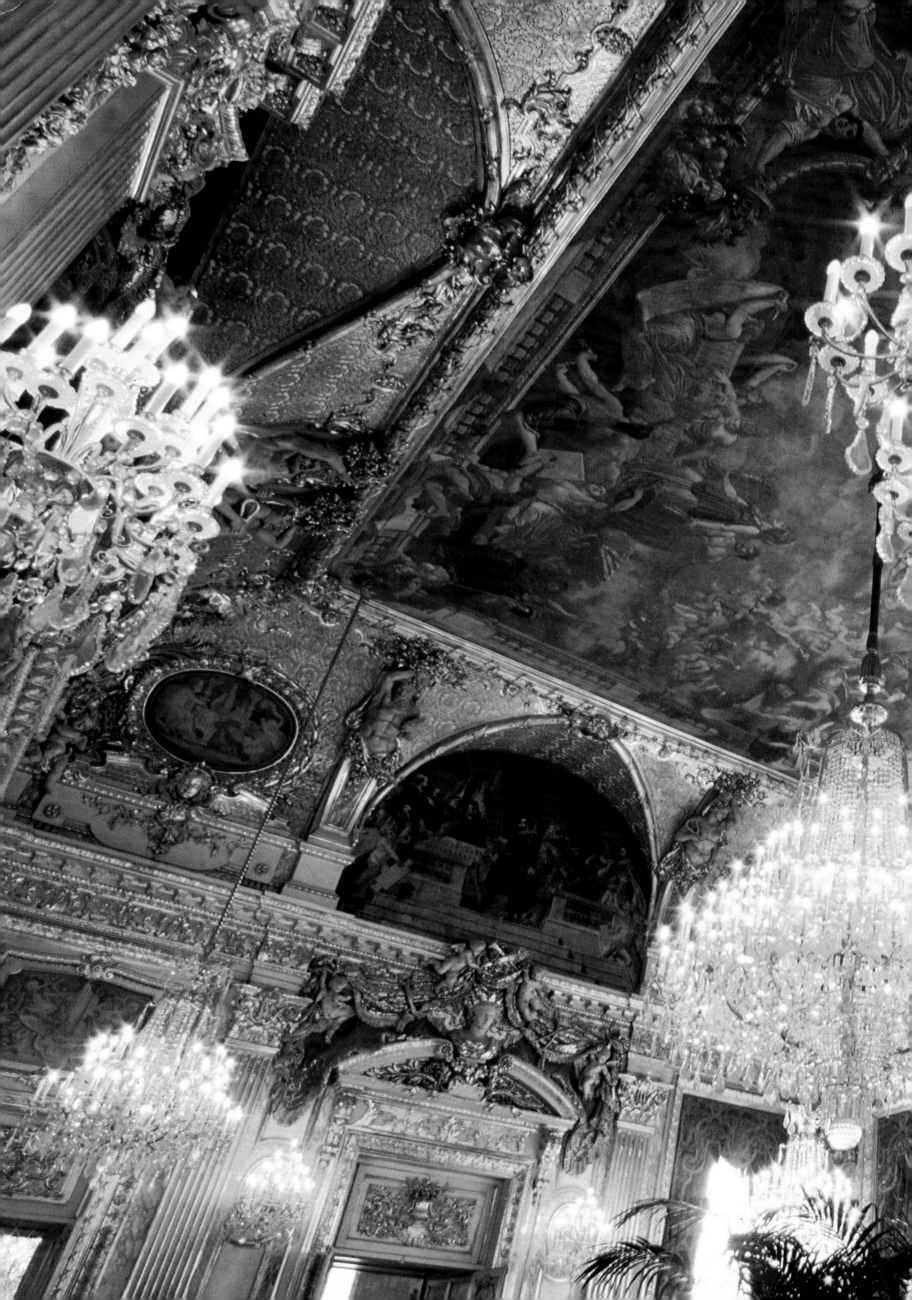

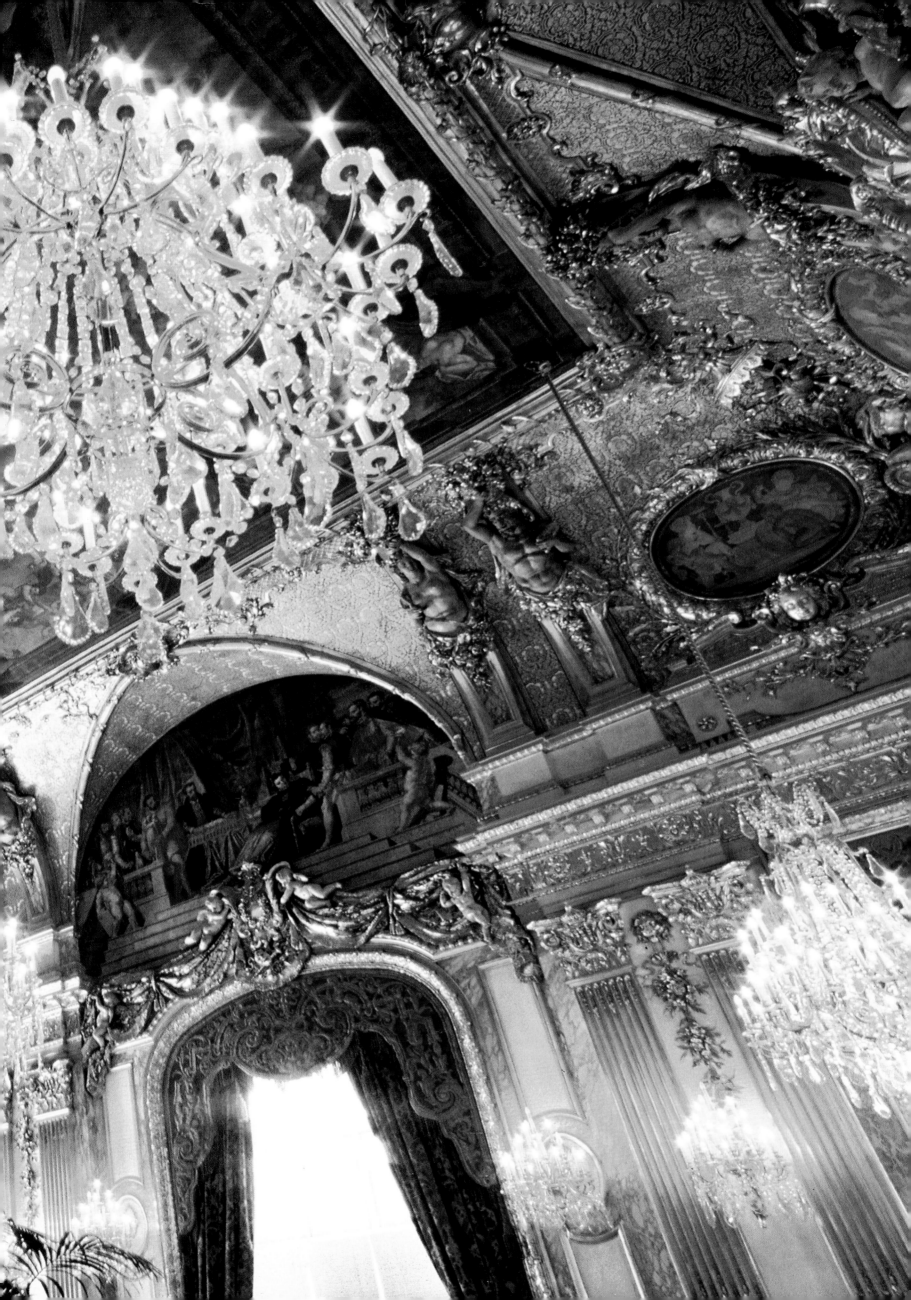

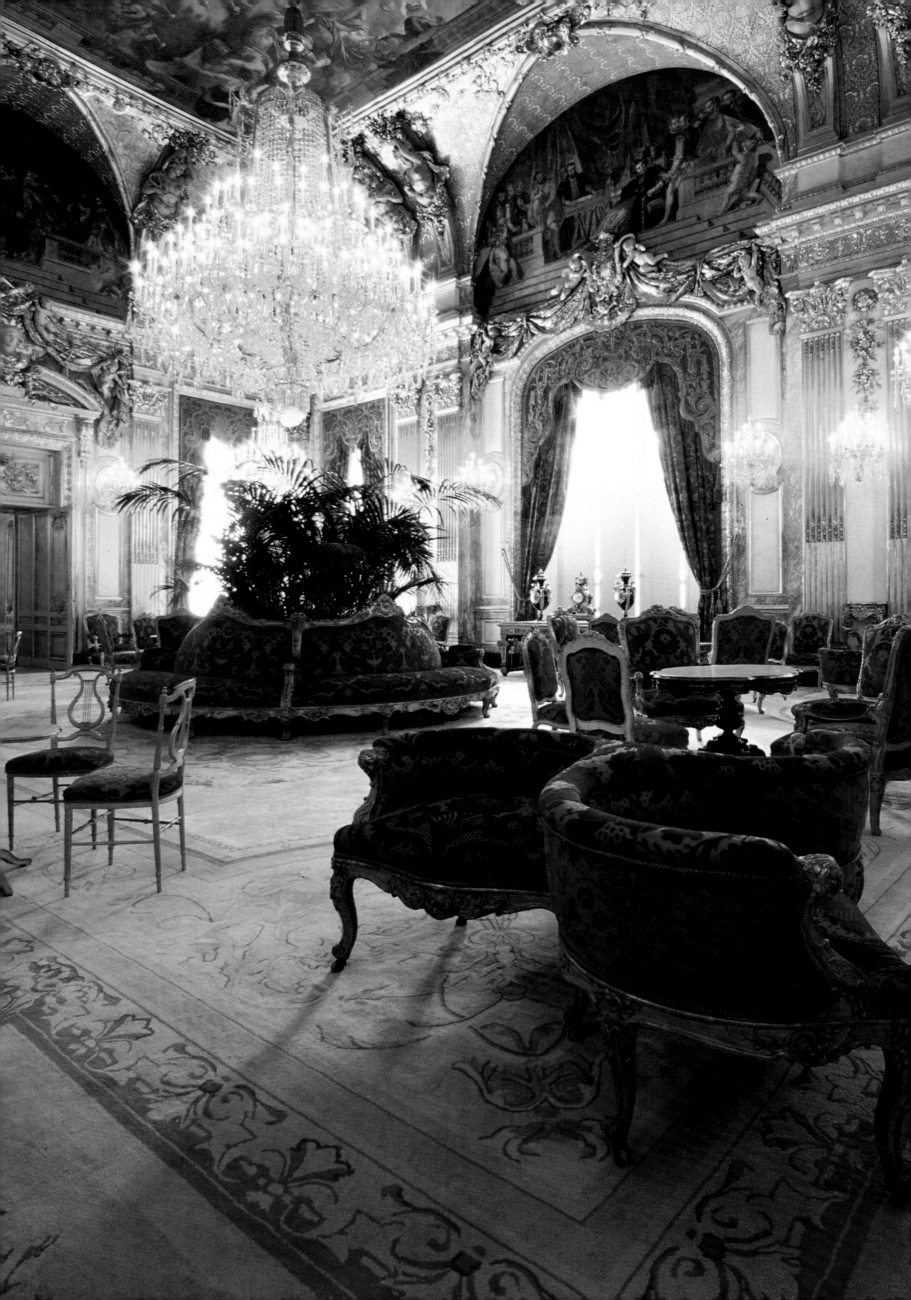

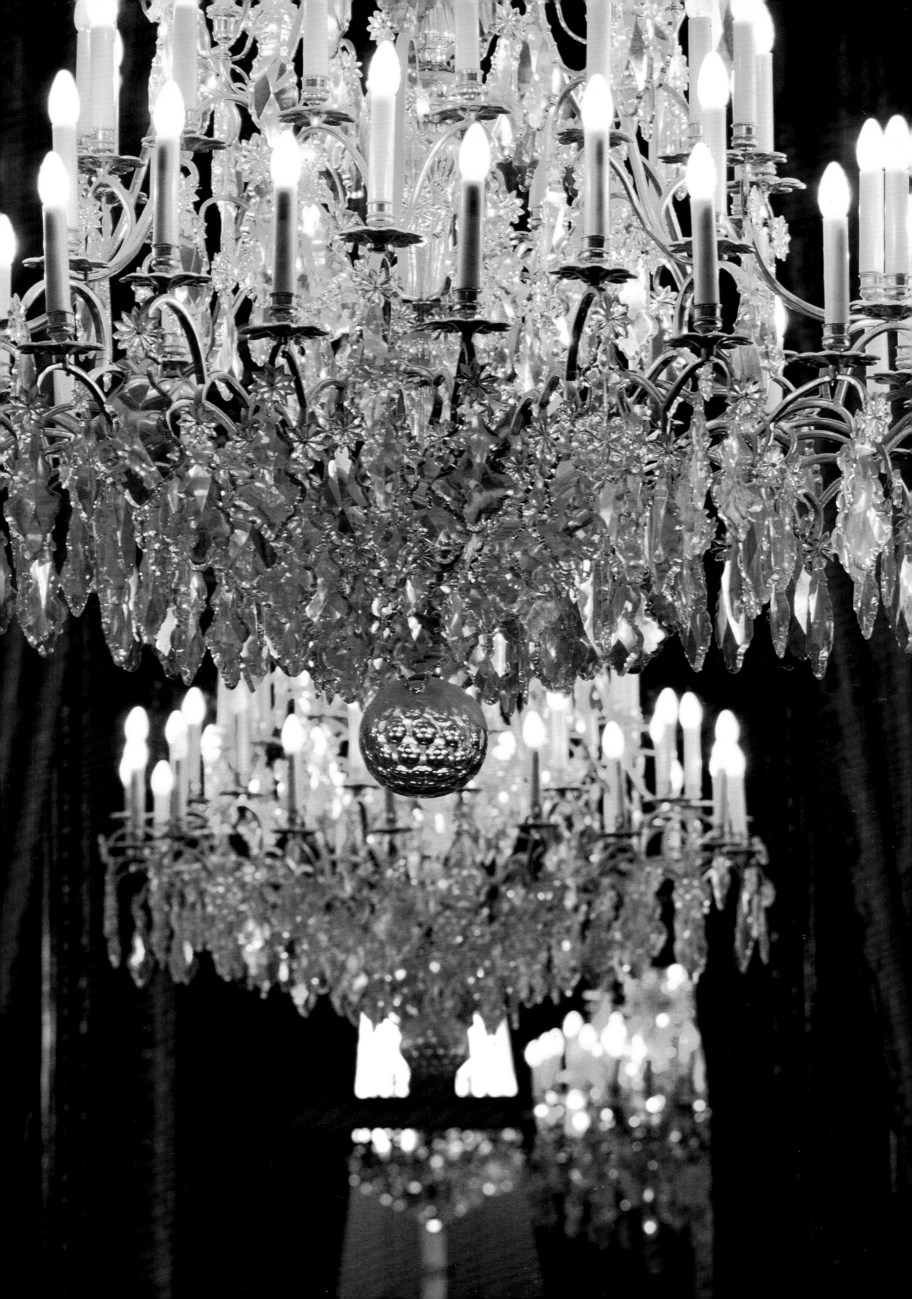

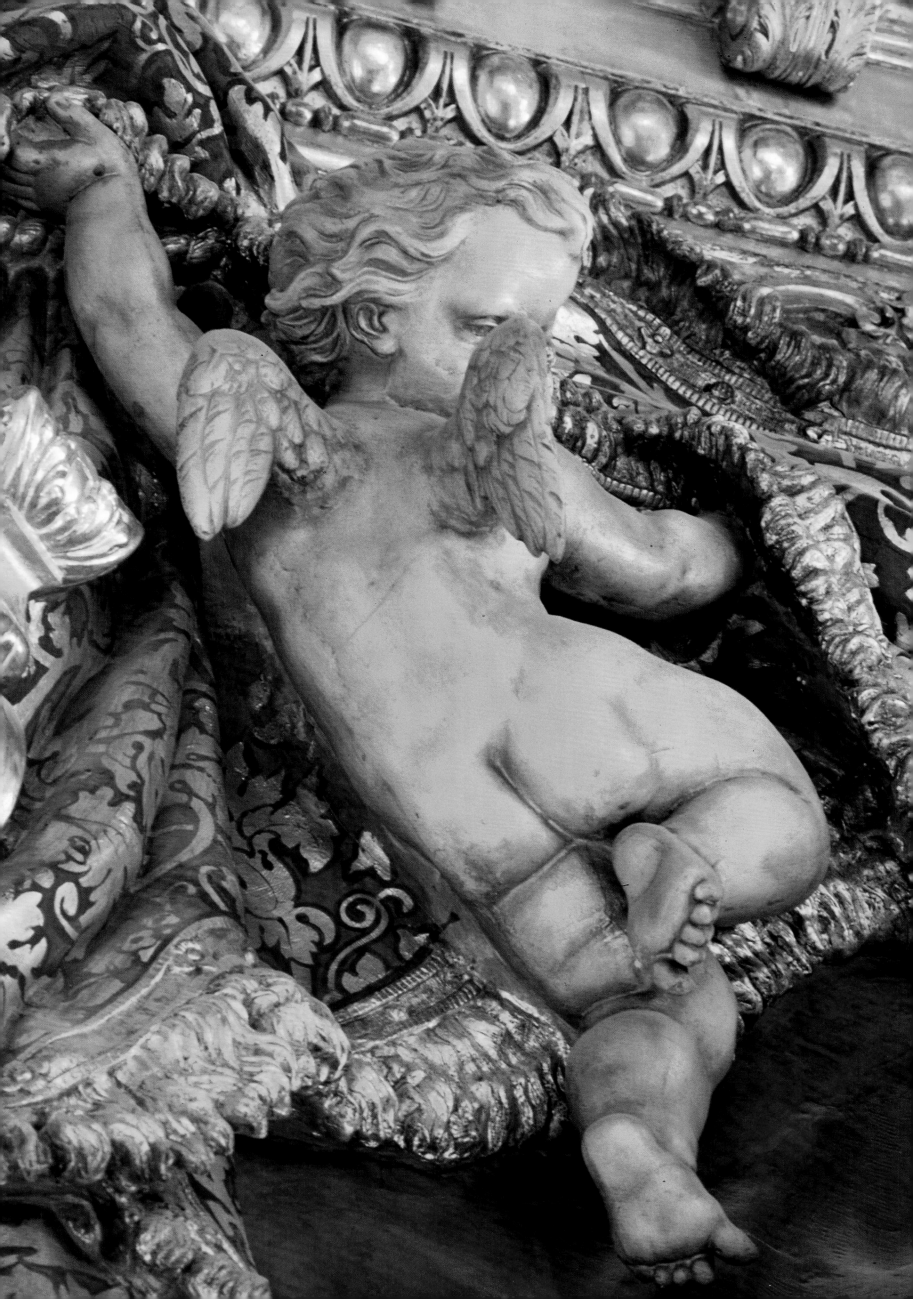

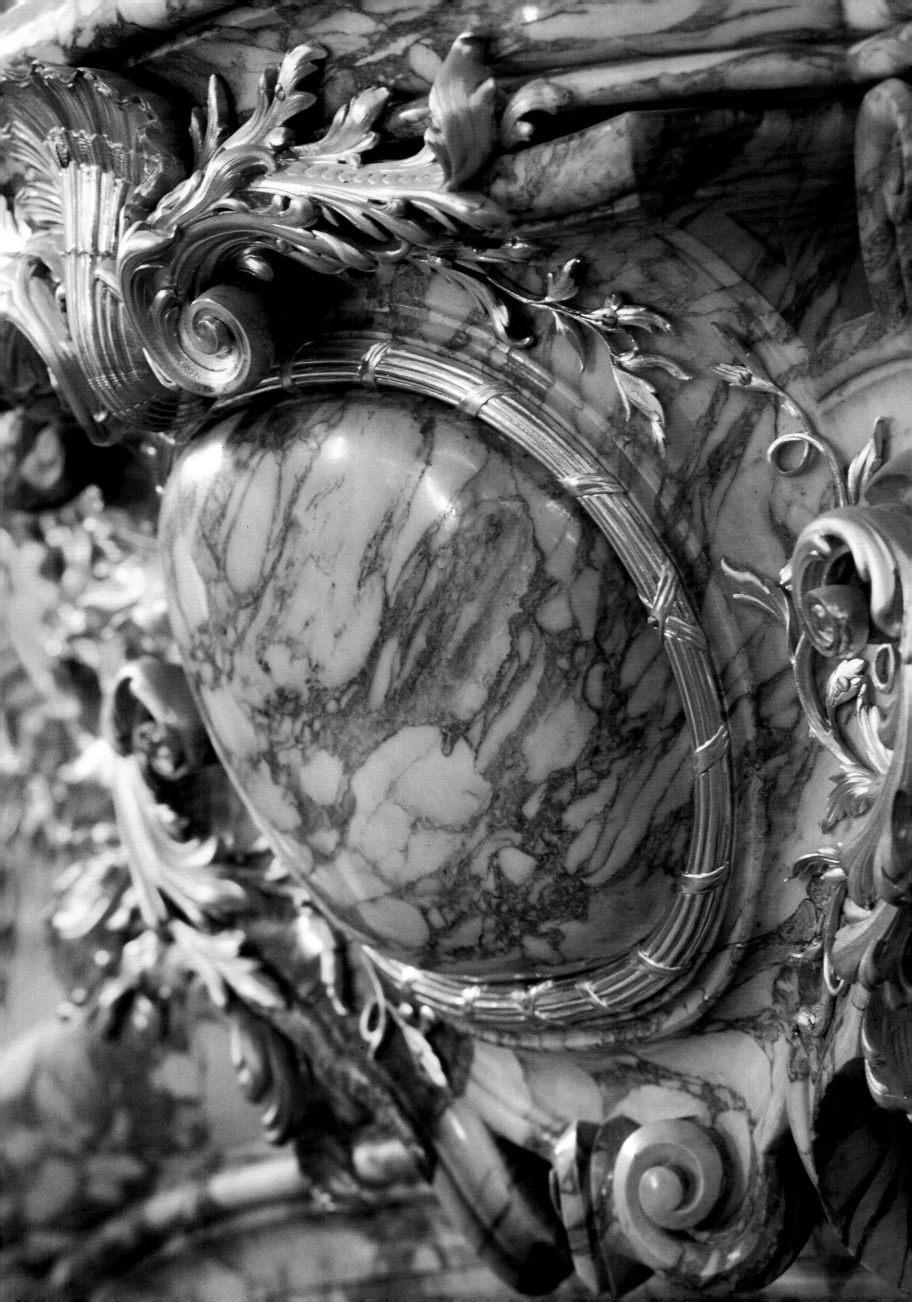

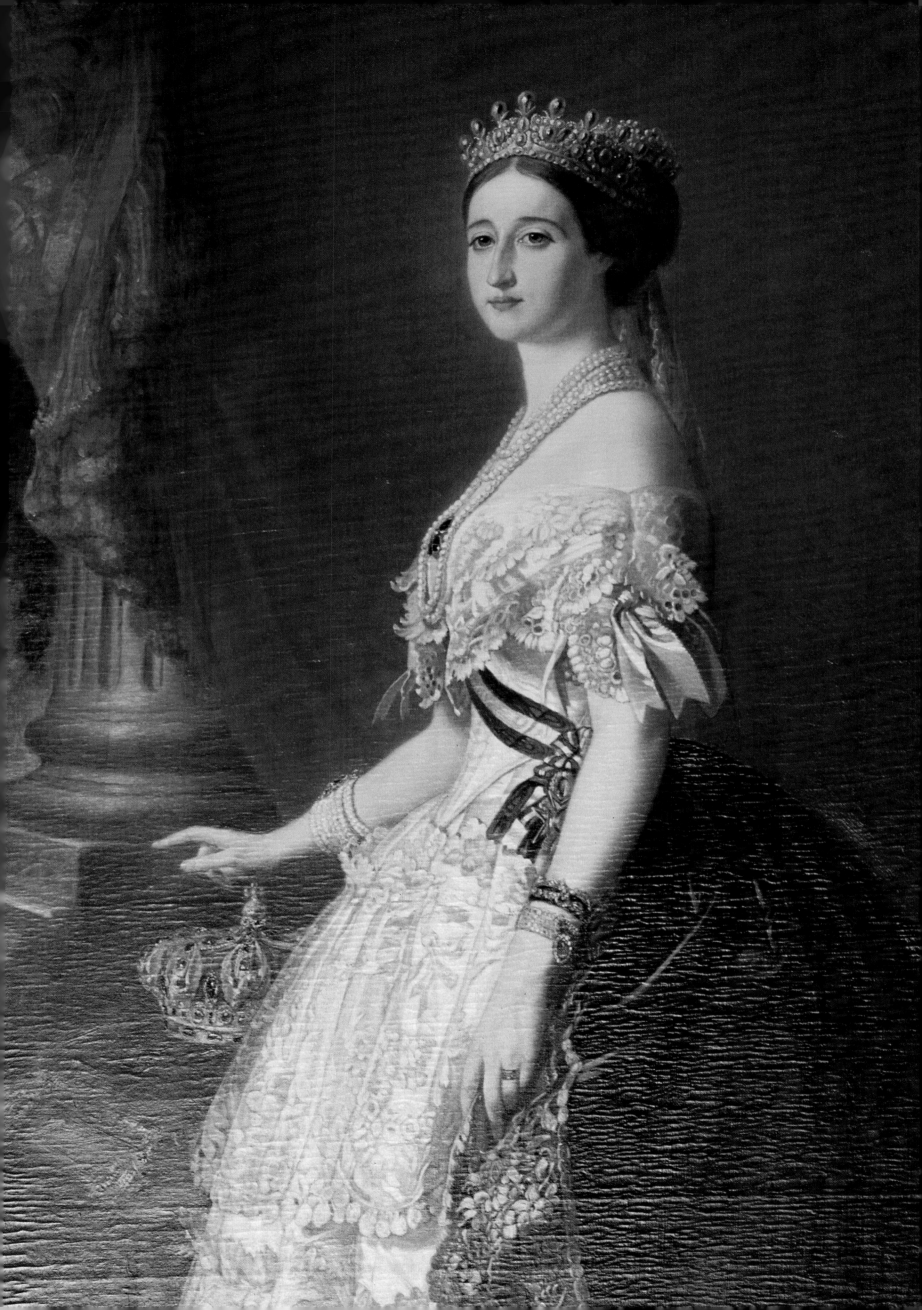

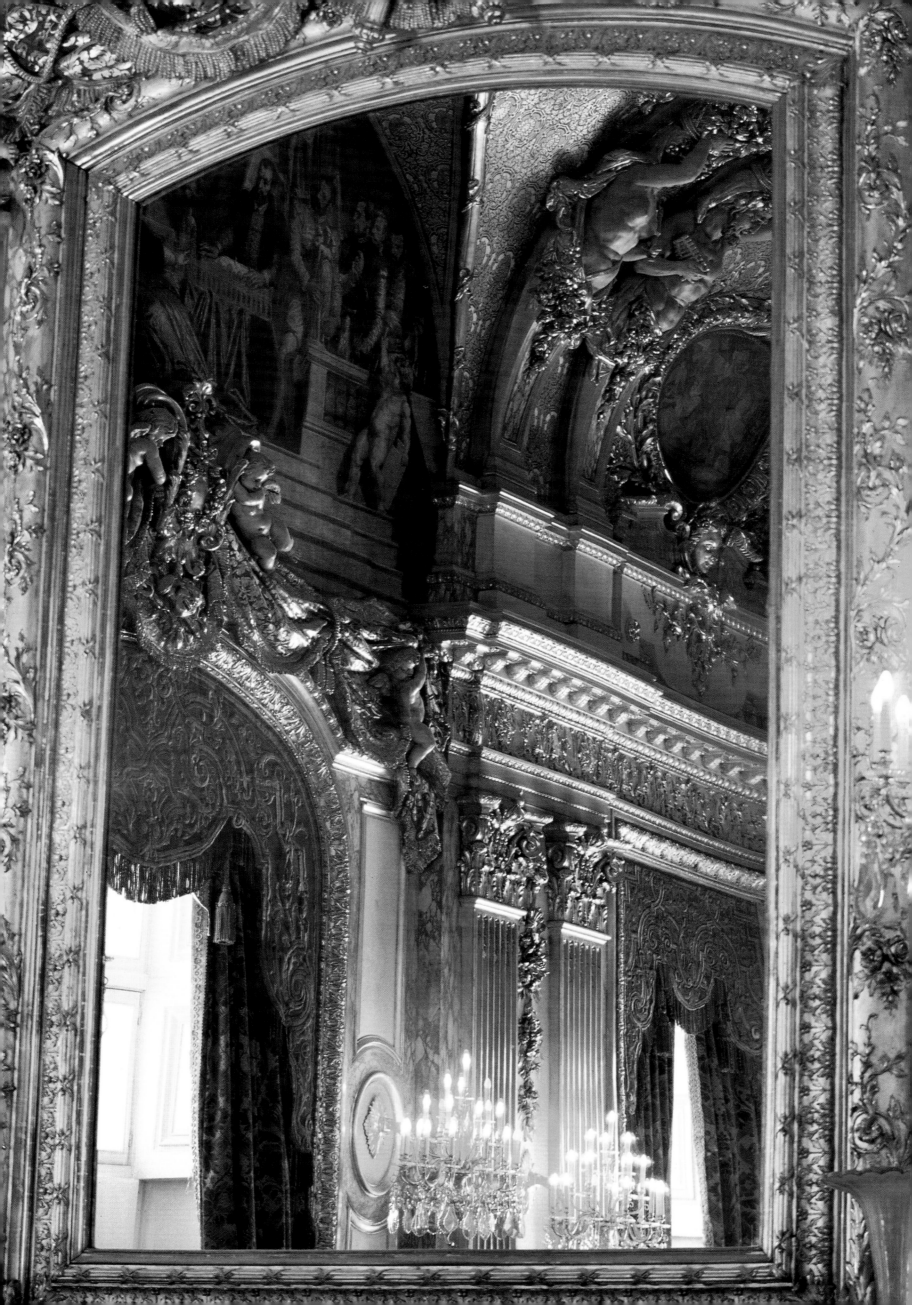

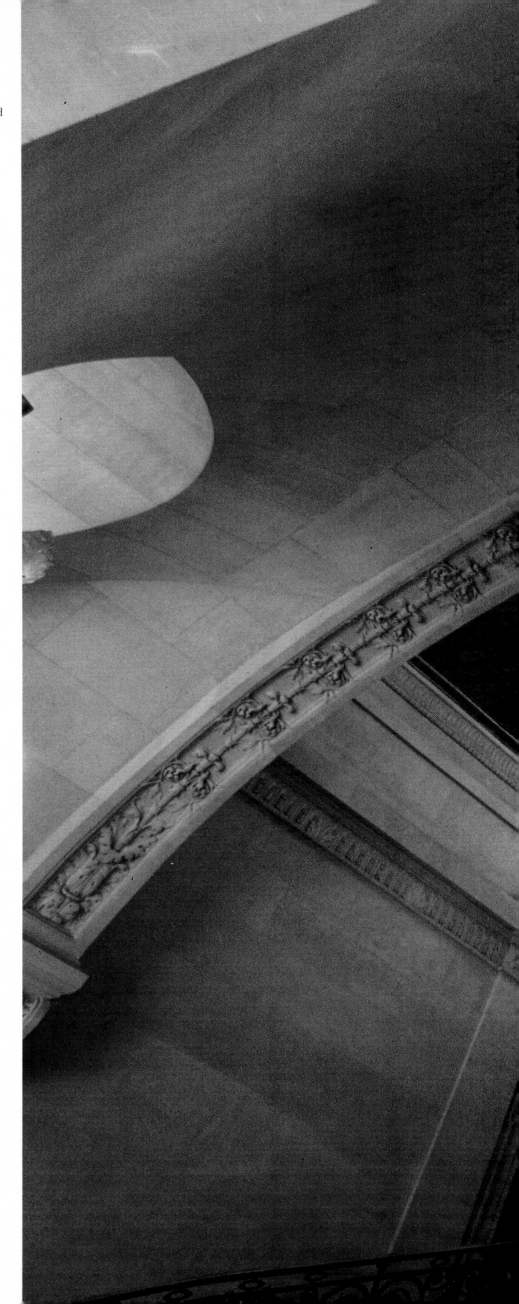

Pages 160–64 Grand Salon of the 'Napoleon III Apartments', decorated by Lefuel, with paintings by Maréchal, for the Minister of State. This formed part of the offices of the Finance Ministry from 1872 to 1989.

Page 165 A detail of ornament in the Napoleon III Apartments.

Page 166 Corner of a small *salon* in the Napoleon III Apartments.

Page 167 Portrait of the Empress Eugénie.

Page 168 A door and pilaster in the Great Dining Room of the Napoleon III Apartments.

Page 169 The Grand Salon in the Napoleon III Apartments, reflected in one of its mirrors.

Opposite The Minister's Staircase, by Lefuel, which leads to the Napoleon III Apartments.

Page 172 The Lefuel Staircase, in the Richelieu wing, was built by Lefuel for the former Imperial Library.

Page 173 The Great Dining Room of the Napoleon III Apartments.

Pages 174–75 The students' room of the Department of Prints and Drawings. This was originally the upper part of Lefuel's Escalier des Souverains in the Flore wing, which remained unfinished; the painted decoration is by Cabanel, the sculpture by Guillaume. The space was transformed and restored in 1968.

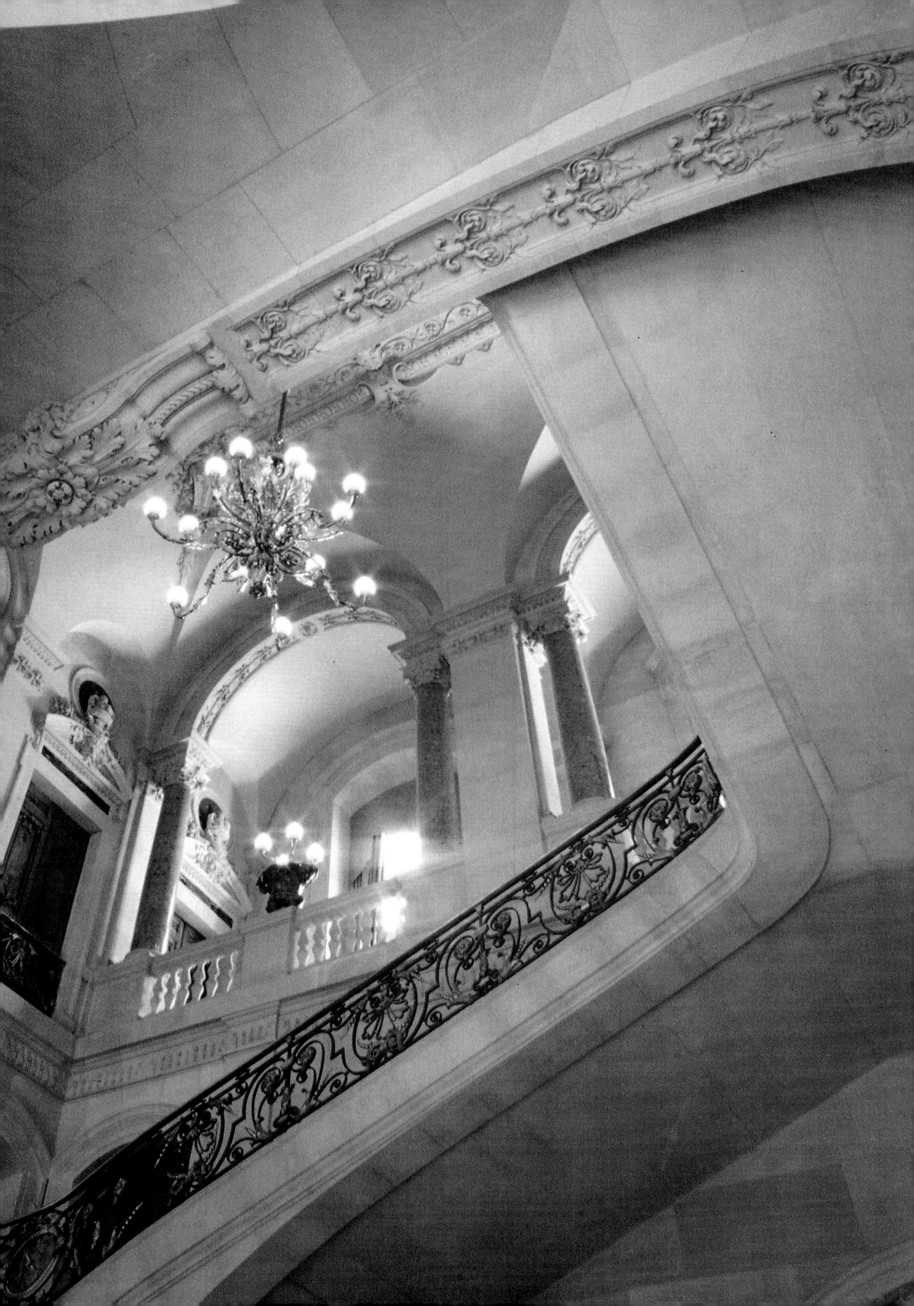

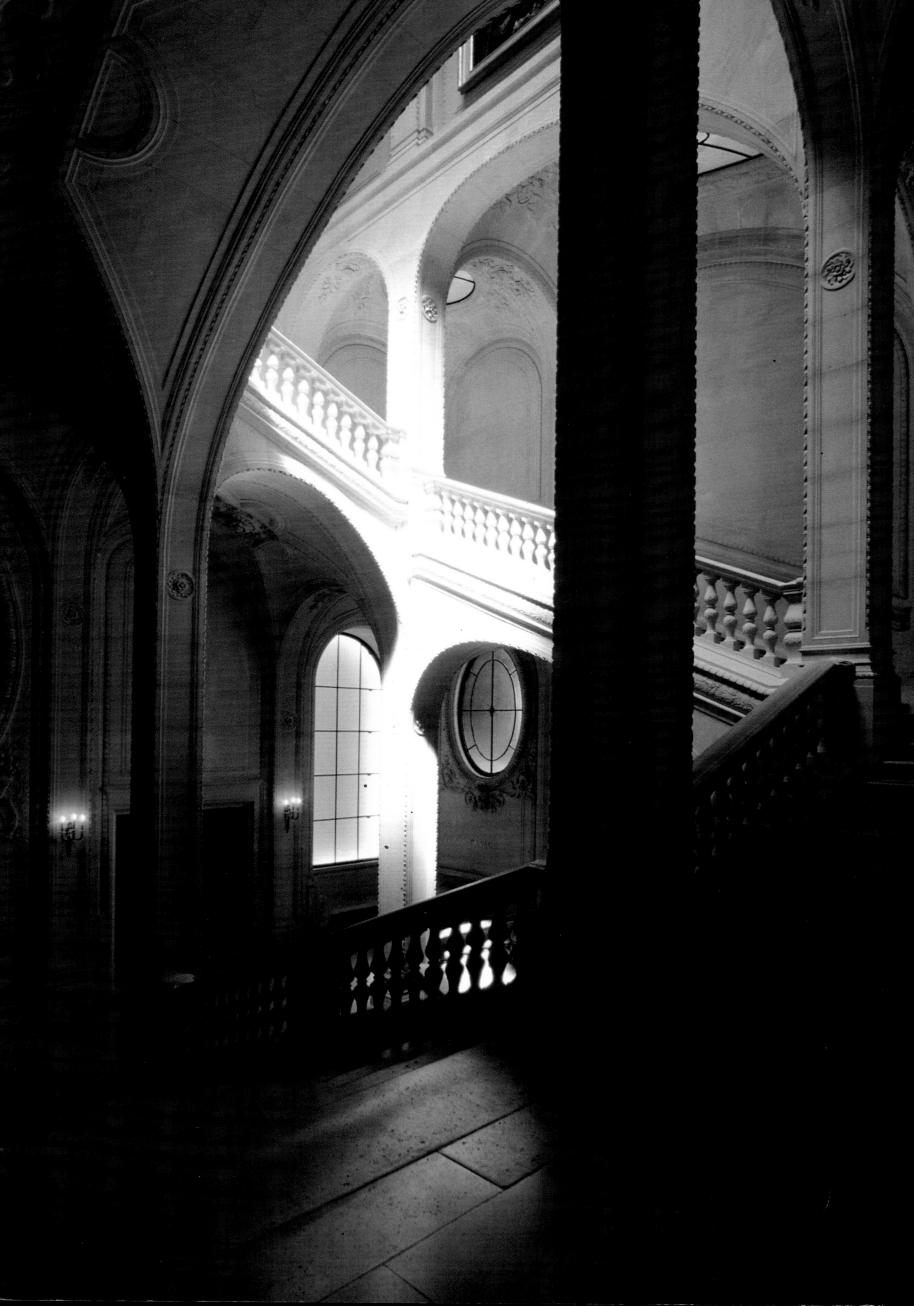

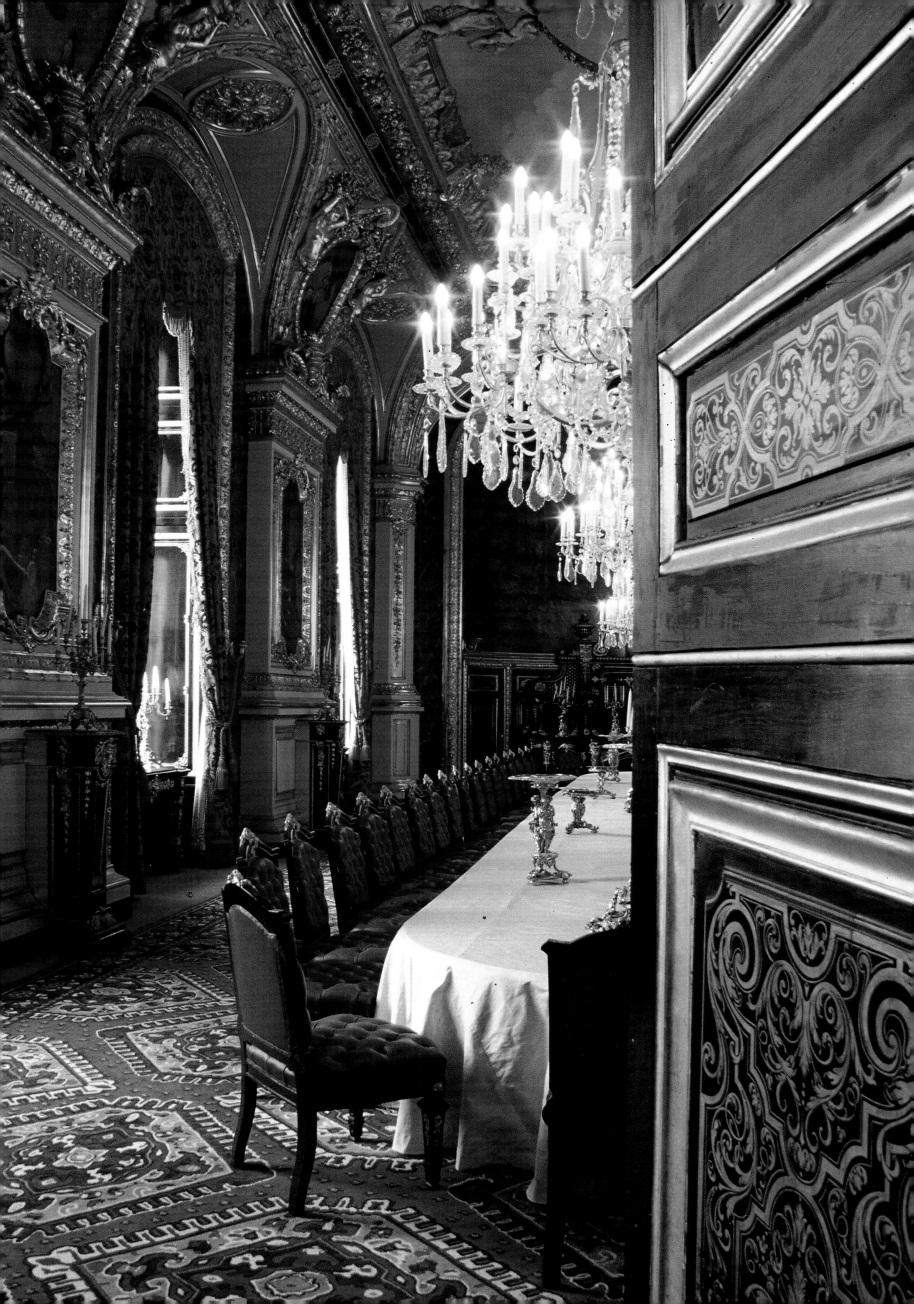

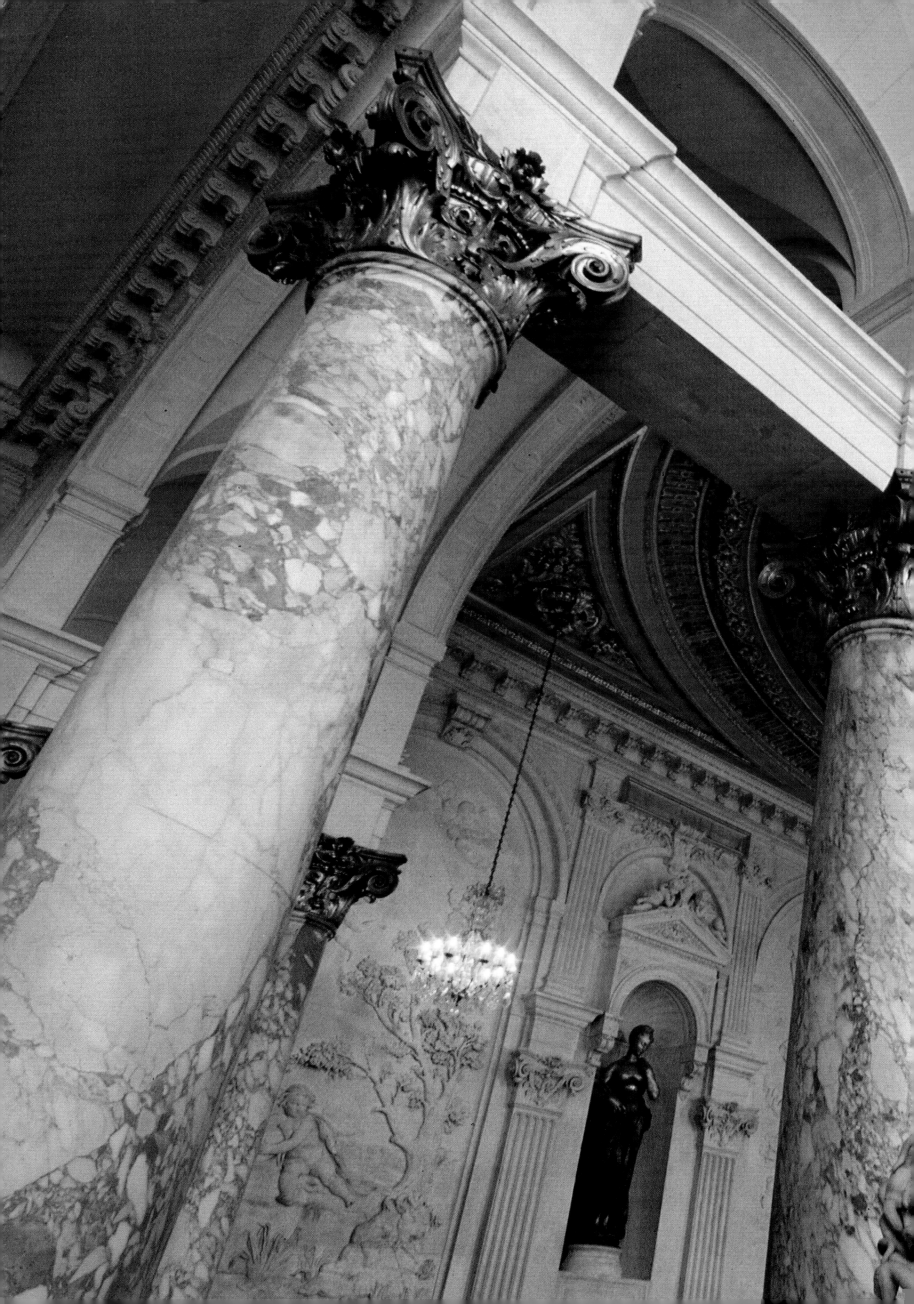

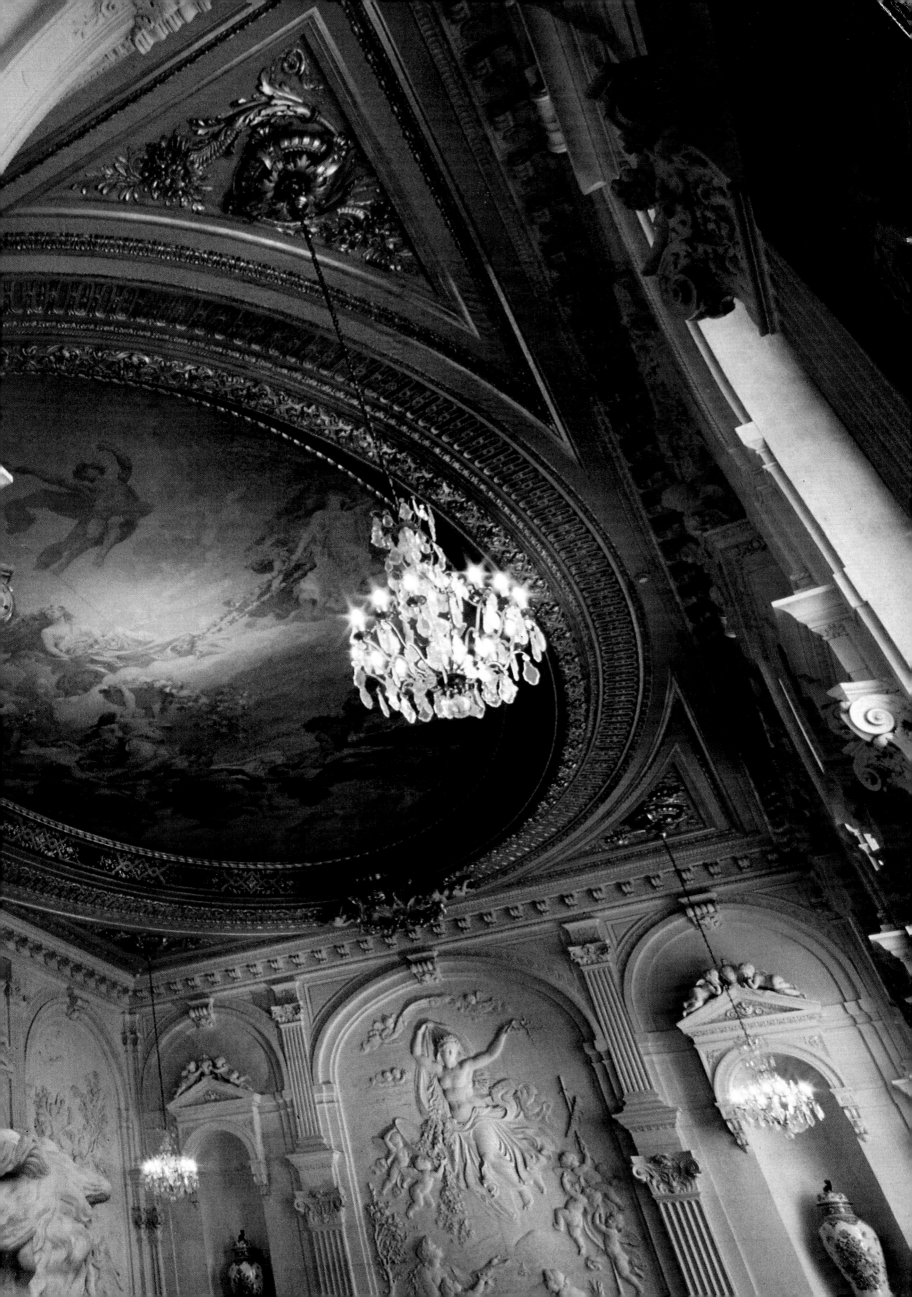

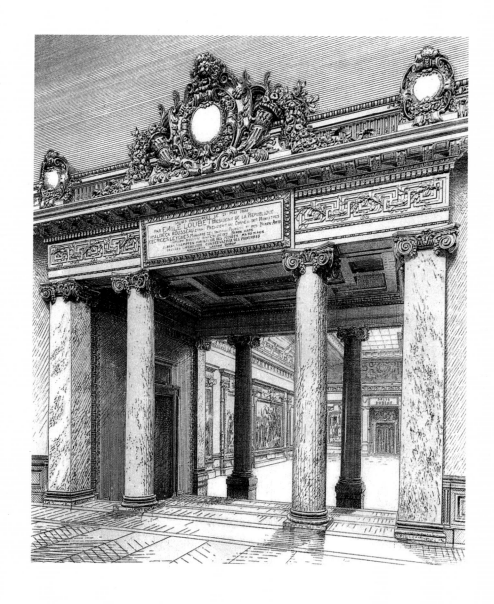

The portico leading from the vestibule to the Rubens Room, by Gaston Redon. Finished in 1900, this complex was the last palace-like interior created in the Louvre.

Triumph
of the Museum

With the fall of the Empire, the Louvre lost its political role. When the Empress Eugénie fled from the Tuileries along the Grande Galerie, she left behind forever what had been the seat of absolute rulers. In her place came ambulances, tending the wounded during the oppressive days of the Siege of Paris. The Commune did, however, manage to organize a few concerts in the imperial apartments to mark the assumption by the people of the privileges of power.

Disaster came in May 1871. At the end of the 'bloody week', at the height of the civil war between the Commune and the Versailles government, a few Communards set out to burn down the centres of power, such as the Chambre des Comptes, the Palais Royal, the Finance Ministry and the Hôtel de Ville. The Tuileries was set alight, together with the library of the Louvre, opposite the Palais Royal, but the museum was saved, thanks to the initiative and bravery of the warders and a few curators, and reinforcements from the army.

The wing along the Rue de Rivoli was quickly restored to house the Finance Ministry, which had lost its own building, but the blackened ruins of the Tuileries remained standing for more than ten years, looming above the squalid shacks where the central Paris post office camped while awaiting the construction of its headquarters in the rue de Rivoli. Many projects for the reconstruction of the royal palace were put forward, but in the end, although the burnt-out shell was still in sound condition, the decision was taken not to restore it. It was an ideological move: when with the encouragement of Jules Ferry the National Assembly voted for the demolition of the Tuileries in 1882, they did so out of a determination to obliterate a visible emblem of monarchy. Henceforth the great axis of Paris would start from the Louvre – and it would be skewed, for the Louvre had been built in line with the river, and it was not parallel to the Tuileries.

The museum was theoretically master of the Louvre, but several other official institutions wormed their way in. First came the Ministry of Finance, which had taken over the Rivoli wing in 1871. The Pavillon de Flore was occupied by the Prefecture of Paris in the days of the Prefect Poubelle (whose encouragement of the introduction of dustbins ensured that they are still known by his name today). Then it, too, was handed over to the Finance Ministry.

The sad story of the work of Edmond Guillaume

The Republic was finding it hard to get established, but while people may have been divided over the régime, they were united in regarding the Louvre as a national symbol. No longer the seat of the executive power, it was to become a temple of the arts. Restoration work was to ensure that it was as splendid as it had been before the fire; and moreover, the new Republic determined to take up where the Second Republic had left off, and to extend to other parts of the museum the sumptuous level of decoration seen in the Salon Carré and Salon des Sept Cheminées. The work was entrusted to the architect Edmond Guillaume.

Born in Valenciennes and trained as an archaeologist, Guillaume taught architectural theory at the Ecole des Beaux-Arts. Before being placed in charge of the Louvre, he had been appointed architect of Versailles, where he carried out work at the Jeu de Paume. At the Louvre, where like his predecessors he was determined to transform the museum into a palace, he was a particular advocate of red walls and luxuriant decoration. All these eclectic interiors of the late nineteenth century were to be swept away during the great renovation work of the 1930s–60s.

Guillaume himself, however, had also been a destroyer. Starting in 1882, he removed the ornament of the Salle des Etats, which had been a hymn of praise for imperial power. Müller's ceiling painting was replaced by a skylight, and the fluted columns and gallery made way for partitions blocking up the side windows. In 1886 the room reopened: it was lit from above, had red walls with long picture rods from which the paintings were hung, and was crowned by a lavish stucco scheme, comprising two large statues, of old or monarchic France (by Gabriel-Jules Thomas) and modern, republican France (by Ernest-Eugène Hiolle), medallions of artists, all of them French (Clouet, Poussin, Claude, Le Brun, Mignard, Watteau, Boucher, Delacroix, etc.), capitals, swags, putti and friezes. The régime may have changed, but the message was as strong as ever. The *Revue de l'Architecture* commented approvingly in 1887 that 'in France genius always has been, and always should be, protected and honoured by a strong government'. Although the artists who produced it were respected figures, this heavy though characteristic ornament soon appeared out of date. It was destroyed without a second thought in 1947, when a purist ethic was proving disastrous for much official art.

Guillaume's second major decorative scheme has just been restored after a long period of neglect. The great saloon of the Pavillon de Beauvais was remodelled in 1889–91 to serve for the display of Flemish and Dutch drawings. Guillaume had found a painting by Emile-Auguste Carolus-Durand executed in 1878 for the Luxembourg but never used: the subject was *The Triumph of Marie de Médicis*, in allusion to the series of paintings that Rubens had made for the decoration of the palace. A splendid setting was now created for the canvas, made of carton-pierre (a kind of papier mâché) and echoing the design of Louis XIV's Bedchamber. In the small adjoining room, which was to be used to show pastels, Guillaume installed three compositions by Hector Leroux. All this decoration was viewed with horror in the purist years, and it was discreetly concealed in 1962. In 1993, however, the ceiling by Carolus-Durand was rediscovered and restored; Leroux still awaits rehabilitation.

On the same floor, major restructuring in 1937 led to the total destruction of a complete painted scheme celebrating the archaeology of the Middle East. The arrival at the Louvre of Sumerian antiquities discovered by Ernest de Sarzec at Telloh (site of the ancient Lagash) in 1881, followed by material recovered from Susa in subsequent years by Marcel Dieulafoy and his wife, had led to the creation of new galleries to present these acquisitions – most notably the famous frieze of archers from Susa. Three rooms on the first floor of the Colonnade wing were given impressive decoration by Guillaume and opened in 1888 by President Carnot as the Salle Sarzec and the Grande Salle de Suse and Petit Salle de Suse. Motivated by a desire to instruct, by the wish to create a sense of atmosphere, and no doubt also by his awareness of tradition, Guillaume commissioned large decorative paintings. The Salle Sarzec was entrusted to Charles Lameire, who created a ceiling with the repeated figure of the god Assur, and a series of friezes on the walls with lions, fig-trees and figures of kings inspired by the glazed ceramic ornamentation of the palace of Khorsabad. The Grande Salle de Suse next door, with glazed friezes from the palace of Darius on all its walls, had a ceiling in similar style by Chauvin. In the Petite Salle de Suse, the upper part of the walls was painted by Chapron and Jambon with landscapes to serve as background to a reconstruction of the palace of Artaxerxes, and in particular of the Apadana. For lovers of bright colours and bold, simple designs, these rooms offered a remarkable repertory of forms: these, and the ancient glazed tile panels on display, were to influence the development of contemporary art.

Guillaume's last executed work was similarly doomed. This was the African Gallery, on the mezzanine level of the Galerie des Sept Mètres, which provided a setting for antiquities from North Africa, notably rich Roman mosaics, displayed against a Pompeian red ground. The room was altered in 1934, leaving only the mosaic floor.

Detail of *The Triumph of Marie de Médicis*, by Carolus-Duran (1878), inserted in the ceiling of the great saloon in the Pavillon de Beauvais by Guillaume in 1889.

178

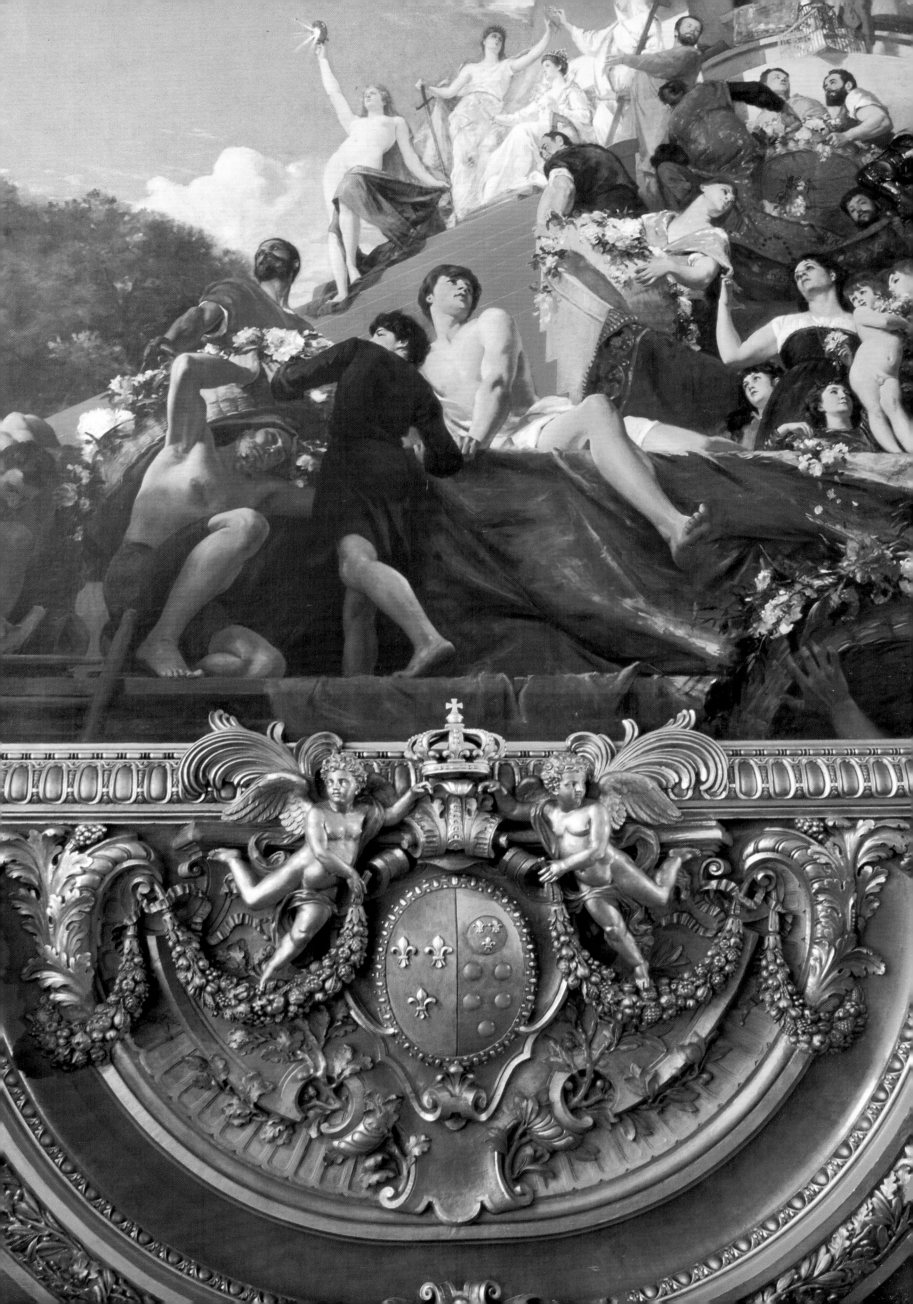

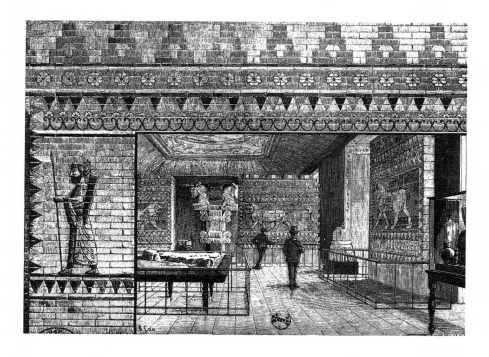

Finally, there is the saga of the staircase in the Pavillon Daru. The Louvre, as we have noted, is a palace of staircases, and this one had been left unfinished on the death of Lefuel. It was a potentially prestigious feature, the more so since the *Winged Victory* had been placed here in 1882. Guillaume decided to tackle its decoration, a project in which he was assisted by the new national ceramics workshop headed by Gerspach, who had already carried out large-scale decorative work in the Panthéon. In 1883 the Commission des Travaux Publics – which included Charles Garnier, architect of the Opéra – agreed in principle to mosaic decoration, and proposed an ambitious scheme for which the patterns were to be provided by the painter Jules-Eugène Lenepveu. It was the beginning of a long and tragicomic enterprise, marked by quarrels between individuals (Guillaume vs. Gerspach), by political tensions (the proposed decoration included a figure of Germany, to whom France had just lost a war, and as if that was not enough, Germany was depicted holding a model of a medieval church, in France, the land of Gothic cathedrals), and by aesthetic disagreements. Above all, there was a fundamental difference of opinion between the architect and the curator of antique sculpture, Félix Ravaisson-Mollien: the latter had placed the *Winged Victory* on the staircase, and he did not welcome the prospect of competition between busy, brilliantly coloured decoration and the proud Greek marble in its time-worn state.

At first, it seemed that the architect and the Commission had won. The programme was a summary of the history of art: there were to be a small cupola above the *Winged Victory* and two larger elliptical cupolas, providing spaces in which to celebrate three periods of art – Antiquity, the Renaissance, and modern times. All around, in bays and smaller cupolas, the lands and artists involved in those three ages would be represented. Allegorical compositions relied on fairly predictable clichés: France was shown as 'slender and very elegant', holding a Limoges enamel and the statuette of *Mercury* by Giambologna (who counted as a French artist because he came from Boulogne); Flanders had a 'fresh complexion' in the manner of Rubens; Germany was blonde; and Italy was 'a handsome brunette type'. In addition, there were to be medallions showing patrons and artists, from Gudea of Lagash through Phidias to Poussin. For a period of ten years there was excitement in the press, the public came and went below the scaffolding, and the mosaicists slowly built up tiny cubes of colours and gold until the cupolas representing Antiquity and the Renaissance were completed. The project had its moment of glory in 1889, when the Universal Exposition was held in Paris, but gradually it fell into a slumber. Guillaume sent his designs to the World's Columbian Exposition in Chicago in 1893, but he died the following year, and his Byzantine dream of mosaic decoration was abandoned. The part that had been completed was totally covered over in 1934. Its appearance is recorded in Guillaume's designs and in the preparatory drawings by Lenepveu (Angers, Musée), and in old photographs.

The Petite Salle de Suse and Grande Salle de Suse.

180

The last decorative work in the Louvre: the Rubens Room

The old Salle des Sessions designed by Lefuel had also remained unfinished. It was used in 1875 for the International Geographical Congress, then from 1879 to 1883 it housed the meetings of the Municipal Council of Paris while the Hôtel de Ville was being reconstructed, and it had been used for exhibitions – for one celebrating the centenary of the Revolution in 1889 and, more importantly, in May 1887, when the crown jewels, which had been confiscated at the Revolution, were shown before being sold at auction. The loss to the national heritage caused by that sale is incalculable, but the gains are clear, for the proceeds went into a fund to pay for acquisitions by museums and resulted in the establishment in 1895 of the Réunion des Musées Nationaux.

Edmond Guillaume had already outlined a project to convert the vast hall into a display gallery for the museum, and his successor, Blondel, inserted a skylight. Realization of the scheme begun in 1896 fell to Gaston Redon, brother of the painter Odilon Redon. He divided the room up into a number of different spaces. First came a vestibule which was used to hang large Flemish paintings, notably Van Dycks. This was separated by a columned portico and steps from a long top-lit room, flanked by eight small cabinets for Flemish and Dutch pictures. The large gallery was to house the great cycle by Rubens on the life of Marie de Médicis, painted for the Luxembourg in 1622. The enterprise was marked by a characteristic lack of agreement between the architect, concerned with style, and the curator of paintings, who was anxious to display the complete cycle in a single space. The architect won. In the interests of symmetry, the chronological sequence of the cycle was disturbed, and several of the canvases were hung in a neighbouring room so that the others could be given rich gilded stucco frames separated by coloured panels imitating sixteenth-century stamped leather. The Rubens Room was the last great example of architectural decoration in the Louvre. Opened by President Loubet on 21 May 1900, it was destroyed fifty years later in the interests of a more museologically satisfactory display.

Although fashion turned against him and he was mercilessly dismissed from the Louvre in 1910, Gaston Redon was nevertheless an elegant designer, as can still be seen in the main space of the Musée des Arts Décoratifs. The Union Centrale des Arts Décoratifs had been founded in 1877 on the model of the South Kensington Museum – later Victoria and Albert Museum – in London. In that year a temporary display of part of its collections was installed at the Louvre in the Pavillon de Flore, which had been restored after the fire of 1871. In 1897 the decision was taken to give it a permanent home in the Louvre, in the Pavillon de Marsan and the adjacent wing which had also been restored, by Lefuel, after the fire. The move signalled official recognition of the importance of the decorative arts as both aesthetic and technical achievements: the museum was to be not only a repository of products of the past, but a laboratory for contemporary creation. Redon remodelled the unpromising space in 1900-1905 on a principle that recalls the contrast between the large Rubens Room and the small flanking cabinets: in the centre he devised two superimposed circulation halls, of which the lower one is spacious and airy and extraordinarily high, lit through its ceiling by openings in the floor of the skylit hall above, where they appear as circular balconies. On either side came tiered storeys with lower ceilings, divided up into smaller rooms for the display of furniture, tapestries and objects.

With the minor exception of the completion of the lower part of the Mollien Staircase by Auguste Blavette on the eve of the First World War, Redon's interiors were the last to receive eclectic, rich historicist decoration. From now on, it was not great showplaces that were decorated but rooms for the display of the collections. In the Rubens Room Redon had insisted on a historical setting for the pictures, but when he came to fit out the newly acquired ground floor of the Pavillon des Etats to display the finds from Jacques de Morgan's recent expedition to Susa, he returned to the didactic approach expressed in the decoration of the earlier Susa rooms, and commissioned large murals showing the site before and during the dig, painted by Jules-Georges Bondoux, who had been a member of the team.

Overleaf Detail of *The Triumph of Marie de Médicis* by Carolus-Duran, in the great saloon of the Pavillon de Beauvais.

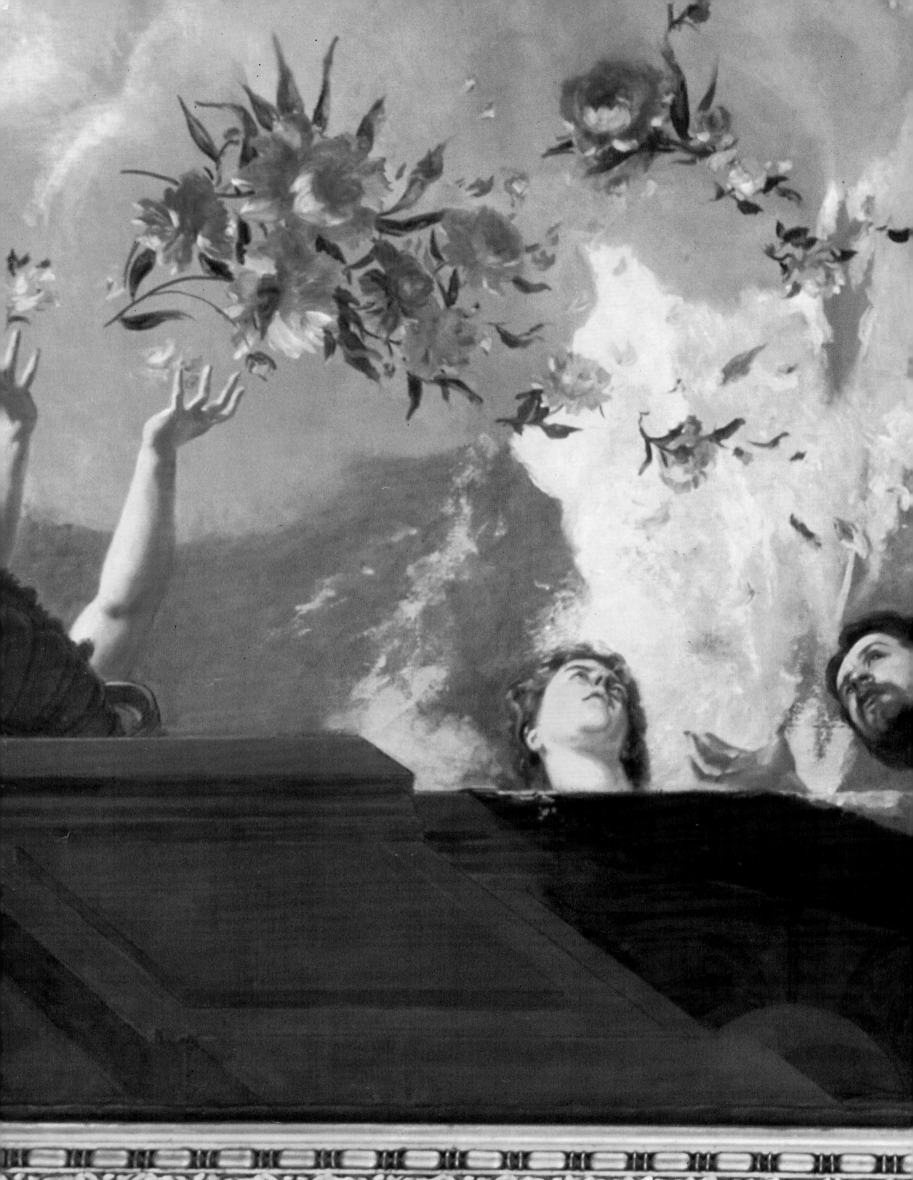

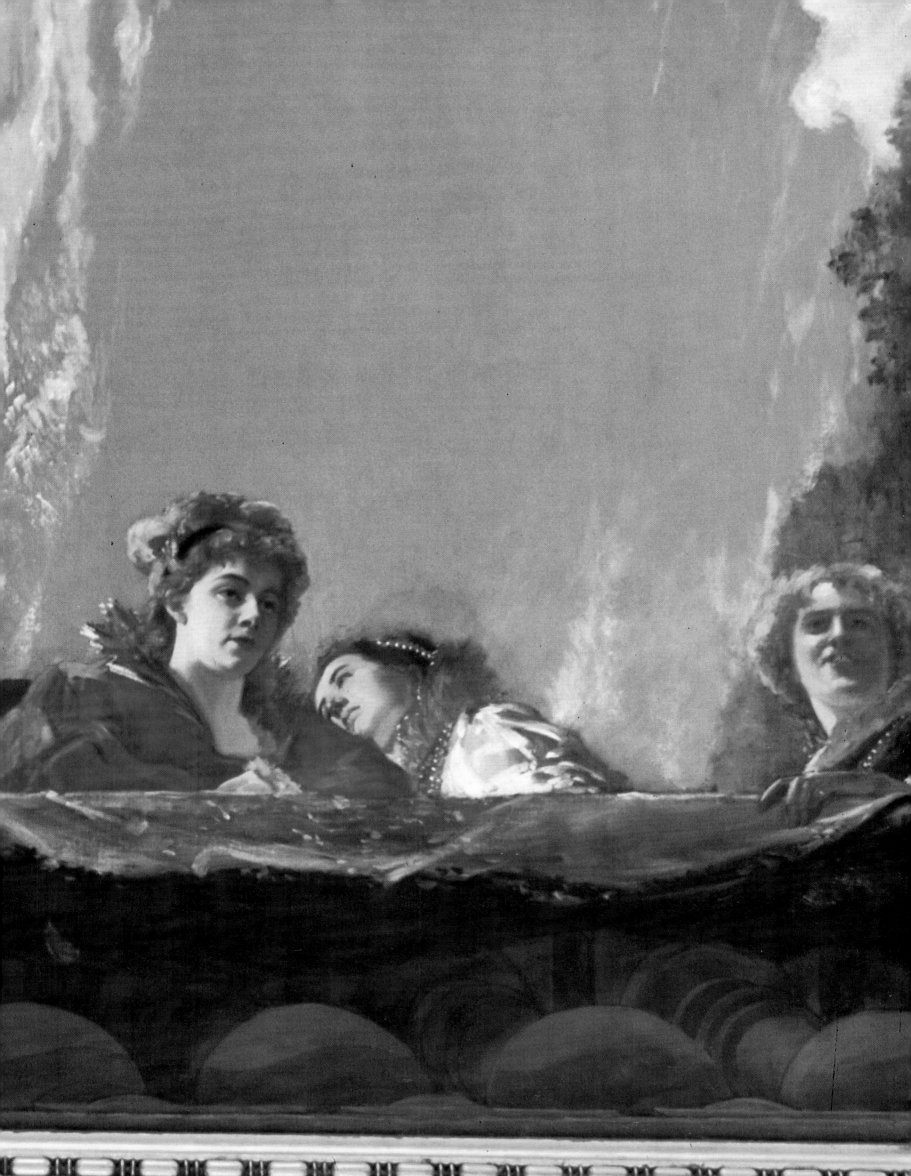

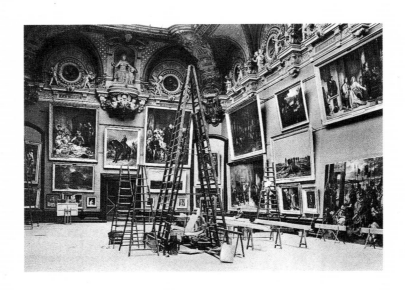

A museum of museums

The desire to keep their name alive after their death, and to preserve the distinctness of their collections, had led many private individuals to make bequests to the museum on condition that these would be displayed in self-contained rooms. Under the Second Empire, the Opéra violinist Sauvageot (on whom Balzac modelled his Cousin Pons) served as curator of 'his' collection on the first floor of the Cour Carrée, jealously watching over it from 1856 until his death in 1861. Shortly before the fall of the Empire, the collection of paintings bequeathed by the philanthropic art-lover Dr La Caze had displaced part of the 'Musée Napoléon III' from the former Salle des Séances in the Lescot wing. The phenomenon blossomed under the Third Republic, with numerous individual rooms and even small 'museums' devoted to particular bequests. The His de La Salle rooms were fitted out to display that collector's drawings at a time when the Cabinet des Dessins still showed their treasures in rooms around the Cour Carrée. When Madame Thiers died in 1881, the collections of objets d'art that she and her husband, the statesman Adolphe Thiers, had assembled were housed in the great saloon of the Pavillon Marengo. After this, it was a matter of finding rooms for the collections of Adolphe de Rothschild (1900), Thomy-Thiery (1902), Alfred Chauchard, proprietor of the Grands Magasins du Louvre (1909), Baron Basile Schlichting (1914), and the Marchesa Arconati-Visconti, who made her gift on impulse when she heard of the bombing of Reims Cathedral in 1916. The display of the Camondo collection had opened in 1914 on the second floor of the Mollien wing: here, great masterpieces of Impressionism such as Manet's *Le Fifre* and Degas' *Classe de Danse* were hung in interiors lined with eighteenth-century panelling, in the atmosphere of an elegant private drawing-room. Outstanding among them all was the immense gift made in 1906 by Etienne Moreau-Nélaton, whose family had tragically died in a dramatic fire at the Bazar de la Charité: initially there was no space for it in the Louvre, so his remarkable collection of nineteenth-century and Impressionist paintings first went on show in the Musée des Arts Décoratifs.

Another story is that of specialized collections such as the Chinese museum of Ernest Grandidier, which began in 1894 with his gift of thousands of Oriental ceramics, and was completed in 1912 by a bequest of eight thousand pieces. Under the régime of the curator of objets d'art, Gaston Migeon, Grandidier's museum transformed the Louvre into one of the world's great museums of Oriental art. Migeon was also concerned to promote Islamic art: in 1912 came the gift of the collections of the Baronne Delort de Gléon, and ten years later a vast display opened in the upper part of the Pavillon de l'Horloge, where the tiered galleries were decorated with mouchrabiehs like the façade of an Arab palace.

The former Salle des Etats as it looked in 1921 (*above*),
and during work on the skylight (*opposite*).

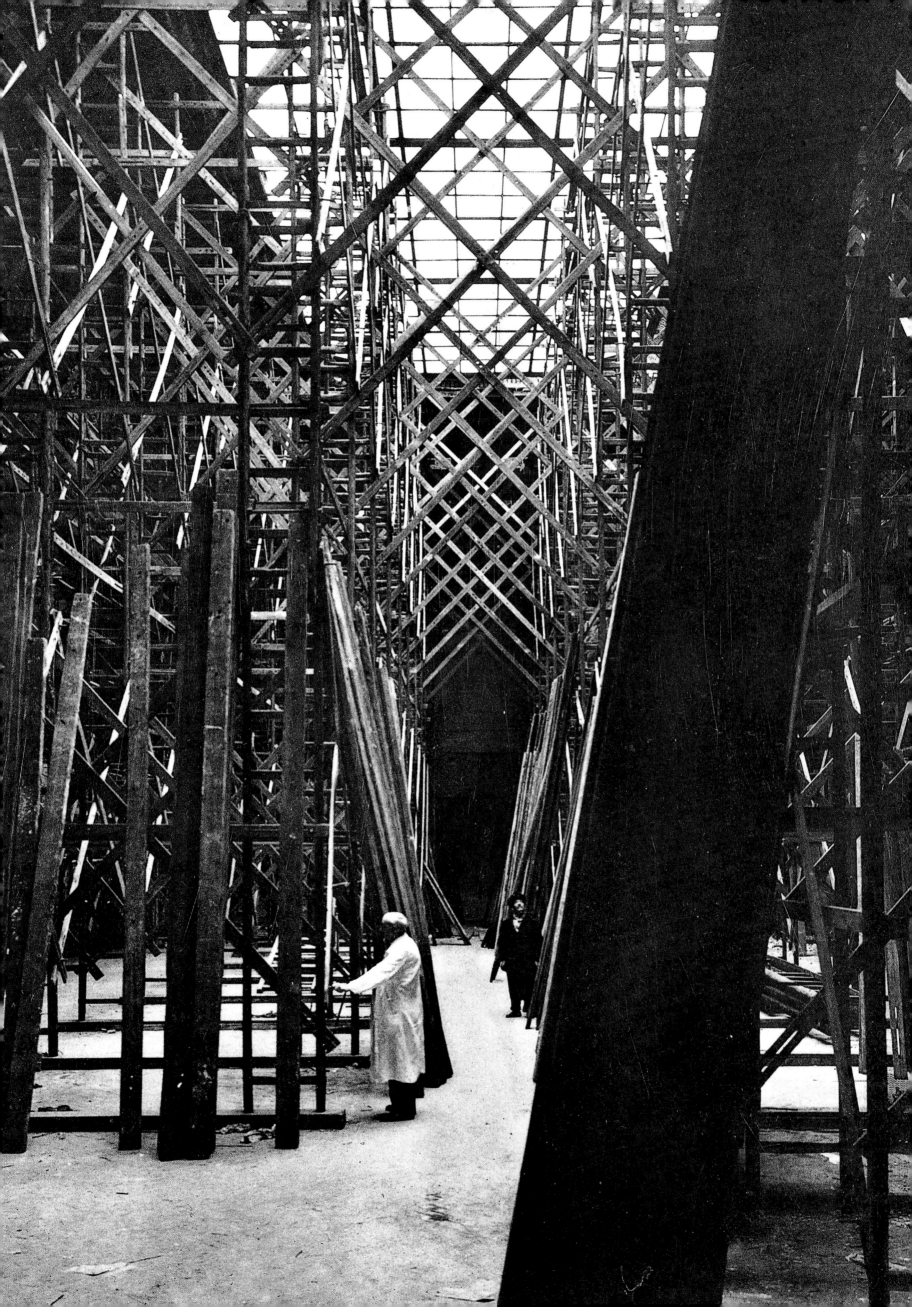

1930s purism

An institution thus divided into separate collections and 'museums' jumbled up one with another could not display its holdings in a coherent way. Visitor routes had to be reorganized, within a functional architectural setting. The first great campaign got under way in the 1930s. It had been initiated in 1927 under the impulse of the director, Henri Verne, and continued thanks to the great job-creation policies of the Popular Front government during the Depression; interrupted by the Second World War, it really came to an end only in the 1970s.

Verne had a twofold plan to solve the problems of the Louvre. His first proposal, which he was able to realize, consisted in reorganizing the collections in those areas of the palace that had been made over to the museum (less a few spaces where a change of purpose was intended). Verne's second proposal was revolutionary: it envisaged no less than the taking over by the museum of all the premises still occupied by the Finance Ministry in the Pavillon de Flore and Rivoli (now Richelieu) wing. The idea had broad public support, and detailed plans were repeatedly drawn up, but nothing happened until 1989.

Between 1927 and 1939 the Louvre as a building and all the departments, especially those of sculpture and Oriental antiquities, were completely transformed. The new style was very modern and very pure. The first architect in charge was Camille Lefèvre; he was succeeded by Albert Ferran, who had trained and taught in the United States. Ferran remodelled the staircase on which the *Winged Victory* stands, and also created very austere and simple galleries on the ground floor around the Cour Carrée for the display of Oriental and Egyptian antiquities. Much of the nineteenth-century ornament disappeared, as did Pompeian red walls and black skirting boards. The fashion was for sober, light-coloured stone walls and for a new purist functionalism that did not reject elegance, but expressed it in tunnel vaults, strongly moulded arches, monumental volumes, and staircases with curved, often elliptical forms. Ferran's architecture was in keeping with the new principles of display: fewer works on show, airy and well-lit spaces, separation between the main visitor routes and 'study galleries' – functionalism, simplicity and grandeur.

The modernization of the nineteenth-century palace also involved technical innovations. The use of skylights was extended, and the Cour du Sphinx was glazed over to allow the display of large Greek and Roman sculptures intended to be seen in the open air. Most revolutionary was the introduction of electricity, which made it possible for the museum to remain open after dark, and for lighted crypts to link the four wings of the Cour Carrée below ground level; showcases were illuminated, as were stairways.

Opposite and *pages 188–89* The Daru staircase, with the *Winged Victory* on the landing.
The structure was built by Lefuel, decorated by Guillaume, and stripped to its present appearance by Ferran.

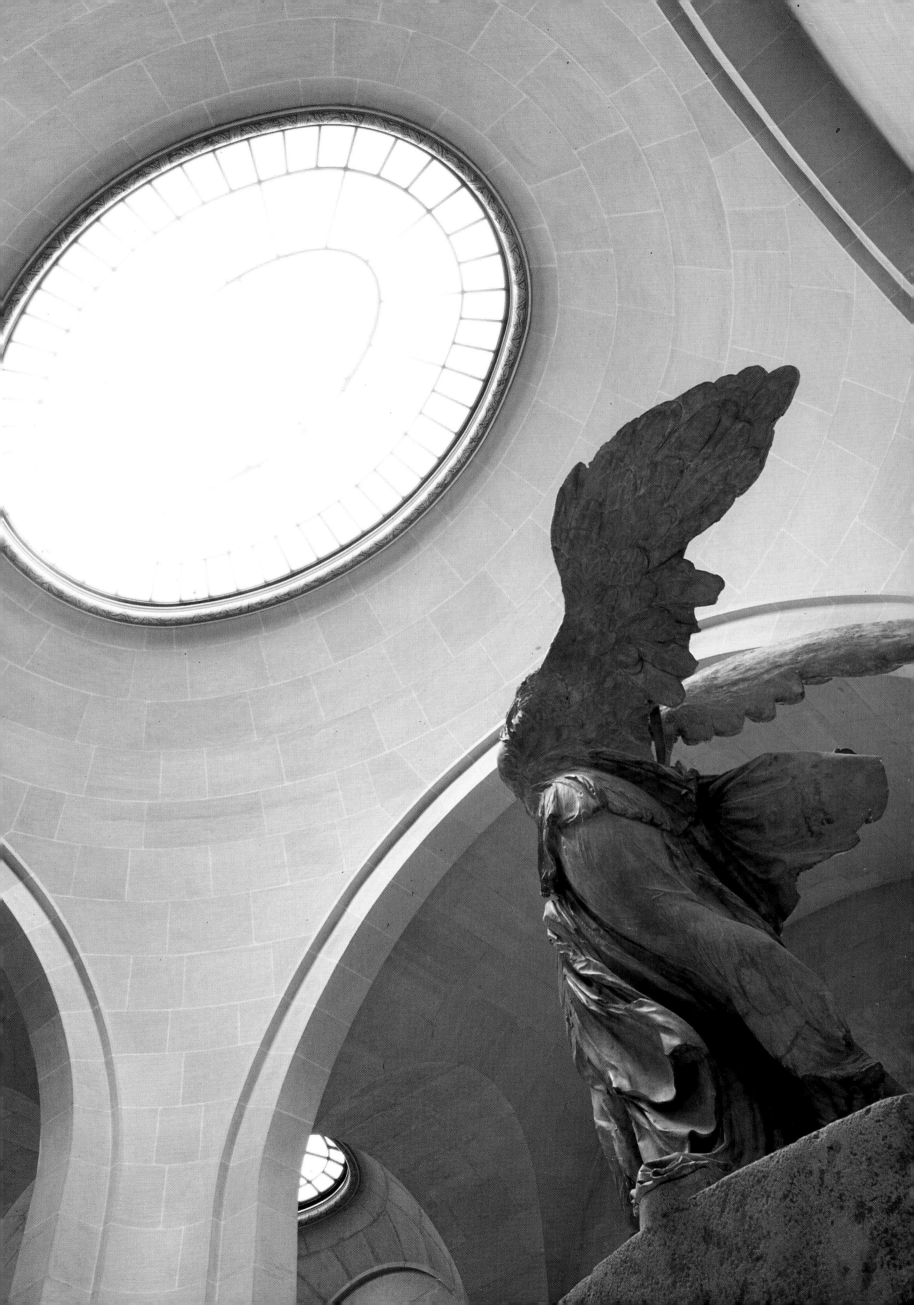

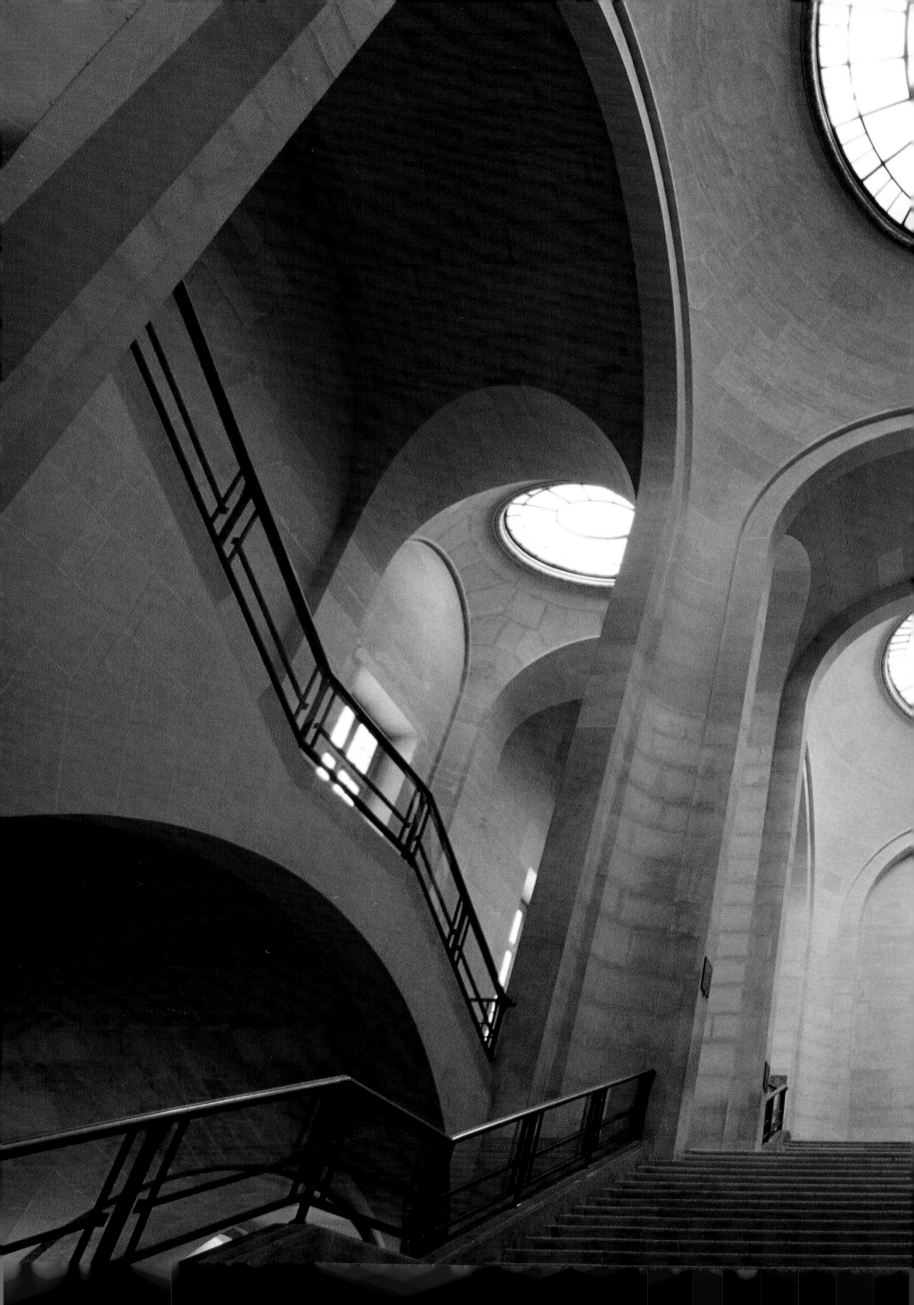

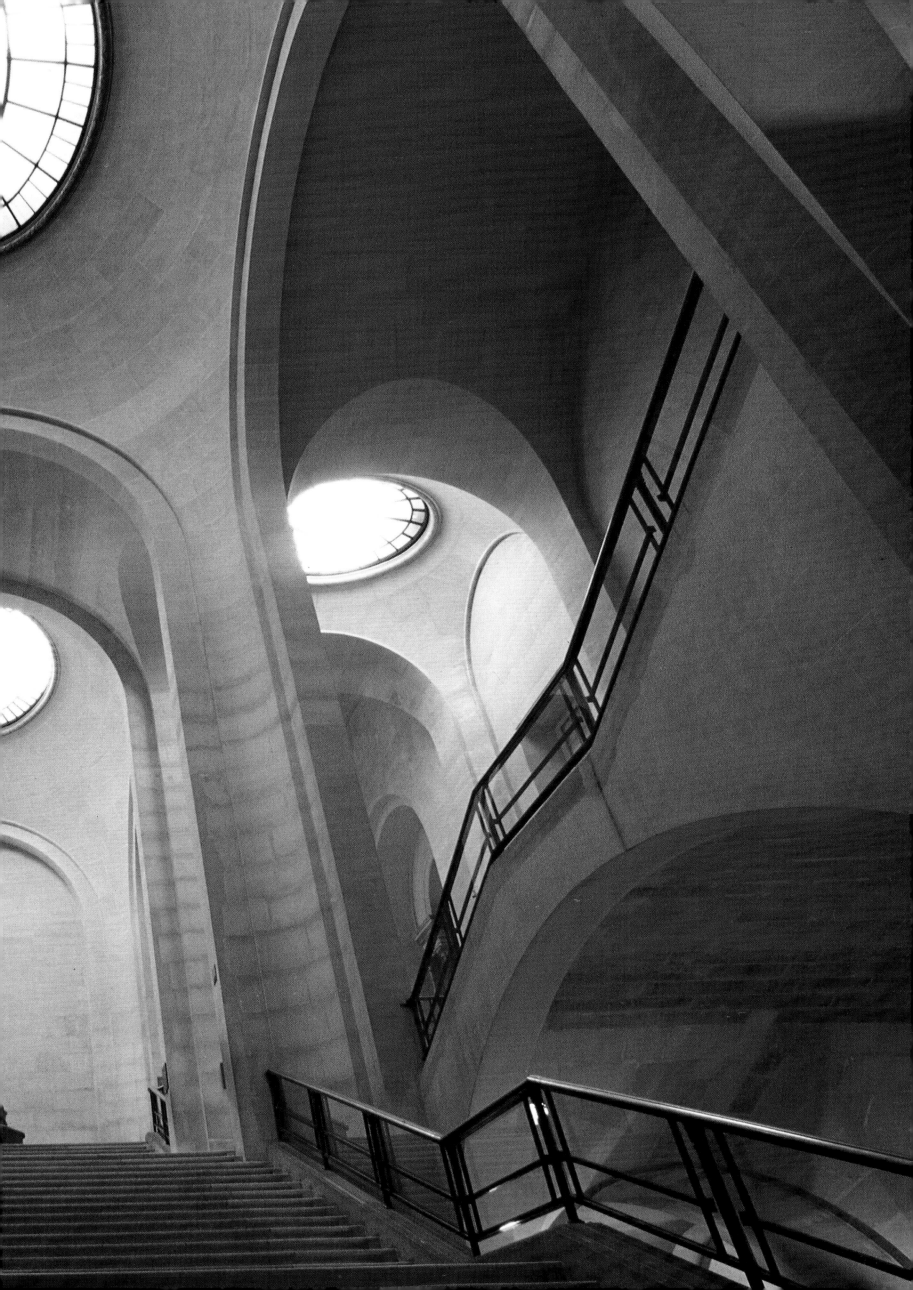

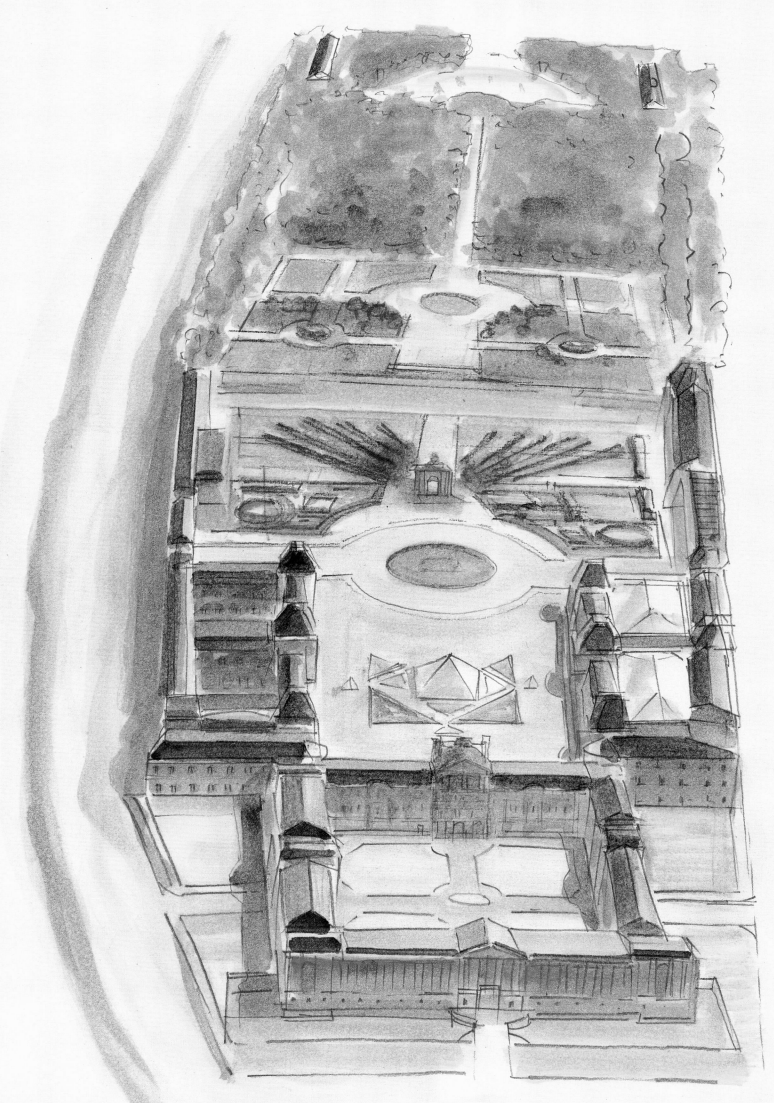

The Grand Louvre. In the centre of the Cour Napoléon stands the Pyramid by I. M. Pei.
His inverted pyramid lies on axis between that and the Arc de Triomphe du Carrousel. On the right,
the two courtyards of the Rivoli or Richelieu wing (formerly used by the Finance Ministry) have been glazed over.

Towards the 'Grand Louvre'

From the Second World War to the Malraux years

Henri Verne's plan for the building and the collections was accompanied by major changes in the nature of those collections. In the 1930s it was decided to transfer the naval section to a new Musée de la Marine in the Palais de Chaillot, a move effected during the war. The Precolumbian material – originally part of the antiquities department – and the 'Musée Ethnographique' had already been moved in 1878 to the Trocadéro Museum, eventually to become the Musée de l'Homme. In 1945, the Asiatic holdings were sent to the Musée Guimet. From 1947, the Impressionist paintings were displayed in the Jeu de Paume, which was regarded as an extension of the Louvre; in 1986, however, the separate new Musée d'Orsay was opened to house all the post-1848 collections.

Thus little by little the Louvre ceased to be a museum of universal scope. Today it consists of seven departments. Three of them are 'ancient': Egyptian; Oriental; and Greek, Etruscan and Roman. Four are 'modern', covering the period from the Middle Ages to 1848: Painting; Sculpture; Objets d'Art; and Prints and Drawings (the Cabinet des Dessins).

Between 1950 and 1980 the aim was to complete the reorganization of these departments along the general lines of the Verne plan. The process of 'cleansing' the pre-war building of its despised nineteenth-century plasterwork was pursued with enthusiasm. In 1945–52 Jean-Jacques Haffner, the architect of the Louvre, remodelled the Salon Carré (while retaining the stucco ceiling), the Salle Daru, the Salle Mollien, the former Salle des Etats, and the Grande Galerie, where an attempt was made to realize Hubert Robert's vision with stucco pilasters and cornicing.

A new system was introduced whereby the architect in charge of the building as a whole was joined by two architects concerned with the interiors, Jean-Charles Moreux and Emilio Terry. In 1953, Moreux completely redesigned the Rubens Room: this time the arrangement was curator-led and the pictures were hung in chronological sequence, but a sense of monumental decorum was maintained by substantial black wooden frames around the paintings, red velvet on the walls, and a high plinth of coloured marble. Moreux also redecorated the small cabinets around the Rubens Room and some rooms used to show nineteenth-century paintings on the second floor of the south wing of the Cour Carrée, and he devised the presentation of the collection that Carlos de Beistegui had generously presented to the Louvre, which was displayed on panels of red velvet suspended from gilt poles.

By now, grand decorative schemes were dead. What architects relied on instead was evocative pastiche, a 'period style' created out of mouldings, panelling and columns, mostly made of light-weight materials, wood and stucco. There was only one exception – but that was spectacular: in 1953, under pressure from the director, Georges Salles, it was decided to replace the paintings by Blondel in the Renaissance ceiling of the Henri II Vestibule with compositions by Georges Braque. The Cubist painter's large blue birds fly around in the middle of Scibecq de Carpi's carved ceiling, proclaiming the continuity of artistic creation in the palace. It was the first expression of an attempt to enact a marriage between ancient and modern, something that was to be taken up again ten years later by André Malraux at the Opéra and the Odéon.

Overleaf An architect's drawing shows the spaces clustered around the Pyramid under the Cour Napoléon, including the auditorium, the bookshop, and (at the right) the Salles d'Histoire du Louvre.

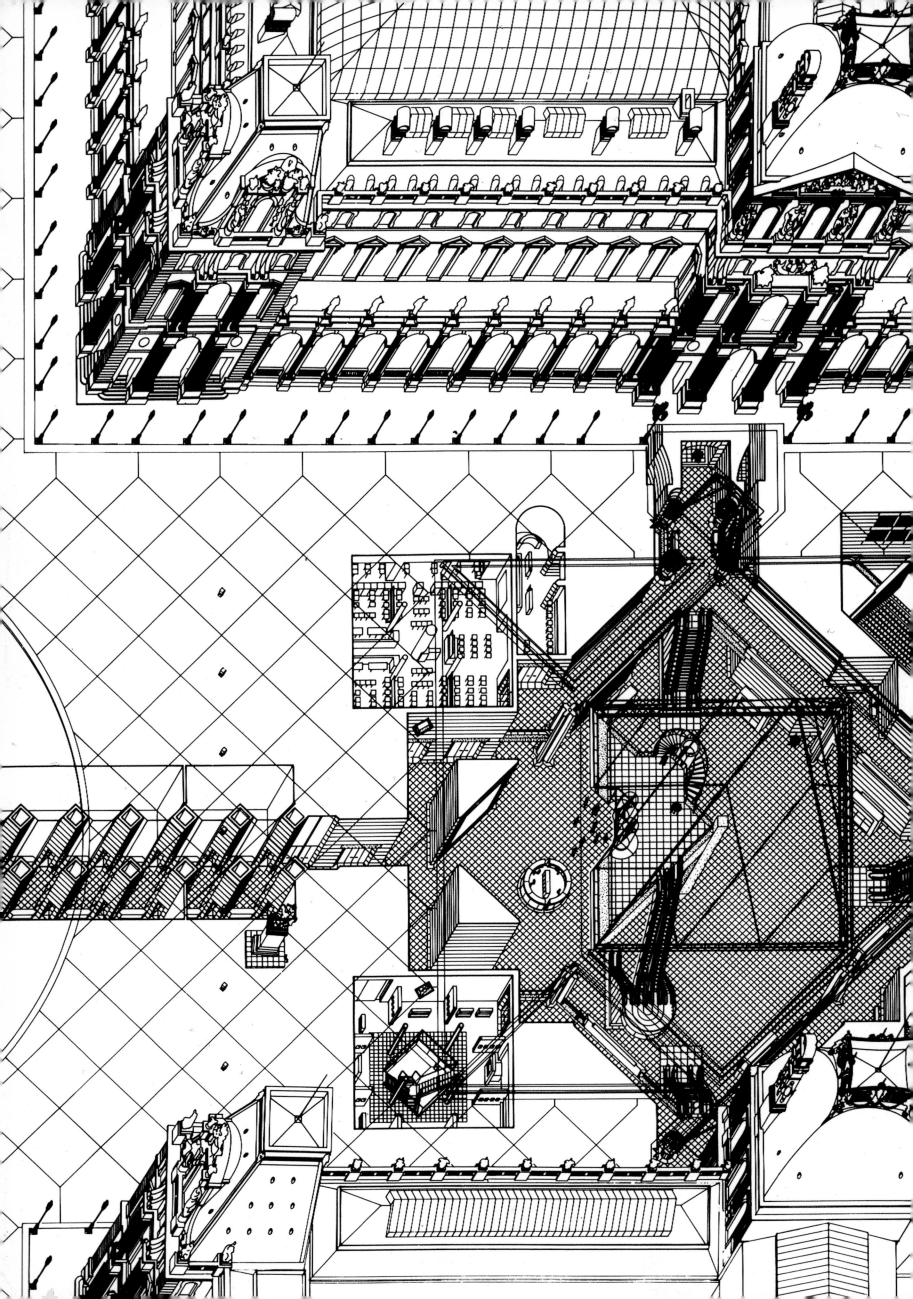

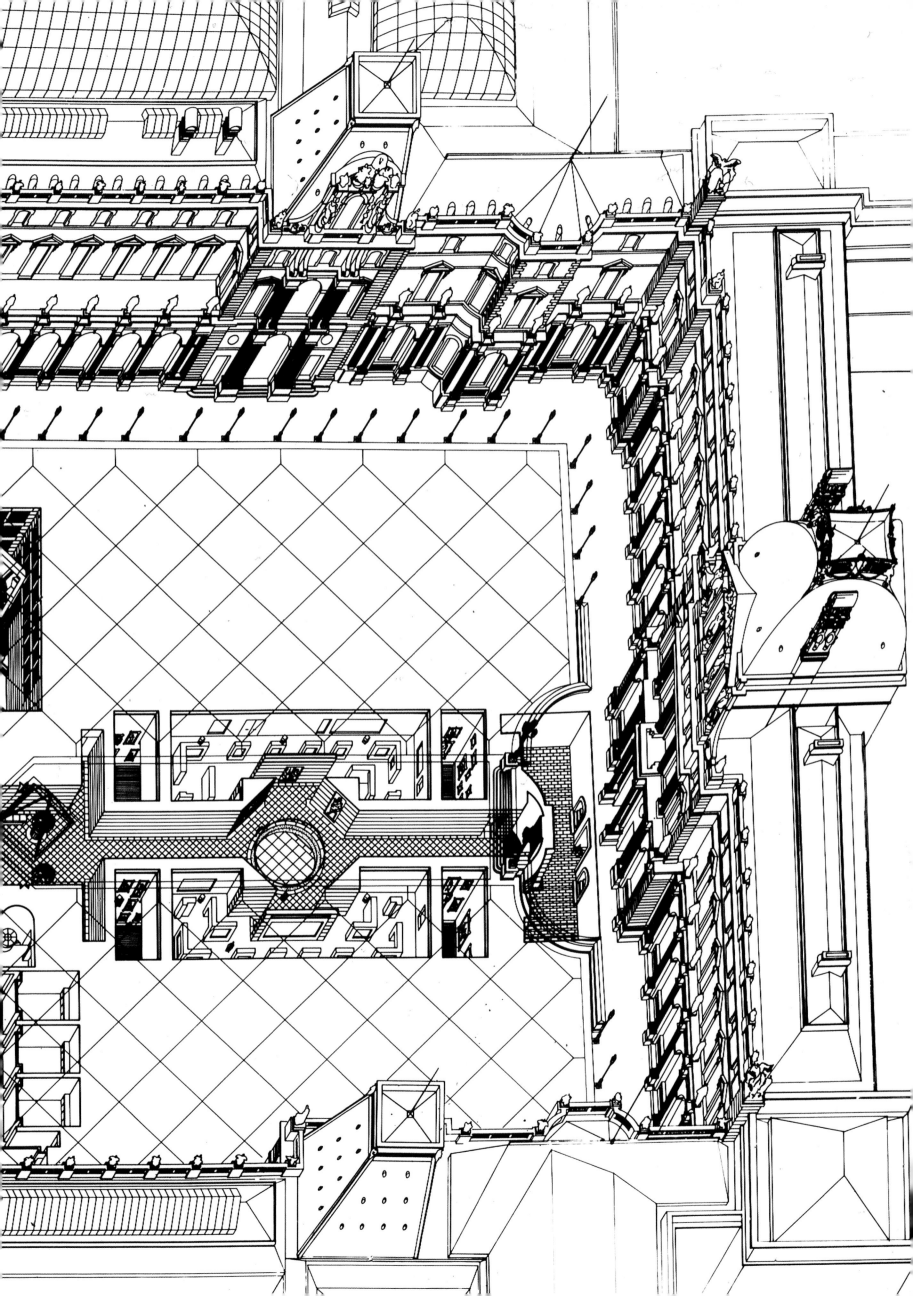

In 1961, an official ceremony marked the formal handing over to the museum of the keys of the Pavillon de Flore. (A similar ceremony had taken place in 1910, but nothing had come of it.) Priority was now given to the conversion of the pavilion and the adjacent wing: the long task (1961–71) was carried out by the two architects of the Louvre, first Olivier Lahalle and then Marc Saltet. The Department of Prints and Drawings took over the Lefuel Staircase as a students' room; the research laboratory of the Musées de France moved in to the upper storeys, and the Sculpture Department was at last able to exhibit eighteenth- and nineteenth-century works that had been in store since the early 1930s.

The design of new accommodation for the Department of Paintings was carried out in several phases between 1966 and 1972 with the assistance of the architect-decorators Pierre Paulin, Joseph Motte and André Mompoix. A new scheme for the overall rearrangement of the collections called for major changes, which were being closely studied by André Malraux, the Minister for Culture. It had been his decision to excavate the moat in front of the Colonnade in 1964, and it was he who sanctioned the admission of French painting into the Grand Galerie. The new aesthetic was discreetly modern, with walls painted in quiet colours such as light brown and dull rose, floors of sandstone or wooden parquet, and furniture conceived by Paulin working on guidelines from the Mobilier National (the body concerned with furniture belonging to the State). Artificial lighting and new showcases were designed with care and intended not to conflict with the existing architecture. New display arrangements in the Salon Carré were confined to the lower part of the room and were devised as an inner facing which would leave the old mouldings undisturbed.

In 1972 the project came to a temporary halt, but a law passed by the Barre government allowed the continuation of the work to complete the Verne scheme, or at least the scheme in its final modified form. The department that benefited most was that of Greek and Roman Antiquities, whose Etruscan, Roman, and finally Greek galleries were modernized. At this time the decision was taken to set up the new Musée D'Orsay, devoted to the art of the second half of the nineteenth century, and the sculptures of Carpeaux and the paintings of Courbet moved across the river into the old Gare d'Orsay, which opened as a museum in 1986. By then the decision had been taken to create the 'Grand Louvre'.

The 'Grand Louvre'

On 26 September 1981 President Mitterrand had announced the decision to hand over to the Louvre the Rivoli wing, occupied by the Finance Ministry. This meant yet another radical transformation of the museum: the concept of the 'Grand Louvre' entailed the establishment of logical visitor routes, with an eye both to the convenience of the public and to the enhanced presentation of the works. To this end, a detailed programme was drawn up by Jérôme Dourdin (who had been chosen by competition), and the complex task of constructing the new spaces was entrusted to the Etablissement Public du Grand Louvre, set up in 1983.

I. M. Pei, designer of new wings for the National Gallery in Washington and the Museum of Fine Arts in Boston, was appointed to oversee the first stage, which involved the creation of a single central entrance to the museum, under the Cour Napoléon. It was a solution which had already been considered in the past, but had always seemed impossibly expensive. Pei now conceived the famous Pyramid, a steel and glass web thrown over a luminous hall. The controversy that it aroused was eagerly seized on by the press. Historicists and modernists were passionately divided over its design, and reservations were expressed about its technical properties; underlying those dissensions, there was unease over the political significance of the choice of design, with its pharaonic symbolism, and of the princely way in which the choice had been made, without a competition.

Drawings of I. M. Pei's Pyramid.

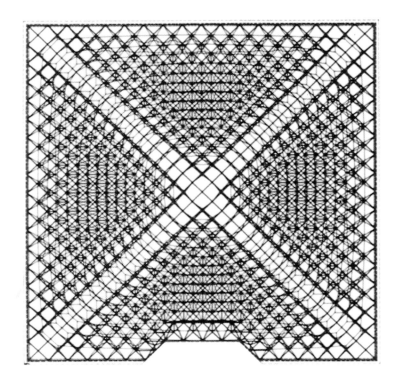

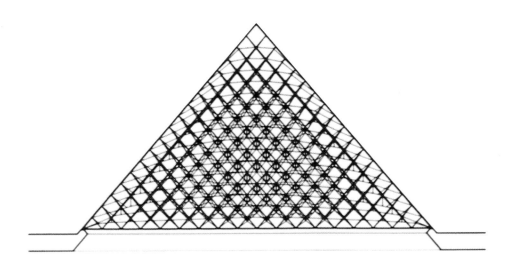

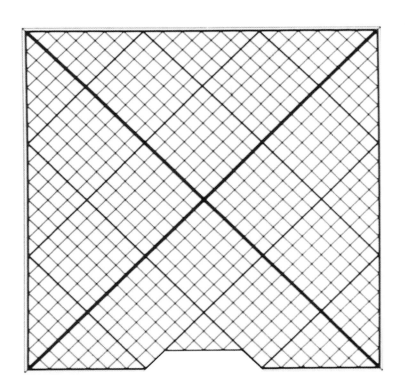

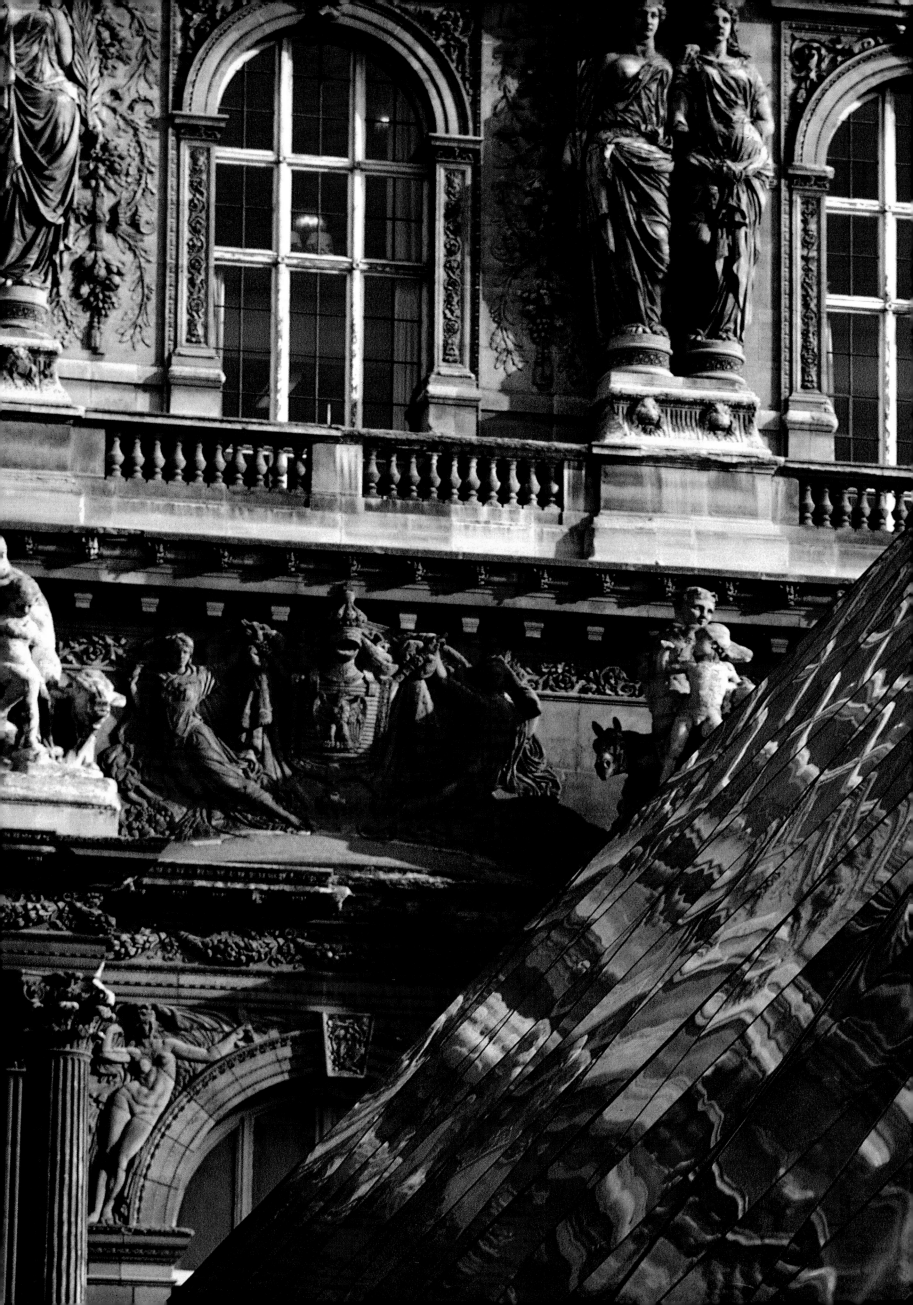

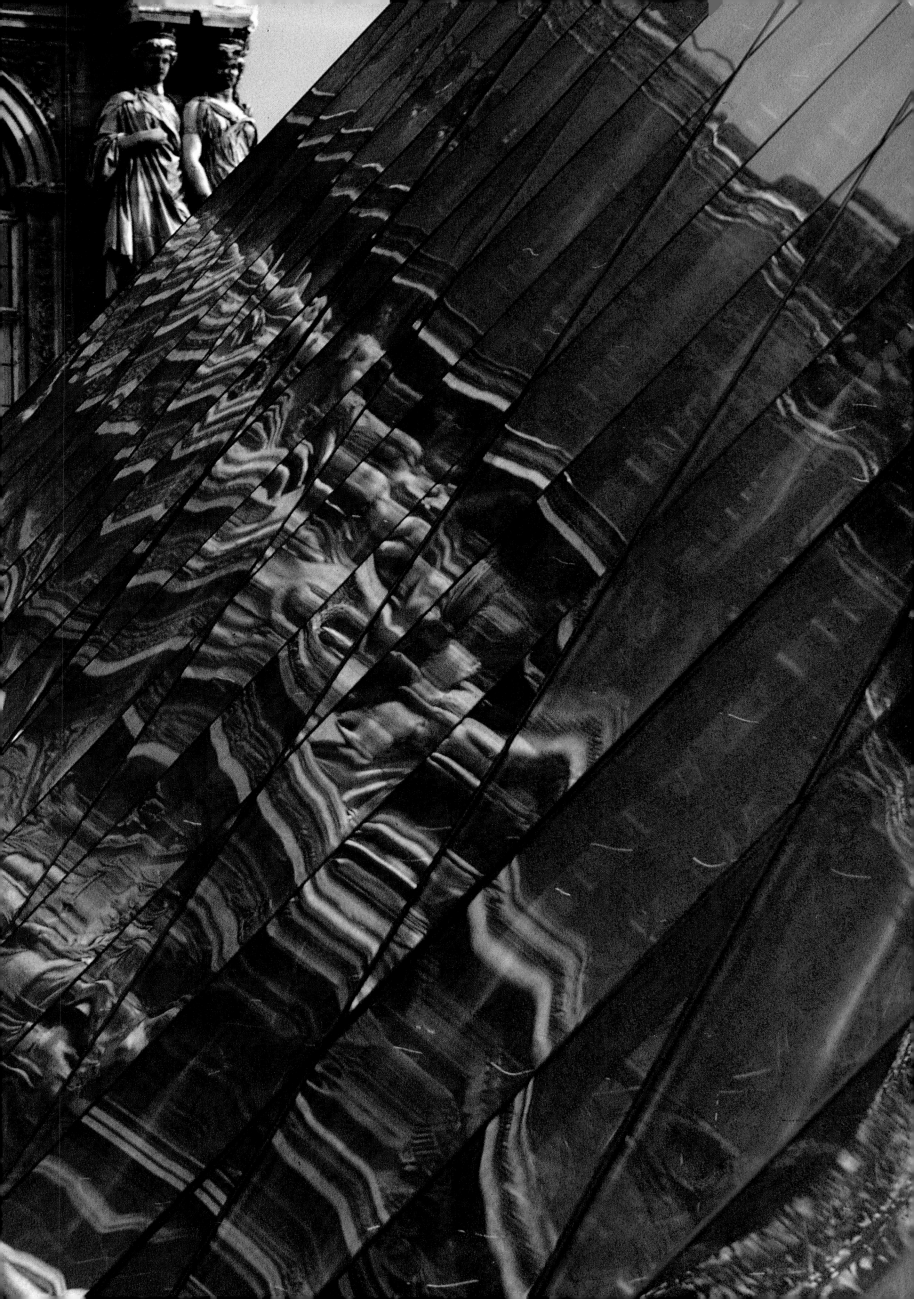

Pages 196–97 The Pyramid, in the foreground, reflects the façade of the Pavillon Richelieu, with its sculptural decoration designed by Lefuel. The groups on the projecting entablatures flanking the imperial arms are copies of Barye's ariginals, installed in 1988.

Opposite The Pavillion Denon, seen through the Pyramid. Its sculpture, again devised by Lefuel, includes groups by Barye which like those on the Pavillion Richelieu are copies; the caryatids are by Brian and Jacquot, and the pediment by Simart.

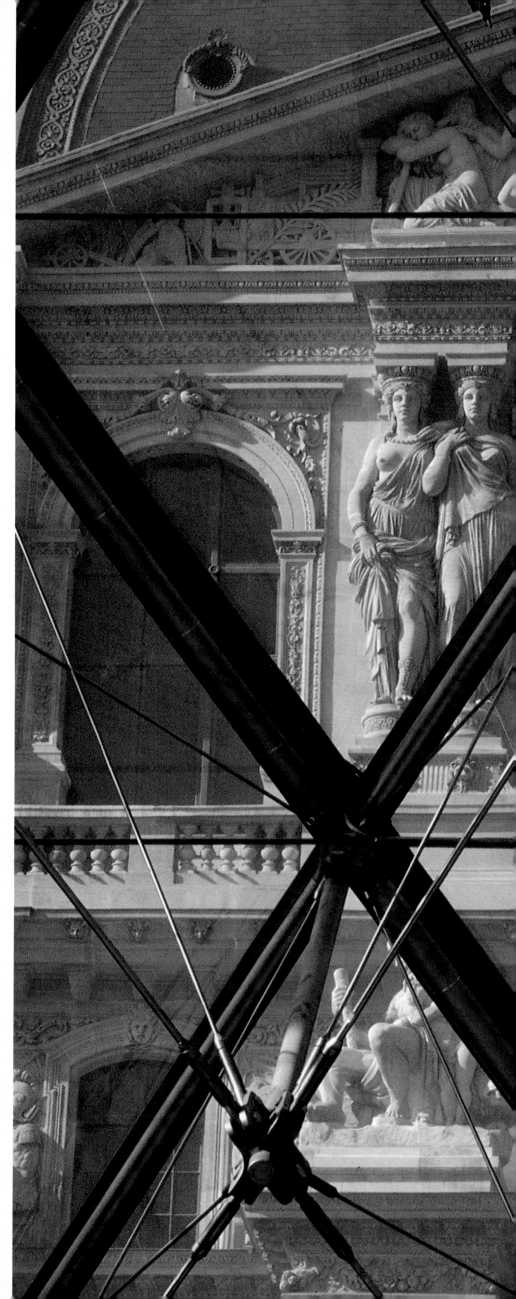

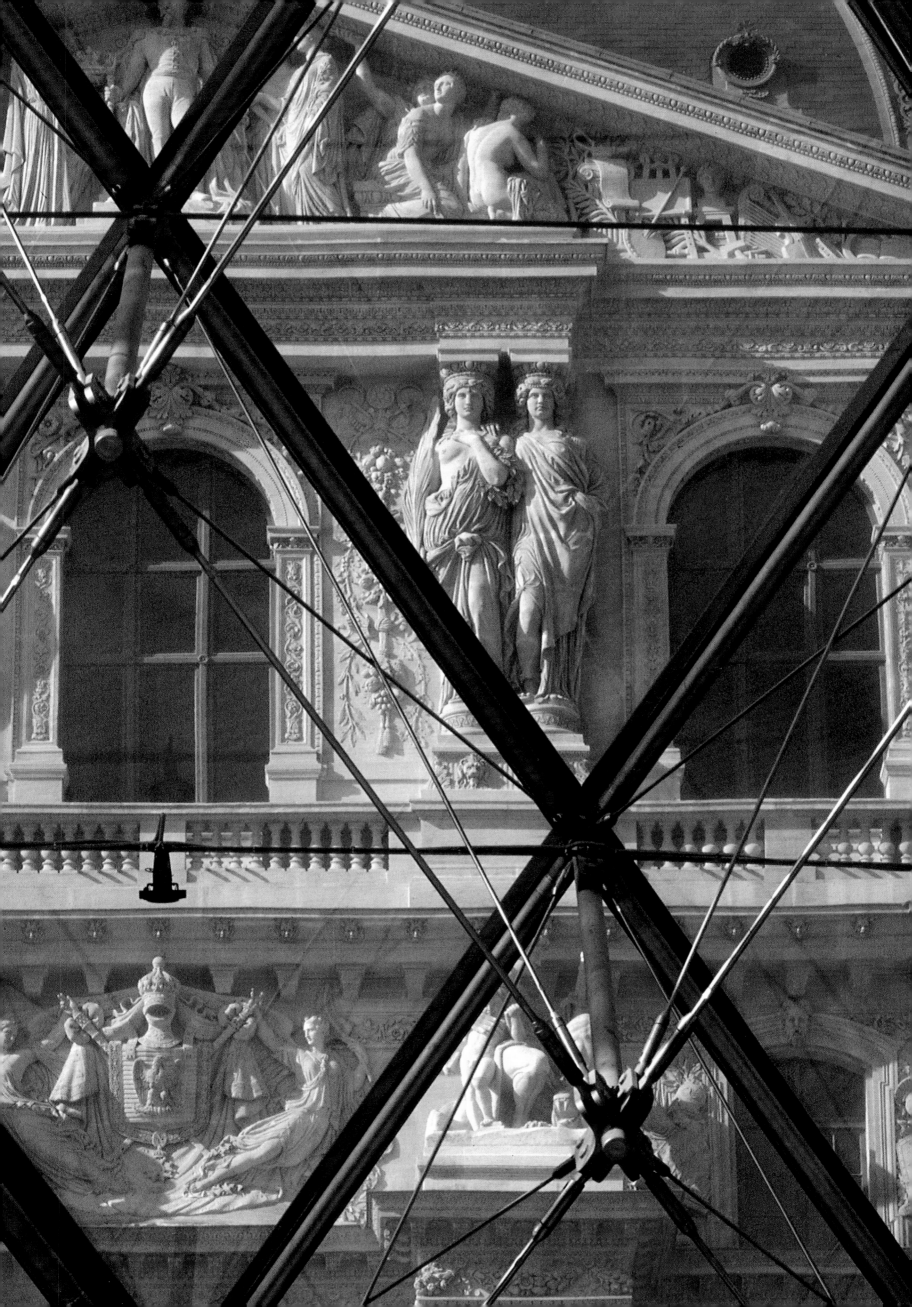

What happened first, however, was that the façades of the Cour Carrée were cleaned under the direction of the chief architect Georges Duval, while the remains of the early castle/palace were studied and restored. Archaeological investigations in 1984–85 led by Michel Fleury and Venceslas Kruta laid bare the spectacular medieval Louvre, while at the same time teams led by Yves De Kisch and Pierre-Jean Trombetta explored the quartier of the Louvre from Gallo-Roman times up to its destruction, and also the tile-works which had given their name to the palace of Catherine de Médicis. The significance of the discoveries made during the various excavations is reflected in the many objects that were found – among them the medieval parade helmet and the material from Bernard Palissy's workshop – and in the architectural remains of the medieval castle.

The vast entrance hall built under the Cour Napoléon at last gave the Louvre a heart and lungs: Pei, in association with Michel Macary, devised a layout that both welcomed incoming visitors and channelled them into new circulation routes that irrigated the museum; at the same time, it provided space for technical departments, an auditorium, rooms for temporary exhibitions, a permanent display on the history of the Louvre, and such essential public services as bookshops and refreshment areas. Associated designers involved were Richard Peduzzi, for the Salles d'Histoire du Louvre; Georges Duval, for the arrangement of the medieval remains; and Jean-Michel Wilmotte, for the temporary exhibitions, bookshop and restaurants.

The glass Pyramid, inaugurated in 1989, was the perfectly proportioned tip of the iceberg. It was more than just a way of illuminating the new underground universe of the Louvre: it was a statement of continued architectural vitality in a great complex that had seen the evolution of Classicism, Neoclassicism and Eclecticism.

The next stage came in 1992, with the design by the Italian architect Italo Rota of new galleries for French paintings. These were linked up to the rooms already renovated by Moreau and Motte, to provide a single sequence from what was now called the Richelieu wing right round the second floor of the Cour Carrée. The work was carried out simultaneously with the restoration of the façades, roofs, and statuary of the palace under the direction of the new chief architect, Guy Nicot.

The third stage coincided with the bicentenary of the museum, celebrated in November 1993. It comprised the complete remodelling of all the spaces in the Richelieu wing that had formerly belonged to the Finance Ministry. The architect in charge was still Pei, in association with Macary for sculpture, Wilmotte for objets d'art, and Stephen Rustow for Oriental antiquities. The latter were now displayed around a covered courtyard containing a reconstruction of the eighth-century BC palace of the Assyrian ruler Sargon II at Khorsabad. Islamic antiquities were given new spaces of their own in the basement. Large-scale French sculpture could now be shown in daylight in two glazed courtyards – the Cour Puget and Cour Marly – while the rest of the collection had adjacent gallery space. Objets d'art were housed in showcases glamorously lit by fibre optics (devised by Wilmotte's firm) in a succession of rooms culminating in the great apartment of Napoleon III's Minister of State. Finally, Flemish and Dutch paintings were brought together around a new display of the Luxembourg Rubens series. The great escalator in the Richelieu wing with its gigantic oculi, the gleaming skylights over the courtyards, and the shopping precinct of the Carrousel around its inverted pyramid are Pei's latest contributions to a building that has seen eight hundred years of architectural transformation.

The Carrousel complex, designed by Michel Macary, forms an extension of the main entrance hall under the Cour Napoléon. Here too, new work had been preceded by archaeological investigations: led by Paul Van Ossel, these revealed the history of the area from Neolithic times right up to the fall of the Tuileries in 1871. The city wall, now exposed, was preserved, to impress visitors with its early sixteenth-century masonry dominating the great moat built by Charles V to protect the western approaches of Paris. The wall now marks the division between two newly excavated commercial areas – parking to the west and shops to the east. Space was also made for a new amphitheatre for the Ecole du Louvre (by Guy Nicot), for the research laboratory of the

Reflections playing on Pei's Pyramid.

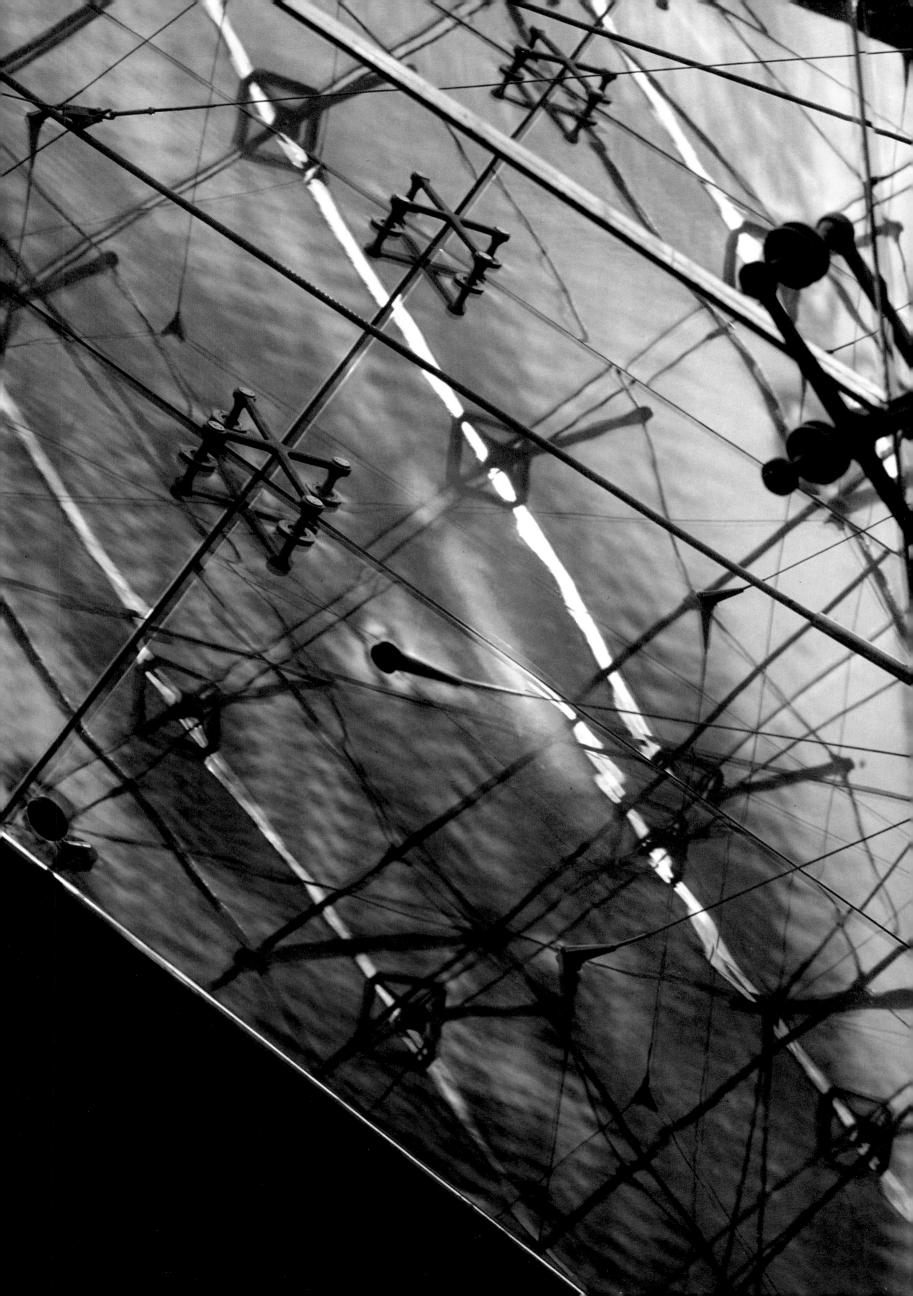

Musées de France (by Jérôme Bunet and Eric Saunier) which opened in 1995, and for new exhibition galleries intended primarily for costume. The standard of design and construction set by the architectural team is maintained throughout this area, which is signalled by a second Pei pyramid, suspended as it were inside-out, its tip poised 1.40 metres (4½ feet) above the ground.

The fourth stage came at the end of 1994 with the opening of the foreign sculpture rooms. Under the direction of the architects François Pin and Catherine Bizouard, two storeys were given over to the presentation of Italian and Northern European sculpture: the old stables beside the Lefuel court became the Donatello Gallery, where Quattrocento Italian works stand out against large grey stone paving slabs, while the predominantly Gothic works from Flanders and the German lands are housed in showcases where the light is controlled to suit polychromed wooden sculpture. The former Galerie Mollien on the first floor, which had retained its rich inlaid pavement of coloured marbles and its vaults carved of luminous white stone, was chosen to display major pieces of Italian sculpture, from Michelangelo's *Slaves* to Canova's *Cupid and Psyche*.

Even now, however, the Grand Louvre is not completed. The Egyptian Antiquities Department is moving into new spaces in the Colonnade wing and the eastern half of the south wing of the Cour Carrée. The Musée Charles X and the Campana Gallery are to be restored and modernized for Egyptian antiquities to the east and Greek to the west. New Archaic Greek galleries are to be created on the ground floor around the Cour Visconti, and new Coptic galleries on the former site of the Ecole du Louvre. A route is to be devised around the court so as to show together Late Antique works from the Mediterranean world, which are at present dispersed between three departments. The Department of Objets d'Art is to find new exhibition space in the Rohan wing, while the Department of Paintings looks to an updating of the display of Italian works in the Grande Galerie and especially to the refurbishment of the Salle des Etats. The Cabinet des Dessins is to be remodelled and reached by the Porte des Lions. The Musée des Arts Décoratifs in the Marsan wing and the Musée des Arts de la Mode in the Rohan wing are also in the process of major reorganization.

While all this work is going on inside, the final touches are being given to the restoration of the façades, the Carrousel garden is taking new shape at the hands of Jacques Wirtz, and the Tuileries Gardens too are being remodelled by Pascal Cribier and Louis Benec to frame the terrace that marks the site of the vanished palace.

From castle to palace to museum to 'New Louvre' and finally to 'Grand Louvre', the complex of buildings – focus of admiration and of controversy for eight hundred years – is in our time seeing its ultimate metamorphosis. The Louvre is sometimes called the greatest and largest museum in the world, but that is only one aspect of it. It is itself rich in history, and it brings together the wealth of a nation for display to all who choose to come. Its key concerns are respect for the works of art, and provision of pleasure to the visitor – conservation and presentation. Centuries old but ever new, the palace distils and transmits the consciousness of art.

The inverted pyramid in the Carrousel concourse, also designed by Pei.

(For captions to *pages 204–9*, see page 210.)

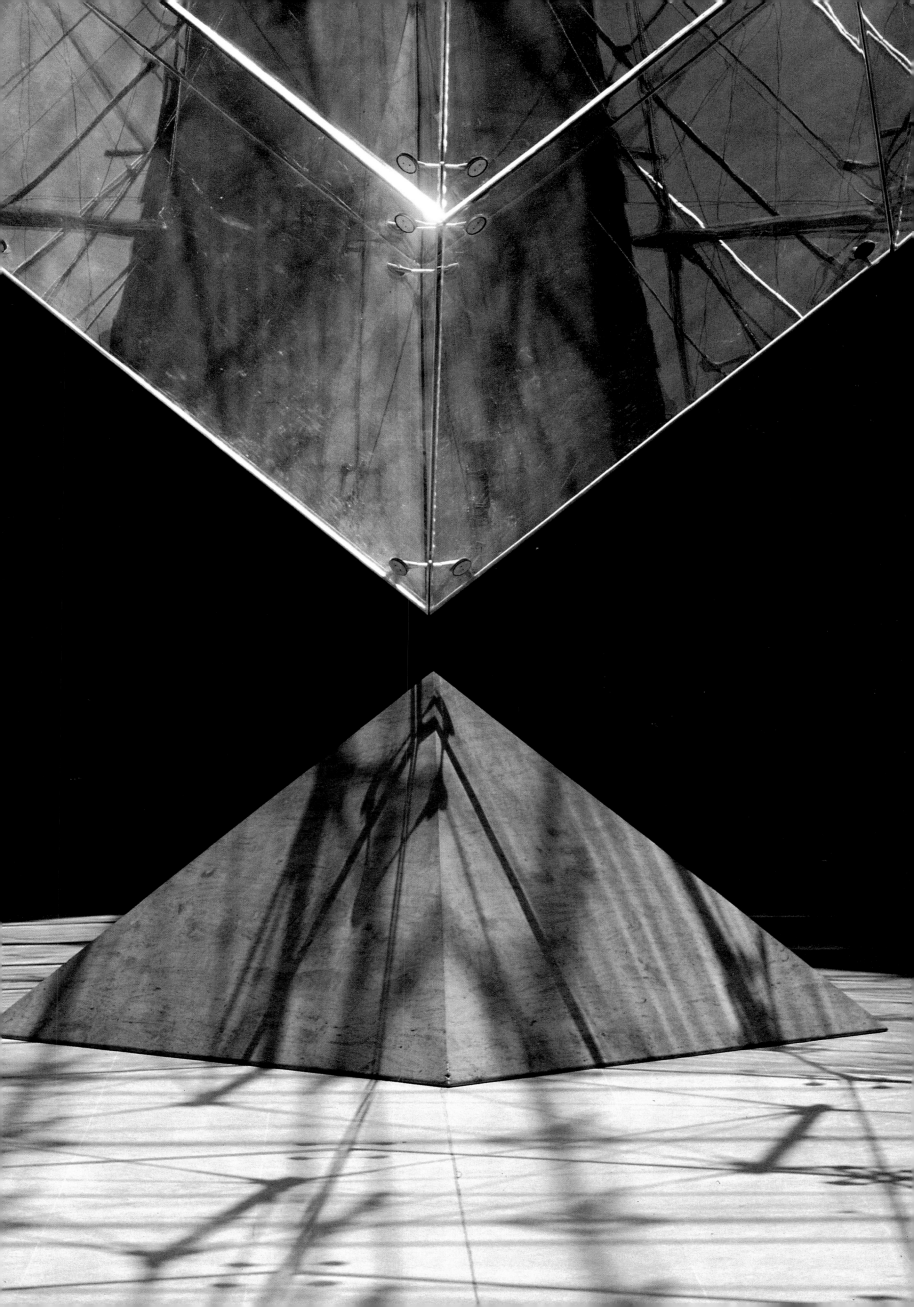

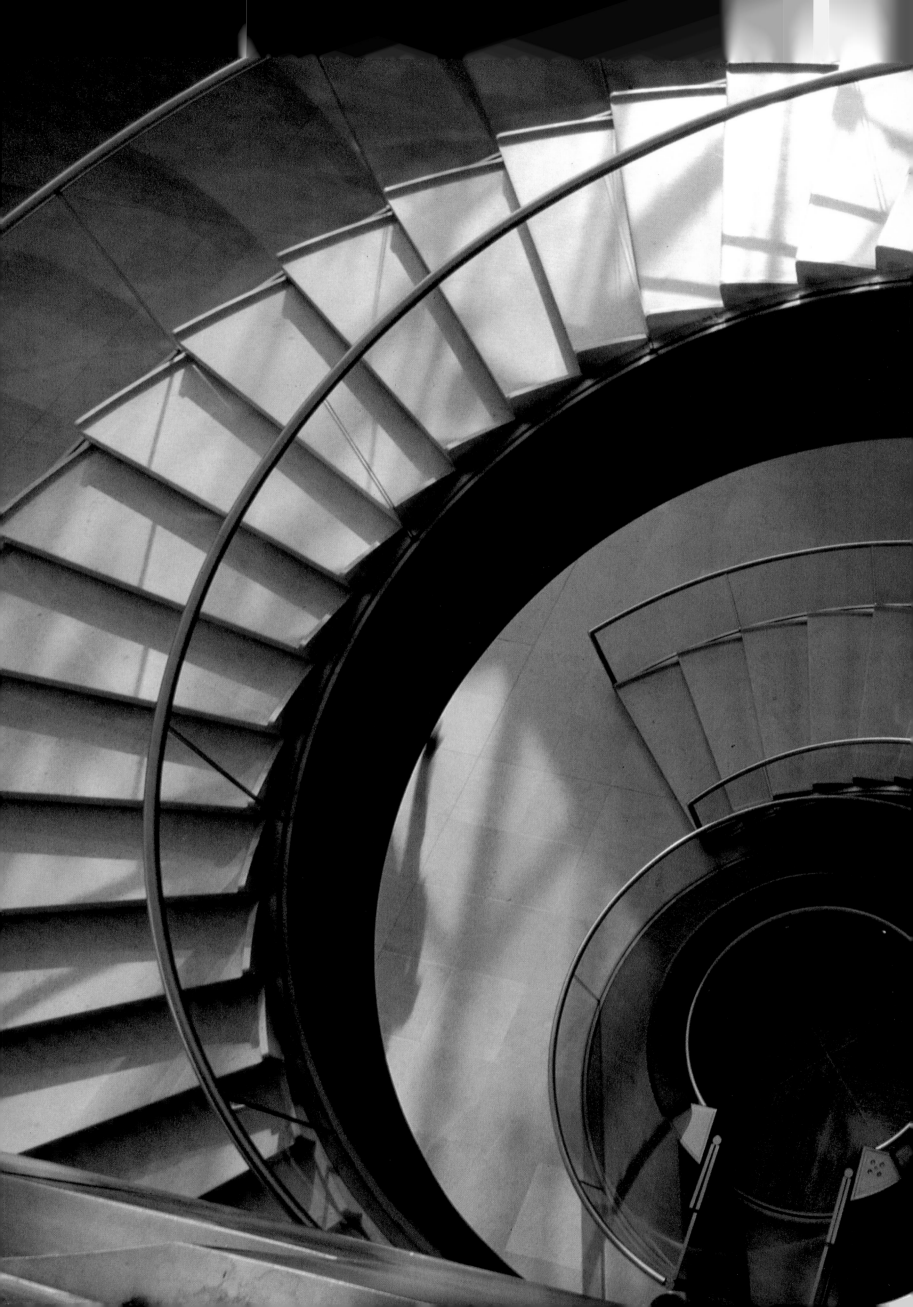

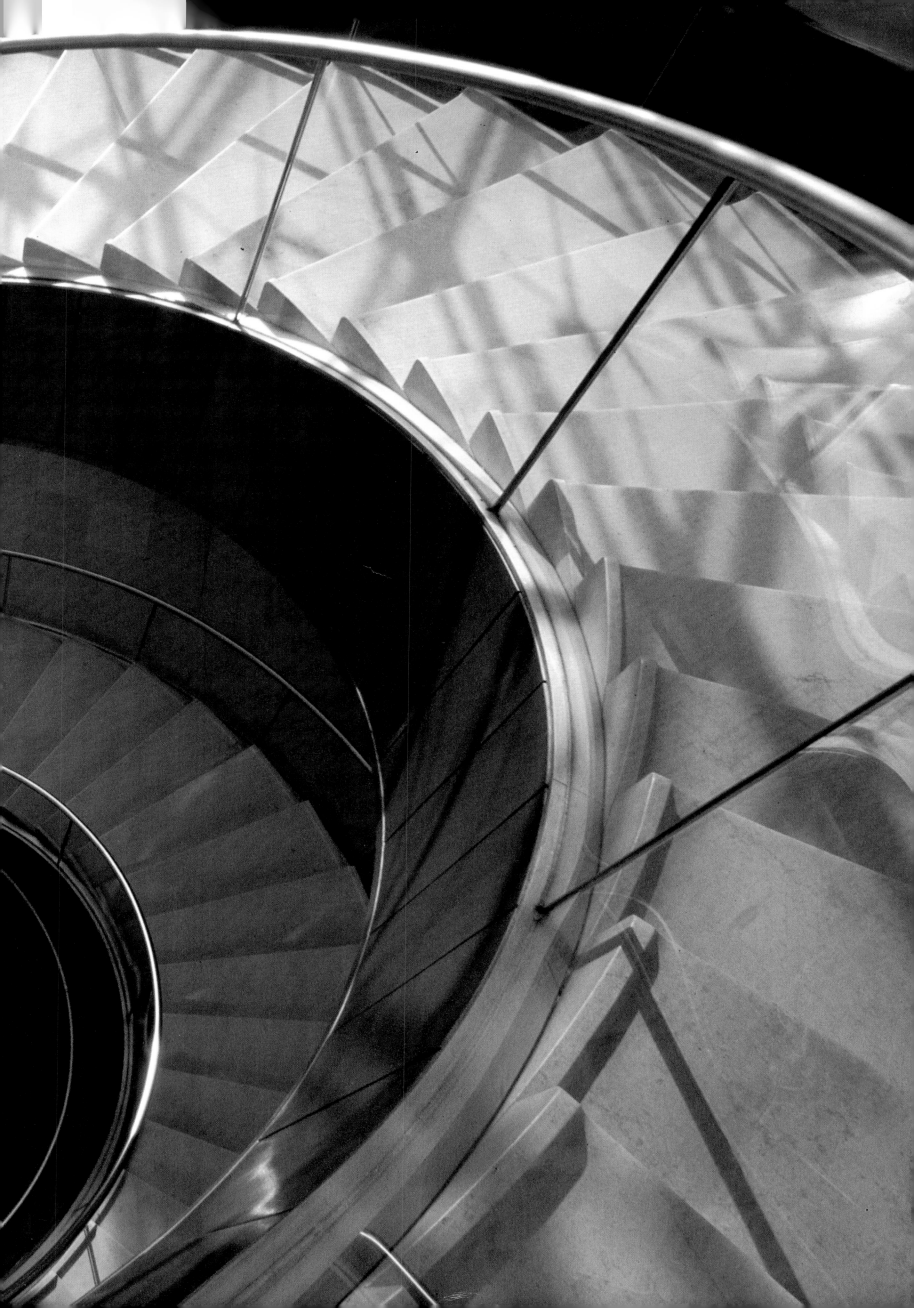

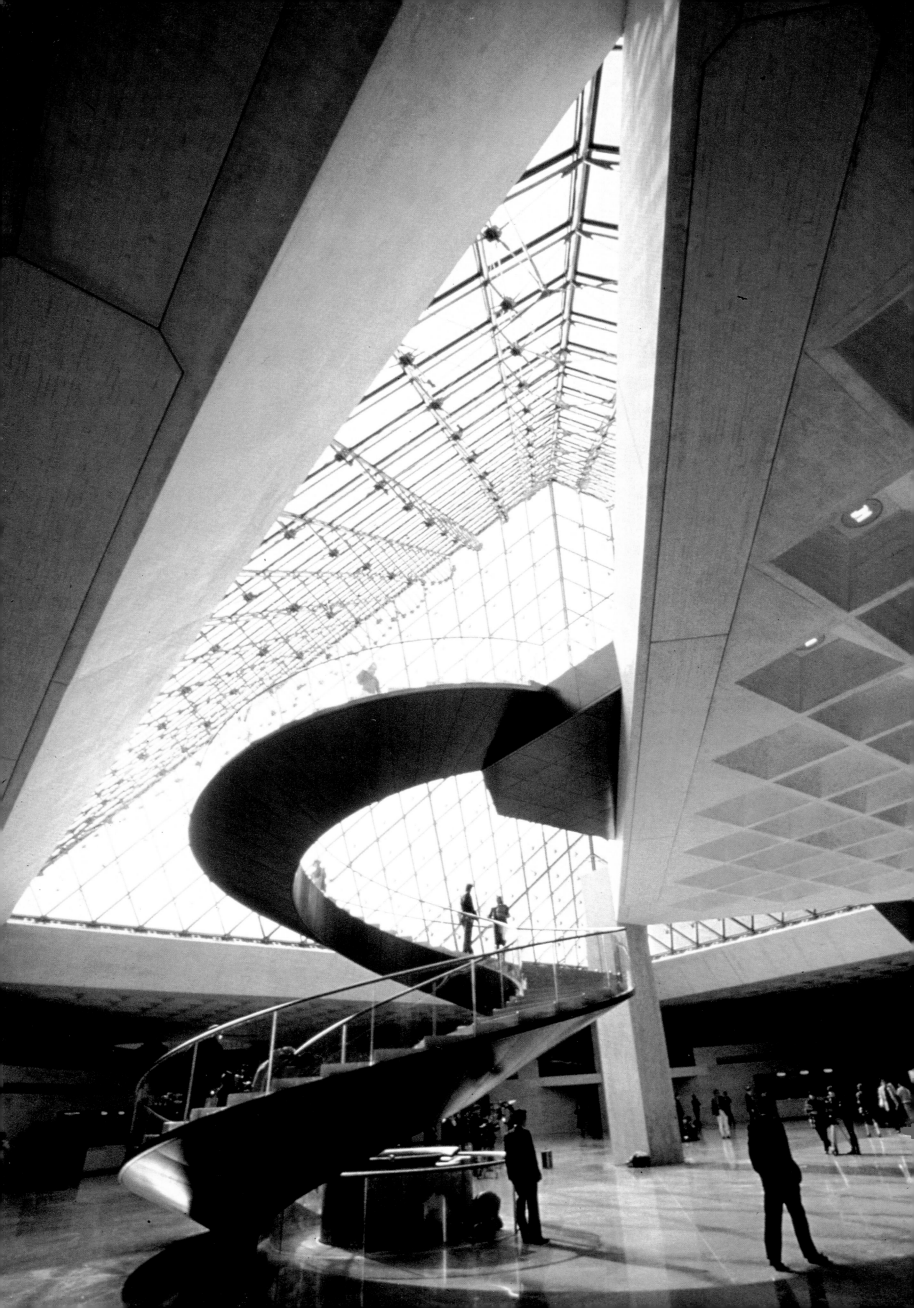

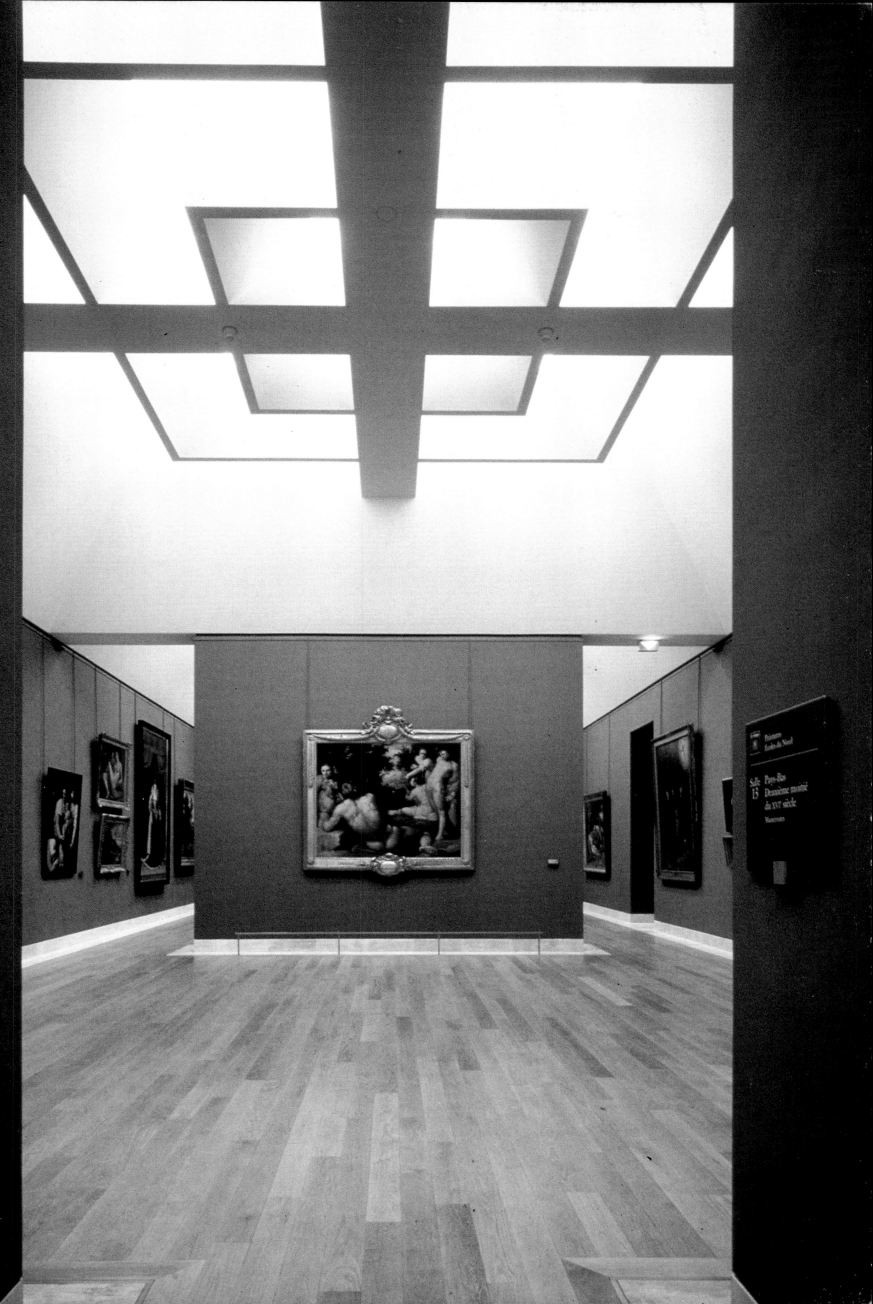

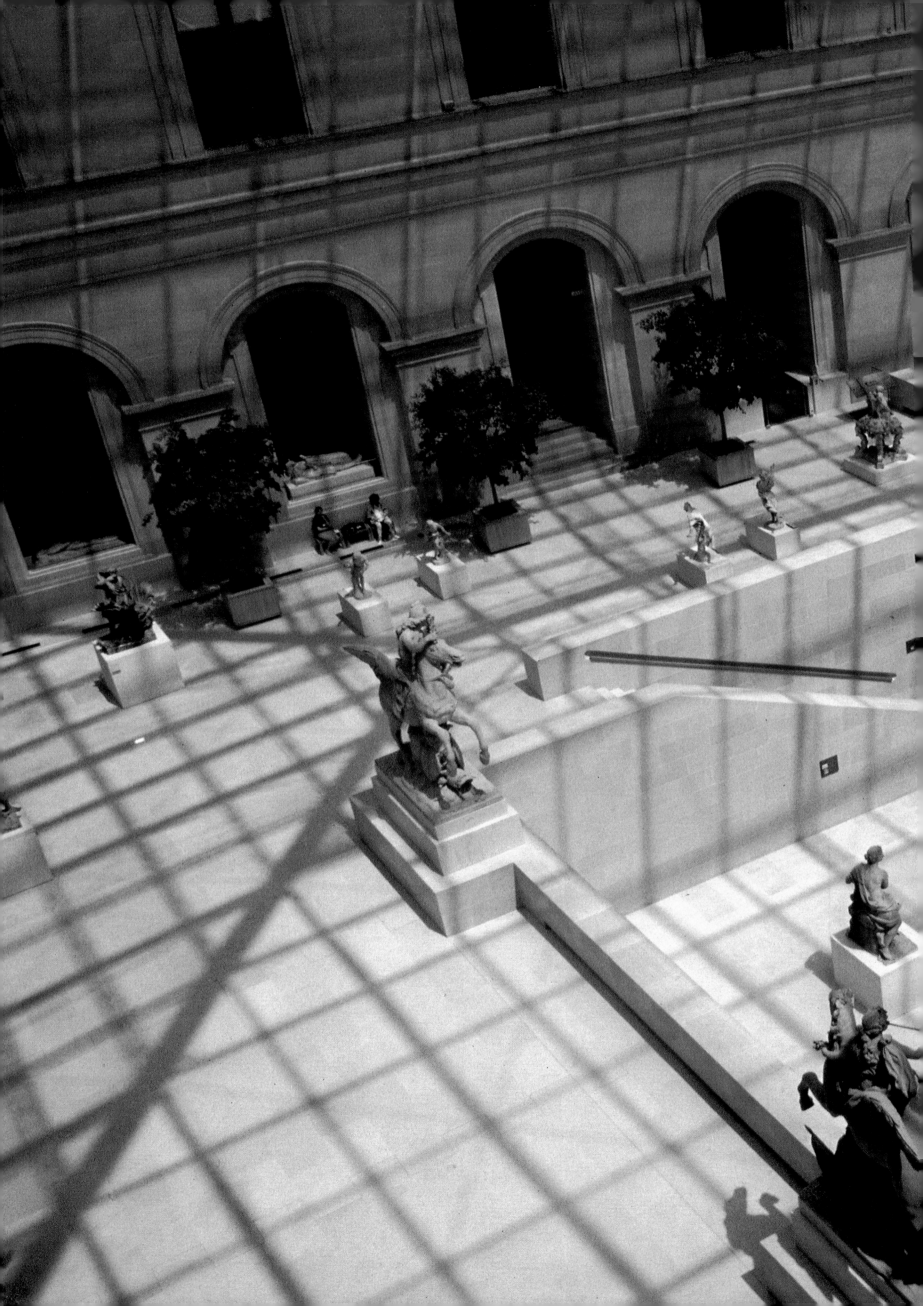

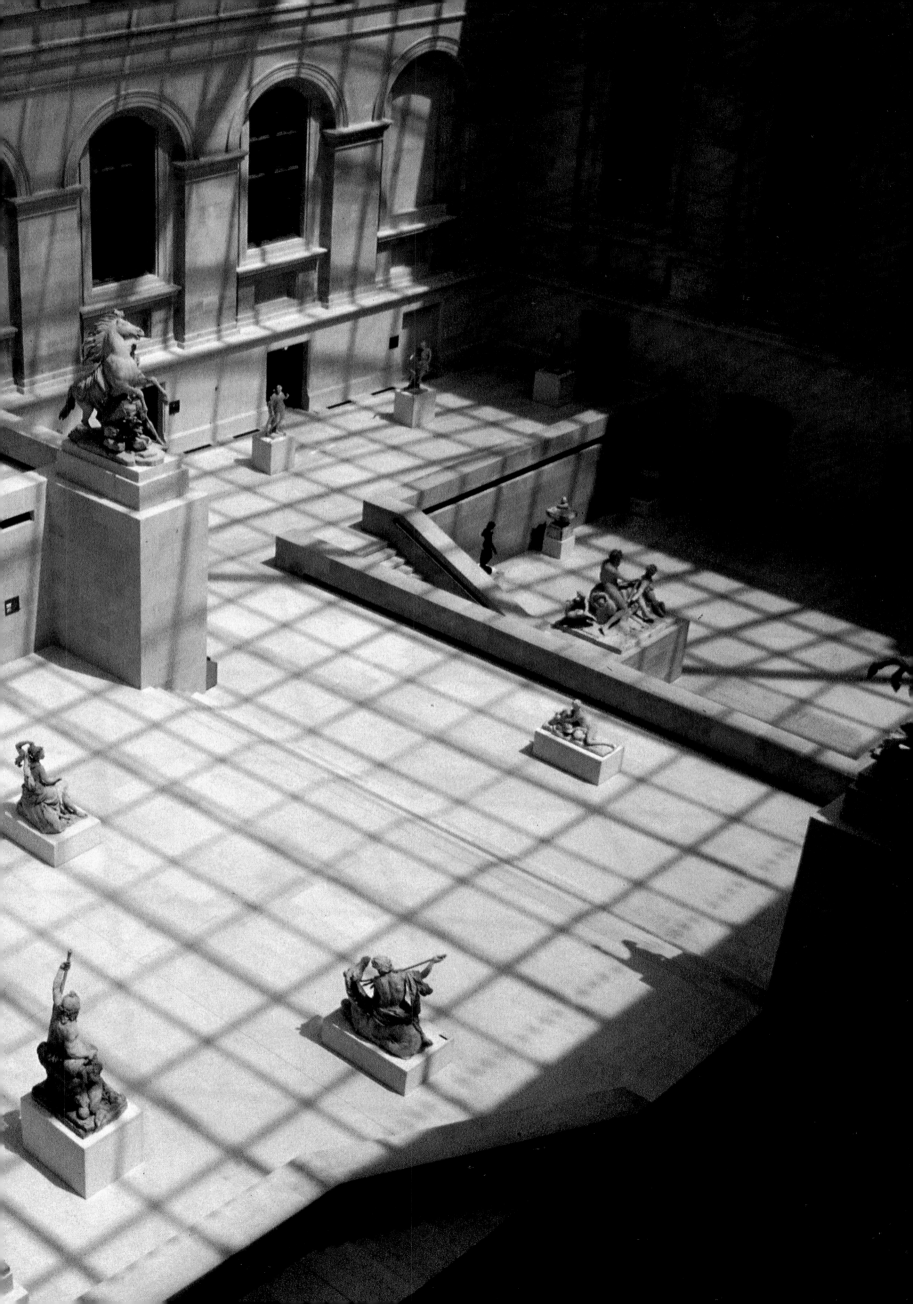

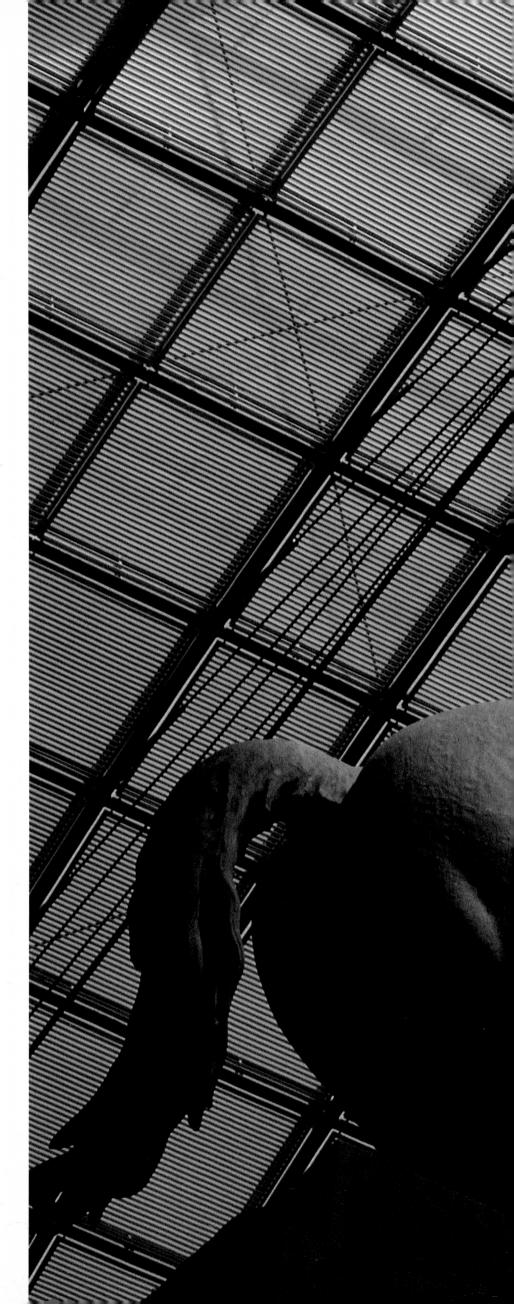

Pages 204–6 Inside the Pyramid, a spiral staircase, coiling round a lift, leads down to the great entrance hall.

Page 207 The new display of the Northern Schools of painting in the Richelieu wing.

Pages 208–9 and *opposite* The new Cour Marly, with its glass roof and display arrangement designed by Pei and Macary. All the sculpture comes from Louis XIV's park at Marly, laid out in 1695–1715 – with the exception of the Horses of Marly by Guillaume Coustou (left on page 209, and opposite). These were carved for the horse-pond of the château (1739–45).

Page 212 Sculpture by François Jouffroy in the Grands Guichets.

Page 213 Looking from the Passage Richelieu towards the Pyramid.

Pages 214–15 View looking west, with the Pyramid in the foreground, the Pavillon Mollien on the left, and in the distance the Arc de Triomphe du Carrousel.

Page 216 A room in the Department of Paintings. On the far wall is *The Two Sisters* by Théodore Chassériau (1843).

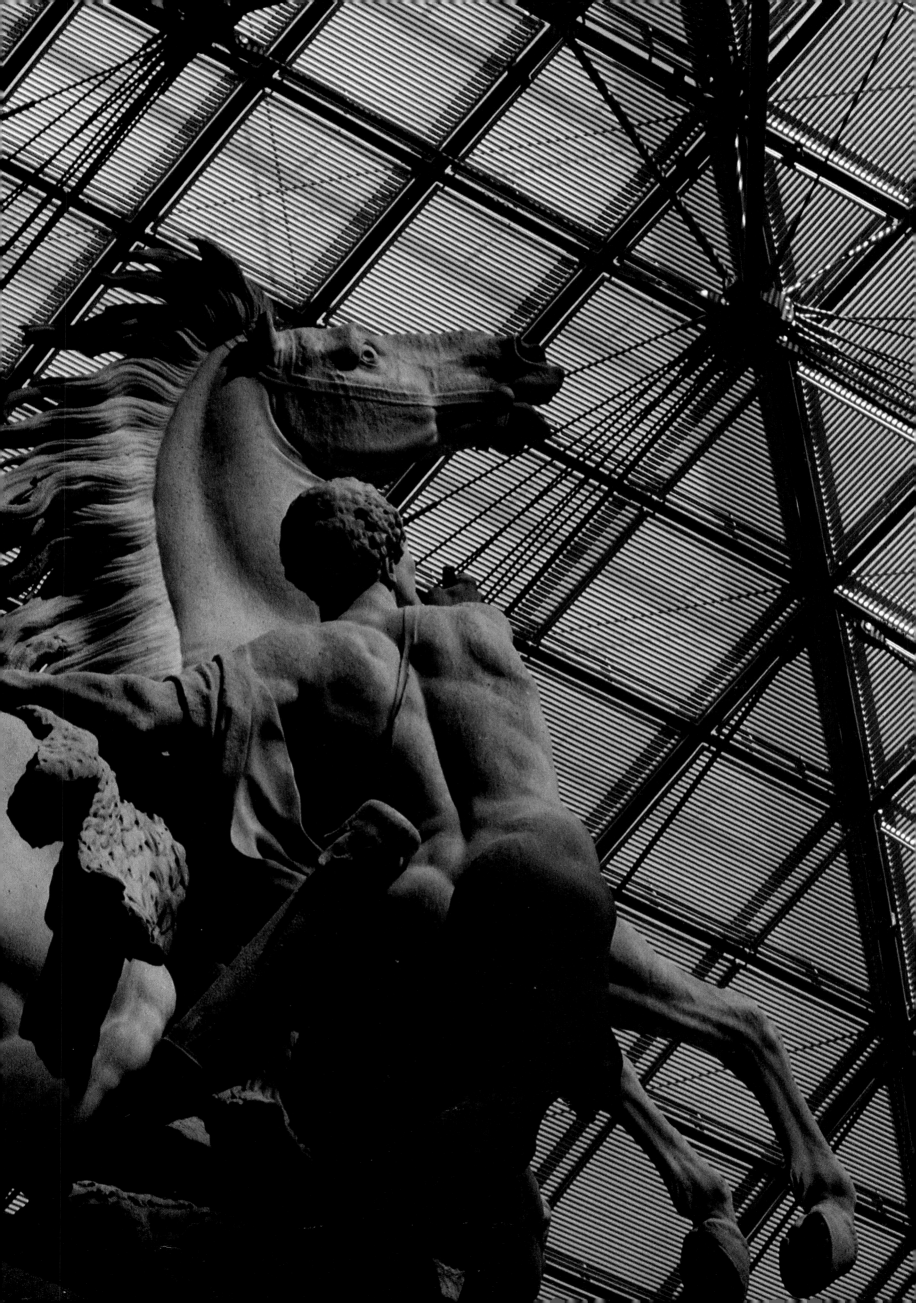

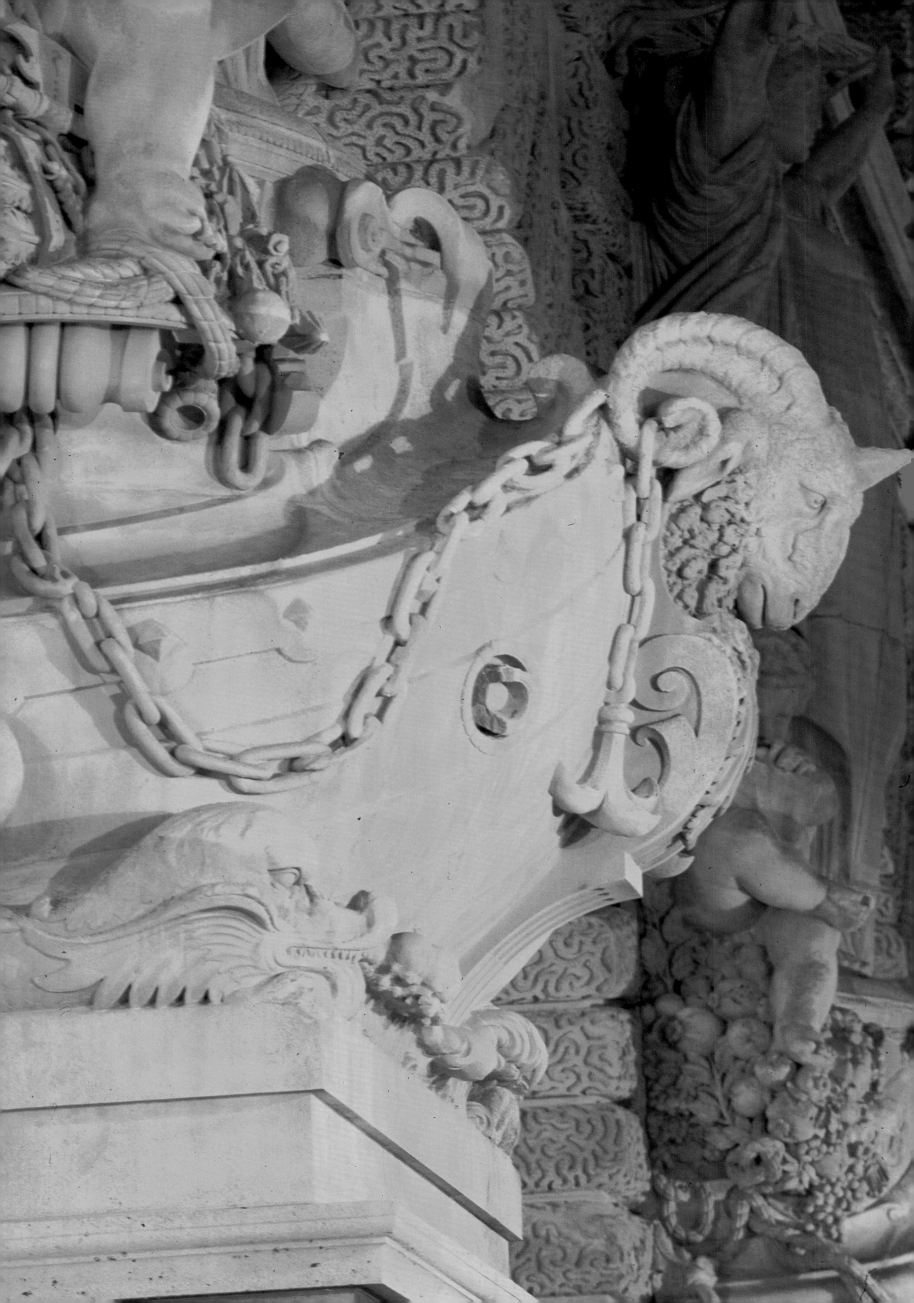

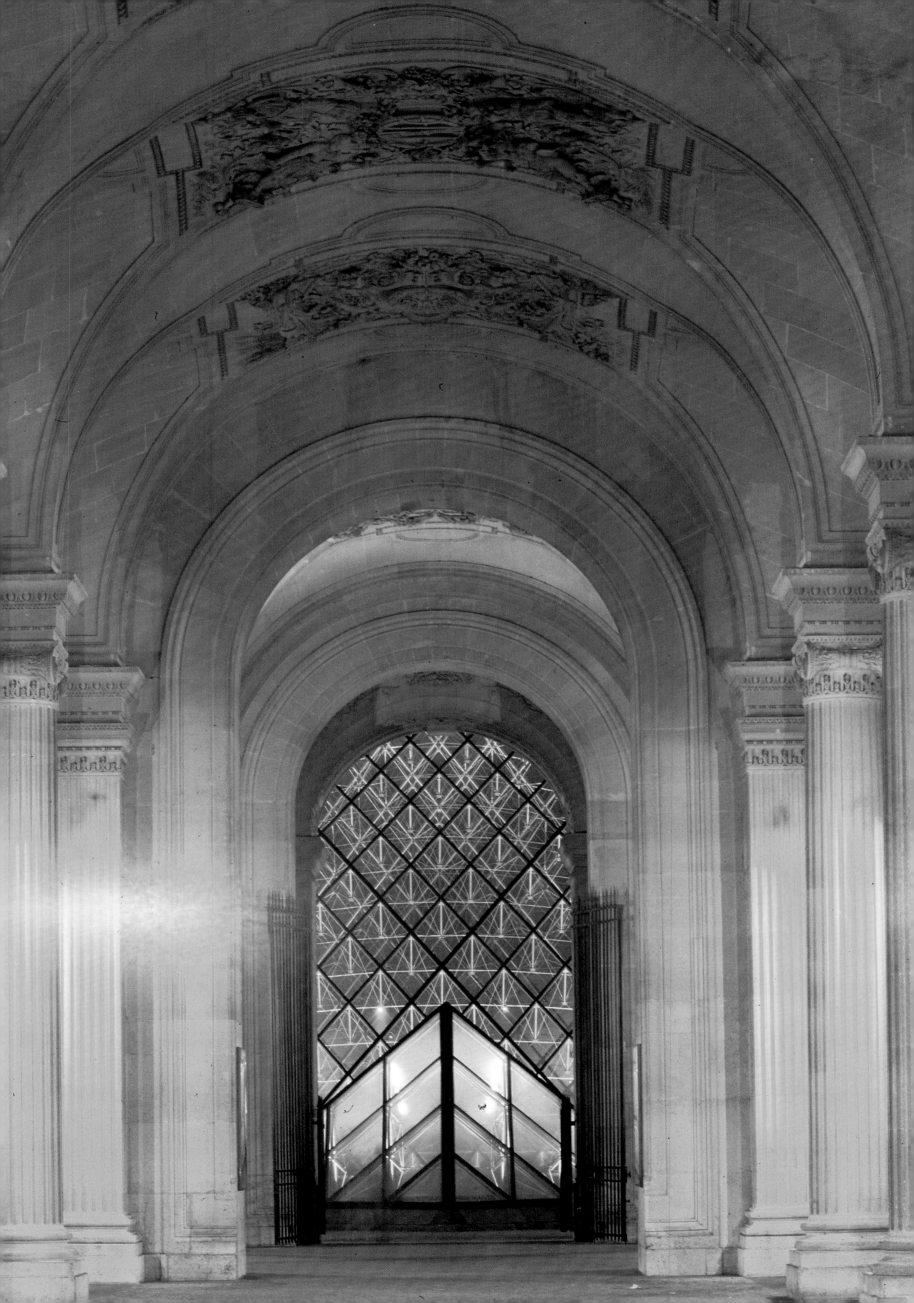

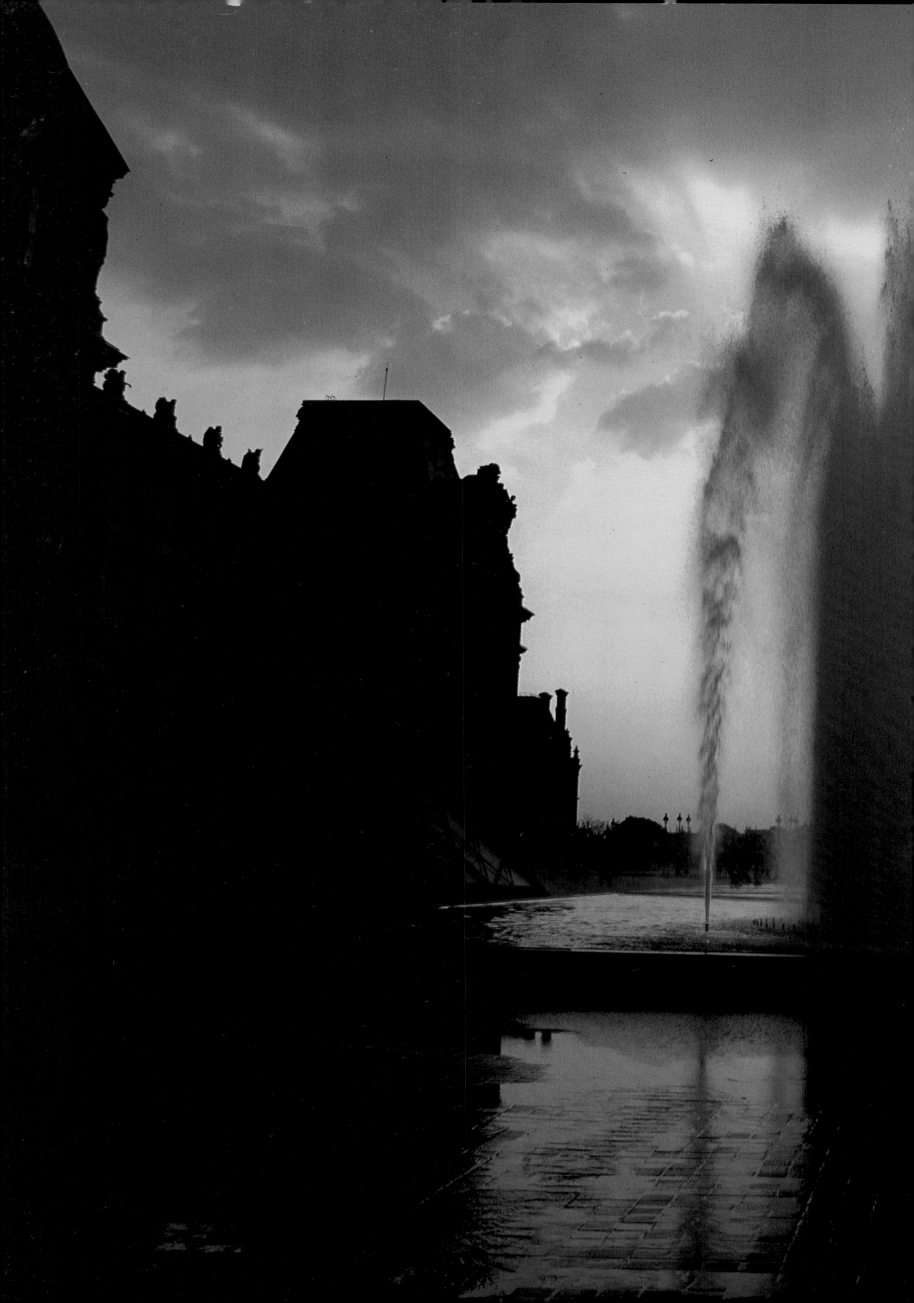

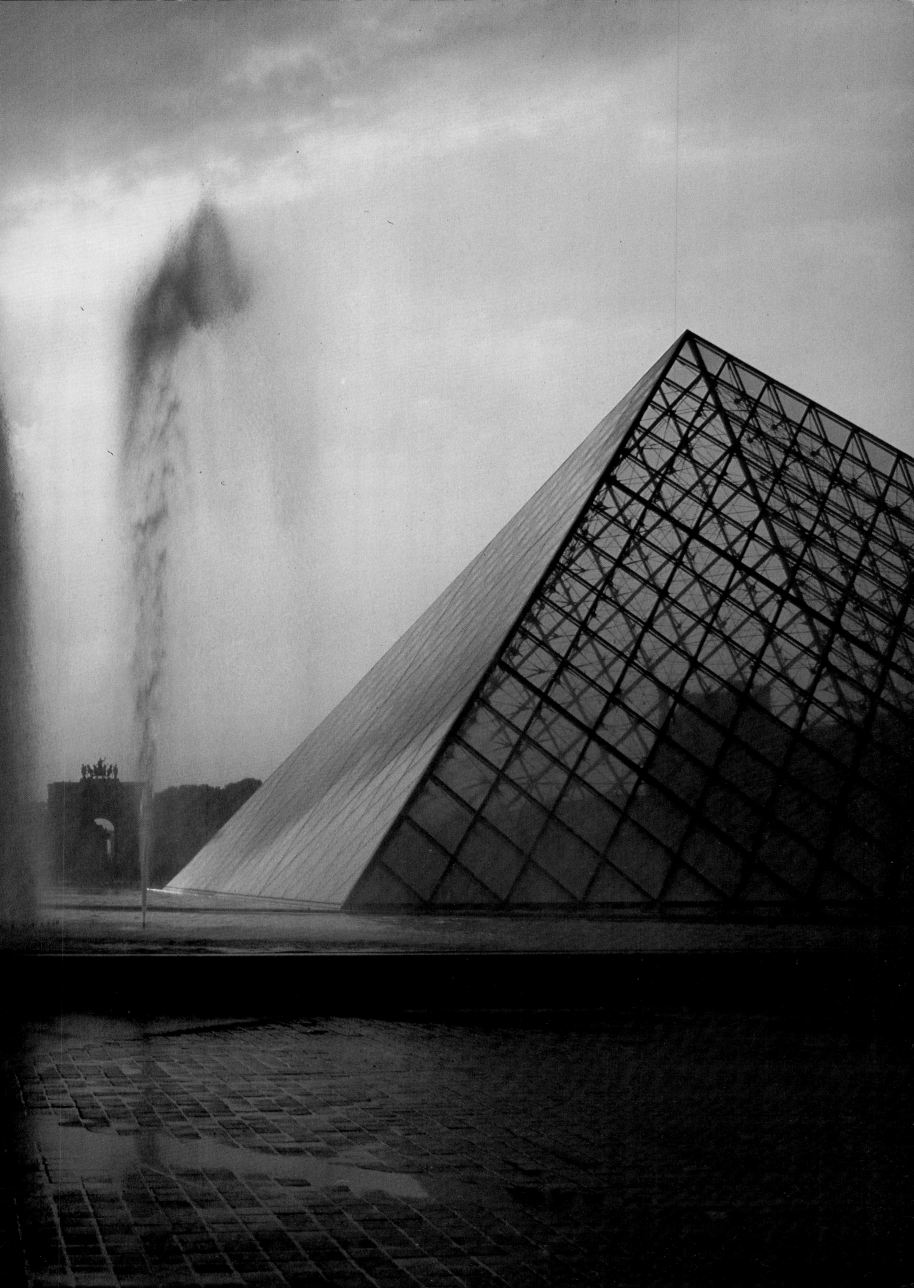

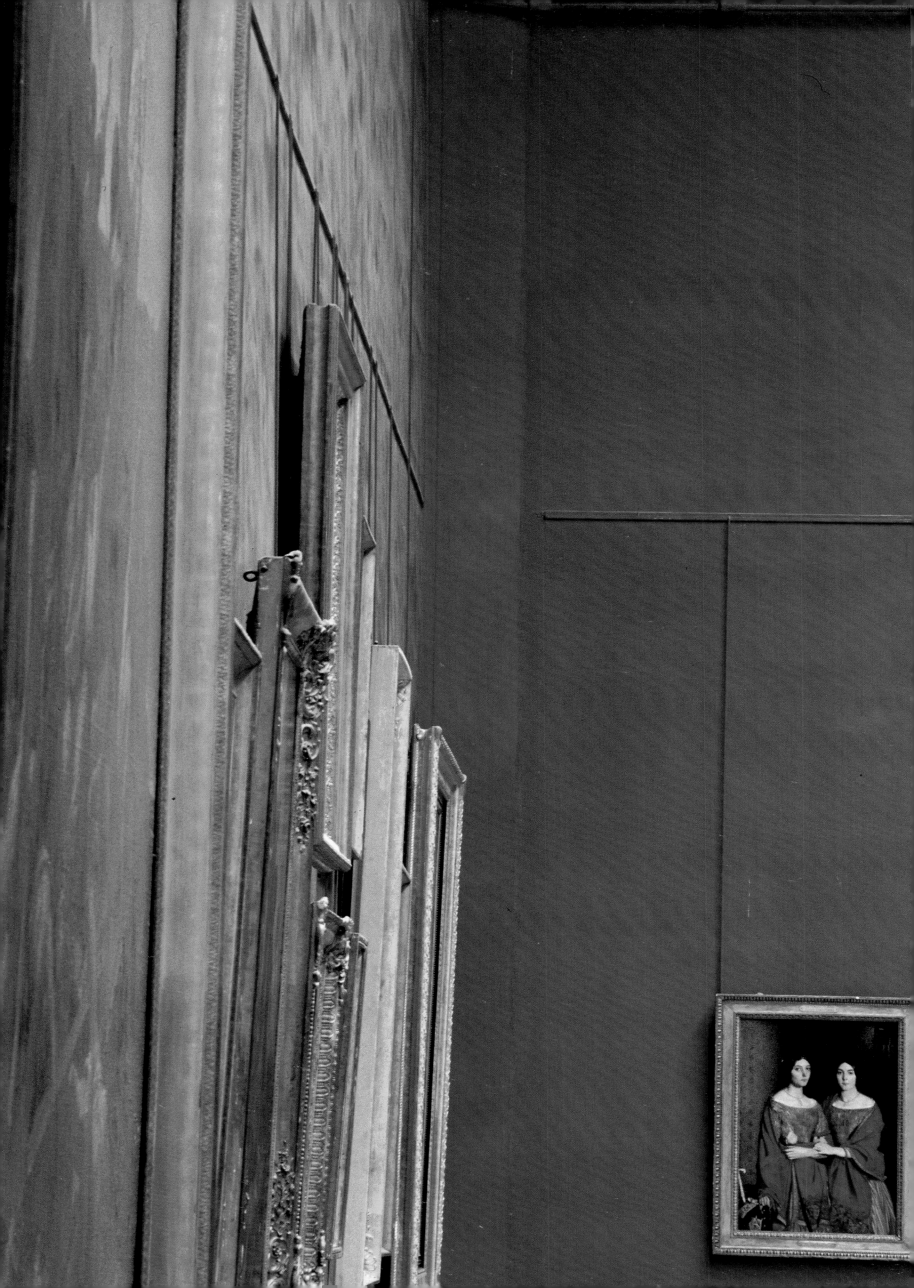

Chronology

1180—1223 Reign of Philippe Auguste

1190   Before setting off on crusade, Philippe Auguste orders the burghers of Paris to build a wall around the city.

1202   First mention of the 'Tower of the Louvre'.

1214   Ferdinand of Portugal, Count of Flanders, is held prisoner at the Louvre.

1364–1380 Reign of Charles V

1364–69   Remodelling of the Louvre for the King by Raymond du Temple; construction and decoration of the 'Grande Vis'.

1515–1547 Reign of François I

1528   Demolition of the round tower of the Louvre.

1540   The Emperor Charles V is received at the Louvre.

1546   Construction begins on the new Renaissance range of lodgings, designed for the King by Pierre Lescot.

1547–1559 Reign of Henri II

1549   The King decides on a change of plan: the intended central staircase is moved to the north.

1550   Jean Goujon sculpts the caryatids in the great hall.

1553   Construction of the attic storey. Work begins on the staircase.

1554   Contract with Goujon for the reliefs of the attic stage.

1556   The ceiling of the State Bedchamber of Henri II is carved by Scibecq de Carpi.

1560–1574 Reign of Charles IX

1560–65   Construction and decoration of the southern wing.

1564   Château des Tuileries begun for Catherine de Médicis.

1566   First stone of the Petite Galerie, and of a gallery designed to link that to the Tuileries, laid by the King. New fortifications built around Paris.

1572   St Bartholomew's Day Massacre.

1574–1589 Reign of Henri III

1588   Journée des Barricades. Flight of Henri III.

1589–1610 Reign of Henri IV

1593   The States of the Parisian League meet in the Louvre.

1595   Grande Galerie begun for the King.

1608   Royal artists are lodged in the Grande Galerie.

1610   Assassination of the King, who dies in the Louvre.

1610–1643 Reign of Louis XIII

1617   Murder of Concini at the Louvre.

1624   The King orders the resumption of building works.

1639   Le Mercier begins decoration of the Pavillon de l'Horloge.

1641–42   Poussin makes designs for the painted decoration of the Grande Galerie.

1643–1715 Reign of Louis XIV

1652   Anne of Austria and Louis XIV move into the Louvre.

1653–54   Decoration of the Winter Apartment of Anne of Austria.

1654   Ceiling of the King's Bedchamber, by Guérin.

1655–59   Decoration of the Summer Apartment of Anne of Austria.

1659   Construction of the Salle des Machines at the Tuileries.

1660   Le Vau submits his plan for the Louvre.

1661   Fire damages the Petite Galerie.

1661–63   Extension of the south wing of the Cour Carrée.

1662   *Carrousel* held to celebrate the birth of the Dauphin.

1662–64   Decoration of the Galerie d'Apollon.

1663   Pediment of the Cour de la Reine (du Sphinx).

1664   Le Nôtre begins work on the Tuileries Gardens.

1665   Bernini in Paris. The first stone of his projected east wing is laid.

1666   Anne of Austria dies in the Louvre.

1667   Work begins on the Colonnade wing.

1668   Widening of the southern wing.

1672   Installation of the pediment of the Colonnade wing. The Académie Française moves into the Louvre.

1674   Louis XIV leaves the Louvre for good.

1692   The royal collection of antique sculptures is transferred to the Salle des Cariatides. The Academy of Painting and Sculpture and Academy of Architecture move into the Louvre.

1699   First exhibition held by the Academy of Painting and Sculpture in the Louvre.

1715–1774 Reign of Louis XVI

1715–23   Regency. The young King is settled in the Tuileries.

1722   The Infanta of Spain, betrothed to Louis XV, resides at the Louvre.

1756   Space in front of the Colonnade wing cleared.

1767   Soufflot presents a design for the Louvre.

1768   Project for a 'museum' in the Louvre.

1774–1792 Reign of Louis XVI

1774–89   Plans for a 'museum' by the Comte d'Angiviller.

1789   French Revolution. The King is housed in the Tuileries.

1792   Fall of the monarchy. The Convention meets in the Tuileries.

1792–1795 Convention

1793   The 'museum' in the Grande Galerie opens to the public.

1795   Foundation of the Institut de France, at the Louvre.

1795–1799 Directoire

1798   Paintings and antiquities arrive from Italy.

1798–99   Transformation of the Summer Apartment of Anne of Austria into the Musée des Antiques.

1800–1804	**Consulate**
1800	Inauguration of the Musée des Antiques.
1802	Vivant Denon appointed director of the museum.
1803	Musée Napoléon.

1804–1815	**Reign of Napoleon**
1806	Arc de Triomphe du Carrousel. Expulsion of the Institut and resident artists from the Louvre.
1807	Decoration of the attic stage of the Lemercier wing.
1808–10	Decoration of the façade of the Colonnade wing by Lemot and Cartellier.
1810	Marriage of Napoleon and Marie-Louise, held at the Louvre.
1811–14	Decoration of the staircases at the ends of the Colonnade wing.

1814–1824	**Reign of Louis XVIII**
1815	Restoration of the monarchy. Looted works of art are restored to the Allies.
1819–24	Ceiling paintings in the Salle Duchâtel and Rotonde d'Apollon.
1821	The *Venus de Milo* arrives in Paris.
1824	Inauguration of the Galerie d'Angoulême, for the display of sculpture from the Renaissance to the eighteenth century.

1824–1830	**Reign of Charles X**
1826	Champollion is curator of Egyptian antiquities.
1827	Inauguration of the Musée Charles X on the first floor of the Cour Carrée. Creation of the Musée Dauphin.

1830–1848	**Reign of Louis-Philippe**
1831	Creation of a private garden in front of the Tuileries Palace.
1831–33	Completion of the decoration of the southern gallery of the Cour Carrée (the future Campana Gallery).
1847	Arrival of the first Assyrian antiquities.

1848–1852	**Second Republic**
1848	Decision to complete the Louvre. Last Salon held there.
1850	Opening of the Mexican – later American – Museum, followed by the Algerian and Ethnographical Museum. Restoration of the façades of the Grande Galerie and Petite Galerie.
1851	Inauguration of the Salon Carré, Salon des Sept Cheminées and Galerie d'Apollon restored by Duban.
1852	Beginning of the work on the Cour Napoléon by Visconti. Creation of the Musée des Souverains.

1852–1870	**Reign of Napoléon III**
1854	Lefuel replaces Visconti.
1857	Inauguration of the buildings surrounding the Cour Napoléon.
1859	First session in the Salle des Etats.
1861	Work resumes. Demolition of the Pavillon de Flore. Decoration of the Salle du Manège.
1863	Musée Napoléon III. Campana collection presented to the Louvre. Acquisition of the *Winged Victory*.
1866	Excavations in the Cour Carrée by Berty, exposing the medieval castle.

1869	Stucco decoration by Carrier-Belleuse in the rebuilt section of the Grande Galerie. Bequest of the La Caze collection.

1870–1940	**Third Republic**
1871	Paris Commune. Burning of the Tuileries. Rivoli wing allocated to the Ministry of Finance.
1875–78	Reconstruction of the Pavillon de Flore and Pavillon de Marsan.
1881	Creation of the Department of Oriental Antiquities.
1882	Demolition of the ruins of the Tuileries.
1900	Opening of the Rubens Room.
1905	Opening of the Musée des Arts Décoratifs.
1914	The museum is evacuated during the war.
1922	Opening of the Islamic Art Room (Delort de Gléon gift).
1927	The director, Henri Verne, devises a restructuring plan.
1932	Beginning of work to realize the Verne plan.
1934	First phase of the Verne plan, in the departments of Sculpture and Egyptian Antiquities. Daru Staircase, Ecole du Louvre.
1936	Second phase of the Verne plan, affecting Egyptian, Greek and modern sculpture.
1938	Third phase of the Verne plan, in the departments of Oriental Antiquities, Objets d'Art and Paintings.
1939	Evacuation of a substantial part of the collections during the war.

1945–1958	**Fourth Republic**
1947	Inauguration of the Musée du Jeu de Paume, displaying the collections of Impressionist paintings.
1953	Ceiling by Georges Braque.
1958–	Fifth Republic
1961	The Pavillon de Flore is handed over to the Louvre.
1964	Excavation of the moat in front of the Colonnade wing, revealing the foundations of an earlier scheme by Le Vau.
1968	Inauguration of the Pavillon de Flore.
1981	Decision to create the 'Grand Louvre'.
1983	Etablissement Public du Grand Louvre set up. I. M. Pei chosen as architect.
1984–86	Excavations in the Cour Carrée (exposing the mediaeval castle) and in the Cour Napoléon (uncovering the *quartier* of the Louvre and the 'Mur Le Vau').
1986	Opening of the Musée d'Orsay, displaying works of the period 1848–1914.
1989	The first phase of the project, and the Pyramid, opened to the public. The Finance Ministry moves to Bercy.
1990	Archaeological investigation of the Carrousel area; clearance of the moat of Charles V.
1992	Opening of the French painting galleries on the second floor of the Cour Carrée.
1993	The Louvre Museum becomes a completely public institution. Bicentenary of the museum; opening of the Richelieu wing.
1994	Opening of the foreign sculpture galleries.
1995	Opening of the new premises of the research laboratory of the Musées de France.

The Architects

Raymond du Temple
active 1360–1403
Master mason of Charles V, for whom in 1364–69 he transformed the medieval castle of Philippe Auguste into a royal residence. His most notable work there was the monumental spiral staircase known as the 'Grande Vis'.

Pierre Lescot
Paris, *c.* 1510–Paris, 1578
Worked with Jean Goujon on the rood screen of Saint-Germain-l'Auxerrois (1541–44) before being placed in charge of building at the Louvre in 1546. The years between then and 1560 saw the erection of the west wing of the old Louvre courtyard (the 'Lescot wing'), the Pavillon du Roi, and the beginning of a new south wing. A humanist, mathematician and man of letters, he applied Vitruvian principles in a pragmatic way to produce the innovations of the Renaissance Louvre: the staircase with straight flights and a carved stone vault, the great Salle des Cariatides, and the double-pitch roof.

Pierre II Chambiges
1545–1616
Member of a family of master masons. He is credited with the ground storey of the Petite Galerie.

Louis Métézeau
Dreux, *c.* 1562–Paris, 1615
Descendant of the architects Clément I and Thibaut Métézeau, who had gone on from work at Dreux to produce the tomb of Henri II in Saint-Denis, Louis Métézeau and his brother Clément II were instrumental in establishing the Classical language of architecture in France under Henri IV and Louis XIII. On commission from Henri IV, Louis Métézeau built the eastern half of the Grande Galerie, begun in 1595. The two faces of his building had different elevations: to the south, along the Seine, was a complex pattern of superimposed storeys decorated with elaborate relief sculpture incorporating royal emblems, and a frieze of gambolling putti; to the north, the design comprised an arcaded ground storey with ornaments alluding to victory and the arts, and an upper storey with tall windows lighting the gallery within.

Jacques II Androuet du Cerceau
c. 1550–1614
Brother of Baptiste Androuet du Cerceau (*c.* 1545–90), who succeeded Lescot as Architecte du Roi from 1578 until his death; both belonged to a dynasty of Royal Architects. For Henri IV he designed the western half of the Grande Galerie and the Pavillon de la Rivière, subsequently known as the Pavillon de Flore. Du Cerceau chose to use the same elevation, with a giant order of pilasters, on both façades. His building was destroyed by Lefuel in 1861, but the design can still be seen on the wing to the north of the Carrousel, where it had been replicated by Percier and Fontaine.

Jacques Lemercier
Pontoise, *c.* 1585–Paris, 1654
Scion of a family of master masons and architects from the Vexin in Normandy, Lemercier worked for Richelieu at his château in Poitou, at the Sorbonne and the Palais Cardinal in Paris, and at the church of Rueil. As Premier Architecte du Roi he was in charge of work at the Val-de-Grâce and provided designs for Saint-Roch. At the Louvre, he was responsible for the Pavillon de l'Horloge (1639–42) and the wing extending from it to the north, as well as the lower storey of the Pavillon de Beauvais and the wing returning at right angles along the north side. Inside the palace, he designed the Appartement du Conseil (1653) and the Appartement des Bains or Winter Apartment of Anne of Austria (1653–54). He had visited Rome in 1607, but while his style shows an awareness of Italian innovations, it is considered to mark the beginning of French Classicism.

Louis Le Vau
Paris, 1612–Paris, 1670
One of the principal representatives of French Classicism under Louis XIV, Le Vau was nevertheless often tempted by the more exuberant forms of Baroque. He worked in monumental masses, enlivening them by the play of columns, openings and decoration derived from the antique. Appointed Premier Architecte du Roi in 1654, Le Vau built a great deal for private clients, sometimes in collaboration with his brother François (Hôtel Bullion, Hôtel Lambert and Hôtel de Lauzun). He introduced a Baroque grandeur with the great dome and the decoration of the château of Vaux-le-Vicomte, which aroused the jealousy of the Surintendant Fouquet. A love of curves is reflected again in the Collège des Quatre Nations (now the Institut de France). For the Queen Mother he built a new wing at the château of Vincennes

and remodelled the Summer Apartments at the Louvre (1655–59). From 1661 onwards he was in charge of extensive works at the Louvre, reconstructing the upper floor of the Petite Galerie to form the Galerie d'Apollon, building another wing parallel to it, and quadrupling the size of the Cour Carrée, before beginning work on the east front (subsequently the Colonnade). He remodelled the façade of the Tuileries, and designed the first stages of Versailles – the Orangery, the first Trianon de Porcelaine, and the rhythmical façade with its terrace that would later be extended and completed by Jules Hardouin-Mansart.

François d'Orbay
Paris, 1634–Paris, 1697
D'Orbay joined forces with Le Vau after a journey to Rome in 1660. He began by preparing designs under his direction, then succeeded him as head of work at the Louvre, and in that capacity helped to build the Colonnade in collaboration with Claude Perrault, who was a doctor. He also designed the cathedral of Montauban and the Hôpital de la Trinité at Lyons.

Claude Perrault
Paris, 1613–Paris, 1688
Doctor and architect, brother of Charles Perrault, Claude had an enquiring spirit and an open mind, avid for knowledge. He translated Vitruvius and worked on the building of the Observatory in Paris and the château of Sceaux. He was involved in the construction of the Colonnade wing, where his technical skills made it possible to lift the huge blocks of stone forming the sloping sides of the central pediment.

Ange-Jacques Gabriel
Paris, 1698–Paris, 1782
Brought up in the midst of a group of Royal Architects – the Gabriels, the Mansarts, the De Cottes – Gabriel was appointed Premier Architecte du Roi himself in 1742. For Louis XV he built the Petit Trianon and the Opera at Versailles, the buildings of the present Place de la Concorde and the Ecole Militaire, as well as new wings at Fontainebleau and Compiègne. In 1755–57 he undertook the demolition of the structures that cluttered the Cour Carrée, and freed the Colonnade from buildings around it. He finished the east side of the Cour Carrée, which forms the back of the Colonnade. Faithful to the spirit of French Classicism, he became director of the Academy of Architecture, whose premises were in the Louvre.

Jacques-Germain Soufflot
Irancy, 1713–Paris, 1780
The architect of Sainte-Geneviève (later the Panthéon), Soufflot succeeded Gabriel at the Louvre, where the King wished to install first the Grand Conseil and then the museum. Most of his major works are not connected with the Louvre, but he was responsible for the opening and the decoration of the passage leading from the Cour Carrée to the Rue de Rivoli.

Maximilien Brébion
1716–96
Architect of the Louvre from 1780 to 1792. He built the Museum Staircase, which was destroyed under the Second Empire.

Auguste Cheval de Saint-Hubert, known as **Hubert**
Paris, 1755–Paris, 1798
After winning the Grand Prix d'Architecture he spent the years 1784–87 in Rome. After his return he became a close friend of the painter David, whose sister-in-law he married, and with whom he helped to organize Revolutionary festivities. He put forward a plan for the improvement of the Tuileries Gardens, and, in the year of his death, planned the installation of the Musée des Antiques in the former Summer Apartment of Anne of Austria.

Jean-Arnaud Raymond
1742–1811
Architect of the Louvre from 1797 to 1803, he carried through the Musée des Antiques on the lines planned by Hubert, and directed the work.

Charles Percier
Paris, 1764–Paris, 1838
After a stay in Rome as the winner of the Grand Prix d'Architecture (1786–92) he collaborated with his friend Fontaine first as architect of the Tuileries and then of the Louvre, from 1801 to 1812. Even after he had officially resigned he remained Fontaine's trusted adviser. A man of the most Classical tastes and a remarkable draughtsman, he also organized many of Napoleon's public celebrations, including his wedding to Marie-Louise in 1810.

Pierre-François-Léonard Fontaine
Paris, 1762–Paris, 1853

After travelling in Italy with his friend Percier at his own expense (1785–90) he became, with him, joint architect of the Tuileries and then of the Louvre from 1801 to 1848. In this capacity he was responsible for the great transformations that took place under the Empire and the Restoration: the north wing along the Rue de Rivoli, the Arc de Triomphe du Carrousel, the sculptural decoration of the Cour Carrée (pediments, attic stage of the Lemercier wing, oculi), of the Colonnade wing, and of the Pavillon Marengo and Pavillon des Arts. In the interior, he built the grand Museum Staircase of which an upper landing survives as the Salles Percier et Fontaine), the north and south staircases of the Colonnade wing, the remodelled Salle des Cariatides, the gallery of antique sculpture in the south wing of the Cour Carrée, the Galerie d'Angoulême on the ground floor of the Lemercier wing, the Musée Charles X, the present Campana Gallery, the rooms of the Conseil d'Etat (now used by the Department of Objets d'Art), the Salle des Bijoux and the Salle des Séances Royales. His work at the Tuileries included a new staircase and a theatre. He left a diary which minutely records his tireless activity at the Louvre.

Félix-Louis-Jacques Duban
Paris, 1797–Bordeaux, 1879

A pupil of Percier, Duban won the Prix de Rome in 1823. As the leader of the Romantic Rationalists, he was extremely active, both in the restoration of historic buildings (the château of Blois, the Sainte-Chapelle, the Louvre) and the design of prestigious new ones (Ecole des Beaux-Arts, château of Dampierre). At the Louvre he restored the Galerie d'Apollon, the river front of the Grande Galerie, and the exterior of the Petite Galerie, and worked on the Cour Carrée. His major contribution remains the decoration of the Salon Carré and of the Salon des Sept Cheminées. He designed the installation of the Musée des Souverains on the first floor of the Colonnade wing. After protracted disagreement with Napoleon III, he resigned in 1853.

Louis-Tullius-Joachim Visconti
Rome, 1791–Paris, 1853

Son of the Roman archaeologist Ennio Quirino Visconti, the first curator of antiquities at the Louvre, Visconti was a pupil of Percier and had a prolific architectural practice in Paris (Fontaine Louvois, Fontaine Molière, Fontaine Saint-Sulpice, tomb of Napoleon in the Invalides, and several large private houses). In May 1848 he was commissioned to link the Louvre and the Tuileries, a project initiated by the Second Republic but only begun in 1852 under Napoleon III, in which he intended faithfully to follow the spirit of the existing architecture. He was prevented from completing the work by his sudden death on 29 December 1853.

Hector-Martin Lefuel
Versailles, 1810–Paris, 1880

The son of a contractor in the royal works, he succeeded his father before winning the Prix de Rome in 1839. Napoleon III noticed him when he was architect at the palace of Fontainebleau and he was put in charge of the Louvre and the Tuileries, which he completed. From 1854 to 1857 he carried out the first phase, which was the construction of the wings and courts surrounding the Cour Napoléon. Then from 1861 to 1868 he reconstructed part of the Grande Galerie and the Pavillon de Flore. In the interior, his talents as a decorator were expressed in the staircases (of the Library, the Minister of State and the Flore, Mollien, Daru and Colbert pavilions), large halls (Salle des Etats, Salon Denon, Salle du Manège), and suites of apartments (in the Tuileries, destroyed; in the

Louvre, apartments of the Minister of State and of the Grand Ecuyer). He also remodelled the eastern part of the Tuileries Gardens. His eclectic and exuberant style turned away from the more classical designs of Visconti towards greater elaboration. After the fall of the Second Empire he remained in charge of the Louvre, reconstructing the Pavillon de Marsan and the north façade of the Pavillon de Flore.

Edmond-Jean-Baptiste Guillaume
Valenciennes, 1826–94

Winner of the Prix de Rome in 1856, he began his connection with the Louvre by archaeological expeditions in Asia Minor. As architect of the palace from 1880 to 1894, he remodelled the Salle des Etats, added mosaic decoration to the Daru Staircase, and designed the African Gallery on the ground floor of the Salle des Sept Mètres, the Sarzec and Susa rooms, and the great saloon of the Pavillon de Beauvais and the room next to it. He laid out the Carrousel Gardens on the site of the destroyed Tuileries Palace.

Gaston Redon
Bordeaux, 1853–1921

Brother of the painter Odilon Redon, he was architect of the Louvre from 1897 to 1910. He created the Rubens Room (1900) and redesigned the Musée des Arts Decoratifs (1905). He also made several fine visionary drawings.

Victor-Auguste Blavette
1850–1933

Architect of the Louvre from 1910 to 1921. He completed the Mollien Staircase, left unfinished in 1870.

Camille Lefèvre
1876–1946

Architect of the Louvre from 1922 to 1929. He prepared the plan for the restructuring of the museum conceived by Henri Verne. It is to him that we owe the display of Monet's *Water Lilies* in the Orangerie.

Albert Ferran
San Francisco, 1886–Paris, 1952

Winner of the Prix de Rome in 1914, he taught in Boston (1922–24) before being commissioned to carry out the reorganization planned by the director of the national museums, Henri Verne. In the course of his great works (1930–43) he brought to the Louvre a sense of purist grandeur, notably in the Daru (*Winged Victory*) Staircase, displays for the Departments of Sculpture and of Oriental Antiquities, the display of Egyptian antiquities on the ground floor, the Salle des Sept Mètres, and the curatorial offices in the south wing of the Cour Carrée. He excavated crypts under the wings of the Cour Carrée, thus making it possible for visitors to make the complete circuit of the ground floor.

Ieoh Ming Pei
Canton, 1917–

After studying at Boston and at the Graduate School of Design at Harvard, Pei became famous for his additions to museums in America: enlargement of the Des Moines Museum (1968), east wing of the National Gallery of Art, Washington (1979), and west wing of the Museum of Fine Art in Boston (1981). Put in charge of the Grand Louvre in 1983, he built the Hall Napoléon and the Pyramid (1988), and the new interiors of the Rivoli or Richelieu wing and the Carrousel concourse (1993).

The Painters

Nicolas Poussin
Les Andelys, 1594–Rome, 1665

Poussin, who had settled in Rome in 1624 and was established as the most famous Classical painter in Europe, was invited by Louis XIII to carry out large-scale decorative work at the Louvre. He arrived in 1640 and was lodged on site, in the Tuileries Gardens. For the decoration of the vault of the Grande Galerie he designed a scheme of medallions and atlantes based on the Labours of Hercules. Work began, but it was interrupted by the deaths of Richelieu and of the King. It could never have been congenial to Poussin, who was by temperament a painter of single, carefully composed and considered canvases, not a decorator. He returned to his family in Rome; and although he promised to continue supplying designs, the project was never completed. A few drawings survive. A circular painting of *Time rescuing Truth* executed by Poussin for the Palais Cardinal (Palais Royal) was brought to the Louvre in the seventeenth century and inserted in the

ceiling of the Grand Cabinet du Roi; it was subsequently taken down and incorporated in the collections of the museum.

Giovanni Francesco Romanelli
1610–62

A pupil of Pietro da Cortona in Rome, Romanelli was brought to Paris in 1646 by Cardinal Mazarin, that champion of Baroque art. There he decorated the gallery of the Palais Mazarin with episodes from the Trojan War and Ovid's *Metamorphoses*, with such success that he was summoned again to direct the decorative work in the Summer Apartment of Anne of Austria in the Louvre (1655–57). He designed the stuccos, realized by Michel Anguier, and himself painted the frescoes – subjects from Roman history in the Grand Cabinet (*Mucius Scaevola, Cincinnatus, Scipio*, etc.), heroic women in the Bedchamber (*Judith* and *Holofernes*, etc.), and in the antechamber or Salle des Saisons scenes of Apollo and Diana and the Seasons.

Eustache Le Sueur
Paris, 1617–Paris, 1655
At the Hôtel Lambert Le Sueur painted scenes from the life of St Bruno and decorated the Cabinet de l'Amour and the Chambre des Muses (the paintings, executed c. 1652–55, are all now in the Louvre collections). He was then commissioned to decorate the King's Apartment in the Louvre, but of that work only a few preparatory drawings survive.

Charles Le Brun
Paris, 1619–Paris, 1690
Premier Peintre of Louis XIV. In 1661, after the fire in the Petite Galerie, Le Brun was entrusted with the decoration of what was to become the Galerie d'Apollon, for which he conceived a scheme celebrating the Sun God, Time and the Muses. The paintings were left unfinished, or have subsequently been damaged or restored, and the character of his original concept is best seen in a small number of preparatory drawings and a series of engravings made by Saint-André in 1695. Still visible today, however, are *The Triumph of the Waters*, showing Neptune and his train, on the wall at the far southern end of the Gallery, and two canvases in compartments of the vault: *Evening* or *Morpheus*, and *Night* or *Diana*.

Hughes Taraval
Paris, 1729–Paris, 1785
His painting of *Autumn* or *The Triumph of Bacchus*, painted on the orders of the Academy of Painting and Sculpture as his reception piece in 1769, was installed in one of the vault compartments of the Galerie d'Apollon.

Louis-Jacques Durameau
Paris, 1733–Paris, 1796
Prix de Rome in 1757, admitted to the Academy of Painting and Sculpture in 1766, for his reception piece in 1774 he was required to paint a canvas for the vault of the Galerie d'Apollon: *Summer*, or *Ceres and her Companions invoking the Sun*. He was extensively patronized by the royal administration, and was one of the leading decorators of official buildings, providing *Apollo crowning the Arts* for the ceiling of the Opera at Versailles, two ceilings for the Opera in the Palais Royal (destroyed), and a ceiling for the Orléans Chancellery. At the same time he pursued a career as a curator, first in charge of the royal collection of paintings (1784–92), then as curator of the special museum of the French School (1795–96).

Antoine-François Callet
Paris, 1741–Paris, 1823
Prix de Rome in 1764, admitted to the Academy of Painting and Sculpture in 1777. For his reception piece in 1780 he was required to paint *Spring*, or *Zephyr and Flora crowning Cybele with Flowers*, for the Galerie d'Apollon.

Michel-Martin Drölling
Paris, 1756–Paris, 1851
Commissioned under Charles X to paint two ceilings for the Louvre: *Law coming down to Earth* for the Conseil d'Etat (1827) and *Louis XII proclaimed 'Father of the People'* (1828) for the southern gallery of the Cour Carrée (now the Campana Gallery).

Pierre-Paul Prud'hon
Cluny, 1758–Paris, 1823
Son of a stone-mason at Cluny, Prud'hon received most of his training at Dijon, where he won the Academy prize and was enabled to study in Rome. Back in Paris, he supported the Revolution, but when the tide turned he had to take refuge at Gray. Eventually he returned to Paris, and as the protégé of Bonaparte received his first official commissions. At the Louvre he painted a medallion for the former Bedchamber of Anne of Austria, which had been enlarged to form the last room at the southern end of the Musée des Antiques (*Study guiding the Flight of Genius*, 1800), and in the following year he was commissioned to paint *Diana imploring Jupiter to exempt her from the Laws of Hymen* for the ceiling of the Salle de Diane. He painted portraits of Josephine (1805) and of Napoleon and went on to great success with works such as *Innocence prefers Love* and *Vengeance pursuing Crime* (1808) and *Psyche borne up by the Zephyrs* (1808). He was then left behind by fashion, though a few Romantic painters, including Delacroix, continued to admire him.

Etienne-Barthélemy Garnier
Paris, 1759–Paris, 1849
After studying with Durameau and Vien, Garnier won the Grand Prix in 1788 and set out for Rome; in 1793, an anti-French riot forced him to leave the city, and he eventually returned to France. He worked with Mérimée and Prud'hon on the decoration of the Salle de Diane, and in a tympanum painted *Hercules obtaining from Diana the Doe with Golden Horns* (1802).

Guillaume Guillon-Lethière
Sainte-Anne (Guadeloupe), 1760–Paris, 1832
Guillon, known as Guillon-Lethière, studied with Doyen and went on to become a portraitist and a history painter. He was committed to the ideas of the Revolution, and worked with Hennequin, who had similar views, on the first decorative scheme commissioned for the Louvre as a museum. Further compartments were needed to complete the ceiling of the Bedchamber of Anne

of Austria in its enlarged state as the last room of the Musée des Antiques and in 1800 he painted a tympanum with the subject of *Victory and the Genius of the Arts*. He became an official artist, director of the Villa Medici in Rome, where one of his pupils was Ingres (1807–16), professor at the Ecole des Beaux-Arts (1819) and member of the Institut (1825).

Philippe-Auguste Hennequin
Lyons, 1763–Leuze (Belgium), 1833
Hennequin was one of the artists most profoundly committed to the Revolution: a Jacobin, he was imprisoned in 1796–97 and after his release reiterated his ideals in the immense *Triumph of the French People* (1799) and *The Remorse of Orestes*. At the Louvre, he contributed to the decoration of the former Bedchamber of Anne of Austria, transformed into the last room of the Musée des Antiques, with a medallion of *The French Hercules*.

Charles Meynier
Paris, 1768–Paris, 1832
After studying with Vincent, Meynier won the Prix de Rome in 1789, and remained in the city until the anti-French riot of 1793. He became one of the official artists of the Empire, producing paintings of religious subjects and especially of great events in Napoleon's reign. It was to him that Vivant Denon turned for designs for the statues and reliefs of the Arc de Triomphe du Carrousel, which were then carved by various sculptors. He received many commissions for work at the Louvre, both under the Empire and after the Restoration, and designed a number of ceilings in which seemingly weightless figures float among clouds. In 1801, for the former Summer Apartment of Anne of Austria, now Musée des Antiques, he painted *The Emperors Hadrian and Justinian Presenting to the World the Codes of Roman Laws*. In 1819, he decorated the ceiling of the Museum Staircase (the part that is now the Salles Percier et Fontaine) with *France protecting the Arts*, then in 1822 that of the adjacent room (the Salle Duchâtel) with *The Triumph of French Painting*. His last work there, in 1827, was a ceiling in the Musée Charles X, where his composition of *The Nymphs of Parthenope bearing their Penates* celebrated the installation in the Louvre of antiquities from Pompeii and Herculaneum. Three studies for these ceilings can be seen in the Salles d'Histoire du Louvre.

François Gérard
Rome, 1770–Paris, 1837
Gérard grew up in Rome, where his father was intendant at the French Embassy, then came to Paris where he studied with the sculptor Pajou and afterwards with the painter David. He did not compete for the Prix de Rome, but thanks to David he was allocated quarters in the Louvre. Early successes in the Salon (*Cupid and Psyche*, 1798) established his reputation. As official portraitist under the Consulate and then the Empire, he painted all the great figures of Europe; at the same time, he maintained a career as a history painter, with works such as the vast *Battle of Austerlitz* (1810, Musée de Versailles). During the reign of Charles X, it was proposed to transform the Salon des Sept Cheminées into a 'Salon Gérard' displaying large compositions including The *Coronation of Charles X* (Musée de Versailles). Louis-Philippe first revised the choice of subject-matter, rejecting depictions of the former King in favour of themes celebrating the Orléans family, and in 1832 commissioned as overdoors colossal representations of Courage, Mercy, Genius and Constancy. In the end the works were never installed, and were instead displayed at Versailles.

Antoine-Jean Gros
Paris, 1771–Meudon, 1835
The son of miniaturists, Gros became the pupil of David, thanks to whom he was able to travel in Italy, where he spent time chiefly in Milan and Genoa. There he met Bonaparte, and painted one of the most famous portraits of the general, *Bonaparte at Arcole* (1796, Versailles). He celebrated great contemporary events of Napoleonic history, such as *The Plague Victims at Jaffa*, *The Battle of Aboukir* and *The Battle of Eylau*, but then, apparently without too much heart-searching, he became official portrait-painter to Louis XVIII. Charles X created him a baron, and Gros took the leading role in the decoration of the Musée Charles X. For the ceiling of the Salle des Colonnes, at the centre of the enfilade, he painted three large compositions with subjects alluding, in a suitably courtly way, to kingly virtues: *True Glory resting on Virtue*, *Mars crowned by Victory listening to the Discourse of Moderation*, and *Time raising Truth to the Steps of the Throne where she is received by Wisdom*; around these, six trompe-l'oeil busts depict famous patrons, from Pericles via Augustus, Leo X, François I and Louis XIV to – naturally – Charles X, in a tacit celebration of State patronage. The same subject recurs in another ceiling that Gros painted for this suite of rooms, in 1827: *The King presents the Musée Charles X to the Arts*. That painting was taken down under Louis-Philippe (it is now in the Musée de Versailles) and replaced by another, also by Gros: the subject this time was less monarchistic but equally nationalistic – *The Genius of France giving Life to the Arts and protecting Humanity*. A standard-bearer of the new style in his youth, Gros now turned to formal Classicism at a time when Romanticism, with its colour and movement, was sweeping the field. He grew increasingly out of step with contemporary trends, and after hostile criticism of his work at the Salon of 1835 he committed suicide by drowning in the Seine.

Alexandre-Evariste Fragonard
Grasse, 1780–Paris, 1850
Son of the painter Jean-Honoré Fragonard, he trained with his father and with

David, and in his style a feeling for simplicity of line characteristic of Neoclassicism is combined with a sense of light and movement. During the Empire he celebrated the reign of Napoleon and took part in the decoration of the National Assembly, turning increasingly to historical subject-matter which after 1819 tended to be French. *François I armed as a Knight by Bayard*, shown at the Salon of 1819, was bought by the King on the spot, and in 1828 was incorporated in the decoration of the southern gallery of the Cour Carrée (now the Campana Gallery). After this early success, he was commissioned by the Ministère de la Maison du Roi to paint *François I and Marguerite of Navarre receiving the Paintings and Statues brought from Italy by Primaticcio*, which was first used in 1827 in the Musée Charles X and then moved to the southern gallery. Fragonard's sketches for these Romantic celebrations of the chivalrous king are exhibited in the Salles d'Histoire du Louvre. He also painted several trompe-l'oeil reliefs in grisaille for the Musée Charles X.

Jean-Auguste-Dominique Ingres
Montauban, 1780–Paris, 1867
Ingres studied in Toulouse at the Academy and also with the Orchestra of the Capitole (the story of the 'violon d'Ingres' is true), and then moved on to the atelier of David in Paris in 1797. He won the Prix de Rome in 1801 but went there only five years later, so that he had already developed his own style, characterized by simplicity of contour and primacy of line, and a belief that art transcends conventional attitudes. He spent a long time in Rome and then in Florence, producing many drawings, scenes in the medievalizing 'Troubadour' style, and portraits, but this extended absence abroad did not prevent him from receiving major commissions for France. After his return home in 1824 he enjoyed an official success that led to his return to Rome as director of the French Academy (1835–41). During a stay in Paris in 1826 he received a commission for the ceiling in the first room of the Musée Charles X: the result was *The Apotheosis of Homer*, destined to become the most famous of all the paintings in this section of the Louvre. It was taken down in 1855 to be displayed with the main collection of paintings, and replaced by a copy executed by Paul Balze (1815–84) and his brother Raymond (1818–1909).

Merry-Joseph Blondel
Paris, 1781–Paris, 1853
Winner of the Prix de Rome in 1803, Blondel was very active at the Louvre under the Restoration. The paintings commissioned from him in 1818 for the Henri II Vestibule (*The Dispute between Minerva and Neptune*, *War* and *Peace*) were taken down and replaced by Braque's canvases, but part of his work in the Rotonde d'Apollon can still be seen (*The Fall of Icarus*, *Air*), as well as two ceilings for rooms of the Conseil d'Etat, now used by the Department of Objets d'Art, commissioned in 1829 (*France receiving the Charter from Louis XVIII*, and *France victorious at Bouvines*).

Jean-Baptiste Mauzaisse
Corbeil, 1784–Paris, 1844
In 1822 Mauzaisse executed both the large grisaille figures in the vault of the Rotonde d'Apollon and the ceiling of the Salle des Bijoux, where a giant figure of Time rises above the ruins of Antiquity, from which we see emerging the *Venus de Milo*, acquired by the Louvre in 1821. He completed the decorations in 1828 with allegories of the Seasons in the coving and eight panels between the windows and above the doors, in which genii represent the Elements, Arts, Sciences, Commerce and War.

Alexandre-Denis Abel de Pujol
Valenciennes, 1785–Paris, 1861
At the age of twelve he entered the Ecole des Beaux-Arts in Valenciennes, founded by his natural father, whose name he later adopted. He then went to Paris to study with David, won the Prix de Rome in 1811, and embarked on a long career as an official painter. He provided paintings for a number of State buildings, including the Musée de Versailles, the Luxembourg Palace and the Bourse. For the Musée Charles X, he was commissioned in 1826 to decorate a room for the display of Egyptian antiquities: for the ceiling he devised an allegorical scene of *Egypt saved by Joseph* in the centre, surrounded by compartments in which episodes from the story of Joseph were painted to look like bronze reliefs, while the upper part of the walls had eleven scenes of daily life in ancient Egypt, rendered in grisaille. Simultaneously in another room, where the ceiling and coving had been painted by Vernet, he contributed eight panels with medallions of leading figures of the Renaissance (Rabelais, Tintoretto, Titian, Erasmus, Montaigne, etc.).

Joseph Alaux
Bordeaux, 1786–Paris, 1864
Executant in 1832 of one of the ceilings commissioned in 1828 for the southern gallery (now the Campana Gallery): *Poussin presented to Louis XIII on his Arrival from Rome* in the centre, flanked by allegorical figures of Philosophy and Truth.

François-Joseph Heim
Belfort, 1787–Paris, 1865
After studying with Vincent and winning the Prix de Rome in 1807, Heim became an outstanding history painter, specializing in public commissions – chiefly for churches, but also for royal residences. He was twice called on for

the decoration of the Louvre. First in 1827, for a room in the Musée Charles X devoted to Pompeii and Herculaneum, he painted the main ceiling picture (*The Personification of Vesuvius receiving from Jupiter the Fire...*) and six subjects in the coving, four of them showing scenes of desolation while the other two illustrate the death of Pliny as he observed the eruption. Then in 1828 he was commissioned to decorate a room in the southern gallery (now the Campana Gallery): his composition, executed in 1833, consists of a long main scene representing *The Rebirth of the Arts in France*, surrounded in the coving by eight scenes from the lives of French kings, from Charles VIII to Henri II.

Charles de Steuben
Bauerbach (Baden), 1788–Paris, 1856
In response to a commission in 1828, Steuben painted one of the ceilings of the Conseil d'Etat rooms with the subject of *The Clemency of Henri IV at the Battle of Ivry*, accompanied by medallions in the coving depicting Henri IV's main collaborators, including Sully and Lesdiguières.

Horace Vernet
Paris, 1789–Paris, 1863
Born in the Louvre, a scion of the famous dynasty that had produced the painters Joseph and Carle Vernet, related to the architect Chalgrin and a pupil of Vincent, Vernet was well placed at the heart of the artistic world. He was a painter of both history subjects and portraits, and though he was a Bonapartist with a keen nostalgia for the Empire, his sympathies were not held against him by the Ministère de la Maison du Roi: in 1826 he became an officer of the Legion of Honour and a member of the Institut (where he occupied David's chair), and was commissioned to paint *Julius II giving Orders to his Artists for the Works at St Peter's in Rome* for a ceiling in the Musée Charles X (executed in 1827). In 1828 he became director of the French Academy in Rome.

Eugène Delacroix
Charenton-Saint-Maurice, 1798–Paris, 1863
Delacroix was the great hero of Romantic art; he had already painted *The Massacre at Chios* by 1827, when his *Death of Sardanapalus* caused a sensation at the Salon. At the same Salon he exhibited his *The Pandects of Justinian*, commissioned for a room of the Conseil d'Etat at the Louvre (destroyed). It was not until the middle of the century, however, when he was already widely recognized and admired, that he received a major commission for the Louvre from Duban: this was the central painting for the ceiling of the Galerie d'Apollon, *Apollo vanquishing the Python*, which he executed in two years with the help of assistants (1850–51).

Eugène Devéria
Paris, 1805–Pau, 1865
Devéria was a painter of historic subjects and genre scenes. He attracted favourable attention at the Salon of 1827 (where Delacroix had shown his *Sardanapalus*) with *The Birth of Henri IV*. His colouristic, Romantic style was congenial to the friends who met at his house, among them Delacroix, Victor Hugo, Alfred de Musset, Liszt, Alfred de Vigny and Théophile Gautier. In 1832 he painted a room in the southern gallery of the Cour Carrée (now the Campana Gallery) devoted to Louis XIV as a patron: the main subject of the ceiling is Puget presenting his statue of *Milo of Crotona* to Louis XIV, while the coving below illustrates various aspects of the King's patronage of savants and artists.

Louis Matout
Renwez (Ardennes), 1811–Paris, 1888
Painter in 1865 of the gigantic ceiling of the Salle des Empereurs (now the Salle d'Auguste), which shows the gods of Olympus seated languorously on clouds, against an expansive background of blue sky.

Charles-Louis Müller
Paris, 1815–Paris, 1892
A history painter who specialized in large-scale compositions, Müller received the most prestigious commissions for Napoleon III's Louvre. He began in 1850 by painting *Aurora* for one of the vault compartments of the Galerie d'Apollon, carefully copying Le Brun's original, and went on to produce the painted decoration of the Salle des Etats (1859), Salon Denon (1863–66), and Mollien Staircase (1869). All that survives of the Salle des Etats is a fine series of preparatory drawings and a painted tympanum depicting *The Triumph of Napoleon I*, but the Salon Denon is still complete: here the lunettes represent St Louis, François I, Louis XIV and Napoleon as patrons, while large allegorical figures illustrate the characteristic qualities of art in those times – Naivety, Taste, Observation, Invention, etc. For the Mollien Staircase he painted only the central scene, *Glory distributing Palms*.

Victor Biennoury
Bar-sur-Aube, 1823–Paris, 1893
After studying with Drölling and winning the Prix de Rome in 1842, Biennoury went on to become an official painter extensively involved with the decoration of the imperial palaces. His work can still be seen in the grand schemes of Napoleon III's Louvre (1860–67): in the Grand Salon of the Minister of State, his are the corner medallions; in the Salle d'Auguste,

formerly the Salle des Empereurs, there are tympana in grey monochrome against a red background representing the Roman Empire and the French Empire; the first room in the former Summer Apartment of Anne of Austria displays his *Roman Sculpture*, *Greek Sculpture* and *French Sculpture*; and the ceiling compartments of the following room include paintings by Biennoury of *Sacred History* and *Secular History*.

Georges Braque
Argenteuil-sur-Seine, 1882–Paris, 1963
In response to a commission in 1953 for new subjects for the ceiling of the Henri II Vestibule, the great Cubist painted the three now-famous blue-toned *Birds*. The collection of his works bequeathed to the Louvre at his death was displayed in this room in 1965.

The Sculptors

Jean Goujon
active Rouen, 1540–Bologna, c. 1568
The most famous French Renaissance sculptor. First recorded at Rouen in 1540, he came to Paris to work with the architect Pierre Lescot on the rood screen of Saint-Germain-l'Auxerrois, then carved the reliefs for the Fontaine des Innocents. His most famous works are those he executed at the Louvre: the reliefs on the façade of the Lescot wing, and the stone caryatids supporting the musicians' gallery in the Salle des Cariatides.

Jacques Sarazin
Noyon, 1592–Paris, 1660
After eighteen years' training in Rome, Sarazin settled into the circle of court artists in Paris, and introduced them to the Roman early Baroque style. He was given lodgings in the Louvre, and provided models for the caryatids of the Pavillon de l'Horloge by Jacques Lemercier, decorated in 1639–40.

Philippe De Buyster
Antwerp, 1595–Paris, 1688
A Fleming come to work in Paris, he joined the team of Sarazin, under whose direction, with Gilles Guérin, he executed the decoration of the Pavillon de l'Horloge. The friezes of putti playing among garlands have a refined delicacy, while the robust caryatids and figures of Fame on the upper parts of the pavillon are remarkable for their monumentality.

Gérard van Opstal
Brussels, 1605–Paris, 1668
Van Opstal trained in Antwerp but joined Sarazin's team at an early age. To his master's design he carved *The Riches of the Earth and of the Sea* for one of the oculi in the Lemercier wing – the only one executed in the seventeenth century. Later, he was to be noted for his work including figures of children (those from the château of Maisons now at Vaux-le-Vicomte, also the marble reliefs in the Cabinet du Roi at the Louvre).

Gilles Guérin
c. 1611–78
Under the direction of Sarazin he worked as a part of a team with De Buyster, producing half the decoration for the Pavillon de l'Horloge. He continued to work for Sarazin at the château of Maisons. Major commissions for the King were the ceiling for the King's Bedchamber at the Louvre (1654) and a marble statue of the young Louis XIV (château of Chantilly), and work in the park at Versailles.

Michel Anguier
Eu, 1614–Paris, 1686
Trained first in Picardy and then in Rome, where with his elder brother François he stayed for many years before returning to France in 1651 to work on major projects for the King and for Fouquet. His most celebrated works are the sculptural decoration of the Summer Apartment of Anne of Austria in the Louvre (designed by the Roman painter Romanelli) and of the Val-de-Grâce church, founded by Anne: in their consummate quality they combine Italian Baroque influences with the moderating effect of French taste. In his artistic personality he was both energetic and reflective, a combination expressed particularly in the large figures of a *Nativity* for the Val-de-Grâce (now at Saint-Roch) and in a series of small bronzes of antique gods and goddesses, each endowed with the appropriate temperament and expression.

Thomas Regnaudin
Moulins, 1622–Paris, 1706
Pupil of François Anguier, and collaborator and friend of Girardon, with whom he worked on Louis XIV's first commissions. He executed a quarter of the stucco decoration in the Galerie d'Apollon, the other figures being modelled by Girardon and the Marsy brothers, and the same team came together again to produce the group of the *Horses of the Sun* in the Grotto of Thetis at Versailles, and to carve one of the fountains of the Seasons (Ceres) and marble sculptures commissioned in 1674.

Gaspard Marsy
Cambrai, 1624–Paris, 1681
Balthazar Marsy
Cambrai, 1628–Paris, 1674
After studying first with their father in Cambrai and then with Sarazin in Paris, the Marsy brothers joined the team of royal sculptors. At the Louvre, they executed the pediments of the Grande Galerie (destroyed) and, more significantly, half the stucco decoration of the Galerie d'Apollon, where under the direction of Le Brun they executed highly remarkable figures of Muses. The rest of their careers, as might be expected, was spent at Versailles, where their skill can still be enjoyed in the Bassin de Latone and the Bassin de l'Encélade.

François Girardon
Troyes, 1628–Paris, 1715
After a stay in Rome, the young Girardon joined the team headed by Gilles Guérin, who employed him particularly on the sculpture of the ceiling of the King's Bedchamber. His rise to fame began with his work in the Galerie d'Apollon, where he carried out a quarter of the stucco decoration and was singled out for praise as having excelled the other sculptors involved in the task. Thenceforth he was to become, with Coysevox, the leading sculptor at the court of Louis XIV. Stages in his brilliant career are marked by the group of *Apollo attended by Nymphs*, the Bassin de Saturne, *Winter* and *The Rape of Proserpine* in the park at Versailles, by many funerary monuments, and by the equestrian statue of Louis XIV for the Place Vendôme. In the end, he assumed the unofficial role of director of all the sculptors at court, in matters moral as well as technical.

Guillaume II Coustou
Paris, 1716–Paris, 1777
Son of Guillaume I, whom he assisted in the creation of the Horses of Marly, that fiery masterpiece of the French Baroque. He was active in all types of sculpture, producing funerary monuments (notably that of the Dauphin in Sens Cathedral) and mythological and religious subjects, but he made a speciality of large-scale pediments – most important in the present context that of the inner façade of the Colonnade wing at the Louvre, but also those of the Gabriel buildings in the Place de la Concorde, all of which survive, and those no longer extant on the château of Bellevue and the church of Sainte-Geneviève (now the Panthéon).

Philippe-Laurent Roland
Marcq-en-Pevèle, 1746–Paris, 1816
A versatile artist, Roland produced ambitious statues (*Homer*), busts both quietly intimate (*Lise Roland*) and full of dash (*Pajou*), and also large reliefs (for the Hôtel de Salm). At the Louvre, he contributed to the decoration of the Museé des Antiques (relief in the Salle des Empereurs Romains, 1798) and to that of the Lemercier wing, where he carved the reliefs for the central bay of the attic storey (*Victory* and *Plenty*, *Minerva* and *Hercules*, *Tiber* and *Nile*, 1807).

Jean-Guillaume Moitte
Paris, 1746–Paris, 1810
Like his contemporary Roland, before the Revolution he sculpted ambitious reliefs (for the Hôtel de Salm and for Ledoux's Barrière d'Enfer). In 1807 he worked alongside Roland on the decoration of the attic of the Lemercier wing, Moitte carving the left-hand bay on the theme of Law and religious law-givers (Moses, Isis, Numa Pompilius and Manco Capac).

Pierre Cartellier
Paris, 1757–Paris, 1831
From beginnings as a goldsmith, Cartellier went on to practise in every genre of Neoclassical sculpture, from portraits to statues with allegorical and mythological subjects. He carved one of the reliefs on the Arc de Triomphe du Carrousel, and the space over the central door of the Colonnade wing of the Louvre, where the symmetrical composition of *Victory distributing Crowns* is derived from an antique cameo.

Antoine-Denis Chaudet
Paris, 1763–Paris, 1810
Winner of the Grand Prix for Sculpture in 1784, Chaudet was an excellent Neoclassical sculptor whose manner alternated between the high 'moral seriousness of groups such as *Belisarius* and the poetic vein of subjects such as Cupid playing with a butterfly. At the Louvre, he modelled the stucco decoration of medallions in the Rotonde de Mars (*The Genius of the Arts, The Union of the Three Arts*), and worked alongside Moitte and Roland in 1807 on the attic storey of the Lemercier wing, sculpting the bay that includes a figure of Homer.

François-Frédéric Lemot
Lyons, 1772–Paris, 1827
After winning the Prix de Rome in 1790, Lemot enjoyed a successful career both under the Empire and after the Restoration, when he received the commission for the equestrian statues of Henri IV for the Pont Neuf in Paris (1818) and Louis XIV in the Place Bellecour at Lyons, his native city. His work at the Louvre comprised the gilt lead Victories flanking the quadriga on the Arc de Triomphe du Carrousel and the east-facing pediment of the Colonnade wing.

François Rude
Dijon, 1784–Paris, 1855
Best known for his figure of the Marseillaise on the Arc de Triomphe and for the statue of Marshal Ney in the Place de l'Observatoire, Rude was invited near the end of his life to participate in the decoration of the Place Napoléon (now the Cour Napoléon): his contribution was two of the statues of famous men on the terraces, those of Poussin and Houdon.

Antoine-Louis Barye
Paris, 1795–Paris, 1875
This great *animalier* sculptor played a major a major role in the decoration of the Louvre. During the Restoration period he had developed a particular skill at depicting wild animals, which was founded on a knowledge of anatomy gained from studies at the Museum of Natural History, but fired by a Romantic spirit. Whether he was portraying animals at rest or locked in fierce and muscular struggle, he displayed a perfect mastery of bronze.

Lefuel first commissioned him to execute four large groups for the centres of the Pavillon Denon and Pavillon Richelieu: Peace and War, Strength and Order appear in the guise of youthful figures riding respectively on a horse, a lion, a panther and an ox, accompanied by young genii. These famous groups have tended to overshadow the work he went on to do at the Pavillon Sully, where he provided the pediment sculpture, and on the Grands Guichets. From the latter scheme, the bronze equestrian figure of Napoleon III was taken down in 1870 and exists only in fragments at Compiègne, but two young reclining figures on the parapet, representing rivers, still invite our admiration.

Francisque-Joseph Duret
Paris, 1804–Paris, 1865
After winning the Prix de Rome in 1823, Duret was at first drawn to Romanticism, producing works inspired by the writings of Chateaubriant (*Chactas*, in the museum at Lyons) and by a vision of the joys of life in Italy (*Fisherman dancing the Tarantella*). He received commissions for major works from the State and also from the City of Paris, such as the giant bronze group of St Michael and the dragon on the Fontaine Saint-Michel, and became involved at the Louvre when Duban commissioned him to decorate the Salon des Sept Cheminées, opened in 1851. Lefuel then chose him for the external sculpture on the Pavillon Richelieu. The Pavillon Denon opposite was entrusted to Simart, the sculptor of the Salon Carré, so that the two major pediments facing each other across the Cour Napoléon are by the artists responsible for Duban's two great *salons*. Duret was a professor at the Ecole des Beaux-Arts and a member of the Institut de France, and the master of Carpeaux.

Pierre-Charles Simart
Troyes, 1806–Paris, 1857
Winner of the Prix de Rome in 1833, Simart was encouraged in his classical leanings by Ingres. He sculpted noble and idealistic works for the Salons, and also created the great chryselephantine *Athena* at the château of Dampierre, an attempt to reproduce Phidias' lost masterpiece, realized for the Duc de Luynes, who was an archaeologist and patron of the arts. He became friends with Duban on the site at Dampierre, and was commissioned by the architect to decorate the Salon Carré of the Louvre, opened in 1851. The following year he was elected a member of the Institut and given the task of sculpting one of the two major pediments of the Cour Napoléon, that of the Pavillon Denon. He also sculpted caryatids for the Pavillon Sully.

François Jouffroy
Dijon, 1806–Laval, 1882
Prix de Rome in 1832, member of the Institut in 1857, and professor at the Ecole des Beaux-Arts in 1863, Jouffroy was involved in many Parisian building projects – providing among other things the group of *Harmony* for the façade of the Opéra – and statues for the Gare du Nord and Palais de Justice – and also created major Salon sculptures. At the Louvre, he was responsible for the decoration of the crowning stage of the Pavillon Mollien and the large sculptural groups on the Grands Guichets (1868).

Auguste Préault
Paris, 1809–Paris, 1879
Préault is regarded as one of the greatest Romantic sculptors, and his intensity is reflected in his most anguished works – *La Tuerie* (The Slaughter, in the museum at Chartres) and *Ophelia* (Musée d'Orsay). At the Louvre, his first commission was for the crowning stage of the Pavillon de la Bibliothèque facing the Rue de Rivoli, depicting *The Arts*; this was followed by two immense allegories of Peace and War in the corners at the inner end of the Cour Napoléon (1857).

Pierre-Jules Cavelier
Paris, 1814–Paris, 1894
The sequence of Cavelier's official distinctions, from Prix de Rome in 1842 to professor at the Ecole des Beaux-Arts and member of the Institut in 1856, ran parallel to his involvement in major building projects of the period of Napoléon III and the Third Republic. He was responsible for the statuary on the Palais Longchamp at Marseilles, and contributed to the decoration of the church of Saint-Augustin and the Gare du Nord. At the Louvre he played a very large role, first in the 1850s, with the pediment of the garden front of the Petite Galerie (1850), the crowning stage of the Pavillon Turgot, the caryatids of the Pavillon Richelieu, the reliefs around the clock on the Pavillon Sully, and a statue of Abelard, all around the Cour Napoléon (1855–56), and then again, after a break, in the 1860s when he realized all the sculpture on the west façade of the Pavillon de Flore (1864) and great atlantes for the Mollien Staircase (1869).

Eugène Guillaume
Montbard, 1822–Rome, 1905
Guillaume was one of the few sculptors who succeeded in reaping all the honours of academic life: Prix de Rome (1845), member of the Institut (1862), professor (1863) then director (1865) of the Ecole des Beaux-Arts, director of the French Academy in Rome, and finally member of the Académie Française (1899). Despite those various activities, he was involved in work on a number of buildings in Paris (the Opéra and the church of the Trinité) and in Marseilles. In 1854, at an early age, he received his first significant commission at the Louvre, for the crowning stage of the Pavillon Turgot; he may have got the job through the influence of Lefuel, who was his father-in-law. He then went on to produce one of the most elegant of the oculi in the Cour Napoléon (*Art and Beauty*) and carved the large reliefs on the former Escalier de Flore (now the students' room of the Department of Prints and Drawings), but his equestrian statue of Napoleon, projected to stand in the courtyard, remained unrealized.

Albert Carrier-Belleuse
Anzy-le-Château, 1826–Sèvres, 1887
Carrier-Belleuse, who was brought up by his uncle, the scientist François Arago, never broke out of the academic mould. He turned to modelling figures for porcelain manufacture, and ended his career at the Sèvres factory, of which he became director in 1876. Friend of Carpeaux and teacher of Rodin, he had a very free, eclectic and vital manner, which is well displayed in the bacchic figures that he created in stucco for the two rotundas of the Grande Galerie (1869).

Jean-Baptiste Carpeaux
Valenciennes, 1827–Courbevoie, 1875
Carpeaux was the protégé of Napoleon III and the most famous sculptor of the age; he was also a painter. Two groups now in the Musée d'Orsay – the sensuous and lively *Dance* from the façade of the Opéra (1865–69) and *Ugolino and his Children* – are, in their drama and intensity, the most characteristic expressions of his many-faceted genius. He could be by turns light and delicate, grave and Michelangelesque, and was also a brilliant portraitist. Though he followed the prescribed course at the Ecole des Beaux-Arts (winning the Prix de Rome in 1856), he was an independent creative spirit and he refused to recognize the authority of the Institut or that of any architect. At the Louvre, where he was thus out of sympathy with the rigorous mechanical approach of Lefuel, he sculpted a group symbolizing *The Navy* for the attic of the Pavillon de Rohan (1854), and was then responsible for the decoration of the upper part of the south front of the Pavillon de Flore (1864–66), giving it vitality with his group of *Imperial France enlightening the World* and his high relief of *The Triumph of Flora*.

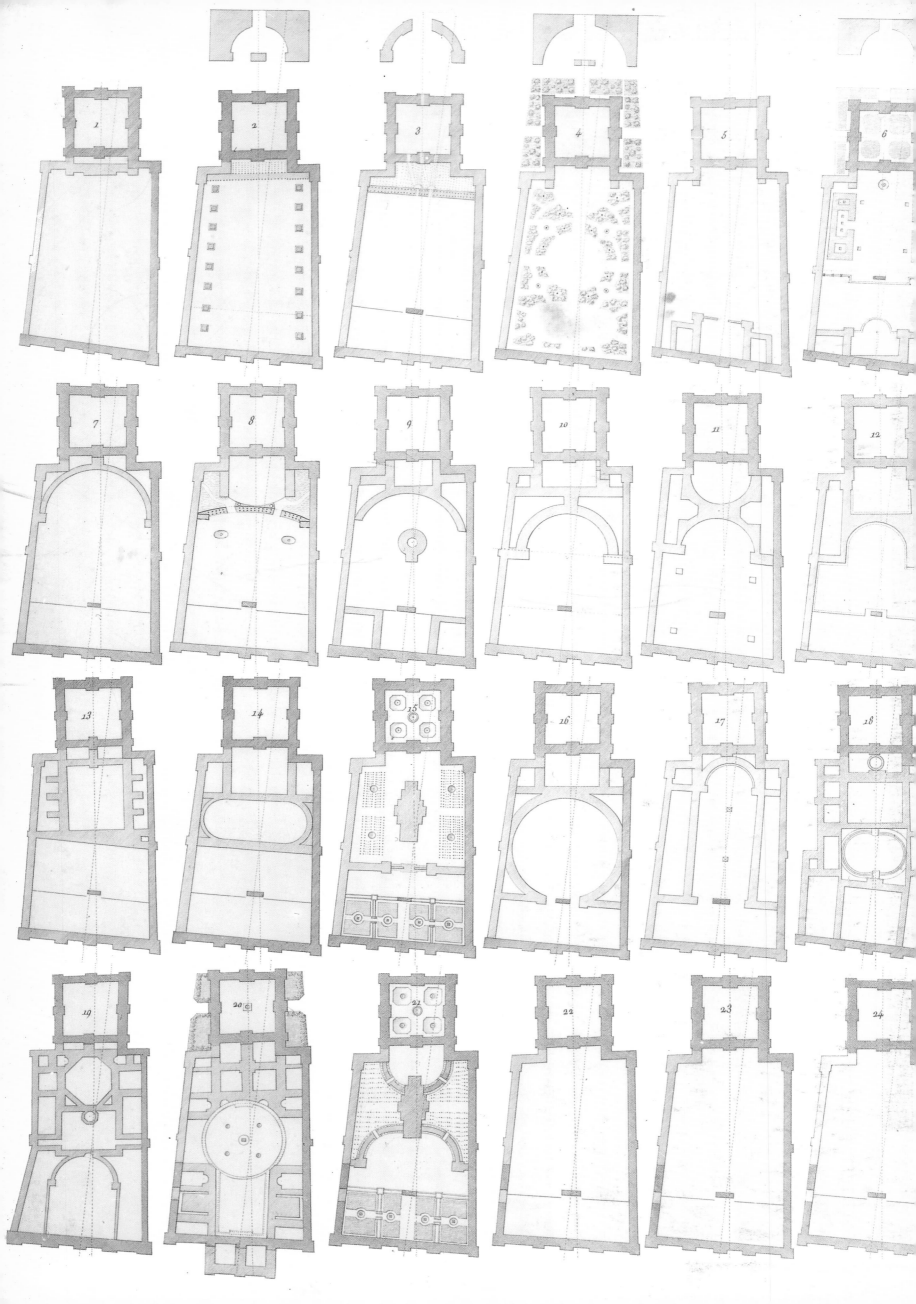